THE IVP

BIBLE
BACKGROUND
COMMENTARY

GENESIS–DEUTERONOMY

John H. Walton &
Victor H. Matthews

InterVarsity Press
Downers Grove, Illinois

InterVarsity Press
P.O. Box 1400, Downers Grove, IL 60515-1426
World Wide Web: www.ivpress.com
E-mail: mail@ivpress.com

InterVarsity Press® *is the book-publishing division of InterVarsity Christian Fellowship/USA*®*, a student movement active on campus at hundreds of universities, colleges and schools of nursing in the United States of America, and a member movement of the International Fellowship of Evangelical Students. For information about local and regional activities, write Public Relations Dept., InterVarsity Christian Fellowship/USA, 6400 Schroeder Rd., P.O. Box 7895, Madison, WI 53707-7895.*

ISBN 0-8308-1456-6

Printed in the United States of America ∞

Library of Congress Cataloging-in-Publication Data

Walton, John H., 1952-
The IVP Bible background commentary: Genesis—Deuteronomy/John
  H. Walton and Victor H. Matthews.
   p.   cm.
  Includes bibliographical references.
  ISBN 0-8308-1406-X (cloth: alk. paper)
  ISBN 0-8308-1456-6 (paper: alk. paper)
  1. Bible. O.T. Pentateuch—Commentaries.   I. Matthews, Victor
  Harold.   II. Title.
  BS1225.3.W34   1997
  222'.107—dc21   *97-11777*
                                                                                  CIP

20	19	18	17	16	15	14	13	12	11	10	9	8	7	6	5	4	3	2
17	16	15	14	13	12	11	10	09	08	07	06	05	04	03	02			

Preface

This book is an attempt to fill a particular niche in the vast field of commentaries on the Bible. Rather than addressing all the varied elements of theology, literary structure, word meanings and history of interpretation, it focuses on the task of providing background information to the text.

Some might wonder what significance background information has for the interpretation of the text. What can we gain from knowing what this commentary seeks to convey? It has been rightly observed that the theological message of the Bible is not dependent on knowing where the places are or what the cultural background was. It is also correct that one could gather all the proofs from history and archaeology that there actually were, for example, for an Israelite exodus from Egypt, but that would still not prove that God orchestrated it—and it is God's involvement that is the most important point of the biblical author. So why should we spend so much time and effort trying to understand the background of Israelite culture, history, geography and archaeology?

The purpose of this book is not apologetics, though certainly some of the information we present could find use in apologetic discussions. Nevertheless, it was not an apologetic agenda that dictated our selection or presentation of the data. Instead, we are trying to shed light on the Israelite culture and worldview. When we read the Bible as a community of faith, we want to draw as much theological content out of the text as possible. As a result we tend to read theological significance into the details. If we are not alerted to the differences that existed in the Israelite way of thinking, we are inclined to read our own cultural biases and our own perspectives and worldview into the text as a basis for understanding its theological significance. The larger ancient Near Eastern world becomes significant in that many times it can serve as a window to the Israelite culture. In many cases, by offering insight into the Israelite or ancient Near Eastern way of thinking, this book can help the interpreter avoid erroneous conclusions. So, for instance, the theological significance of the pillar of fire, the scapegoat or the Urim and Thummim can be understood in new ways once we make connections to the general culture of the ancient Near East.

The issue is not a question of whether the Israelites "borrowed" from their neighbors or not. God's process of revelation required that he condescend to us, accommodate our humanity and express himself in familiar language and metaphors. It should be no surprise that many of the common elements of the culture of the day were adopted—at times adapted, at times totally converted—and used to accomplish God's purposes. Indeed, we would be surprised if this were not the case. Therefore, if *circumcision is to be understood in Israel's context, it is helpful to understand its ancient Near Eastern form. If sacrifice is to be appreciated for what it represented in Israel, it is helpful to contrast what it represented in the ancient world. While sometimes this search for knowledge can result in problems that are difficult to resolve, maintaining ignorance of those problems would not mean they did not exist. And more often than not, our new knowledge has positive results.

Sometimes the information we provide is simply to satisfy curiosity. As teachers, however, we have found that much of our task is taken up with developing in our students a curiosity about the text and then attempting to satisfy, in some degree, that curiosity, so that they may become alert and informed readers.

This book is intended to serve the nonprofessional market rather than the academic and scholarly communities. If we were to footnote every piece of information here so that readers could find and check the original publications, we would end up with a multivolume work too detailed to be of any use to the laypeople for whom we are seeking to provide a service. So we have made the difficult decision to omit footnotes. But we gladly acknowledge our debt to our colleagues and trust that the few bibliographic references we do provide can lead you to their work. We have additionally tried to be very careful with proprietary information and ideas so that a standard of integrity can be maintained.

Another consequence of targeting the nonprofessional market is that our references to the primary literature have of necessity been somewhat vague. Rather than citing text reference and publication resource, we have have said, "Hittite regulations include . . ." or "Egyptian reliefs show . . . ," concentrating our efforts on giving the pertinent information rather than on offering a research trail. We recognize that this will create some frustrations for those who would like to track the reference for further information. We can only recommend going back to the bibliography and tracing the information from there.

Other Resources for the Cultural Context of the Pentateuch

General Reference
Biblical Archaeologist
Biblical Archaeology Review
Boardman, J., et al., eds. *The Cambridge Ancient History.* Cambridge: Cambridge University Press, 1970.
Douglas, J. D., ed. *The Illustrated Bible Dictionary.* Wheaton: Tyndale House, 1980.
Freedman, D. N., ed. *The Anchor Bible Dictionary.* New York: Doubleday, 1992.
Meyers, E. M., ed. *The Oxford Encyclopedia of Archaeology in the Near East.* New York: Oxford University Press, 1997.
Pritchard, James, ed. *Ancient Near Eastern Texts.* Princeton, N.J.: Princeton University Press, 1950.
Sasson, Jack, ed. *Civilizations of the Ancient Near East.* New York: Scribner's, 1980.
Stern, E., ed. *The New Encyclopedia of Archaeological Excavations in the Holy Land.* New York: Simon & Schuster, 1993.
van der Toorn, K., et al., eds. *Dictionary of Deities and Demons in the Bible.* Leiden: Brill, 1995.

Books on Particular Aspects of Bible Background
Aharoni, Y. *The Land of the Bible.* Philadelphia: Westminster Press, 1979.
Baines, John, and Jaromír Málek. *Atlas of Ancient Egypt.* New York: Facts on File, 1980.
Beitzel, Barry. *The Moody Atlas of Bible Lands.* Chicago: Moody Press, 1985.
Cansdale, George. *All the Animals of the Bible Lands.* Grand Rapids: Zondervan, 1970.
de Vaux, Roland. *Ancient Israel.* New York: McGraw-Hill, 1965.
Dearman, Andrew. *Religion and Culture in Ancient Israel.* Peabody, Mass.: Hendrickson, 1992.
Fritz, Volkmar. *The City in Ancient Israel.* Sheffield, U.K.: Sheffield Academic Press, 1995.
Gower, Ralph. *The New Manners and Customs of Bible Times.* Chicago: Moody Press, 1987.
Hepper, F. Nigel. *Baker Encyclopedia of Bible Plants.* Grand Rapids: Baker, 1992.
Hoerth, A., G. Mattingly and E. Yamauchi. *Peoples of the Old Testament World.* Grand Rapids: Baker, 1994.
King, Philip. *Hosea, Amos, Hosea, Micah: An Archaeological Commentary.* Philadelphia: Westminster Press, 1988.
Kitchen, Kenneth A. *Ancient Orient and Old Testament.* Downers Grove, Ill.: InterVarsity Presss, 1966.
————. *The Bible in Its World.* Downers Grove, Ill.: InterVarsity Press, 1977.
Matthews, Victor. *Manners and Customs in the Bible.* Peabody, Mass.: Hendrickson, 1988.

Matthews, Victor, and D. Benjamin. *The Social World of the Old Testament*. Peabody, Mass.: Hendrickson, 1993.

Mazar, Amihai. *Archaeology of the Land of the Bible*. New York: Doubleday, 1990.

Millard, Alan. *Treasures from Bible Times*. Tring, U.K.: Lion, 1985.

Paul, Shalom, and William Dever. *Biblical Archaeology*. Jerusalem: Keter, 1973.

Rasmussen, Carl. *NIV Atlas of the Bible*. Grand Rapids: Zondervan, 1989.

Roaf, Michael. *Cultural Atlas of Mesopotamia and the Ancient Near East*. New York: Facts on File, 1990.

Rogerson, John. *Atlas of the Bible*. New York: Facts on File, 1985.

Saggs, H. W. F. *The Greatness That Was Babylon*. New York: Mentor, 1962.

———. *The Might That Was Assyria*. London: Sidgwick and Jackson, 1984.

Selms, A. van. *Marriage and Family Life in Ugaritic Literature*. London: Luzac, 1954.

Thompson, J. A. *Handbook of Life in Bible Times*. Downers Grove, Ill.: InterVarsity Press, 1986.

van der Toorn, K. *From Her Cradle to Her Grave*. Sheffield, U.K.: JSOT, 1994.

———. *Sin and Sanction in Israel and Mesopotamia*. Assen, Netherlands: Van Gorcum, 1985.

Walton, John H. *Ancient Israelite Literature in Its Cultural Context*. Grand Rapids: Zondervan, 1989.

Weinfeld, Moshe. *Social Justice in Ancient Israel*. Minneapolis: Fortress, 1995.

Wright, Christopher J. H. *God's People in God's Land*. Grand Rapids: Eerdmans, 1990.

Wright, David. *The Disposal of Impurity*. Atlanta: Scholars, 1987.

Zohary, Michael. *Plants of the Bible*. Cambridge: Cambridge University Press, 1982.

Commentaries

Genesis

Hamilton, Victor. *The Book of Genesis*. New International Commentary on the Old Testament. Grand Rapids: Eerdmans, 1995.

Wenham, Gordon. *Genesis*. 2 vols. Word Biblical Commentary. Dallas: Word, 1994.

Exodus

Beegle, Dewey. *Moses, the Servant of Yahweh*. Grand Rapids: Eerdmans, 1972.

Davis, John. *Moses and the Gods of Egypt*. Grand Rapids: Baker, 1971.

Durham, John. *Exodus*. Word Biblical Commentary. Dallas: Word, 1987.

Kelm, George. *Escape to Conflict*. Fort Worth, Tex.: IAR, 1991.

Sarna, Nahum. *Exodus*. JPS Torah Commentary. Philadelphia: Jewish Publication Society, 1991.

———. *Exploring Exodus*. New York: Schocken, 1986.

Leviticus

Grabbe, Lester. *Leviticus*. Old Testament Guides. Sheffield, U.K.: Sheffield Academic Press, 1993.

Hartley, John. *Leviticus*. Word Biblical Commentary. Dallas: Word, 1992.

Levine, Baruch. *Leviticus*. JPS Torah Commentary. Philadelphia: Jewish Publication Society, 1989.

Milgrom, Jacob. *Leviticus 1—16*. Anchor Bible. New York: Doubleday, 1991.

Wenham, Gordon. *The Book of Leviticus*. New International Commentary on the Old Testament. Grand Rapids: Eerdmans, 1979.

Numbers

Ashley, Timothy. *The Book of Numbers*. New International Commentary on the Old Testament. Grand Rapids: Eerdmans, 1993.

Levine, Baruch. *Numbers 1—20*. Anchor Bible. New York: Doubleday, 1993.

Milgrom, Jacob. *Numbers*. JPS Torah Commentary. Philadelphia: Jewish Publication Society, 1990.

Wenham, Gordon. *Numbers*. Tyndale Old Testament Commentaries. Downers Grove, Ill.: InterVarsity Press, 1981.

Deuteronomy

Tigay, Jeffrey. *Deuteronomy*. JPS Torah Commentary. Philadelphia: Jewish Publication Society, 1996.

Weinfeld, Moshe. *Deuteronomy 1—11*. Anchor Bible. New York: Doubleday, 1991.

GENESIS

Introduction

Genesis is typically divided into two main sections (1—11, 12—50). The background material most helpful for understanding the first section is the mythological literature of the ancient Near East. Both Mesopotamian and Egyptian mythology provide a wealth of materials concerning contemporary perspectives on the creation of the world and of human beings. These works include the Enuma Elish and the Atrahasis Epic, as well as a number of *Sumerian myths from the region of Mesopotamia. From Egypt there are three main creation texts, one each from Memphis, Heliopolis (in the Pyramid Texts) and Hermopolis (in the Coffin Texts). Additionally, there are several flood stories available from the region of Mesopotamia, found in the Gilgamesh Epic and in the Atrahasis Epic. Examination of this literature helps us to observe many similarities and differences between ancient Near Eastern and Israelite concepts. Similarities will make us aware of the common ground that existed between Israel and her neighbors. Sometimes the similarity will be in the details of the narrative (such as sending out birds from the ark) or in aspects of the text we might not have noticed before (such as the naming of things in conjunction with their creation). Some similarities might lead us to question whether we have read too much theological significance into certain elements in the text (e.g., the creation of woman from a rib), while in other cases we might find that we have not seen enough of the theological significance (e.g., God's coming to the garden in the "cool of the day"). In general such similarities help us to understand the biblical accounts in broader perspective.

The differences between the ancient Near Eastern and biblical literatures will help us to appreciate some of the distinctives of both the Israelite culture and the biblical faith. These will again include specific details (shape of the ark, length of the flood) as well as foundational concepts (the contrast between the biblical view of creation by the spoken word of God and the Mesopotamian view that the creation of the world was associated with the birth of the cosmic deities). In many cases the differences are related (either directly or indirectly) to the unique monotheistic faith of Israel.

It is not unusual for the similarities and the differences to come together in a single element. The concepts of humankind's being created (1) from clay and (2) in the image of deity are both familiar in the ancient Near East, but Israel puts a unique twist on the idea that moves it into an altogether different sphere.

We cannot always account for the similarities and the differences as clearly or as conclusively as we might wish. Different scholars will have varying opinions of the implications based on some of their own presuppositions. The issues are often complex, and any individual scholar's conclusions may be highly interpretive. For this reason it is easier to offer information than it is to offer satisfying answers.

Finally, the comparative literature not only provides parallel accounts to some of those found in Genesis 1—11 but also provides a parallel to the overall structure of this section. The Mesopotamian Atrahasis Epic, like Genesis 1—11, contains a summary of creation, three threats and a resolution. Such observations can help us to understand the literary aspects to how this portion of the Bible is pieced together. Additionally, if this parallel is legitimate, it can help us see the genealogies in a different light, because when the biblical text has genealogies it reflects the Genesis blessing of being fruitful and multiplying, while in the comparable sections of Atrahasis the gods are distressed by the growth of human population and try to curb it.

Finding literary parallels to Genesis 12—50 presents more of a challenge. Though scholars have attempted to attach various descriptive terms to the patriarchal narratives (such as "sagas" or "legends"), any modern terminology is inadequate to encompass the nature of the ancient literature and is bound to mislead as much as it helps. There is nothing in the literature of the ancient Near East to parallels the stories about the patriarchs. The closest material is found in Egypt in works such as the *Story of *Sinuhe*, but that account covers only the lifetime of one man, rather than following several generations, and has nothing to do with resettlement or relationship with God. Even the Joseph story, considered on its own, is difficult to classify and compare. Again comparisons could be made to the stories of Sinuhe, *Wenamon or *Ahiqar (all dealing with the life and times of royal courtiers), but the similarities are quite superficial.

The background information for understanding these narratives comes from a different set of materials. These chapters concern the lives of the patriarchs and their families as they move from Mesopotamia to Canaan to Egypt in the process of the formation of the covenant. A number of archives (*Nuzi, *Mari, *Emar, *Alalakh) that have been discovered in Syria and Mesopotamia have provided information about the history, culture and customs of the ancient Near East in the second millennium. Often these materials can shed light on the political events or settlement history of the region. They can also help us to see how families lived and why they did some of the things that appear odd to us. In the process we gain important information that can help us process the biblical materials. For instance, we commonly seek ethical guidance in the behavior of biblical characters (though this is not always a productive procedure). In order to understand why people do what they do and to understand the decisions they make, it is important to become familiar with the norms of culture. We may find, then, that some of the behavior of the patriarchs is driven by norms that we have misunderstood or that we could easily misconstrue. Corrective information can often be provided by the archives.

One of the interesting conclusions that can be drawn from this kind of analysis is the understanding that there was not much in the world-view of the patriarchs and their families that differentiated them from the common ancient Near Eastern culture of the day. Again, then, an understanding of the general culture may help us to sort out what elements in the text have theological significance and what elements do not. For instance, an understanding of the practice of *circumcision in the ancient Near East may provide helpful guidelines to our assessment of it in the Bible. Observations about the use of the torch and censer in ancient Near Eastern *rituals may open up the meaning of Genesis 15. Even Abraham's understanding of God can be illuminated by information from the ancient Near Eastern documents.

As we encounter all of this information, we must be impressed with how often God uses the familiar to build bridges to his people. As what was familiar to them becomes more familiar to us, we can understand more of the text. On the other hand it is important to realize that the purposes of the book of Genesis go far beyond any of the literature available in the ancient Near East. The presence of similarities does not suggest in any way that the Bible is simply a secondhand, second-class repackaging of ancient Near Eastern literature. Rather, the background material helps us understand Genesis as a unique theological product linked to people and events embedded in a specific cultural and historical context.

1:1—2:3
Creation

1:2. formless and empty. In Egyptian views of origins there is the concept of the "nonexistent" that may be very close to what is expressed here in Genesis. It is viewed as that which has not yet been differentiated and assigned function. No boundaries or definitions have been established. The Egyptian concept, however, also carries with it the idea of potentiality and a quality of being absolute.

1:1-5. evening and morning. The account of creation does not intend to give a modern scientific explanation of the origin of all natural phenomena, but rather to address the more practical aspects of creation that surround our experiences of living and surviving. In the course of this chapter the author relates how God set up alternating periods of light and darkness—the basis for time. The narrative speaks of evening first because the first time period of light is just coming to a close. The author does not attempt an analysis of the physical properties of light, nor is he concerned about its source or generation. Light is the regulator of time.

1:6-8. firmament. In a similar way the expanse (sometimes called "the firmament") set up in day two is the regulator of climate. The ancient Near Eastern cultures viewed the cosmos as featuring a three-tiered structure consisting of the heavens, the earth and the underworld. Climate originated from the heavens, and the expanse was seen as the mechanism that regulated moisture and sunlight. Though in the ancient world the expanse was generally viewed as more solid than we would understand it today, it is not the physical composition that is important but the function.

1:9-19. function of the cosmos. Just as God is the One who set time in motion and set up the climate, he is likewise responsible for setting up all the other aspects of human existence. The availability of water and the ability of the land to grow vegetation; the laws of agriculture and the seasonal cycles; each of God's creatures, created with a role to

Ancient Near Eastern Mythology and the Old Testament

Mythology in the ancient world was like science in our modern world—it was their explanation of how the world came into being and how it worked. The mythological approach attempted to identify function as a consequence of purpose. The gods had purposes, and their activities were the causes of what humans experienced as effects. In contrast, our modern scientific approach identifies function as a consequence of structure and attempts to understand cause and effect based on natural laws that are linked to the structure, the composite parts, of a phenomenon. Because our scientific worldview is keenly interested in structure, we often go to the biblical account looking for information on structure. In this area, however, the biblical worldview is much more like its ancient Near Eastern counterparts in that it views function as a consequence of purpose. That is what Genesis 1 is all about—it has very little interest in structures. This is only one of many areas where understanding ancient Near Eastern culture, literature and worldview can help us understand the Bible.

Many parallels can be identified between ancient Near Eastern mythology and Old Testament passages and concepts. This is not to suggest that the Old Testament is to be considered simply as another example of ancient mythology or as being dependent on that literature. Mythology is a window to culture. It reflects the worldview and values of the culture that forged it. Many of the

play—all of this was ordered by God and was good, not tyrannical or threatening. This reflects the ancient understanding that the gods were responsible for setting up a system of operations. The functioning of the cosmos was much more important to the people of the ancient world than was its physical makeup or chemical composition. They described what they saw and, more important, what they experienced of the world as having been created by God. That it was all "good" reflects God's wisdom and justice. At the same time the text shows subtle ways of disagreeing with the perspective of the ancient Near East. Most notable is the fact that it avoids using names for the sun and moon, which to the neighbors of the Israelites were also the names of the corresponding deities, and refers instead to the greater light and the lesser light.

1:20-25. zoological categories. The zoological categories include various species of (1) sea creatures, (2) birds, (3) land-based creatures, which are divided into domestic and wild animals and "creatures that move along the ground" (perhaps the reptiles and/or amphibians), and (4) humans. Insects and the microscopic world of creatures are not mentioned, but the categories are broad enough to include them.

1:26-31. function of people. While the organizational or functional focus of the account may have similarities with the ancient Near Eastern perspective, the reason for it all is quite different. In the ancient Near East, the gods created for themselves—the world was their environment for their enjoyment and existence. People were created only as an afterthought, when the gods needed slave labor to help provide the conveniences of life (such as irrigation trenches). In the Bible the cosmos was created and organized to function on behalf of the people that God planned as the centerpiece of his creation.

1:26-31. creation of people in ancient Near Eastern myths. In creation accounts from Mesopotamia an entire population of people is created, already civilized, using a mixture of clay and the

writings we find in the Old Testament performed the same function for ancient Israelite culture that mythology did for other cultures—they provided a literary mechanism for preserving and transmitting their worldview and values. Israel was part of a larger cultural complex that existed across the ancient Near East. There are many aspects of that cultural complex that it shared with its neighbors, though each individual culture had its distinguishing features. When we seek to understand the culture and literature of Israel, we rightly expect to find help in the larger cultural arena, from mythology, wisdom writings, legal documents and royal inscriptions.

The community of faith need not fear the use of such methods to inform us of the common cultural heritage of the Near East. Neither the theological message of the text nor its status as God's Word is jeopardized by these comparative studies. In fact, since revelation involves effective communication, we would expect that whenever possible God would use known and familiar elements to communicate to his people. Identification of similarities as well as differences can provide important background for a proper understanding of the text. This book has only the task of giving information and cannot engage in detailed discussion of how each individual similarity or difference can be explained. Some of that type of discussion can be found in John Walton, *Ancient Israelite Literature in Its Cultural Context* (Grand Rapids: Zondervan, 1987).

blood of a slain rebel god. This creation comes about as the result of conflict among the gods, and the god organizing the cosmos had to overcome the forces of chaos to bring order to his created world. The Genesis account portrays God's creation not as part of a conflict with opposing forces but as a serene and controlled process.

1:26-27. image of God. When God created people, he put them in charge of all of his creation. He endowed them with his own image. In the ancient world an image was believed to carry the essence of that which it represented. An idol image of deity, the same terminology as used here, would be used in the worship of that deity because it contained the deity's essence. This would not suggest that the image could do what the deity could do, nor that it looked the same as the deity. Rather, the deity's work was thought to be accomplished through the idol. In similar ways the governing work of God was seen to be accomplished by people. But that is not all there is to the image of God. Genesis 5:1-3 likens the image of God in Adam to the image of Adam in Seth. This goes beyond the comment about plants and animals reproducing after their own kind, though certainly children share physical characteristics and basic nature (genetically) with their parents. What draws the idol imagery and the child imagery together is the concept that the image provides the capacity not only to serve in the place of God (his representative containing his essence) but also to be and act like him. The tools he provided so that we may accomplish that task include conscience, self-awareness and spiritual discernment. Mesopotamian traditions speak of sons being in the image of their fathers (*Enuma Elish) but do not speak of man created in the image of God; but the Egyptian *Instructions of Merikare* identi-

fies humankind as the god's images who came from his body. In Mesopotamia a significance of the image can be seen in the practice of kings setting up images of themselves in places where they want to establish their authority.

2:1-3. seventh-day rest. In the Egyptian creation account from Memphis, the creator god Ptah rests after the completion of his work. Likewise the creation of man is followed by rest for the Mesopotamian gods. In Mesopotamia, however, the rest is a result of the fact that people have been created to do the work that the gods were tired of doing.

2:1. sabbath divisions. Dividing time into seven-day periods was a practice that is so far unattested in the other cultures of the ancient Near East, though there were particular days of the month in Mesopotamia that were considered unlucky, and they were often seven days apart (that is, the seventh day of the month, the fourteenth day of the month, etc.). Israel's sabbath was not celebrated on certain days of the month and was not linked to the cycles of the moon or to any other cycle of nature; it was simply observed every seventh day.

2:4-25
Man and Woman in the Garden

2:5. botanical categories. Only the most general descriptions of plants are found. Trees, shrubs and plants are listed, but no specific species. We know, however, that the principal trees found in the Near East were acacia, cedar, Cypress, fig, oak, olive, date palm, pomegranate, tamarisk and willow. Shrubs included the oleander and juniper. The principal cultivated grains were wheat, barley and lentils. The description in this verse differs from day three in that it refers to domesticated or cultivated plants. The reference then is not to a time before day three but to the fact that agriculture was not taking place.

2:6. watering system. The word used to describe the watering system in verse 6 (NIV: "streams") is difficult to translate. It occurs elsewhere only in Job 36:27. A similar word occurs in *Babylonian vocabulary drawn from early *Sumerian in reference to the system of subterranean waters, the primordial underground river. The Sumerian myth of *Enki and Ninhursag likewise mentions such a watering system.

2:7. man from dust. The creation of the first man out of the dust of the earth is similar to what is found in ancient Near Eastern mythology. The Atrahasis Epic portrays the creation of humankind out of the blood of a slain deity mixed with clay. Just as dust in the Bible represents what the body becomes at death (Gen 3:19), so clay was what the body returned to in *Babylonian thinking. The blood of deity represented the divine essence in mankind, a similar concept to God's bringing Adam into being with the breath of life. In Egyptian thinking it is the tears of the god that are mixed with clay to form man, though the *Instructions of Merikare* also speak of the god's making breath for their noses.

2:8-14. location of Eden. Based on the proximity of the Tigris and Euphrates Rivers and the *Sumerian legend of the mystical, utopian land of *Dilmun, most scholars would identify Eden as a place in or near the northern end of the Persian Gulf. *Dilmun has been identified with the island of Bahrain. The direction that it is "in the east" merely points to the general area of Mesopotamia and is fairly typical of primordial narratives. This, plus the direction of flow of the rivers (the location of the Pishon and Gihon being uncertain), has caused some to look in the Armenia region, near the sources of the Tigris and Euphrates. However, the characteristics of a well-watered garden in which humans do little or no work and in which life springs up without cultivation fits the marshy areas at the base of the Gulf and may even be an area now covered by the waters of the region.

2:8. The "garden of Eden." The word *Eden* refers to a well-watered place, suggesting a luxuriant park. The word translated "garden" does not typically refer to vegetable plots but to orchards or parks containing trees.

2:9. tree of life. The tree of life is portrayed elsewhere in the Bible as offering extension of life (Prov 3:16-18), which sometimes can be viewed as having rejuvenating qualities. Various plants with such qualities are known from the ancient Near East. In the *Gilgamesh Epic there is a plant called "old man becomes young" that grows at the bottom of the cosmic river. Trees often figure prominently in ancient Near Eastern art and on cylinder seals. These have often been interpreted as depicting a tree of life, but more support from the literature would be necessary to confirm such an interpretation.

2:11. Pishon. Analysis of sand patterns in Saudi Arabia and satellite photography have helped identify an old riverbed running northeast through Saudi Arabia from the Hijaz Mountains near Medina to the Persian Gulf in Kuwait near the mouth of the Tigris and Euphrates. This would be a good candidate for the Pishon River.

2:11. Havilah. Perhaps because gold is mentioned in relation to Havilah, it is named in several other passages (Gen 10:7; 25:18; 1 Sam 15:7; 1 Chron 1:9). It has most often been placed in western Saudi Arabia near Medina along the Red Sea, an area that does produce gold, bdellium and onyx. Genesis 10:7 describes Havilah as the "brother" of Ophir, a region also known for its wealth in gold.

2:21-22. rib. The use of Adam's rib for the creation of Eve may find illumination in the *Sumerian language. The Sumerian word for rib is *ti*. Of interest is the fact that *ti* means "life," just as *Eve* does (3:20). Others have suggested that a connection should be seen with the Egyptian word *imw*, which can mean either clay (out of which man was made) or rib.

2:24. man leaving father and mother. This statement is a narrative aside, which provides a comment on the social world of the people in later times. It uses the story of Eve's creation as the basis for the legal principle of separate households. When a marriage was contracted, the wife left her parents' home and joined the household of her husband. New loyalties were established in this way. Furthermore, the consummation of the marriage is associated here with the idea of the couple becoming one flesh again, just as Adam and Eve come from one body. The statement here that the *man* will leave his family does not necessarily refer to a particular sociology, but to the fact that in this chapter it is the man who has been seeking a companion. It also may reflect the fact that wedding ceremonies, including the wedding night, often took place in the house of the bride's parents.

3:1-24
The Fall and the Pronouncement

3:1. significance of serpents in ancient world. From the very earliest evidence in ancient Near Eastern art and literature, the serpent is presented as a significant character. Perhaps because its poison was a threat to life and its lidless eyes provided an enigmatic image, the serpent has been associated with both death and wisdom. The Genesis account evokes both aspects in the wisdom dialogue between the serpent and Eve and with the introduction of death after the expulsion from Eden. Similarly, *Gil-gamesh is cheated out of perpetual youth when a serpent consumes a magical plant the hero had retrieved from the sea bottom. The sinister image of the serpent is graphically displayed by the intertwining coils of a snake encompassing a *cult stand found at Beth-Shean. Whether as a representative of primeval chaos (*Tiamat or *Leviathan) or a symbol of sexuality, the serpent harbors mystery for humans. Of particular interest is the *Sumerian god Ningishzida, who was portrayed in serpent shape and whose name means "Lord of the Productive/Steadfast Tree." He was considered a ruler in the nether world and "throne-bearer of the earth." He was one of the deities that offered the bread of life to *Adapa (see next comment). Even when not related to a god, the serpent represented wisdom (occult), *fertility, health, chaos and immortality, and was often worshiped.

3:2-5. temptation to be like God. Aspiration to deity and lost opportunities to become like the gods figure prominently in a few ancient myths. In the tale of *Adapa an offer of the "food of life" is inadvertently refused. Adapa, the first of the seven sages before the flood, is attempting to bring the arts of civilization to the first city, Eridu. As a fisherman, he had an unfortunate escapade with the south wind one day that eventuated in an audience with the chief god, Anu. Under the advice of the god *Ea, when Anu offered him food he refused it, only to discover that it was food that would bring immortality. Eternal life also eludes *Gilgamesh. In the famous epic about him, the death of his friend Enkidu leads him in a search for immortality, which he discovers is unattainable. In both of these accounts, being like the gods is viewed in terms of achieving immortality, whereas in the biblical account it is understood in terms of wisdom.

3:7. fig leaf significance. Fig leaves are the largest found in Canaan and could provide limited covering for the shamed couple. The significance of the fig's use may lie in its symbolism of fertility. By eating the forbidden fruit, the couple have set in motion their future role as parents and as cultivators of fruit trees and grain.

3:8. cool of the day. *Akkadian terminology has demonstrated that the word translated "day" also has the meaning "storm." This meaning can be seen also for the Hebrew word in Zephaniah 2:2. It is often connected to the deity coming in a storm of judgment. If this is the correct rendering of the word in this passage, they heard the thunder (the word translated "sound" is often connected to thunder) of the Lord moving about in the garden in the wind of the storm. In this case it is quite understandable why they are hiding.

3:14-15. curses on serpents. The Egyptian Pyramid Texts (second half of third millennium) contain a number of spells against serpents, but likewise include spells against other creatures considered dangers or pests who threaten the dead. Some of these spells enjoin the serpent to crawl on its belly (keep its face on the path). This is in contrast to raising its head up to strike. The serpent on its belly is nonthreatening, while the one reared up is protecting or attacking. Treading on the serpent is used in these texts as a means of overcoming or defeating it.

3:14-15. all snakes poisonous. While it would have been observable that not all snakes were poisonous, the threat provided by some would, in the haste to protect oneself, attach itself to all. Of thirty-six species of snake known to the area, the viper (*vipera palaestinae*) is the only poisonous snake in northern and central Israel. Snakes are associated occasionally with fertility and life (bronze serpent in the wilderness). However,

they most often are tied to the struggle for life and the inevitability of death. The poisonous snakes would be the most aggressive, so an attack by a snake would always be viewed as a potentially mortal blow.

3:16. labor pains. Perhaps displaying the dual character of life, the joy of motherhood can be gained only through labor pain. Without modern medicine, these pains are described as the worst possible agony for humans (see Is 13:8; 21:3) and gods (note the *Babylonian goddess *Ishtar's cry in the *Gilgamesh flood epic when she sees the horror of the flood unleashed). *Babylonians associated demons such as Lamashtu with the pain of childbirth and the tenuous condition of life for both mother and child in the birth process.

3:16. husband-wife relationship. Arranged marriages downplayed the role of romantic love in ancient Israelite society. However, in this labor-poor society men and women had to work together as a team. While pregnancy and child care periodically restricted the woman's work in the fields or the shop, a couple's survival was largely based on shared labor and the number of children they produced. Domination of the wife by her husband, while evident in some marriages, was not the ideal in ancient relationships. Both had their roles, although the legal rights with regard to making contracts, owning property and inheritance rights were primarily controlled by males. It is also a fact that concern over female chastity led to restrictions on associations by females and male control of the legal process.

3:17. toil. In Mesopotamian thinking people were created to be slaves and to do the work that the gods had tired of doing for themselves, much of it concerned with the agricultural process. In *Enuma Elish the entire purpose for creating people was to relieve the gods of their toil, unlike the biblical account, in which people were created to rule and became burdened with toil only as a result of the fall.

3:20. significance of naming. Adam earlier had named the animals, which was a demonstration of his authority over them. Here his naming of Eve suggests Adam's position of rule, as referred to in verse 16. In the ancient world when one king placed a vassal king on the throne, a new name would often be given to demonstrate the overlord's dominion. Likewise, when God enters *covenant relationships with Abram and Jacob, he changes their names. A final example occurs in the *Babylonian account of creation, *Enuma Elish, which opens with the situation before heaven and earth were named. The account proceeds to give names, just as God names the things he creates in Genesis 1.

3:21. skin garments. The long outer tunic is still the basic garment for many people in the Middle East. This replaces the inadequate fig leaf covering made by Adam and Eve. God provides them with these garments as the type of gift given by a patron to a client. Gifts of clothing are among the most common presents mentioned in the Bible (see Joseph in Gen 41:42) and other ancient texts. It also prepares them for the rigors of weather and work which await them. In the *Tale of Adapa* (see comment on 3:2-5), after *Adapa loses the opportunity to eat from the bread and water of life, he is given clothing by the god Anu before being sent from his presence.

3:24. cherubim. The cherubim are supernatural creatures referred to over ninety times in the Old Testament, where they usually function in the capacity of guardians of God's presence. From the guardian of the tree of life, to the ornamental representation over the mercy seat on the ark of the covenant, to the accompaniment of the char-

iot/throne in Ezekiel's visions, the cherubim are always closely associated with the person or property of deity. Biblical descriptions (Ezek 1, 10) agree with archaeological finds that suggest they are composite creatures (like griffins or sphinxes). Representations of these creatures are often found flanking the throne of the king. Here in Genesis the cherubim guard the way to the tree of life, now forbidden property of God. An interesting Neo-Assyrian seal depicts what appears to be a fruit tree flanked by two such creatures with deities standing on their backs supporting a winged sun disk.

4:1-16
Cain and Abel

4:1-7. sacrifices of Cain and Abel. The sacrifices of Cain and Abel are not depicted as addressing sin or seeking atonement. The word used designates them very generally as "gifts"—a word that is most closely associated with the grain offering later in Leviticus 2. They appear to be intended to express gratitude to God for his bounty. Therefore it is appropriate that Cain should bring an offering from the produce that he grew, for blood would not be mandatory in such an offering. It should be noted that Genesis does not preserve any record of God requesting such offerings, though he approved of it as a means of expressing thanks. Gratitude is not expressed, however, when the gift is grudgingly given, as is likely the case with Cain.

4:11-12. nomadic lifestyle. The wandering nomadic lifestyle to which Cain is doomed represents one of the principal economic/social divisions in ancient society. Once animals had been domesticated, around 8000 B.C., herding and pastoral nomadism became a major economic pursuit for tribes and villages. Generally, herding was part of a mixed village economy, including agriculture and trade. However, some groups concentrated more of their efforts on taking sheep and goats to new pasture as the seasons changed. These seminomadic herdsmen followed particular migration routes which provided adequate water for their animals as well as grazing. Contracts were sometimes made with villages along the route for grazing in harvested fields. These herdsmen occasionally clashed with settled communities over water rights or because of raiding. Governments tried to control nomadic groups within their area, but these attempts were not usually successful over long periods of time. The result is the composition of stories which describe the conflict between herders and farmers as they compete for use of the land.

4:14-15. blood vengeance. In areas where the central government had not gained full control, blood feuds between families were common. They were based on the simple principle of "an eye for an eye," which demanded the death of a murderer or the death of a member of his family as restitution. There was also an assumption that kinship ties included the obligation to defend the honor of the household. No hurt could be ignored, or the household would be considered too weak to defend itself and other groups would take advantage of them. Cain's comment assumes that there is a more extensive family in existence and that some from Abel's line would seek revenge.

4:15. mark of Cain. The Hebrew word used here does not denote a tatoo or mutilation inflicted on a felon or slave (referred to in the Laws of *Eshnunna and the Code of *Hammurabi). It best compares to the mark of divine protection placed on the foreheads of the innocents in Jerusalem in Ezekiel 9:4-6. It may be an external marking that would cause others to treat him with respect or caution. However, it may represent a sign from God to Cain

that he would not be harmed and people would not attack him.

4:17-26
The Line of Cain

4:17. city building. Because the founding of a city is tied so intimately to the founding of a nation or people in the ancient world, stories about the founder and the circumstances surrounding its founding are a part of the basic heritage of the inhabitants. These stories generally include a description of the natural resources which attracted the builder (water supply, grazing and crop land, natural defenses), the special attributes of the builder (unusual strength and/or wisdom) and the guidance of the patron god. Cities were constructed along or near rivers or springs. They served as focal points for trade, culture and religious activity for a much larger region and thus eventually became political centers or city states. The organization required to build them and then to keep their mud-brick and stone walls in repair helped generate the development of assemblies of elders and monarchies to rule them.

4:19. polygamy. The practice of a man marrying more than one wife is known as polygamy. This custom was based on several factors: (1) an imbalance in the number of males and females, (2) the need to produce large numbers of children to work herds and/or fields, (3) the desire to increase the prestige and wealth of a household through multiple marriage contracts and (4) the high rate of death of females in childbirth. Polygamy was most common among pastoral nomadic groups and in rural farming communities, where it was important that every female be attached to a household and be productive. Monarchs also practiced polygamy, primarily as a means of making alliances with powerful families or other nations. In such situations the wives might also end up as hostages if the political relationship soured.

4:20. animal domestication. Raising livestock is the first stage in animal domestication, which involves human control of breeding, food supply and territory. Sheep and goats were the first livestock to be domesticated, with the evidence extending back to the ninth millennium B.C. Larger cattle came a bit later, and evidence for pig domestication begins in the seventh millennium.

4:21. musical instruments. Musical instruments were among the first inventions of early humans. In Egypt the earliest end-blown flutes date to the fourth millennium B.C. A number of harps and lyres as well as a pair of silver flutes were found in the royal cemetery at *Ur dating to the early part of the third millennium. Flutes made of bone or pottery date back at least to the fourth millennium. Musical instruments provided entertainment as well as background rhythm for dances and *ritual performances, such as processions or *cultic dramas. Other than simple percussion instruments (drums and rattles), the most common instruments used in the ancient Near East were harps and lyres. Examples have been found in excavated tombs and painted on the walls of temples and palaces. They are described in literature as a means of soothing the spirit, invoking the gods to speak and providing the cadence for a marching army. Musicians had their own guilds and were highly respected.

4:22. ancient metal technology. As part of the account of the emergence of crafts and technology in the genealogy of Cain, it is appropriate that the origin of metalworking would be mentioned. *Assyrian texts mention Tabal and Musku as the early metalworking regions in the Taurus Mountains (of eastern Turkey). Copper tools, weapons and implements began to be smelted and forged in the fourth millennium B.C. Subsequently, alloys of copper, principally bronze, were introduced in the early third millennium as sources of tin were discovered outside the Near East and trade routes expanded to bring them to Egypt and Mesopotamia. Iron, a metal which requires much higher temperatures and skin bellows (portrayed in the Egyptian Beni Hasan tomb paintings) to refine and work, was the last to be introduced, toward the end of the second millennium B.C. *Hittite smiths seem to have been the first to exploit it, and then the technology spread east and south. Meteorite iron was cold-forged for centuries prior to its smelting. That would not represent as large an industry as the forging of terrestrial deposits, but it would explain some of the early references to iron prior to the *Iron Age.

5:1-32
The Line of Seth

5:1. the account of (toledoth). This chapter begins by introducing "the written account of Adam's line"—just as 2:4 had referred to the account of the heavens and earth. Genesis uses this label eleven times throughout the book. Earlier translations used the word "generations" in place of "account." In other places in the Bible this word is most often associated with genealogies. Some believe that in Genesis they indicate written sources that the author used in compiling the book. Alternatively, they could simply be understood as introducing the people and events that "eventuated" from the named individual. In any case they serve as convenient division markers between the sections of the book.

5:1-32. importance of genealogies. Genealogies represent continuity and relationship. Often in the ancient Near East they are used for purposes of power and prestige. Linear genealogies start at point A (the creation of Adam and Eve, for example) and end at point B (Noah and the flood). Their intention is to bridge a gap between major events. Alternatively they can be vertical, tracing the descendants of a single family (Esau in Gen 36:1-5, 9-43). In the case of linear genealogies, the actual amount of time represented by these successive generations does not seem to be as important as the sense of completion or adherence to a purpose (such as the charge to be fertile and fill the earth). Vertical genealogies focus on establishing legitimacy for membership in the family or tribe (as in the case of the Levitical genealogies in Ezra 2). Mesopotamian sources do not offer many genealogies, but most of those that are known are linear in nature. Most of these are either of royal or scribal families, and most are only three generations, with none more than twelve. Egyptian genealogies are mostly of priestly families and are likewise linear. They extend to as many as seventeen generations but are not common until the first millennium B.C. Genealogies are often formatted to suit a literary purpose. So, for instance, the genealogies between Adam and Noah, and Noah and Abraham, are each set up to contain ten members, with the last having three sons. Comparing biblical genealogies to one another shows that there are often several generations skipped in any particular presentation. This type of telescoping also occurs in *Assyrian genealogical records. Thus we need not think that the genealogy's purpose is to represent every generation, as our modern family trees attempt to do.

5:3-32. long lives. Although there is no satisfactory explanation of the long life spans before the flood, there are *Sumerian lists of kings who purportedly reigned before the flood with reigns as long as 43,200 years. The Sumerians used the sexagesimal number system (a combination of base six and base ten), and when the numbers of the Sumerian king list are converted to decimal, they are very much in the range of the age spans of the preflood genealogies of Genesis. The Hebrews, like most other Semitic peoples, used a base-ten decimal system as far back as writing extends.

5:21-24. God took Enoch. Seventh in the line, Enoch was the most outstanding individual in the line of Seth. As a result of walking with God (a phrase expressing piety) he was "taken"—an alternative to dying, the stated fate of all the others in the genealogy. The text does not say *where* he was taken, a possible indication that the author did not profess to know. We can properly assume that he was believed to have been taken to a better place, for this fate was seen as a reward for his close relationship to God, but the text stops short of saying he went to heaven or to be with God. In the Mesopotamian lists of preflood sages, the seventh in the list, Utuabzu, is said to have ascended to heaven. In the Egyptian Pyramid Texts, Shu, the god of the air, is instructed to take the king to heaven so he does not die on earth. This simply represents the transition from mortality to immortality. Jewish writings after the time of the Old Testament offer extensive speculation about Enoch and portray him as an ancient source of revelation and apocalyptic visions (*1, 2* and *3 Enoch*).

6:1-4
The Sons of God and the Daughters of Men

6:2. sons of God. The term "sons of God" is used elsewhere in the Old Testament to refer to angels, but the idea of sonship to God is also portrayed corporately for the Israelites and individually for kings. In the ancient Near East kings were commonly understood as having a filial relationship to deity and were often considered to have been engendered by deity.

6:2. marrying whom they chose. The practice of marrying "any of them they chose" has been interpreted by some to be a reference to polygamy. While it is not to be doubted that polygamy was practiced, it is difficult to imagine why that would be worthy of note, since polygamy was an acceptable practice even in Israel in Old Testament times. It is more likely that this is a reference to the "right of the first night," cited as one of the oppressive practices of kings in the *Gilgamesh Epic. The king could exercise his right, as representative of the gods, to spend the wedding night with any woman who was being given in marriage. This presumably was construed as a *fertility rite. If this is the practice referred to here, it would offer an explanation of the nature of the offense.

6:3. 120 years. The limitation of 120 years most likely refers to a reduction of the life span of humans, since it is in the context of a statement about mortality. While the verse is notoriously difficult to translate, modern consensus is moving toward translating it "My spirit will not remain in man forever," thus affirming mortality. Just as the offense can be understood in light of information from the Gilgamesh Epic, so this statement may refer to the never-ending quest for immortality; a quest such as is at the core of the Gilgamesh Epic. Though Gilgamesh lived after the flood, these elements of the narrative resonate with universal human experience.

6:4. Nephilim. *Nephilim* is not an ethnic designation but a description of a particular type of individual. In Numbers 13:33 they are identified, along with the descendants of Anak, as some of the inhabitants of the land of Canaan. The latter are described as giants, but there is no reason to consider the Nephilim to be giants. It is more likely that the term describes heroic warriors, perhaps the ancient equivalent of knights errant.

6:5—8:22
The Flood

6:13. violence as cause of flood. In the Atrahasis Epic's account of the flood the reason that the gods decide to send the flood is the "noise" of mankind. This is not necessarily different from the biblical reason in that "noise" can be the result of violence. Abel's blood cries out from the ground (4:10) and the outcry against Sodom and Gomorrah is great (Gen 18:20). The noise could be generated either by the number of petitions being made to the gods to respond to the violence and bloodshed or by the victims who cry out in their distress.

Ancient Near Eastern Flood Accounts

The most significant ancient Near Eastern flood accounts are found in the Atrahasis Epic and the Gilgamesh Epic. In these accounts the chief god, Enlil, becomes angry at mankind. The Atrahasis Epic portrays him as disturbed over the "noise" of mankind (see comment on Gen 6:13) and, after trying unsuccessfully to remedy the situation by reducing the population through things like drought and disease, persuades the divine assembly to approve a flood for the total elimination of humankind. The god Ea manages to forewarn one loyal worshiper, a king, who is instructed to build a boat that will preserve not only him and his family but representatives skilled in the various arts of civilization. The other people of the city are told that the gods are angry with the king and he must leave them. The pitch-covered boat has seven stories shaped as either a cube or, more likely, a ziggurat (see comment on 11:4). The storm lasts seven

6:14. gopher wood. *Gopher* is the Hebrew word translated "cypress wood" in the NIV. This is an unknown type of material, although it undoubtedly refers to some sort of coniferous tree thought to possess great strength and durability. Cypress was often used by shipbuilders in the ancient Near East. Similarly, the cedars of Lebanon were prized by the Egyptians for the construction of their barques for transport on the Nile, for instance in the eleventh century B.C. *Diary of *Wenamon*.

6:14-16. size of the ark. Based on a measurement of one cubit equaling eighteen inches or forty-five centimeters, the ark Noah constructs is approximately 450 feet (135 meters) long, 75 feet (22 meters) wide, and 45 feet (13 meters) deep. If it had a flat bottom, the total surface capacity would be about three times that of the tabernacle (100 by 50 cubits in Ex 27:9-13), with a displacement of 43,000 tons. In comparison, the ark constructed by *Utnapishtim in the *Babylonian version of the *Gilgamesh epic is either a cube or ziggurat-shaped (120 by 120 by 120 cubits), with a displacement of three or four times that of the Genesis ark. Noah's ark was not designed to be navigated—no rudder or sail is mentioned. Thus the fate of the company aboard was left in the hands of God. Although *Utnapishtim does employ a navigator,

the shape of his ark may be magical, since he could not depend on the gods to preserve him.

6:14. boats in the ancient world. Prior to the invention of seaworthy vessels that could carry sailors and cargo through the heavy seas of the Mediterranean, most boats were made of skin or reeds and were designed to sail through marshes or along the river bank. They were used for fishing or hunting and would not have been more than ten feet in length. True sailing ships, with a length of 170 feet, are first depicted in Old Kingdom Egyptian art (c. 2500 B.C.) and are described in *Ugaritic (1600-1200 B.C.) and Phoenician (1000-500 B.C.) texts. Remains of shipwrecks from the mid-second millennium (*Late Bronze Age) have also been found in the Mediterranean. They still generally navigated within sight of land, with trips to Crete and Cyprus as well as the ports along the coasts of Egypt, the Persian Gulf and Asia Minor.

6:15-16. length measurements. The standard measurement unit for length was the cubit, which was eighteen inches (forty-five centimeters). This was based on the length of a man's forearm, from his fingertips to his elbow. Other units include the span, the handbreadth/palm and the finger. Use of a "four-finger equals one palm" and of a

days and nights, after which the boat comes to rest on Mount Nisir. Birds are sent out to determine the time for leaving the ark. Sacrifices are made, for which the gods are very thankful since they have been deprived of food (sacrifices) since the flood began.

The Atrahasis Epic is dated to the early second millennium B.C. The Gilgamesh Epic came into its present form during the second half of the second millennium but used materials that were already in circulation at the end of the third millennium. From the short summary above one can detect a number of similarities as well as a number of differences. There is no reason to doubt that the ancient Near Eastern accounts and Genesis refer to the same flood. This would certainly account for the similarities. The differences exist because each culture is viewing the flood through its own theology and worldview.

"twenty-four-finger equals one cubit" measure is common throughout the ancient Near East. Some variations do occur, such as seven palms equals one cubit in Egypt and thirty fingers equals one cubit in *Babylonia until the *Chaldean period (perhaps based on their use of a sexagesimal mathematics system).

6:17. archaeological evidences of flood. There is presently no convincing archaeological evidence of the biblical flood. The examination of silt levels at the *Sumerian cities of *Ur, Kish, Shuruppak, *Lagash and *Uruk (all of which have occupation levels at least as early as 2800 B.C.) are from different periods and do not reflect a single massive flood that inundated them all at the same time. Similarly, the city of Jericho, which has been continuously occupied since 7000 B.C., has no flood deposits whatsoever. Climatological studies have indicated that the period from 4500 to 3500 B.C. was significantly wetter in this region, but that offers little to go on. The search for the remains of Noah's ark have centered on the Turkish peak of Agri Dagh (17,000 feet) near Lake Van. However, no one mountain within the Ararat range is mentioned in the biblical account, and fragments of wood that have been carbon-14 dated from this mountain have proven to come from no earlier than the fifth century A.D.

7:2-4. seven of every kind. Though Noah takes two each of most animals into the ark, he is instructed in verse 2 to take seven pairs of every clean animal and of every bird. Additional clean animals would be needed both for the sacrifice after the flood and for quicker repopulation for human use. In some sacrificial *rituals seven of each class of designated animal are offered (cf. 2 Chron 29:21), but, of course, Noah is not going to sacrifice all of them.

7:2. clean and unclean before Moses. The distinction between clean and unclean animals was not an innovation established at Sinai but is seen as early as Noah. Evidence from Egypt and Mesopotamia offer no system equivalent to the Israelite system of classification. While there are dietary restrictions in those cultures, they tend to be much more limited, that is, certain animals restricted only to certain classes of people or on certain days of the month. Even here one cannot assume that the classification has implications for their diet. Up to this time no permission had been granted to eat meat (see 1:29). When meat was granted to them as food after the flood (9:2-3), there were no restrictions along the lines of clean and unclean. As a result it appears that the classification concerned sacrifice, not diet, in this period.

7:11. floodgates opened. The text uses the poetic phrase "windows of heaven" to describe the openings through which the rain came down. This is not scientific language but reflects the perspective of the observer, much as we would speak of the sun "setting." The only other occurrence of such a term in ancient Near Eastern literature is in the Canaanite myth of *Baal building his house, where the "window" of his house is described as a rift in the clouds. But even here it is not associated with rain.

7:11—8:5. time periods of flood. The total elapse of time in the flood narrative can be viewed in different ways depending on how the given information is merged. From the information given in 7:11 and 8:14 it can be determined that Noah and his family were in the ark for twelve months and eleven days. The exact number of days would depend on how many days were counted in a month and whether any adjustments were being made between lunar and solar reckonings. The eleven days has been found interesting by some, since the lunar year of 354 days is eleven days shorter than the solar year.

8:4. Ararat. The mountains of Ararat are located in the Lake Van region of eastern Turkey in the area of Armenia (known as Urartu in *Assyrian inscriptions). This range of mountains (the highest peak reaching 17,000 feet) is also mentioned in 2 Kings 19:37, Isaiah 37:38 and Jeremiah 51:27. The *Gilgamesh epic, however, describes the flood hero's ark coming to rest on a specific mountaintop, Mount Nisir in southern Kurdistan.

8:6-12. use of birds in ancient Near East. One of the enduring pictures of the Noah account is that of Noah sending out the birds to gain information about the conditions outside the ark. The flood stories in the *Gilgamesh Epic and the Atrahasis Epic feature a similar use of birds. Rather than a raven and three missions for the dove, we find a dove, swallow and raven sent out. The dove and swallow return without finding a place, while the raven is pictured, as in 8:7, as flying about cawing and not returning (*Gilg.* 11.146-54). Ancient navigators were known to use birds to find land, but Noah is not navigating, and he is on land. His use of the birds is not for purposes of finding direction. It is also known that the flight patterns of birds sometimes served as omens, but neither Genesis nor Gilgamesh make observations from the flight of the birds sent out.

8:7. habits of ravens. Unlike pigeons or doves, which will return after being released, a raven's use to seamen is based on its line of flight. By noting the direction it chooses, a sailor may determine where land is located. The most sensible strategy is to release a raven first and then use other birds to determine the depth of the water and the likelihood of a place to land. A raven, by habit, lives on carrion and would therefore have sufficient food available.

8:9. habits of doves. The dove and the pigeon have a limited ability for sustained flight. Thus navigators use them to determine the location of landing sites. As long as they return, no landing is in close range. The dove lives at lower elevations and requires plants for food.

8:11. olive leaf significance. The olive leaf retrieved by the dove suggests the amount of time it would take for an olive tree to leaf out after being submerged—a clue to the current depth of the flood waters. It is also symbolic of new life and fertility to come after the flood. The olive is a difficult tree to kill, even if cut down. This freshly plucked shoot shows Noah that recovery has begun.

8:20-22. use of altars. Altars are a common element in many religions, ancient and modern. In the Bible altars were usually constructed of stone (hewn or unhewn), but in certain circumstances even a large rock would suffice (Judg 13:19-20; 1 Sam 14:33-34). Many believe that the altar would have been understood as the table for the deity, since sacrifices were popularly understood as providing a meal for the god, though that imagery is not easily recognized in the Old Testament.

8:20. purpose of Noah's sacrifice. The purpose of Noah's sacrifice is not stated. The text calls them "burnt offerings," which served a broad function in the sacrificial system. It may be more important to note what the text does not call the sacrifice. It is not a sin offering, nor specifically designated a thank offering. The burnt offerings are usually associated with petitions or entreaties set before God. In contrast, the sacrifice offered after the flood in the *Gilgamesh Epic and in the earlier *Sumerian version of the flood story feature libations and grain offerings as well as meat sacrifices in order to provide a feast for the gods. The general purpose for sacrifice in the ancient world was to appease the anger of the gods by gifts of food and drink, and that is probably the intention of the flood hero in the Mesopotamian accounts.

8:21. pleasing aroma. Sacrifice here, as well as throughout the Pentateuch, is said to produce a pleasing aroma—terminology that was retained from the ancient contexts in which sacrifice was viewed as food for deity. This account falls far short of the graphic description in the *Gilgamesh Epic, where the famished gods (deprived of food for the duration of the flood) gather around the sacrifice "like flies," glad to find reprieve from starvation.

9:1-17
The Covenant with Noah

9:2-4. meat eating in ancient world. Meat was not a common dish on ancient dinner tables. Animals were kept for their milk, hair and wool, not specifically for their meat. Thus meat was only available when an animal died or was killed as a sacrifice. While meat is now put on the list of acceptable foods, there is still a restriction on eating meat with the blood. In ancient times blood was considered a life force (Deut 12:23). The prohibition does not require that no blood at all be consumed, but only that the blood must be drained. The draining of the blood before eating the meat was a way of returning the life force of the animal to the God who gave it life. This offers recognition that they have taken the life with permission and are partaking of God's bounty as his guests. Its function is not unlike that of the blessing said before a meal in modern practice. No comparable prohibition is known in the ancient world.

9:5-6. capital punishment. Human life, because of the image of God, remains under the protection of God. The accountability to God for preserving human life is put into humanity's hands, thus instituting blood vengeance in the ancient world and capital punishment in modern societies. In Israelite society blood vengeance was in the hands of the family of the victim.

9:8-17. covenant. A *covenant is a formal agreement between two parties. The principal section of a covenant is the stipulations section, which may include requirements for either party or both. In this covenant God takes stipulations upon himself, rather than imposing them on Noah and his family. Unlike the later covenant with Abraham, and those that build on the covenant with Abraham, this covenant does not entail election or a new phase of revelation. It is also made with every living creature, not just people.

9:13. rainbow significance. The designation of the rainbow as a sign of the *covenant does not suggest that this was the first rainbow ever seen. The function of a sign is connected to the significance attached to it. In like manner, *circumcision is designated as a sign of the covenant with Abraham, yet that was an ancient practice, not new with Abraham and his family. In the *Gilgamesh Epic the goddess *Ishtar identified the lapis lazuli (deep blue semiprecious stones with traces of gold-colored pyrite) of her necklace as the basis of an oath by which she would never forget the days of the flood. An eleventh-century *Assyrian relief shows two hands reaching out of the clouds, one hand offering blessing, the other holding a bow. Since the word for rainbow is the same word as that used for the weapon, this is an interesting image.

9:18-28
Noah's Pronouncement
Concerning His Sons

9:24-27. patriarchal pronouncements. When Noah discovered that Ham had been indiscreet, he uttered a curse on Canaan and a blessing on Shem and Japheth. In the biblical material the patriarchal pronouncement generally concerns the destiny of the sons with regard to the fertility of the ground, the fertility of the family and relationships between family members. Other examples in Genesis can be seen in 24:60; 27:27-29, 39-40; 48:15-16; 49:1-28. From this practice we can draw several conclusions concerning this passage. First of all, Ham's indiscreet action need not be seen as the "cause" for the curse, only the occasion that evoked it. Compare, for example, when Isaac asked Esau to prepare a meal so that he could bless him; the meal was not the cause of blessing, it only created a suitable environment for it. Second, we need not be concerned that Canaan appears to be singled out without cause. We could well assume that the pronouncement was much more comprehensive, including some unfavorable statements about Ham. The biblical writer has no need to preserve the whole—he merely chooses those sections that are pertinent to his point and relevant to his readers, since the Canaanites were the Hamites with whom Israel was most familiar. Third, we need not understand these as prophecies originating from God. There is no "Thus says the Lord . . ." They are the patriarch's pronouncement, not God's (cf. the use of the first person in 27:37). Even so, they were taken very seriously and considered to have influence in the unfolding of history and personal destiny.

10:1-32
The Table of Nations

10:1. criteria of division. The genealogy of Noah's family provides information on the future history and geographical distribution of peoples in the ancient Near East. Clues are given about the settlement of the coastal areas, northern Africa, Syria-Palestine and Mesopotamia. All of the major regions are thus represented, as well as most of the nations who will in some way interact with the Israelites, among them Egypt, Canaan, the Philistines, the Jebusites, *Elam and Asshur. This suggests the political division of the "world" at the time this list was written and provides a definite indication that the roots of the Israelites are in Mesopotamia. There is no attempt, however, to link these peoples to racial divisions. Ancient peoples were more concerned with distinctions based on nationality, linguistics and ethnicity.

10:2-29. names: personal, patronymic, political. The names of Noah's descendants listed in the "Table of Nations" are designed to reflect the totality of humanity and to give at least a partial sense of their geopolitical divisions and affiliations. A total of seventy peoples are listed, a number found elsewhere in the text for the number of Jacob's family to enter Egypt (Gen 46:27) and as the representatives of the nation (seventy elders, Ex 24:9; Ezek 8:11). Other examples of seventy representing totality are found in the number of gods in the *Ugaritic pantheon and the number of sons of Gideon (Judg 8:30) and of Ahab (2 Kings 10:1). The kinship ties established in the list of peoples have been considered by some to reflect political affiliation (lord-vassal relationships) rather than blood tie. Kinship language is sometimes used in the Bible to reflect political associations (1 Kings 9:13). Some of the names in the list appear to be the names of tribes or nations rather than of individuals. In *Hammurabi's genealogy a number of the names are tribal or geographical names, so this would not be unusual in an ancient document. As a vertical genealogy, this list is simply trying to establish relationships of various sorts.

10:2-5. Japhethites. Although not all of the descendants of Japheth are tied to contiguous regions, they could all be defined from an Israelite perspective as coming from across the sea (NIV: "maritime peoples" in v. 5). A *Babylonian world map from the seventh or eighth century illustrates the geographical worldview that there were many peoples considered on the outskirts of civilization beyond the sea. Many named here can be identified with sections or peoples in Asia Minor (Magog, Tubal, Meshek, Tyras, Togarmah) or the Ionian islands (Dodanim), as well as Cyprus (Elisha and Kittim). There are also several that seem, based on *Assyrian and *Babylonian records, to originate in the area to the east of the Black Sea and in the Iranian plateau—Cimmerians (Gomer), Scythians (Ashkenaz), Medes (Madai), Paphlagonians (Riphat). Tarshish presents the most problems, since it has generally been identified with Spain and that takes it out of the geographic sphere of the others. However, the theme of Greek or Indo-European peoples for these "nations" would make a tie to Sardinia or perhaps Carthage possible.

10:6-20. Hamites. The common theme in the genealogy of the Hamites is their close geographical, political and economic importance to the people of Israel. These nations serve as major rivals and literally surround Israel (Egypt, Arabia, Mesopotamia, Syro-Palestine). Most important here is the political placement of groups within the Egyptian sphere (Cush, Put, Mizraim and his descendants) and the Canaanite sphere (various peoples like the Jebusites and Hivites), and, interestingly, several are classified ethnically as Semitic peoples (Canaanites, Phoenicians, *Amorites). The list is also marked by brief narratives (Nimrod and Canaan) which break up the stereotypical genealogical framework and tie in areas (*Babylon, *Nineveh, Sidon, Sodom and Gomorrah) which will be significant in later periods of Israelite history.

10:8-12. Nimrod. Interpreters over the years have attempted to identify Nimrod with known historical figures such as Tukulti-Ninurta I (an *Assyrian king during the period of the biblical judges), or with Mesopotamian deities such as Ninurta, a warrior god and patron of the hunt, who in one myth hunts down a number of fantastic creatures and defeats or kills them. In Genesis, however, Nimrod is clearly a human hero rather than divine or even semidivine. Late Jewish tradition picked up occasionally by church fathers envisioned him as the builder of the Tower of Babel and the originator of idolatry, but these ideas have no basis in the text. The extension of his kingdom from southern Mesopotamia (v. 10) to northern Mesopotamia (v. 11) corresponds to the growth of the first known empire in history, the dynasty of Agade ruled by Sargon and Naram-Sin (about 2300 B.C.), among the greatest of the heroic kings of old. Nimrod's kingdom included Erech (=*Uruk), the city where *Gilgamesh reigned and one of the oldest and greatest centers of *Sumerian culture.

10:21-31. Semites. Even though Shem is the oldest son of Noah, his genealogy appears last, as is typical in Genesis for the son the text seeks to follow most closely. There is a mixture of Semitic and non-Semitic nations (by our ethnic criteria) in this list. For instance, *Elam (east of the Tigris) and Lud (Lydia in southern Asia Minor) are considered non-Semitic, but there are close historical ties to both areas in later periods. Sheba, Ophir and Havilah are all part of the Arabian region, and *Aram originated east of the Tigris and north of Elam but came to be associated with the Aramaeans, who dominated Syria and northwest Mesopotamia at the end of the second millennium B.C.

10:25. dividing of the earth. While this has traditionally been taken to refer to the division of the nations after the Tower of Babel incident (Gen 11:1-9), other possibilities exist. It could, for instance, refer to a division of human communities into sedentary farmers and pastoral nomads; or, possibly a migration of peoples is documented here that drastically transformed the culture of the ancient Near East—perhaps one represented in a break-off group traveling southeast in Genesis 11:2.

11:1-9
The Tower of Babel

11:1. common language tradition. The account of a time when all mankind spoke a single language is preserved in *Sumerian in the epic entitled *Enmerkar and the Lord of Aratta*. It speaks of a time when there were no wild beasts and only harmony among people: "The whole universe in unison spoke to *Enlil in one tongue." It then reports that speech was changed and "contention" was brought into it. There is nothing else in this account that parallels the Tower of Babel, but confusion of language by deity can be seen as an ancient theme.

11:2. Shinar. Shinar is one of the biblical designations for the lower region of the Tigris-Euphrates basin. It has long been identified as linguistically equivalent to "Sumer," the designation for the same region that witnessed the earliest development of civilization. The principal cities of the region in earliest times were *Ur, Eridu, *Uruk and Nippur.

11:3. brick technology. The passage speaks of using kiln-baked bricks in place of stone. In Palestine readily available stone was used for the foundations of important buildings and sun-dried brick for the superstructure. Kiln-fired brick was unnecessary and is not attested in this region. In the southern plains of Mesopotamia, however, stone would have to be quarried some distance away and transported. The technology of baking brick was developed toward the end of the fourth millennium, and the resulting product, using bitumen as a mastic, proved waterproof and as sturdy as stone. Since it was an expensive process, it was used only for important public buildings.

11:4. urbanization. Urbanization in southern Mesopotamia was pioneered by the *Sumerians in the early centuries of the third millennium B.C. The "cities" of this period were not designed for people to live in. They housed the public sector, for the most part religious buildings and storage facilities enclosed by a wall. Since the government of these early cities was made up of elders connected to the temple, there would not even have been separate government buildings, though there may have been residences for these public officials. The determination to build a city suggests a move toward urbanization, which can easily be understood as a course of action that would prevent scattering. The cooperative living available through urbanization would allow more people to live together in a defined region, as it would allow for large-scale irrigation and excess grain production. The need for nonurbanized peoples to scatter is well demonstrated in the story of Abraham and Lot in Genesis 13.

11:4. tower. The central feature of these early cities in southern Mesopotamia was the temple complex. Often, the temple complex *was* the city. The temple complex in this period would have been comprised of the temple itself, where the patron deity was worshiped, and, most prominently, by the ziggurat. Ziggurats were structures designed to provide stairways from the heavens (the gate of the gods) to earth so that the gods could come down into their temple and into the town and bring blessing. It was a convenience provided for the deity and his messengers. These stairways were featured in the mythology of the *Sumerians and also are portrayed in Jacob's dream (Gen 28:12). The ziggurats were constructed of a sun-dried brick frame filled with dirt and rubble and finished off with a shell of kiln-baked brick. There were no rooms, chambers or passageways of any sort inside. The structure itself was simply made to hold up the stairway. At the top was a small room for the deity, equipped with a bed and a table supplied regularly with food. In this way the deity could refresh himself during his descent. None of the festivals or *ritual acts suggest that *people* used the ziggurat for any purpose. It was for the gods. The priests certainly would have to go up to provide fresh supplies, but it was holy ground. The ziggurat served as the architectural representation of the pagan religious developments of this period, when deity was transformed into the image of man.

11:4. making a name. The people were interested in making a name for themselves. This is a desire that God recognized as legitimate in other contexts, saying that he will make a name for Abraham and David. Having descendants was one way of making a name. While there need not be anything evil or sinful about wanting to make a name for oneself, we must also acknowledge that this desire may become obsessive or lead one to pursue wicked schemes.

11:4. avoiding scattering. Likewise, it is logical that the people would want to avoid scattering. Though God had blessed them with the privilege of multiplying so much that they would fill the earth, that did not obligate them to scatter. The filling was to be accomplished by multiplying, not by spreading out. Economic conditions would have eventually forced the breakup of any group of people, which was why they embarked on the course of urbanization. God scattered them not because he did not want them to be together, but because their united efforts were causing

mischief (as we separate children who misbehave).

11:5. came down to see. The ziggurat would have been built so that God could come down into their midst to be worshiped and bring blessing with him. God indeed "came down" to see. But rather than being pleased at their provision of this convenience, he was distressed by the threshold of paganism that had been crossed in the concepts represented by the ziggurat.

11:8. settlement patterns of *Uruk phase. Many of the features of this account point to the end of the fourth millennium as the setting of the narrative. This is the period when receding water allowed settlement of the southern Tigris-Euphrates basin. Many settlements on native soil show that the occupants brought the northern Mesopotamian culture with them. It is likewise in the period known as the Late *Uruk phase (toward the end of the fourth millennium) that the culture and technology known from these settlements in southern Mesopotamia suddenly starts showing up in settlements throughout the ancient Near East. Thus both the migration referred to in verse 2 and the dispersion of verse 9 find points of contact in the settlement pattern identified by archaeologists for the end of the fourth millennium. Urbanization, ziggurat prototypes and experimentation with kiln-baked brick also fit this time period.

11:9. ancient Babylon. The ancient history of *Babylon is difficult to recover. Excavations at the site cannot go back further than the beginning of the second millennium because the water table of the Euphrates has shifted over time and destroyed the lower levels. In the literature of Mesopotamia there is no significant mention of Babylon until it is made the capital of the *Old Babylonian empire in the eighteenth century B.C.

11:10-32
The Line of Shem, the Family of Abraham

11:28. Ur of the Chaldees. Abraham's family is from *Ur of the Chaldees. For many generations the only *Ur that has been known to modern scholars is the famous *Sumerian city on the southern Euphrates. It has been somewhat of a mystery why this southern city would be referred to as *Ur of the Chaldees—since at this time the Chaldeans were settled primarily in the northern section of Mesopotamia. An alternative was provided when textual evidence from Mesopotamia began to produce evidence of a smaller town by the name of *Ur in the northern region, not far from Haran (where Terah moves his family). This town could logically be referred to as *Ur of the Chaldees to differentiate it from the well-known *Ur in the south. This would also explain why Abraham's family is always seen as having its homeland in "Paddan *Aram" or "Aram Naharaim" (24:10; 28:2, descriptions of northern Mesopotamia between the Tigris and Euphrates).

11:30. barrenness in the ancient Near East. Failure to produce an heir was a major calamity for a family in the ancient world because it meant a disruption in the generational inheritance pattern and left no one to care for the couple in their old age. Thus legal remedies were developed which allowed a man whose wife had failed to provide him with a son to impregnate a slave girl (Code of *Hammurabi; *Nuzi texts) or a prostitute (Lipit-Ishtar Code). The children from this relationship could then be acknowledged by the father as his heirs (Code of Hammurabi). Abram and Sarai employ the same strategy when they use the slave girl Hagar as a legal surrogate to produce an heir for the aged couple (see comments on Gen 16:1-4).

11:31. Haran. The city of Haran was located 550 miles northwest of the southern *Ur, on the left bank of the Balikh River (a tributary of the upper Euphrates). Today it is in modern Turkey about ten miles from the Syrian-Turkish border. It is mentioned prominently in the *Mari texts (eighteenth century B.C.) as a center of *Amorite population in northern Mesopotamia and an important crossroads. It was known to feature a temple to the moon god, Sin. There has been very limited excavation at the site due to continuing occupation.

12:1-9
Abraham Travels to Canaan

12:1. father's household. A man was identified in the ancient world as a member of his father's household. When the head of the household died, his heir assumed that title and its responsibilities. It is also identified with ancestral lands and property. By leaving his father's household, Abram was thus giving up his inheritance and his right to family property.

12:1. The *covenant promises. Land, family and inheritance were among the most significant elements in ancient society. For farmers and herdsmen land was their livelihood. For city dwellers land represented their political identity. Descendants represented the future. Children provided for their parents in old age and enabled the family line to extend another generation. They gave proper burial to their parents and honored the names of their ancestors. In some of the ancient Near Eastern cultures these were considered essential to maintaining a comfortable existence in the afterlife. When Abram gave up his place in his father's household, he forfeited his security. He was putting his survival, his identity, his future and his security in the hands of the Lord.

12:6. tree of Moreh. Most likely this was a great Tabor oak *(Quercus ithaburensis),* which served as a landmark at Shechem and perhaps could have functioned as a point where a teacher (the literal meaning of *Moreh*) or judge would come to hear legal cases or provide instruction (such as Deborah's palm tree in Judg 4:5 and Danil's judgment tree in the *Ugaritic epic of *Aqhat). Besides being valued for their shade, such trees also served as evidences of *fertility and were therefore often adopted as places of worship (not often as objects of worship).

12:6. Shechem. The site of Shechem has been identified with Tell Balatah, east of modern Nablus and thirty-five miles north of Jerusalem. Perhaps because of its proximity to two nearby peaks, Mount Gerizim and Mount Ebal, it has had a long history as a sacred site. The strategic position of Shechem, at the east entrance to the pass between these mountains, also made it an important trading center. As early as the *Middle Bronze I period, Shechem is mentioned in the Egyptian texts of Pharaoh Sesostris III (1880-1840 B.C.). Excavations have revealed an apparently unwalled settlement in *Middle Bronze IIA (about 1900 B.C.) with the development of fortifications in Middle Bronze IIB (about 1750).

12:6-9. significance of altars. Altars function as sacrificial platforms. Their construction can also mark the introduction of the worship of a particular god in a new land. Abram's setting up of altars in each place where he camped defines areas to be occupied in the "Promised Land" and establishes these places as religious centers in later periods.

12:10-20
Abraham in Egypt

12:10. famine in the land. Syria-Palestine has a fragile ecology that is based on the rains which come in the winter and spring months. If these rains fail to come

The Religion of Abraham

It is important to notice that Abraham comes from a family that is not monotheistic (see Josh 24:2,14). They would have shared the polytheistic beliefs of the ancient world at that time. In this type of system the gods were connected to the forces of nature and showed themselves through natural phenomena. These gods did not reveal their natures or give any idea of what would bring their favor or wrath. They were worshiped by being flattered, cajoled, humored and appeased. *Manipulation* is the operative term. They were gods made in the image of man. God made a covenant with Abraham in order to reveal what he was really like—to correct the false view of deity that people had developed. But this was projected to take place in stages, not all at once.

The Lord, *Yahweh, is not portrayed as a God that Abraham already worshiped. When he appears to Abraham, he does not give him a doctrinal statement or require rituals or issue demands; he makes an offer. Yahweh does not tell Abraham that he is the only God there is, and he does not ask him to stop worshiping whatever gods his family was worshiping. He does not tell him to get rid of his idols, nor does he proclaim a coming Messiah or salvation. Instead, he says that he has something to give Abraham if Abraham is willing to give up some things first.

In the massive polytheistic systems of the ancient Near East the great cosmic deities, while respected and worshiped in national and royal contexts, had little personal contact with the common people. Individuals were more inclined to focus their personal or family worship on local or family deities. We can best understand this through an analogy to politics. Though we respect and recog-

at the appropriate time, are less or more than is expected, or fail to come at all, then planting and harvests are negatively affected. It was not uncommon for drought and resulting famine to occur in this region.

12:11-12. wife as sister. The wife/sister theme appears three times in Genesis. It functions as (1) a protective strategy by migrants against local authorities, (2) a contest between God and the god-king Pharaoh in Genesis 12 and (3) a literary motif designed to heighten tension in the story when the promise of an heir to the *covenant is threatened. The logic is possibly that if an individual in power desired to take a woman into his harem he might be inclined to negotiate with a brother, but he would be more likely to eliminate a husband. In each case, the ancestral couple are reunited and enriched and the local ruler is shamed. On a personal level this does not speak well of Abram, but it does make him appear more human than in other stories.

12:11. the beauty of aged Sarah. Sarah is described as a beautiful woman, though by this time she is between sixty-five and seventy years of age. The phrase used to describe Sarah here is sometimes used to describe a woman's beauty (2 Sam 14:27), but it does not necessarily refer strictly to feminine allure or attractiveness. It is sometimes used to describe male good looks (1 Sam 17:42), but it may be important to note that the phrase is also used to describe a fine specimen of cow (Gen 41:2). We need not therefore assume that Sarah has miraculously retained the stunning beauty of youth. Her dignity, her bearing, her countenance, her outfitting could all contribute to the impression that she is a striking woman.

12:10-20. Beni Hasan tomb painting. The Twelfth Dynasty (19th century B.C.)

nize the authority of our national leaders, if we have a problem in our community we pursue it with our local government rather than write a letter to the president. In Mesopotamia in the first part of the second millennium an important religious development can be observed that parallels this approach to politics. The people began to relate to "personal gods," who were often then adopted as family gods and worshiped from generation to generation. This was usually the function of minor deities and was at times no more than a personification of luck. The personal god was one that was believed to take special interest in the family or an individual and to be a source of blessing and good fortune in return for worship and obedience. While the personal god was not worshiped exclusively, most of the worship by the individual and his family would be focused on him.

It is possible that Abraham's first responses to Yahweh may have been along these lines—that Abraham may have viewed Yahweh as a personal god that was willing to become his "divine sponsor." Though we are given no indication that Yahweh explained or demanded a monotheistic belief, nor that Abraham responded with one, it is clear that the worship of Yahweh dominated Abraham's religious experience. By making a break with his land, his family and his inheritance, Abraham is also breaking all of his religious ties, because deities would be associated with geographical, political and ethnic divisions. In his new land Abraham would have no territorial gods; as the head of a new people he would have brought no family gods; having left his country he would have no national or city gods; and it was Yahweh who filled this void, becoming the "God of Abraham, Isaac and Jacob."

tomb painting of Khnum-hotep III at Beni Hasan (near Minya in Middle Egypt) depicts one of many caravans of "Asiatics" that brought raw materials and exotic items (frankincense, lapis lazuli). These traders wear multicolored robes, bring their families with them and travel with their weapons and donkeys laden with "ox-hide," ingots of bronze and other trade goods. Their garb and the ease with which they were able to travel to Egypt may well reflect the look of Abram's household. Egypt served as both a market as well as a source of food and temporary employment for many groups driven by war or famine from the rest of the Near East.

12:17. nature of disease. The assumption in the ancient world is that all disease is a reflection of the displeasure of a god or gods. Infectious disease could be coped with through purification and sacrifice and might be treated with herbal medicines, but the root cause was viewed as divine, not physical. Thus disease was considered the direct result of sin or some violation of custom, so the ancients would seek to determine which god might be responsible and how he might be appeased. Medicinal remedies would be augmented by magical remedies and incantations.

13:1-18
Abraham and Lot

13:1-4. Abram's itinerary. Since the household is depicted as pastoral nomads, they would have had to stop periodically to find pasture and water for the herds and flocks. The Negev was more heavily populated in the early second millennium and might have provided specific staging points for this journey (see Ex 17:1). The return to the vicinity of Bethel marks the resumption of the *covenantal narrative and sets the stage for the separation from Lot. From the border of Egypt to the area of Be-

thel/Ai would be a journey of about two hundred miles.

13:5-7. herding needs and lifestyle. The primary requirements for a successful herding group are pasturage and water sources. The hot, dry months from April through September require movement of herds to higher elevations where grass remains and streams and springs can be found. In the colder, wet months of October through March, the animals will be brought back to the plains for grazing. This seasonal movement necessitates long separations of herders from their villages or the establishment of an unconnected, seminomadic lifestyle in which whole families travel with the herds. The knowledge of natural resources along their routes of travel would be their primary lore. Disputes over grazing land and water rights would be the most frequent cause of quarrels between herdsmen.

13:7. Canaanites and Perizzites. See comment on Exodus 3:7-10.

13:10. the plain of the Jordan. It would be possible to get a good view of the Jordan Valley and the northern area of the Dead Sea from the hills around Bethel. While the area around the Dead Sea is not a particularly hospitable region today, this verse makes it clear that prior to the Lord's judgment the area had a far different quality. It should be noted that there are extensive areas along the Jordan Plateau that do provide ample grazing, and this may also be represented in this narrative.

13:12. the boundaries of Canaan. The eastern boundary of Canaan is everywhere identified as the Jordan River (see especially Num 34:1-12 and the comments on it). Thus it becomes clear that by moving to the vicinity of the cities of the plain Lot has gone outside the land of Canaan, leaving it entirely to Abram.

13:18. Hebron. The city of Hebron is located in the Judean hill country (c.

3,300 feet above sea level) approximately nineteen miles southeast of Jerusalem and twenty-three miles east of Beersheba. Ancient roadways converge on this site coming east from Lachish and connecting with the road north to Jerusalem, indicating its importance and continuous settlement. Its springs and wells provide ample water for olive and grape production and would have supported a mixed agricultural-pastoral economy such as that described in Genesis 23. Hebron is said to have been founded "seven years before Zoan" (Avaris in Egypt), dating it to the seventeenth century B.C. (see comment on Num 13:22). The construction of an altar here, as at Bethel, transforms this into an important religious site, and its subsequent use as a burial place for the ancestors established its political importance (reflected in the Davidic narrative—2 Sam 2:1-7; 15:7-12).

14:1-16
Abraham Rescues Lot

14:1-4. the kings of the East. The kings of the East have remained stubbornly obscure despite numerous attempts to link them to historically known figures, though the geographical areas they represent can be identified with some confidence. Shinar refers elsewhere in the Bible to the southern Mesopotamian plains known in earliest times as *Sumer and later connected to *Babylonia. Ellasar corresponds to an ancient way of referring to *Assyria (a.la$_5$.sar). *Elam is the usual name for the region, which in this period comprised the whole of the land east of Mesopotamia from the Caspian Sea to the Persian Gulf (modern Iran). Goiim is the most vague, but it is generally associated with the *Hittites (who were located in the eastern section of present-day Turkey), mostly because the king's name, Tidal, is easily associated with the common Hittite royal name, Tudhaliyas. As a reference to a group of people, Goiim would most likely refer to a coalition of "barbaric" peoples (like the *Akkadian designation, *Umman Manda*). In *Mari it is a designation used to refer to the Hancans. While there were many periods in the first half of the second millennium when the Elamites were closely associated with powers in Mesopotamia, it is more difficult to bring the Hittites into the picture. We do know that *Assyrian merchants had a trading colony in the Hittite region, but there is no indication of joint military ventures. Early Hittite history is very sketchy, and we have little information concerning where the Hittites came from or precisely when they moved into Anatolia. The names of the kings of the East are authentic enough, but none of them have been identified or linked to the kings of these respective regions at this period. So, for instance, there is an Arioch who was prince of Mari in the eighteenth century. We certainly have no information of Elamite control of sections of Palestine as suggested in verse 4, but it must be admitted that there are many gaps in our knowledge of the history of this period. None of the five kings of Canaan are known outside the Bible, for even these cities are yet unattested in other ancient records, despite occasional claims of possible references to Sodom.

14:5-7. the itinerary and conquests of the kings of the East. The itinerary of conquest is given as is common in chronographic texts. The route goes from north to south along what is known as the King's Highway, the major north-south artery in Transjordan, just east of the Jordan Valley. Ashtaroth, neighboring the capital later called Karnaim, was the capital of the region just east of the Sea of Galilee inhabited by the Rephaim. Virtually nothing is known of these peoples, or of the Zuzites and

Emites, though all of them are identified with the giants of the land at the time of the conquest under Joshua (cf. Deut 2). The next stop was Ham in northern Gilead. Shaveh, also known as Kiriathaim, was in Reubenite territory when the land was divided among the tribes and bordered on the Moabite region. The Horites were the people living in the region later known as Edom, the next region south. After reaching the area of the gulf of Aqaba (the town of El Paran= Elath?), the invaders turn northwest to confront the Amalekites in the region of Kadesh Barnea (at that time called En Mishpat) and the *Amorites in the southern hill country. This route then brings them around to the cities of the plain in the region south and east of the Dead Sea. The towns of Sodom and Gomorrah have not been located with any certainty, though some think that their remains are beneath part of the Dead Sea (see comments on Gen 19). After the battle in the Valley of Siddim, the four kings traveled along the west side of the Jordan and got as far as Dan, in the very north of the land of Canaan, before being overtaken by Abraham and his men.

14:10. tar pits. Tar pits are common in this area that is so rich in bitumen that large amounts bubble to the surface and even float on the Dead Sea. The word translated "pits" is the same word used for wells of water throughout the Old Testament and therefore generally refers to a spot that has been dug out. The Valley of Siddim, then, had many pits that had been dug to extract bitumen, and these provided refuge for the kings (they "lowered themselves into them" rather than "they fell into them").

14:13. "the Hebrew." Abram is referred to as "Abram the Hebrew." Typically the designation "Hebrew" in early times was used only as a point of reference for foreigners. Besides the use here, it is used to identify Joseph in Egypt (e.g.,

39:14-17), the Israelite slaves in reference to the Egyptian masters (Ex 2:11), Jonah to the sailors (Jon 1:9), the Israelites to the Philistines (1 Sam 4:6), and other such situations. Some have thought that "Hebrew" is not in these cases an ethnic reference but a designation of a social class of people known as the "Habiru" in many ancient texts, where they are typically dispossessed peoples.

14:14-16. 318 trained men. Here we discover that Abram has a household of significant size (318 recruits or retainers). The word used to describe these men occurs nowhere else in the Old Testament, but does occur in an *Akkadian letter of the fifteenth century B.C. Whether Abram is placed within the early part of the *Middle Bronze Age, when the area was predominantly occupied by herdsmen and villagers, or within the later *Middle Bronze Age when there were more fortified settlements, this army would have been a match for any other armed force in the region. Even as late as the *Amarna period the armies of any particular city state would not have been much larger.

14:15. battle tactics. Abram caught up to the eastern army at the northern border of the land, Dan. Abram uses the strategy of nighttime ambush, which is attested in texts as early as the Judges period in Egyptian as well as in *Hittite documents.

14:17-24
Abraham and Melchizedek

14:17-20. Melchizedek. Melchizedek is introduced as the king of Salem and is portrayed as the principal king of the region in that he receives a portion of the booty. Salem is generally considered to be Jerusalem, though early Christian evidence and the Madeba map associate it with Shechem. (The Madeba map is the earliest map of Palestine. It is a mosaic on the floor of a sixth-century A.D.

church.) Often one city-state would gain predominance over the others in the region, as is seen in the book of Joshua where kings of Jerusalem and Hazor put the southern and northern coalitions together. Whether Melchizedek is Canaanite, *Amorite or Jebusite cannot be easily determined. The name of God that he uses to bless Abram, *El Elyon* ("God Most High"), is well known as a way of referring to the chief Canaanite god, *El, in Canaanite literature.

14:18-19. meeting of Abraham and Melchizedek. Their meeting takes place in the Valley of Shaveh. The designation of it as the King's Valley connects it to the valley just south of Jerusalem, most likely where the Kidron and Hinnom valleys come together. In a later period, Absalom built a monument here (2 Sam 18:18). The communal meal that they share would typically indicate a peaceful agreement between them. *Hittite treaties refer to the provision of food in wartime by allies. Melchizedek is anxious to make peace with such a proven military force, and Abram submits by paying the tithe, thereby acknowledging Melchizedek's status.

14:21-24. agreement between Abraham and kings of Sodom. The king of Sodom acknowledged that Abram had a right to the booty, but asks that the people be returned to him. Abram refuses the booty with the explanation that he is under oath to *El Elyon (whom he identifies as *Yahweh) not to profit from his military action. It is possible that this agreement would have occasioned the formulation of a document to formalize the terms. Such a document could easily have taken the form that this chapter takes and may have even served as a source for this chapter.

15:1-21
Ratification of the Covenant

15:1. visions. Visions were a means used by God to communicate to people. All of the other visions of this category in the Old Testament were given to prophets (the writing prophets as well as Balaam) and often resulted in prophetic *oracles which were then delivered to the people. Visions may be experienced in dreams but are not the same as dreams. They may be either visual or auditory. They may involve natural or supernatural settings, and the individual having the vision may be either an observer or a participant. Visions are likewise part of the prophetic institution in other cultures in the ancient Near East.

15:2-3. inheritance by servant. In those instances where the head of a household had no male heir, it was possible for a servant to be legally adopted as the heir, as particularly demonstrated in an *Old Babylonian text from *Larsa. This would most likely be a course of last resort, since it would mean transference of property to a person (and his line) who was (1) originally a servant or bondsman, and (2) not a blood relative. It signals the frustration of the childless Abram that he tells God that he has designated Eliezer of Damascus as his heir, though it is not clear whether he has actually adopted Eliezer or is simply referring to that as the only remaining course of action.

15:9-10. the ritual of dividing animals. As in the case in Jeremiah 34:18, where a *covenant *ritual is represented by passage between the severed body of a sacrificial animal, here Abram is given the "sign" of the covenant promise for which he asked. Each "three-year old" animal (calf, goat, ram, dove, pigeon, the same animals featured in the sacrificial system described in Leviticus) is cut in half, although the body sections of the birds are not separated. Second-millennium *Hittite texts use a similar procedure for purification, while some first-millennium *Aramaic treaties use such a ritual for placing a curse on any violation of the treaty. Texts from *Mari and *Alalakh feature the killing of animals as part of the ceremony of making a treaty. Walking through this sacrificial pathway could be seen as a symbolic action enacting both the covenant's promise of land and a curse on the one who violates the promise, though interpreters have wondered what significance a self-curse could possibly have for God. Abram's driving away the birds of prey further symbolizes the future protection from their enemies when they take possession of the land.

15:17. smoking firepot and blazing torch. The firepot is made of earthenware and could be of various sizes. It functioned as an oven principally for baking, including the baking of grain offerings (Lev 2:4). The torch could certainly be used to provide light, but it is also used in military contexts or to speak of God's judgment (Zech 12:6). Mesopotamian *rituals of this period usually featured a sacred torch and censer in the initiation of rites, particularly nocturnal rites of purification. Purification would be accomplished by the torch and censer being moved alongside of someone or something. While in Mesopotamia the torch and oven represented particular deities, here they represent *Yahweh, perhaps as the purifier. This would be one of many instances where the Lord used familiar concepts and motifs to reveal himself.

15:18. river of Egypt. The usual designation of Israel's southwestern border is the "brook [wadi] of Egypt," identified with Wadi el 'Arish in the northeastern Sinai (Num 34:5). It is unlikely that it refers to the Nile River. Another possibility is that it refers to the easternmost delta tributary that emptied into Lake Sirbonis.

15:19-21. occupants of Canaan. This is the longest (including ten groups) of seventeen such lists of Canaan's pre-Is-

raelite peoples (see Deut 7:1; Josh 3:10; 1 Kings 9:20). Each of these lists, which usually comprise six or seven names, ends with the Jebusites (perhaps tied to David's conquest of Jerusalem), but the list in Genesis 15 is the only one to exclude the Hivites. For the *Hittites, Perizzites, *Amorites, Canaanites and Jebusites, see the comments on Exodus 3:7-10 and Numbers 13. The Kenites are often associated with the Midianites and appear as a seminomadic people from the Sinai and Negev region. The name suggests that they were metalworkers, tinkerers or smiths. The Kenizzites, Kadmonites and Girgashites are little known, though the latter is also attested in the *Ugaritic texts. The Rephaim are considered to be Anakites in Deuteronomy 2:11, who in turn appear as giants in Numbers 13:33. Aside from these associations, nothing is known of this ethnic group.

16:1-16
The Birth of Ishmael

16:1-4. maidservants. Slave women or bondswomen were considered both property and legal extensions of their mistress. As a result it would be possible for Sarai to have Hagar perform a variety of household tasks as well as to use her as a surrogate for her own barren womb.

16:2. contractual arrangements for barrenness. *Concubines did not have the full status of wives but were girls who came to the marriage with no dowry and whose role included childbearing. As a result concubinage would not be viewed as polygamy. In Israel, as in most of the ancient world, monogamy was generally practiced. Polygamy was not contrary to the law or contemporary moral standards but was usually not economically feasible. The main reason for polygamy would be that the first wife was barren. In the Bible most cases of polygamy among commoners occur prior to the period of the monarchy.

16:3-4. surrogate mothers. Surrogate mothers appear only in the ancestral narratives: Hagar and the two maidservants of Rachel and Leah (Gen 30). There is no contract mentioned here, since these women were all legal extensions of their mistress and any children they bore could be designated as the children of their mistress. The eighteenth century B.C. *Babylonian Code of *Hammurabi does contain surrogate contracts for priestesses who were not allowed to conceive children. As in the biblical examples, these surrogates had a lower legal standing than the wife.

16:5-6. relationship of Sarah and Hagar. Women in the ancient world obtained honor through marriage and children. Although Hagar was a servant, the fact that she had conceived a child and Sarai had not gave her cause to hold her mistress in contempt. Sarai's reaction in abusing Hagar may be based on both jealousy and class difference.

16:7-10. angel as messenger. The word translated "angel" simply means "messenger" in Hebrew and can be used for either human or supernatural messengers. Since these messengers represent God, they do not speak for themselves, but only for God. It is therefore not unusual for them to use the first person, "I." Messengers were granted the authority to speak for the one they represented and were treated as if they were the one they represented.

16:13-14. "seeing God." Hagar affirms a supernatural identity for the messenger and may well believe that the messenger was indeed a deity, but the fact that she expresses incredulity about the likelihood of having seen a deity does not mean that she actually has seen one (additionally the text is very difficult to translate and may not even suggest this much). Most likely Hagar is expressing surprise that she has encountered a deity who is inclined to show favor to her in such an unlikely place.

16:13. naming God. The text identifies the deity as the LORD (*Yahweh) but gives no indication that Hagar knew it was Yahweh. This is the only example in the Old Testament of someone assigning a name to deity. Usually naming someone or something is a way of affirming authority over the one named. Here it is more likely that since she does not know the name of the deity that has shown her favor, she assigns a name to him as an identification of his nature and so that she might invoke him in the future.

16:14. Kadesh and Bered. The location of the well of Beer Lahai Roi, where Hagar experienced a *theophany and was told of her son's future, is most likely in the Negev between Kadesh Barnea and Bered. The oasis of Kadesh Barnea is in the northeast section of the Sinai, on the southern border of the Wilderness of Zin (see comment on Num 13). Since Bered does not appear elsewhere in the text, its location is uncertain, though Jebel umm el-Bared to the southeast is as good a guess as any.

17:1-27
Circumcision, the Sign of the Covenant

17:1-2. El Shaddai. *El Shaddai ("God Almighty") in verse 1 is a relatively common name used for the Lord in the Old Testament (48 times), though the conventional translations are little more than guesses. It appears only once outside the Old Testament in the name "Shaddai-Ammi" on an Egyptian statue from the Judges period, though there may be a reference to Shaddai-beings in the Deir Allah inscription. One of the most frequent suggestions understands Shaddai as related to the *Babylonian *sadu*, "steppe, mountain," but evidence is sparse.

17:3-8. name changing. Names had power in the ancient world. By naming the animals, Adam demonstrated his mastery over them. In a similar way, God's changing Abram's name to Abraham and Sarai's name to Sarah signifies both a reiteration of the *covenant promise and the designation of these people as God's chosen servants.

17:4. covenanting with God. There are no parallels in the ancient world to *covenants between deity and mortal, though certainly gods are known to make demands and promise favorable treatment. In most of these cases kings report their care of the sanctuaries of the god and then tell how the deity responded with blessing. But these fall far short of a covenant relationship initiated by deity for his own purposes.

17:9-14. circumcision. *Circumcision was practiced widely in the ancient Near East as a rite of puberty, fertility or marriage. Although the Israelites were not the only people to circumcise their sons, this sign was used to mark them as members of the *covenantal community. When used in relation to marriage, terminology suggests it was performed by the new male in-laws, indicating that the groom was coming under the protection of their family in this new relationship. Performed on infants, it is more a ritual scarring than something done for health reasons. The fact that blood is shed also signifies that this is a sacrificial *ritual and may function as a substitution for human sacrifice, which was practiced by other people. Waiting until the eighth day to perform this ritual may reflect the high infant mortality rate and the desire to determine if the child was viable. The *Hittites also had a ritual for the seventh day of the newborn's life. Circumcision can be seen as one of many cases where God transforms a common practice to a new (though not necessarily unrelated) purpose in revealing himself and relat-

ing to his people.

17:15-22. divine announcement of sons. The divine announcement of a son to be born is a common motif found throughout ancient Near Eastern literature. Perhaps most notable is the announcement by the Canaanite deity *El to King Danil that he would finally have a son in his old age, in the *Ugaritic story of *Aqhat. Additional examples are found in the *Hittite tale where the sun god tells Appu he will have a son, and in Mesopotamian literature where the god Shamash advises *Etana, king of Kish, how to procure a son. Also notable in this text is the statement that Sarah will be the mother of kings. This would be an indication of long survival of the line and great success for the line.

18:1-15
Abraham's Visitors

18:1. entrance to tent at heat of day. The goatskin tents of pastoral nomadic people were designed to hold in heat at night with the flaps down and to allow a breeze to pass through during the day, when the flaps were up. Sitting at the entrance during the heat of the day would provide needed shade while a person enjoyed the breeze and guarded the tent's contents.

18:2-5. hospitality (meals). Hospitality customs required that all strangers who approached a dwelling were to be offered the opportunity to rest, refresh themselves and eat a meal. This was done to transform potential enemies into at least temporary friends. Protocol required that the meal served to the guest exceed what was first offered. Thus Abraham simply offers a meal, but what he orders prepared is freshly baked bread, a calf and a mixture of milk and yogurt. What is particularly generous here is the fresh meat, an item not usually found in their daily diet. This meal is similar to that offered by Danil to the representative of the gods, Kathar-wa-Hasis (when he comes traveling through town), in the Ugaritic epic of Aqhat.

18:4. foot washing. Washing the feet of guests was a standard act of hospitality in the dry, dusty climate that characterized much of the ancient Near East. Open leather sandals were common, as were enclosed soft leather boots. Neither style succeeded in keeping out the dirt of the road.

18:6-8. flour and baking. The three seahs of flour (c. twenty quarts) used to make bread again reflects Abraham's generosity to his guests. The method of baking, since nomadic people lacked ovens, would be placing the dough on the sides of a heated pot or dutch oven. This produced a slightly raised, circular loaf of bread. Curds (yogurt) and milk are served along with the meal as customary side dishes and normal byproducts of the herd. The fact that Sarah remains in the tent may reflect a custom of women not eating with men.

18:16-33
Discussion of God's Justice and Mercy

18:20-21. judge collecting evidence. There is a combination of anthropomorphism (God being given humanlike qualities) and theodicy (explanation of divine action) in this story and in the Tower of Babel episode (Gen 11). In both cases, to demonstrate divine justice and fairness, God "comes down" to investigate a situation before taking action.

18:22-33. Abraham's bargaining. Haggling is a part of all Middle Eastern business transactions. In this case, however, Abraham's determination of the exact number of righteous persons needed to prevent the destruction of Sodom and Gomorrah provides a repeated demonstration of God's just actions. A just God

will not destroy the righteous without warning or investigation. Even the unrighteous, in this early period, can be spared for the sake of the righteous. On the other hand, however, justice is not served by overlooking wickedness. The discussion of the number of righteous people may concern not whether they can balance the wickedness of the rest but whether, given time, they might be able to exert a reforming influence.

19:1-29
The Destruction of Sodom and Gomorrah

19:1, 24. Sodom and Gomorrah. The "cities of the plain" along the eastern shore of the Dead Sea have not been positively located. Their association with Zoar (Zoara on the sixth-century A.D. Madaba map) and the bitumen pits "in the Valley of Siddim" (Gen 14:10) both point to the southern end of the Dead Sea. Arguments for their identification with the north end are based on the distance to travel from Hebron (eighteen miles versus forty miles to the southern location) and the mention of the "plain of the Jordan" in Genesis 13:10-12. Cities located in this arid region survived and prospered on the salt, bitumen and potash deposits around the Dead Sea and as trading centers for caravans traveling the road north and south. There are five sites of *Early Bronze Age cities on the southeast plain of the Dead Sea, demonstrating that fairly large populations once existed here (occupied from 3300 to 2100 B.C.): Bab-edh Dhra' (Sodom?), Safi (Zoar), Numeira (Gomorrah?), Feifa and Khanazir. Only Bab-edh Dhra and Numeira have been excavated, and the destruction of these cities has been set by archaeologists at about 2350 B.C., too early for Abraham (though chronological reckoning of this period is difficult).

19:1-3. sitting at the gate. In ancient cities the gate area functioned as a public square. Its constant flow of people made it the ideal place for businessmen to set up their booths and for judges to hear cases. The fact that Lot is sitting in the gate suggests he was doing business there and had been accepted in the community of Sodom.

19:1. bowing to the ground. One way to show respect to superiors and to demonstrate peaceful intentions was to bow to the ground. Some Egyptian texts from *El Amarna (fourteenth century B.C.) exaggerate this gesture by multiplying it seven times.

19:2. hospitality (lodging). When a host offered a guest the opportunity to spend the night, he was also accepting responsibility for the safety and well-being of his guest. The offer generally extended for a total of three days.

19:3. bread without yeast. As in the case of the unleavened bread eaten on Passover prior to the exodus (Ex 12) from Egypt, Lot's "bread without yeast" was made quickly. It was evening when his guests arrived, and he did not have time to let his bread rise before baking it.

19:4-10. behavior of men at Sodom. The angels' visit to Sodom was to determine if there were ten righteous men there. The legal formula in verse 4 makes it clear that all of the men of the city confronted Lot about his guests. In addition to the fact that homosexuality was considered a capital offense, their refusal to listen to reason and their unanimous insistence on violence as they rushed toward his house confirmed the fate of the city.

19:8. Lot's offer of his daughters. When Lot offers his virgin daughters to the men of Sodom as a substitute for his guests, he is playing the consummate host. He is willing to sacrifice his most precious possessions to uphold his honor by protecting his guests. He was saved from making this sacrifice by the refusal of the mob and the actions of the angels.

19:24. burning sulfur. The scene is one of divine retribution. Brimstone appears here and elsewhere as an agent of purification and divine wrath upon the wicked (Ps 11:6; Ezek 38:22). The natural deposits of bitumen and the sulfurous smell attached to some areas around the Dead Sea combine to provide a lasting memory of Sodom and Gomorrah's destruction. One can only speculate about the actual manner of this destruction, but perhaps the combustion of natural tars and sulfur deposits and the release of noxious gases during an earthquake are a part of the story (Deut 29:23).

19:26. pillar of salt. The story of the punishment of Lot's wife is often illustrated by some grotesquely humanlike, salt-encrusted objects that have become landmarks in the Dead Sea area (alluded to in the apocryphal Wisdom of Solomon 10:4). This phenomenon is a result of the salt spray that blows off the Dead Sea. Huge salt nodules still appear in the shallow sections of the lake. The mineral salts of the region include sodium, potash, magnesium, calcium chlorides and bromide. An earthquake in the area could easily have ignited these chemicals, causing them to rain down on the victims of the destruction.

19:30-38. origins of Moabites and Ammonites. One primary intent of the ancestral narrative is to demonstrate the origin of all of the peoples that inhabited Canaan and Transjordan. Archaeological survey of the area indicates a resettlement between the fourteenth and twelfth centuries B.C., and the language of both the Moabites and Ammonites is similar to Hebrew. Although both are considered enemy nations for most of their history, it is unlikely that their "birth" as a result of the incestuous union between Lot and his daughters (see Deut 2:9; Ps 83:5-8) is simply a political or ethnic slur. The initiative taken by Lot's daughters in the face of likely childlessness and the extinction of Lot's household may have appeared to them as the only feasible option in their desperate plight.

20:1-18
Abraham and Abimelech

20:1. Kadesh and Shur. Again a story begins with the itinerary of Abraham's travels, this time taking him south on a line between Kadesh (an oasis forty-six miles south of Beersheba in the northeastern Sinai) and Shur. The latter site probably refers to the "wall" (*shur*) of Egyptian fortresses in the eastern Delta region. The Egyptian story of *Sinuhe (twentieth century B.C.) mentions this "Wall of the Ruler" as a barrier to the incursions of Asiatics into Egypt.

20:1. Gerar. Although it is not within the range of the Kadesh-Shur line, Gerar may not have been too far of a journey for pastoral nomads such as Abraham's household. Its exact location, beyond the general area of the western Negev, is uncertain (Gen 10:19), and it may in fact be the name for a territory rather than a city. Most archaeologists, noting strong Egyptian influence in this region between 1550 and 1200 B.C., point to Tell Haror (Tell Abu Hureireh), fifteen miles northwest of Beersheba, as its probable location.

20:3. God speaking to non-Israelite in dream. There are few instances of messages being given in dreams by the Lord to Israelites, but dreams are one of the most common forms divine revelation was believed to take for the uninitiated. In the *Mari texts it is usually those who are not among the professional temple personnel who receive messages by means of dreams. In most places in the Bible where significant dreams are given to individuals the text does not explicitly state that God spoke to the individual in the dream (Pharaoh, Nebuchadnezzar).

20:7. prophet's intercession. Abraham is identified by God as a prophet who is capable of intercession on Abimelech's behalf. The role of prophet was well understood in the ancient Near East, as evidenced by over fifty texts found in the town of *Mari that report messages given by various prophets. Generally the prophet offered a message from deity, but here Abraham is praying for healing (cf. v. 17). This reflects the broader view of a prophet as one who has powerful connections to deity such that he can initiate curses or remove them. A similar prophetic role can be seen in Scripture in 1 Kings 13:6. In the ancient Near East this role would typically be played by an incantation priest.

20:11-13. relationship of Abraham and Sarah. In this repetition of the wife/sister motif, Abraham reveals that Sarah is actually his half sister. There was no incest taboo against such marriages in the ancestral period, and it was a way of insuring that female children from second marriages were cared for by a household. Abraham's deception of Abimelech is reinforced by Sarah's willingness to repeat the half-truth.

20:16. 1000 shekels. A thousand shekels of silver is a sizable sum. In *Ugaritic literature it is the amount of the bride price paid among the gods. In weight it would equal about twenty-five pounds of silver. In value it would be more than a worker could expect to make in a lifetime. The king's generosity should be understood as his guarantee that Sarah had been untouched, but also as appeasing the deity who had virtually cut off all fertility in his family.

20:17. plague on Abimelech's house. The plague of barrenness or sexual dysfunction is placed on Abimelech's house until he returns Sarah to Abraham. Abraham's intercession causes God to open their wombs. The irony is that Abimelech is denied children as long as

Abraham is denied his wife (for information on barrenness in the ancient Near East see comment on 11:30).

21:1-21
The Birth of Isaac and the Expulsion of Ishmael

21:4. 8 days. Initially the eight-day waiting period distinguishes Isaac from Ishmael, who was *circumcised at age thirteen. Subsequently, it serves as a determination of the infant's viability and may be tied to the period of uncleanness after the birth (Lev 12:1-3).

21:14. desert of Beersheba. The southern Negev region around Beersheba, Tell es-Seba', is steppe land and would have been inhospitable enough to be described as a desert. Hagar's wanderings after being expelled from Abraham's camp took her southeast through a relatively flat portion of the Negev toward northern Arabia.

21:8-21. expulsion of wife. There is a contract in the *Nuzi documents that contains a clause prohibiting the expulsion of the children of the secondary wife by the primary wife. The situation in Genesis is different on two counts: first, it is Abraham who sends them away; and second, Hagar is given her freedom, which, according to one ancient law code (Lipit-Ishtar) would mean that her children would forfeit any inheritance rights.

21:20. archer. The expulsion of Hagar and Ishmael and their subsequent life in the desert of Paran would require them to acquire survival skills. As a skilled archer, Ishmael could provide food for his family and perhaps could find occupation as a mercenary (see Is 21:17 for reference to the bowmen of Kedar, Ishmael's son).

21:21. desert of Paran. The arid wilderness of the northeastern Sinai desert was given the name of Paran. Situated west of Edom, it figures prominently in the wilderness period (Num 13:3, 26; Deut 1:1) and is the area where Kadesh is located. Its associations with Egypt are probably based on caravan trade and Egypt's military interest in the Sinai.

21:22-33
Abraham and His Neighbors

21:25-31. wells and water rights. In the semiarid region around Beersheba, water would have been a precious resource. Disputes between herdsmen and farmers over wells and springs would have arisen. To prevent this, treaties like that between Abraham and Abimelech would have established firm ownership or right of usage to wells. Note that Abraham's payment of seven ewe lambs provides the basis for the name Beersheba (well of seven) and serves as a gesture of goodwill toward the people of Gerar.

21:32. land of the Philistines. The first known mention of the Philistines outside the Bible is in the records of Pharaoh Ramses III (1182-1151 B.C.). As part of the invading *Sea Peoples, they settled in five city-states along the southern coast of Canaan and were employed by the Egyptians as mercenaries and trading partners. The picture of Abimelech (a Semitic name) as "king of Gerar" in the land of the Philistines does not match the known history of this people. This story may thus represent contact with an earlier group of Philistines who settled the area prior to the Sea Peoples' invasion, or this may simply be the *anachronistic use of the name Philistines for the area rather than the people Abraham encountered.

21:33. tamarisk tree. The tamarisk grows in sandy soil. It is deciduous and may reach over twenty feet in height, with small leaves that excrete salt. Its bark is used for tanning and its wood for building and making charcoal. Bedouin commonly plant this hearty tree for its shade and the branches which provide grazing for animals. Abraham's action probably signifies the sealing of the treaty with Abimelech—a life-giving plant symbolizing a fertile and prosperous future.

22:1-24
Abraham Requested to Sacrifice Isaac

22:2. region of Moriah. The only indication of Moriah's location given here is that it is three days' journey from Beersheba. That may simply be a conventional number of a completed journey, but in any case no direction is provided. The only other reference to Moriah is in 2 Chronicles 3:1, which refers to the site of the temple in Jerusalem but makes no mention of Abraham or this incident. Since the wooded hills around Jerusalem would not have required the transport of firewood for the sacrifice, it is most likely a coincidence of the same name rather than a reference to the same place.

22:1-2. child sacrifice. In the ancient Near East, the god that provides *fertility (*El) is also entitled to demand a portion of what has been produced. This is expressed in the sacrifice of animals, grain and children. Texts from Phoenician and Punic colonies, like Carthage in North Africa, describe the *ritual of child sacrifice as a means of insuring continued fertility. The biblical prophets and the laws in Deuteronomy and Leviticus expressly forbid this practice, but that also implies that it continued to occur. In fact, the story of Abraham's "sacrifice" of Isaac suggests that Abraham was familiar with human sacrifice and was not surprised by *Yahweh's demand. However, the story also provides a model for the substitute of an animal for a human sacrifice that clearly draws a distinction between Israelite practice and that of other cultures.

22:3. donkey domestication. The wild ass was domesticated about 3500 B.C. Its primary function from the beginning was as a pack animal because of its ability to tolerate heavy loads and to survive for long periods on little water. As a result it was often relied upon for long-distance travel and transport.

22:13-19. sacrifice as replacement. In this section the ram is offered as a sacrifice in the place of Isaac. The concept of substitution in sacrifice is not as common as we might think. In the ancient Near East the sympathetic magic of incantation *rituals would often include substitution of an animal that would be killed to remove a threat to the human subject. But the concept behind the regular institution of sacrifice was generally either to offer a gift to deity or to establish communion with deity. Even in Israel there is little to suggest that the sacrificial institution was understood to have a principally vicarious or substitutionary element. Redemption of the firstborn and Passover would be notable exceptions on the fringe of the sacrificial institution.

22:19. Beersheba. This important city, often identified as the southern limit of Israel's territory (Judg 20:1; 1 Sam 3:20), is traditionally located in the northern Negev at Tell es-Seba' (three miles east of the modern city). Its name derives from its association with the wells dug to provide water for the people and flocks in this area (see Gen 26:23-33). Archaeological evidence has been found of occupation during the monarchy through the Persian periods. The lack of archaeological evidence for the patriarchal period may suggest that the city by this name changed location, but more important is the observation that there is no suggestion here in the text that there was a walled settlement at Beersheba. There are evidences of early settlement under the modern town (Bir es-Saba') about two miles from the *tell, where some now suspect the ancient city of Beersheba was located.

23:1-20
Sarah's Death and Burial

23:2. variant place names. Place names change as new people enter a region or events occur which provide the reason to memorialize them with a name change (see Jebus and Jerusalem, 1 Chron 11:4; Luz and Bethel, Gen 28:19). Hebron's association with the name Kiriath Arba ("village of four") is unclear, but it may be related to either the joining of four villages into a single settlement or the convergence of roads at the site.

23:3-20. Hittites in Palestine. The origin of the *Hittite presence in Canaan is uncertain, although Genesis 10:15 identifies them as descendants of Canaan through their eponymous ancestor Heth. The use of Semitic names and the ease with which Abraham deals with them in Genesis 23 suggest that this particular group of Hittites was either part of the indigenous population or a trading colony that had partially assimilated to the Canaanite culture (see Gen 26:34). The Hittite empire of Asia Minor (Anatolia, modern Turkey) was destroyed during the invasion of the *Sea Peoples around 1200 B.C. A successor kingdom of Neo-Hittites continued to exist in Syria until the seventh century B.C. and is mentioned in *Assyrian and *Babylonian records. These records often refer to Palestine as the "Land of Hatti," confirming an association with these people. The groups known as Hittites occupying sections of Syria and Canaan may or may not be related to these well-known Hittites. The Hittites in Canaan have Semitic names, while the Hittites of Anatolia were Indo-European.

23:4-5. burial practices. Burial practices vary in the ancient Near East. Nomadic groups often practiced secondary burial—transporting the skeletal remains to a traditional site long after death. Burial chambers were used by village cultures. These could be natural or hand-carved caves, or subterranean, multichambered tombs. Most often these tombs were used by several generations. A body would be laid in a prepared shelf, along with grave goods (food, pottery, weapons, tools), and then the skeletal remains were removed and placed in another chamber or an ossuary box or simply swept to the rear of the tomb to accommodate the next burial.

23:7-20. ownership of land. Arable land was so precious a possession that it was not supposed to be sold to anyone outside the kinship group. The lack of a buyer within the family and/or the practicalities of business sometimes required a sale to an unrelated person. This could be legally sidestepped through the adoption of the buyer or the intercession of village elders on his behalf with the owner. The designation of Abraham as "a prince" suggests he would be a desirable neighbor. The offer to receive the land as a gift was refused by Abraham because that would have enabled Ephron's heirs to reclaim the land after Ephron's death.

23:14. 400 shekels of silver. Four hundred shekels of silver was a substantial price. It would be equal to about seven and a quarter pounds of silver. In comparison, Omri bought the site of Samaria for six thousand shekels (1 Kings 16:24), and David bought the site of the temple for six hundred gold shekels (1 Chron 21:25), with the threshing floor itself fetching fifty shekels (2 Sam 24:24). Jeremiah bought property, at greatly deflated prices, for seventeen shekels (Jer 32:7). Abraham's payment would be more likely viewed as exorbitant rather than discounted, for rather than negotiating, he paid the inflated initial quote. It is likely that he was anxious to pay full price because a discounted price could be later connected to family debt problems that would allow the heirs of Ephron to reclaim the land. A laborer or artisan at ten shekels per year would not expect to make this much in a lifetime.

23:5-16. bargaining procedures. Haggling and staged bargaining are typical business procedures in the Middle East. They are both entertaining and competitive. However, when it is clear that the potential buyer is in a situation where a purchase is necessary or highly desired, the seller will use the bargaining to his advantage.

23:16. weight current among merchants. Terminology from roughly contemporary Old Assyrian trade letters suggests that this phrase concerns conformity to the standard for silver that was used in overland trade.

24:1-67
A Wife for Isaac

24:1-9. swearing oaths. An oath is always sworn in the name of a god. This places a heavy responsibility on the one who swears such an oath to carry out its stipulations, since he would be liable to divine as well as human retribution if he did not. Sometimes, as in this case, a gesture is added to the oath. The gesture usually is symbolic of the task to be performed by the oath taker. For instance, by placing his hand inside Abraham's thigh (in the vicinity of or on the genitals), the servant ties his oath of obedience to the acquisition of a wife for Isaac and thus the perpetuation of Abraham's line.

24:4. marrying from same tribe. The practice of marrying within one's own tribe or family is called endogamy. Endogamy could be the result of religious, social or ethnic concerns. In this text it appears to be ethnic in that there are no suggestions that the family of Laban, Rebekah and Rachel shares the religious beliefs of Abraham and his family. Likewise social standing is usually an issue only when nobility and commoners are involved or certain classes of urban society are seen as necessarily distinct. Ethnic concerns usually center around clan traditions or family land holdings. At times they represent long-established hostilities between two groups. In this text the endogamy seems motivated by the *covenant that seeks to prevent Abraham and his family from simply being assimilated into the ethnic melting pot in Canaan.

24:10-11. camel domestication. Although camel remains in Arabia date back to 2600 B.C., domesticated camels were not common in Palestine until 1200 B.C. The occasional references to them in Genesis are authenticated by evidence of domestication in an *Old Babylonian text from *Ugarit from the early second millennium. Evidence that the camel was used as a beast of burden in Arabia dates to the end of the third millennium. The stages of domestication may be traced by the development of the saddles. Camels were extremely valuable animals capable of carrying heavy loads through hostile desert terrains. Thus they were seldom used for food and would have been a sign of wealth.

24:10. Aram Naharaim. *Aram Naharaim (Aram of the two rivers), containing Haran on the Balikh River, includes the general area between the Euphrates River and the Habur River triangle in northern Mesopotamia. The name also appears in Deuteronomy 23:4, in the superscription of Psalm 60 and in 1 Chronicles 19:6. It may be the same as *Nahrima* in the fourteenth-century B.C. *El Amarna letters between the Egyptian Pharaoh and the rulers of Canaanite city-states.

24:11. well at evening time outside of town. The cool of the early morning and evening would have been the best times for women to go to the village well for water. Since the well was often outside the town to accommodate watering of animals, women would normally travel in groups for protection. Strangers could be expected to use the well, but it may be assumed that they would ask permission of the villagers. Hospitality custom would have necessitated offering them a drink.

24:12-21. mechanistic oracle. Abraham's servant is using an *oracular approach to identifying Isaac's bride-to-be. In an oracle a yes/no question is posed to deity, and a mechanism of some binary nature is used so that deity can provide the answer. In post-Sinai Israel the priest carried the Urim and Thummim to use in oracular situations. Abraham's servant must be more creative and uses a natural mechanism for the oracle. His yes/no question is whether the girl that he is about to approach is the right wife for Isaac. His oracular mechanism is based on a question that he will pose to the girl. When asking for a drink, one would normally expect that a drink would be offered. That would be normal behavior in the context of etiquette and hospitality. In this case such a response would indicate a "no" answer to his oracular question. For the alternative the servant chooses something far out of the range of expectation: that prompted by such a common, unimposing request, the girl would volunteer to water all his camels. This unbelievable offer would indicate a "yes" answer to his oracular question. The thought behind this process is that if deity is providing the answer, he can alter normal behavior and override natural instinct in order to communicate his answer. For similar mechanistic oracles, see Judges 6:36-40 and 1 Samuel 6:7-12. The prophets occasionally approach this type of oracular situation from the other side when they provide

signs to verify that they represent God, as in Numbers 16:28-30 or 1 Samuel 12:16-17.

24:11, 13. spring versus well. The difference in terminology between verse 11 ("well") and verse 13 ("spring") may reflect a variety of water sources available. There are examples where a water source originated from a spring but as the water table shrank it became necessary to dig down, thereby forming a well. This is the case at Arad, where a deep well now replaces the original spring.

24:19-20. how much camels drink. Camels drink only as much water as they have lost and do not store it in the hump. The concentration of fat and the coat of hair allows dissipation of heat, less sweating and a wider range of body temperature during the day and night. The camel also is able to maintain a constant amount of water in its blood plasma and thus sustain higher water loss than most animals. A camel that has gone a few days without water could drink as much as twenty-five gallons. In contrast, the jars that were used for water would usually hold no more than three gallons.

24:22. nose rings. Nose rings were especially popular during the *Iron Age (1200-600 B.C.), though there are examples from earlier periods. Made of silver, bronze and gold, and often tubular in design, they were round with two ends for insertion and sometimes included a tiny pendant. The beka is the half-shekel measure of weight, equal to one-fifth of an ounce.

24:22. jewelry. The bracelets would have been bands worn around the wrist as bangles. They were very popular items and are often found on the arms and wrist of females in tombs. By placing them on her arms, the servant may be symbolizing the marriage contract. A ten-shekel bracelet would weigh about four ounces. Legal materials from the first half of the second millennium suggest a worker might expect to make at most ten shekels per year and often less. These would typically be shekels of silver—gold would be more valuable.

24:28. mother's household. It would be natural for a young, unmarried woman to refer to her home as her mother's house until she was wed (see Song 3:4).

24:50-59. presents of betrothal. For a marriage to be arranged, the groom's family must provide a bride price, while the bride's family provided a dowry. The silver and gold objects and the garments presented to Rebekah are part of her transformation into a member of Abraham's household. The word used in the text denotes metal worked into useful items, whether jewelry or plates and other utensils. The presents given to her brother Laban and her mother demonstrate Abraham's wealth and the desirability of the marriage.

24:57-58. Rebekah making decision. It was unusual in the ancient world for the woman to have any part in major decisions. Rebekah was not consulted with regard to the marriage (vv. 50-51), but when the servant asked to leave right away the men looked to Rebekah for consent. Marriage contracts of this general period show a great concern for maintaining the woman's security within her husband's family. The presence of her family was one of the guarantees that she would be cared for and treated properly. The ten days that Rebekah's family requested (v. 55) would have given them a little more opportunity to make sure that everything was as it appeared to be. It is likely that she was consulted because of the substantial risk that was involved in leaving the family protection under such unusual circumstances.

24:59. accompanying nurse. It would have been suitable for a woman be-

trothed to a wealthy man to have an entourage of servants. The nurse, however, would have higher status as the nurturer of the child who would now remain as part of her new household and serve as a chaperon on the return journey.

24:62. Beer Lahai Roi. The place name means "well of the living who sees me" and is first associated with Hagar's *theophany in Genesis 16:14. It would have been southwest of Hebron in the Negev. Either Isaac and Abraham have moved their encampment south or Isaac is now living separately.

24:62-66. use of veil. Since she had gone unveiled during the journey, Rebekah's veiling herself once Isaac is identified to her suggests that this is her way of demonstrating to him that she is his bride. Brides were veiled during the wedding but went unveiled as married women. Veil customs differed in various locations and times. Asiatic women on the Beni Hasan tomb painting (early second millennium) are not veiled, but in the Middle *Assyrian laws (late second millennium) all respectable ladies went about veiled in public.

24:67. tent of his mother. Sarah's tent, due to her status of mistress of the household, would have been empty since her death. By taking Rebekah into his mother's tent, Isaac demonstrates that she is now the mistress of the household. This is similar to the importance placed on entering the house of the bridegroom in *Ugaritic texts.

25:1-11
The Death of Abraham

25:2, 4. Midianite origins. Midian is one of the children born to Abraham and Keturah, and the reference to him shows the writer's continued interest in establishing links between Abraham and all of the peoples of Palestine, Transjordan and Arabia. The Midianites are most frequently mentioned as a pastoral nomadic group of tribes living in the Negev and the Sinai deserts. Midianite traders carry Joseph to Egypt (Gen 37:28). Moses marries the daughter of Jethro, the priest of Midian, after fleeing Egypt (Ex 2:16-21). During the conquest narrative, Midianites are allied with Moab and are targeted as enemies of the Israelites (Num 25:6-18). There is no extrabiblical information about their history or origins.

25:1-4. descendants of Abraham from Keturah. Not all of these sixteen names can be identified, although most are associated with the Syro-Arabian desert to the east of the Jordan and may represent a confederation of tribes involved in the lucrative spice trade. Of the six sons born to Abraham and Keturah, the name of Midian is the most prominent in later narrative as a people living on the fringe of Israelite territory in the Negev and Sinai region. Some of the names appear in the *Assyrian annals (Medan is Badana, south of Tema; Ishbak is the northern Syrian tribe of Iasbuq; Sheba is in the southwestern part of Arabia). Shuah also appears in *cuneiform texts as a site on the middle Euphrates near the mouth of the Habur River (see Job 2:11).

25:1-4. concubines. The *concubines, or secondary wives, of Abraham were Hagar and Keturah. Concubines were usually women who did not possess a dowry, and thus their children did not have primary rights to inheritance. The father may choose to designate one of them as his heir if his primary wife has not produced a son. However, if he does not do so, then any claims they may have on his property would be based on the stipulations of the marriage contracts.

25:5-6. giving gifts. It is the prerogative of the father to designate his heir. However, he must also provide for his other children. Thus by giving his other sons gifts and sending them away he shares his wealth with them but also protects Isaac's position as heir of the household.

25:6. land of the east. The Hebrew *qedem* in this unique phrase may indicate a direction, "east," or an actual place name. The twentieth-century B.C. Egyptian story of the political exile *Sinuhe mentions the land of Qedem as lying near Byblos. In other biblical texts it refers to the peoples who inhabit the desert region on the eastern edges of Israel (Judg 6:3; 7:12; Is 11:14).

25:12-18
Ishmael's Line

25:12-16. Ishmael's descendants. Continuing the listing of those descendants of Abraham who inhabited neighboring regions are the sons of Ishmael. The term *son* sometimes represents political affiliation rather than blood ties, but whatever the case, this list comprises a confederation of tribes living in the Syro-Arabian desert. The occurrence of these names in *Assyrian records, intermixed with names from the Keturah list, suggests both shifts in tribal affiliation and allegiance. Most prominent among the names are Nebaioth, probably the Nabaiati of Ashurbanipal's campaigns against the Arab tribes and possibly to be associated with the later Nabateans of Petra; Tema, an oasis northeast of Dedan on the caravan route between southern Arabia and Mesopotamia; and Kedar, a people mentioned elsewhere as pastoral nomads (Ps 120:5; Is 42:11, 60:7).

25:18. area of Ishmael's descendants. The region from Havilah (see Gen 2:11; 10:7) to Shur (see Gen 16:7) probably represents migration and caravan routes for the descendants of Ishmael. This area is not suitable for large, sedentary populations, but it could support pastoral nomadic groups, and it was the center of the spice trade from southern Arabia traveling west to Egypt and east to Mesopotamia and Syria. Asshur, in this context, would not be the Mesopotamian kingdom of the upper Tigris region, but rather one of the northern Arabian areas (see Gen 10:22; 25:3).

25:19-26
The Birth of Jacob and Esau

25:21. barrenness. Barrenness is used in the ancestral narratives to heighten tension, as the element of the *covenantal promise of descendants (12:2) is thereby endangered. It also marks the son who is eventually born as special, because only God could relieve this infertility.

25:22-23. oracular response. Rebekah's concern about her pregnancy leads her to ask for an *oracle. The text gives no indication of what means Rebekah uses to inquire of the Lord. She is not using a mechanistic oracular device, for that only provides yes/no answers. There is no mention of a prophet, oracular priest, or angel delivering the oracle. In Egypt and Mesopotamia oracles such as this were almost always provided by a priest. Another alternative is that the oracle could be sought in a dream. This usually involved sleeping in a holy place. The text is less interested in the means and more concerned about the content of the oracle. The oracle does not concern the children themselves as much as it addresses the ultimate destiny of the family lines that each will establish. Such an oracle would not have suggested any particular treatment of the children by the parents.

25:24-26. naming children. The giving of names in the ancient world was a significant act. A name was believed to affect a person's destiny; so the person giving the name was exercising some degree of control over the person's future. Often names expressed hopes or blessings. At other times they preserved some detail of the occasion of the birth, especially if the occasion appeared significant. Here Esau is named by a physical characteristic, whereas Jacob is named for his peculiar behavior during birth. The names need not mean the word associated with them, but are often linked by wordplay. So the Hebrew word Jacob does not mean "heel"—it only sounds like the word for heel. The name was expected to play a role in the unfolding destiny of the individual and to take on additional significance and appropriateness throughout his life, though the direction of that appropriateness was impossible to foresee.

25:27-34
Esau Trades His Birthright

25:28. mother's role in inheritance decisions. A Canaanite contract from *Ugarit contains a situation in which the father allows the mother to choose which son receives preferential treatment in the inheritance.

25:29-30. Jacob cooking stew. The incident with the stew appears to take place away from home, otherwise Esau could have appealed to his parents. Jacob is not the hunting type, so it would be unusual for him to be out in the countryside alone. He has been described as a man "staying among the tents," which may indicate he was more closely associated with the shepherding business. The shepherds moved their camps over a broad area of land in order to find water and grazing for the flocks. It is most likely that Jacob would be out supervising some of the shepherds at such a camp when Esau stumbled upon them. Jacob would be the one in charge at the camp, so the decision would be his, and there would therefore be witnesses to the agreement made between Jacob and Esau.

25:31-34. birthright. The birthright concerned only the material inheritance from the parents. The inheritance was divided into the number of sons plus one. The eldest son then received a double share. This was a customary practice throughout the ancient Near East. The stew buys from Esau that additional share (probably not his entire inheritance). There are no examples in the known literature from the ancient Near East of such a deal being made. The closest is in the legal materials from *Nuzi, where one brother sells some already inherited property to one of his brothers.

26:1-16
Isaac and Abimelech

26:1-6. recurrent famine. The uncertainties of rainfall in season and in the proper amount made drought and famine fairly common occurrences in ancient Palestine. The writer here notes this frequent disaster and differentiates between the famine in Abraham's day (Gen 12) and that of Isaac.

26:1. Philistines in Palestine. Large numbers of Philistines entered Canaan after the invasion of the *Sea Peoples (1200 B.C.) broke Egyptian control over the area. In this context they are mentioned in the records of Ramses III (1182-1151 B.C.). They established a pentapolis of five major city-states (Gaza, Gath, Ashdod, Ekron, Ashkelon) along the southern coastal plain and quickly gained political control over nearby regions as well (Judg 15:11). Their mention in Genesis may reflect an earlier group that settled in Canaan prior to 1200 B.C., or it may be an *anachronism based on their presence in the Gerar region in later periods (see Gen 21:32), earlier people of the vicinity being referred to by the name known to later readers. Archaeological evidence of their presence is found in the introduction of new pottery types, grave goods (such as the sarcophagi with human features) and new architectural designs.

26:7-11. wife as sister. The wife/sister theme is used three times in the ancestral narratives (see also chaps. 12 and 20). Here Abimelech (either a throne name or a dynastic name meaning "My father is king") is tricked by Isaac and Rebekah. The result is their obtaining royal protection and the right to farm and to graze his herds in Gerar.

26:12-16. planting crops. It is not unusual for pastoral nomadic tribes to plant a crop or to harvest date palms along their usual line of march. This may be a step toward settling into a village life, but that is not necessarily the case. Generally sedentarism (settling of nomads) is more directly related to the actions of governments or changes in the political boundaries through which they drive their herds. Wealth may also cause them to settle down, but this is not a major factor.

26:17-35
Isaac's Wells

26:17-22. well rights and disputes. Wells are generally dug and protected by villages. The likelihood that they will silt up or collapse requires at least occasional oversight. The labor involved and the necessity of water for humans, crops and animals makes it likely that disputes will arise between villages and/or herdsmen who also wish to claim and use the wells.

26:20. naming wells. One way to designate ownership of a well or other natural resource is to give it a name. Once this has become its traditional name, title is not difficult to establish. It thus prevents later disputes or settles any that may arise. Naming is also part of the traditional lore of a tribe which is passed on to later generations.

26:23-25. build altar, call, pitch tent, dig well. The three acts of verse 25 are all related to possession of the land and are therefore a suitable response to the *covenant promise of verse 24. The altar gave recognition to the holiness of the place where the Lord spoke to him. Pitching a tent and digging a well are generally accepted means by which to establish a right to unclaimed land.

26:26-33. peace treaty. The peace treaty of verses 28-30 would constitute recognition by Isaac's neighbors that his presence in that area was acceptable. The agreement was validated by the sharing of a meal and by the swearing of oaths. Just as Abraham had built altars (chap. 12) and established recognized rights to land (chap. 23), so Isaac is now doing the same.

26:33. folk etymology of town names. Beersheba was named earlier by Abraham (in 21:31). The designation of significance to a name is not necessarily a suggestion that the name originated at that time. Just as people's names can be reinterpreted (for instance, Jacob in 27:36), so a place name can be reinterpreted. The ancients were less concerned with the origin of a name than they were with the significance the name acquired. This town at the southern extreme of the land becomes the home base for Isaac. The site identified by archaeologists as Beersheba has no remains prior to the Judges period (*Iron Age, 1200), but there is no suggestion in the story of Isaac that there was a town on the site in his day, so this is not a problem.

27:1-40
Isaac's Pronouncement on His Sons

27:1-4. deathbed blessings. Blessings or curses pronounced by the patriarch of the family were always taken seriously and considered binding. Such pronouncements from a patriarch's deathbed would be even more momentous. In this text, however, Isaac is not portrayed as being on his deathbed, merely aged

enough that he wants to put his house in order by providing the traditional blessing.

27:4. proper atmosphere for blessings. While the feast that Esau is to prepare may provide a pleasant atmosphere and appropriate mood for the blessing, it also provides the context of celebration that would accompany significant events, much as we might go out to dinner at a fancy restaurant.

27:11-13. curse appropriation. Rebekah responds to Jacob's fears of bringing a a curse on himself by appropriating to herself any curse that may result. Can she do that? As this chapter demonstrates, a blessing is not transferable, and neither is the pronouncement of a curse. But in this case Rebekah is most likely referring to the consequences of the curse rather than the curse itself. Since deity is the enforcer of the curse, this acknowledgment that she has forced Jacob to deceive his father would target her if a curse was to result.

27:14. food preparation. Food preparation was done by both men and women. One way to provide variation of taste to meals (which were often monotonous and meatless) was to hunt wild game. This meat might be tough and gamey-tasting, and thus it would be stewed to tenderize it and mixed with herbs to improve the flavor.

27:27-29. nature of blessing. The blessing that Isaac bestows on Jacob (whom he mistakes for Esau) grants him fertility of the ground, dominion over other nations, including those descended from siblings, and a boomerang effect for curses and blessings. These are typical elements for the patriarchal blessing and have no relationship to either material inheritance or to the *covenant, though some of these features are also present in the covenant benefits that the Lord promises to Israel. They constitute the foundational elements of survival and prosperity.

27:34-40. no negation of blessing. The power of the spoken word was such that it could not be "unsaid"—this is true even outside the realm of superstition in that many words spoken do the benefit or damage they intend regardless of any second thoughts the speaker may have. The pronouncement regarding Esau's destiny thus reflects the realities of the previously uttered blessing on Jacob. It would not be considered a curse because it assumes continuing existence and eventual freedom.

27:37. "I have made." Isaac explains to Esau, "I have made him lord . . . I have sustained him." The first-person forms show that Isaac is not suggesting that this blessing is a prophetic proclamation from deity. Neither does Isaac call on deity to perform it. Similar formulas in Mesopotamia regularly invoke deity in such blessings and curses.

27:41-46
The Outcome of the Deception
27:45. lose both in one day. Rebekah expresses the concern that she might lose both in one day. This could either refer to losing both Isaac and Jacob, that is, Isaac dies and Jacob is killed by Esau; or losing both Jacob and Esau, that is, Jacob would be killed and Esau, as his murderer, would either have to flee or end up the victim of blood vengeance.

27:46. Hittite women. The *Hittite women that Esau married were part of the indigenous culture of Canaan at this time. While it is possible that this group is related to the well-known Hittites of Anatolia, our knowledge of the culture and history of the Canaanite Hittites in the patriarchal period is insufficient to allow informed conclusions. There is a well-established Anatolian Hittite presence in Canaan during the monarchy period, and even as early as the middle of the second millennium the *Amarna

texts contain Hittite and *Hurrian personal names.

28:1-22
Jacob's Dream and Vow
28:2. Paddan Aram. This place name only appears in Genesis. It is either a designation for the general area of northern Mesopotamia (= *Aram Naharaim in 24:10) or perhaps another name for Haran. In *Akkadian, both *padanu* and *harranu* mean "path" or "road." In either case, Jacob is instructed to return to his ancestors' homeland to seek a bride as part of their practice of endogamy (marrying within a select group).

28:5. Aramean. The origin of the *Arameans is problematic. They do not actually appear in Mesopotamian records until the end of the second-millennium *Assyrian annals of Tiglath-pileser I (1114-1076 B.C.). In the ninth century Shalmaneser III mentions kings of Aram in Damascus (including Hazael and Ben-Hadad III). However, this is many centuries after the setting of the ancestor narratives. The mention of Arameans in relation to Abraham and Jacob is likely a reference to scattered tribes of peoples in upper Mesopotamia who had not yet coalesced in the nation of Aram, which appears in later texts. Based on other examples from *cuneiform literature, the name Aram may in fact have originally been that of a region (cf. Sippar-Amnantum of the *Old Babylonian period) and was later applied to people living there. Current evidence suggests that the Arameans inhabited the upper Euphrates throughout the second millennium, first as villagers and pastoralists, then as a political, national coalition.

28:10-12. Jacob's itinerary. Jacob takes the central ridge road that goes through the hill country from Beersheba through Hebron, Bethel and Shechem to join the main artery, the Great Trunk road, in

Beth Shan. It would have taken a couple of days to get from Beersheba to Bethel (about 60 miles), and the trip to Haran would have taken over a month (about 550 miles).

28:13-15. stairway. The ladder or stairway that Jacob sees in his dream is the passageway between heaven and earth. The comparable word in *Akkadian is used in Mesopotamian mythology to describe what the messenger of the gods uses when he wants to pass from one realm to another. It is this mythological stairway that the *Babylonians sought to represent in the architecture of the ziggurats. These had been built to provide a way for the deity to descend to the temple and the town. Jacob's background would have given him familiarity with this concept, and thus he would conclude that he was in a sacred spot where there was a portal opened between worlds. Though he sees the stairway in his dream, and the messengers (angels) are using it to pass between realms (embarking on and returning from missions, not a procession or parade), the Lord is not portrayed as having used it, but as standing beside it (this is the proper translation of the Hebrew idiom).

28:16-17. house of God, gate of heaven. When Jacob awakes he identifies the sacred place as the house of God (beth-el) and the gate of heaven. In *Akkadian mythology the stairway used by the messengers went up to the gate of the gods, while the temple of the deity was located at the bottom. In this way the patron deity could leave the assembly of the gods and descend to the place of worship.

28:18-19. pillars and anointing. The sacred pillars or standing stones are well known in the religious practice of the ancient Near East predating the fourth millennium B.C. They are featured prominently in Canaanite *cultic installations such as the high place at Gezer

and were also used in the Israelite temple at Arad. Other standing stones were simply set up as memorials. From basins sometimes found near the foot of such pillars, it is inferred that libations (liquid offerings) were poured over them, as we see Jacob doing in 35:14. The anointing of the pillar would constitute the dedication of it.

28:19. Bethel/Luz. As noted in Genesis 23:2, place names change based on the appearance of new peoples or significant events. Bethel was an important town located in the central hill country just north of Jerusalem. An important east-west road lay just south of the town, making it a crossroads for travelers and a likely place for the establishment of a *cultic site. There is some speculation that Luz was the original city site and that Bethel (literally "house of God") was a separate cultic site located outside the town. Once the Israelites had established themselves in the region, however, the site's association with Abraham (12:8) and Jacob would have caused the older name to be superseded.

28:20-22. vows. Vows are promises with conditions attached, almost always made to God. In the ancient world the most common context for a vow was when a request was being made to deity. The condition would typically involve God's provision or protection, while that which was vowed was usually a gift to deity. This would most commonly take the form of a sacrifice but could refer to other types of gifts to the sanctuary or priests. Fulfillment of a vow could usually be accomplished at the sanctuary and was a public act. In Jacob's vow the conditions actually extend through the end of verse 21. Jacob promises a tithe upon the fulfillment of the conditions.

28:22. tithe. In the ancient world tithing was often a means of taxation. There were tithes paid to the temple as well as those paid to the king. Since income and personal wealth was often not primarily in money, all goods were included in the calculations of the tithe, as indicated here by Jacob in the phrase "all that you give me." Jacob's tithe is clearly voluntary rather than imposed and therefore would not be associated with taxation of any sort. There is no temple or priesthood at Bethel, so to whom would Jacob give his tithe? It is likely that Jacob anticipates that any wealth coming to him would be in the form of flocks and herds. In such a case the tithe would be represented in sacrifices at Bethel.

29:1-14
Jacob Finds Laban and His Family
29:2, 3, 10. stone over well mouth. The stone served a double function, as a guard against contamination or poisoning of the well and as a social control mechanism, preventing any of the herdsmen in the area from drawing more water than was their right. Apparently water was scarce in this "open country" and thus the right to use the well was a jealously guarded one. Bedouin herders seldom wish to even divulge the location of wells within their territory, so this degree of security is not out of place. The stone may even have served to disguise the location of the well from the casual passerby. Wells of this time were not surrounded by protective walls, so the stone would also have prevented animals (or people) from inadvertently stumbling into it.
29:3. watering agreements. In regions where water sources were scarce, it would have been necessary to make agreements between herdsmen for use of the local well or spring. A lack of trust, however, could result in a scene like the one in the text, where all of the herds had to be assembled before any could drink.
29:6. female shepherd. While it is not uncommon today for women and small children to herd Bedouin flocks, in antiquity women would have done so only when the household had no sons. It was a dangerous practice since they might be molested, but it was also a way of attracting a husband.
29:11. kiss of greeting. The traditional form of greeting for friends and relatives in the Middle East is a warm hug and a kiss on each cheek. This is done with both male and female relatives.

29:15-30
Jacob Works for His Wives
29:17. Leah's eyes. In the comparative description of Rachel and Leah, the only comment about Leah concerns her eyes. The term used is generally considered positive and speaks of fragility, vulnerability, tenderness or a delicate quality (NIV note). Although eyes were a principal component of beauty in the ancient world, Leah's positive features paled in comparison to Rachel's loveliness.
29:18-20. seven years' labor. Typical marriage customs would have included a payment made to the bride's family by the groom or his family. This could provide a sort of trust fund to provide for the wife should the husband die, desert her or divorce her. Alternatively it was at times used by the family to pay the bride price for the bride's brothers. In some cases it was even returned to the bride in the form of an indirect dowry. In the *Nuzi texts a typical bride price is thirty or forty shekels of silver. Since ten shekels of silver is a typical annual wage for a shepherd, Jacob is paying a higher price. That can be understood, however, given the circumstances: Jacob is in no position to negotiate, and the payment is being made in labor.
29:21-24. wedding feast. Since a wedding is based on a contract between two families, it is similar to treaties and to business transactions. Like them, the

marriage would have been consummated with a *ritual meal (a sign of peace between the parties). There would also be a procession to a designated "first home" (usually within the house or tent of the groom's father, although not in Gen 29) and sexual intercourse between the couple. The bride would be veiled during these public festivities, and it may be assumed that the high spirits would have led to drunkenness, both factors in Jacob's inability to recognize the substitution of Leah for Rachel at the feast.

29:24. gift of maidservant. It was quite common for the bride to receive a gift of a maidservant on the occasion of her marriage. In this way she obtained her own personal household or entourage, providing her with both greater prestige and help in performing her duties.

29:26-30. custom of older married first. It is the practice of people of the ancient Near East, and still a tradition today in that area, for the oldest daughter to be married first. This prevents a younger sibling from shaming a sister who may not be as beautiful and also prevents the financial drain on the family caused by spinsters. Females were used, through marriage contracts, to obtain wealth and prestige for the family. If an older sister was bypassed and then never married, her family would be left with the responsibility to support her.

29:27. bridal week. The relationship between the seven-day story of creation and the idea of creating new life through marriage may be the origin of the bridal week. Diverting the bride and groom from other tasks was also designed to insure a pregnancy early in the marriage.

29:31—30:24
Jacob's Children

29:33. naming of children. The naming of children was a significant act and typically represented some circumstance or sentiment at the time of birth. It rarely addressed the supposed fate or destiny of the child directly and was not thought to determine the child's destiny, but it was believed that the name was directly related to a person's essential self and therefore could be expected to find significant associations with the person's nature and experiences.

30:3-13. maidservant as surrogate wife. Just as Sarah gave Abraham her maid Hagar as a surrogate wife (16:1-4), so too the wives of Jacob give him their maids. The object is for a barren (or unloved) wife to have children by means of this legal surrogacy. Provision for this custom is also found in the *Lipit-Ishtar Code and in the Code of *Hammurabi from Mesopotamia.

30:14-15. mandrake plants. *Mandragora officinarum* is a stemless, perennial root in the potato family found growing in stony ground. It resembles the human figure and has narcotic and purgative properties, which explain its medicinal use. Its shape and pungent fragrance may be the origin of its use in *fertility rites and as an aphrodisiac (see Song 7:13-14). It has dark green, wrinkled leaves from which rise a violet, bell-shaped flower. Its fruit is a yellowish berry, approximately the size of a small tomato, which can be consumed. The mandrake is native to the Mediterranean region but is not common in Mesopotamia.

30:25-43
Jacob Employed by Laban

30:22-25. Jacob's request. A woman's status in the family would be very tenuous if she had not borne children. A barren woman could be and often was discarded, ostracized or given a lower status and would find protection in her relatives. Now that Rachel's status in Jacob's family is established, Jacob feels free to request permission to leave.

30:27. divination of Laban. An Israelite reader would have been struck by Laban's suggestion that *Yahweh has given information by means of *divination. There is no mention of what type of divination Laban used, but all divination was later forbidden under the law. Divination assumed that there was knowledge to be gained about the activities and motives of the gods through the use of various indicators (such as entrails of sacrificed animals). It operated in a worldview that was contrary to that promoted in the Bible. Nevertheless, God occasionally chooses to use such methods, as the Bethlehem star attests.

30:32-33. sheep breeding. The coloring chosen by Jacob (dark lambs and variegated goats) generally made up a very small proportion of the herd. Jacob seems to be settling for a share that was far smaller than usual, in that contracts of the day designated sometimes as much as 20 percent of new births for the shepherd (Bedouin studies today suggest that 10 percent is common). Byproducts (wool, milk products) are not mentioned here, but a percentage of those were also often part of the shepherd's compensation.

30:37-43. use of rods. Jacob's solution to Laban's treachery contains elements of scientific breeding and folklore tradition. Clearly, shepherds would have been aware of the estrus cycle of their sheep (which runs from June to September), and observation would have demonstrated that breeding healthy animals would produce vigorous lambs. What is not scientific, however, is the principle that certain characteristics (coloration in this case) can be bred for through visual aids. The stripped rods which Jacob places before the troughs of the sheep cannot genetically affect the sheep. This type of sympathetic magic is found in many folk traditions (including modern tales of col-

ors worn by a mother determining the sex of her child). It plays a part in the trickster theme of this narrative and is reflective of a culture which depended on a mixture of magical and common-sense methods to produce results.

31:1-21
Jacob's Flight

31:1. Laban's sons' complaint. Jacob's success in Laban's employ would naturally result in the reduction of Laban's assets and therefore the depletion of the inheritance his sons could expect to receive. It is no wonder then that they nurse a grudge against their brother-in-law.

31:13. God of Bethel. By identifying himself as the God of Bethel, the Lord has reminded Jacob of the vow of Jacob in 28:20-22. Though it is true that Canaanites would have viewed sacred sites as each having their own separate deities, there is no suggestion in the text that Jacob considers the God of Bethel to be distinct from *Yahweh, and certainly the author of the Pentateuch sees them as one (compare vv. 3 and 13).

31:14-16. Rachel and Leah's complaint. Rachel and Leah express willingness to leave with Jacob because of the way Laban has treated them in his financial dealings. It has been suggested that they are referring to assets that were generally held in escrow for the care of the woman should her husband die or divorce her. Such assets would have been part of the bride price, which, in this case, Jacob had paid in labor rather than tangible assets. If Laban never put aside the value of Jacob's fourteen years of labor, there would be nothing in reserve to provide for the women. As a result they would not enjoy any additional protection in economic terms by staying in the vicinity of their family. They identify this as treating them as foreigners, because Laban had gained from Jacob's labor but had not passed the gain on to them—it is therefore just as if he had sold them.

31:18. Paddan Aram. Paddan Aram seems to refer to the region of northern Mesopotamia and northeast Syria (see comment on 28:2). The inclusion of *Aram suggests connections with the Arameans (see comment on 28:5).

31:19-20. sheep shearing. Shearing domestic sheep of their woolly fleece occurs in the spring a few weeks prior to lambing. This allows wool to grow back during the summer to help protect against extreme temperatures. Shep herds would bring their animals to a central location where the wool was also processed, dyed and woven into cloth. Archaeological excavations at Timnah (see 38:12) have produced large numbers of loom weights, suggesting that this was a center for shearing and weaving. Because this involved a journey, provisions would have had to be made to protect the villagers left behind. There would also be a celebration associated with the event after the hard work of shearing was completed.

31:19. household gods. The *teraphim* or "household gods" were associated with luck and prosperity of the family. One suggestion is that, like the *lares* and *penates* of Roman tradition, these small images guarded the threshold and hearth. They were passed from one generation to the next as part of the inheritance. The fact that Rachel was able to hide them under a saddle suggests their tiny size, though some were larger (see 1 Sam 19:13). Many of these small figurines have been found in Mesopotamia and Syro-Palestine. They were a part of the popular or local religion, not associated with temples or national *cults for the major deities. One recent study has suggested they were figurines of the ancestors, but others see them as more generally related to the family's patron deity. Laban's frantic desire to retrieve

these images suggests their importance to his family, in contrast to Jacob's disposal of them before he departs for Canaan.

31:21. hill country of Gilead. Jacob's departure from the area of Haran takes him south and west across the Euphrates River and into the Transjordanian region known as Gilead. This area comprises most of the Jordanian plateau between the Yarmuk River near the Sea of Galilee and the northern end of the Dead Sea.

31:22-55
The Settlement of Jacob and Laban

31:27. musical instruments. Tambourines and harps were the common musical instruments associated with celebrations in the village culture. They were used to mark major events, such as military victories (Ex 15:20), celebratory and religious dances (1 Sam 10:5), and, as in this case, feasts of departure.

31:35. Rachel's excuse. Rachel's excuse that she had her period would have been sufficient to warn off Laban, for in the ancient world a woman in menstruation was considered a danger because menstrual blood was widely believed to be a habitat for demons.

31:38-42. shepherd's responsibility. Herding contracts have been discovered in excavations in Mesopotamia which spell out the responsibilities and the wages of herdsmen. They describe activities in much the same way as in this passage: taking animals to proper grazing areas and water sources, birthing of lambs, treatment of sick and injured animals, protection from wild predators and retrieval of lost sheep. It was expected that losses through neglect or failure to protect the flock would be deducted from the shepherds' wages. Plus, only animals that had been killed or died of natural causes could be eaten by the shepherds.

31:42. ancestral Deity. Jacob's use of the terms the "God of my father, the God of Abraham" and the "Fear of Isaac" provide a sense of kinship based on the worship of an ancestral deity by these tribal people (see 28:12; Ex 3:6; 4:5). "The Fear of Isaac" appears only in Genesis and may represent a cognomen (nickname) for the patron God as well as an implied threat against any violence by Laban (see 31:29). The reference to divine patrons, "Ashur, the god of your fathers," is also found in Old *Assyrian texts (early second millennium B.C.).

31:45-53. pillar as witness. The use of a heap of stones as a boundary marker or a memorial to an event or to bear witness to a *covenant appears several places in the biblical text (see 28:18; 35:20; Josh 24:27). In Canaanite religion, the massebah, or standing stone, was erected and considered as a guardian or a dwelling place of a god (see Deut 16:21-22; 1 Kings 14:23). The fact that two are erected here and each is given a name is suggestive of an invoking *ritual in which the god(s) of each party are called to witness the treaty-making ceremony and to enforce its stipulations. One possible parallel to this may be the twin pillars, Jachin and Boaz, placed in front of Solomon's temple in Jerusalem (1 Kings 7:15-22).

31:48-53. nature of agreement. Like other treaty documents in the ancient Near East (such as the seventh-century B.C. *Assyrian vassal treaties of Esarhaddon and the thirteenth-century B.C. treaty between Ramses II and Hattusilis III), the gods of each party are invoked as witnesses, a set of exact stipulations is spelled out and a sacrifice and *ritual meal conclude the agreement. While the only explicit charge here is that Jacob not take any more wives, it is suggested by the setting up of the pillars that this is also a boundary agreement and territory is now marked. Parallels to this restriction on taking another wife are found in *Nuzi legal documents (fifteenth century B.C.). The stipulation is intended to protect the rights and status of the current wife/wives, especially in this context where the wives' family would not be there to assure fair and equitable treatment.

31:54. sacrificial meal. It was apparently standard procedure to use a meal to seal an agreement (see 14:18; 26:30; Ex 24:5-11). Just as food is a part of the hospitality *ritual (18:2-5), here it functions as a means of drawing each party into a familial, nonhostile relationship. By adding the element of sacrifice, it also insures the participation of the gods and heightens the solemnity of the occasion.

32:1-21
Jacob's Return to Canaan

32:1. met by angels. Just as Jacob experienced an angelic *theophany as he left the Promised Land (28:12), so too he is met by angels on his return. This forms an *inclusio* (a literary device in which the same events or lines occur at the beginning and the end of a literary segment) in the narrative and signals both divine sanction for the treaty just concluded and a reestablishment of direct contact with the *covenantal heir.

32:2. naming places. Applying names to sites where specific events occur, especially *theophanies, is fairly common in the ancestral narratives (see 16:14; 21:31; 26:20, 33; 28:19). In this way the presence of the deity is established at that site. For instance, Bethel, the location of one of Abraham's altars and the place where Jacob experienced a theophany, later became a major religious site. The name of the place in this passage, Mahanaim, means "two camps," but the reference is obscure. Although it has not been located, this is a fairly important city in the tribal territory of Gad (see Josh 13:26;

21:38; 2 Sam 2:8-9).

32:3. Seir. The land of Seir is generally considered to be the mountainous central region of Edom (elevations generally over 5,000 feet) between Wadi al-Ghuwayr on the north and Ras en-Naqb on the south.

32:3-5. Jacob's communication. Jacob's communication to Esau is intended to make several points. First, he has not been in hiding or sneaking around the land behind Esau's back. Second, and more importantly, he has not come to lay claim to inheritance rights. By describing his success and wealth, he insinuates that he has not returned because he is broke and looking to demand what is due him.

32:13-21. gifts for Esau. The generosity of Jacob's gifts can be understood when compared to tribute paid by one nation to another. So, for instance, in the ninth century B.C. the town of Hindanu paid to *Assyrian king Tukulti-Ninurta II some silver, bread, beer, thirty camels, fifty oxen and thirty donkeys. This gift would be sufficient for Esau to get a good start on a herding operation of his own or, alternatively, to reward any mercenaries in his employ who may have been anticipating booty.

32:13-21. Jacob's strategy. Jacob's gifts to Esau demonstrate that he is as shrewd as ever. Besides being an attempt to gain Esau's favor through generosity, the continuous arrival of the herds of animals will wear out any schemes for ambush and deflate any degree of military readiness that Esau might be planning in his encounter with Jacob. Additionally, traveling with the animals will slow Esau down and make his company much noisier. Finally, the plan adds Jacob's servants to Esau's retinue—a decided advantage if there is to be fighting.

32:22. river fords. River crossings or fords function in much the same way as gates. Both are entranceways giving access in and out of territory. Both have strategic value for armies (see Judg 3:28; 12:5; Jer 51:32). As such, they are tied to power, both physical and supernatural. Thus it is not difficult to imagine a link between Jacob's entrance into the Promised Land and a struggle with a supernatural being beside the fast flowing waters at the ford of the Jabbok River.

32:24-26. detaining for blessing. A *Hittite *ritual text envisions a struggle between the goddess Khebat and the king in which the goddess is detained and there is discussion of who will prevail over whom, leading to a request for blessing by the king.

32:24. leaving at daybreak. The reference to time indicates both the length of the struggle between Jacob and the divine being and serves as an indicator of Jacob's lack of perception during the fight. Daybreak or "cock's crow" are often found in folklore as the moment when powers and creatures of the dark lose their power to affect humans, though this is not a familiar element in ancient Near Eastern literature. In this case the issue is not one of potency, but one of supremacy (as indicated by the naming) and discernment (see v. 29).

32:28-30. name changing. There is, of course, an etiological (explaining how things came to be) aspect to name changes (e. g., Abram to Abraham in 17:5, which reenforces the *covenantal promise of fathering many nations). When the angel asks Jacob his name, this provides the opportunity to highlight the change to Israel. Thus the change serves both an etiological purpose (memorializing this event at Peniel), but it also marks the Jacob/Israel shift from an outcast and usurper to the heir of the covenant and the chosen leader of God's people. Name changing was also a way to exercise authority over an individual. When a suzerain put a vassal on the throne, he sometimes gave him a new name, demonstrating his power over that vassal.

32:31-32. etiological comments. An etiological comment is one that provides an origin for a name, characteristic or practice. In folklore etiological comments are often fanciful (how the camel got its hump), while in ethnic or national traditions they tend to be legendary. While such fanciful or legendary accounts can often be entirely fabricated, etiological comments need not be only the consequence of a creative imagination but may preserve an accurate story of a tradition. The naming of the place where Jacob/Israel wrestled with God draws its name from his exclamation of surprise at "seeing God face to face" (a clear parallel to his earlier encounter at Bethel, 28:16-19). The final notation in this episode provides an explanation for a unique dietary law, which does not appear elsewhere in Jewish law. However, the legal value in forbidding the consumption of the "tendon attached to the socket of the hip" (possibly the sciatic nerve) is found in its memorializing of Jacob/Israel's struggle at the Jabbok—in that sense comparable to the institution of *circumcision (17:9-14)—marking a significant *covenantal reaffirmation.

33:1-20
Jacob's Reunion with Esau

33:1-3. bowing seven times. One way that a person showed respect for a superior in the ancient world was by bowing to the ground. To magnify the honor being given and the subservience of the person who bowed, this gesture could be repeated seven times. Some Egyptian texts from El Amarna (fourteenth century B.C.) portray vassals bowing seven times to Pharaoh.

33:16. Seir. This region comprises the hill country stretching to the southeast of the Arabah, between the Dead Sea and the Gulf of Aqabah, in territory later inhabited by the Edomites (see 36:20; Judg 5:4). Because of its relatively high annual rainfall and elevation, the area has sufficient water and snow melt to support scrub forests and brushes. This may be the origin of the name Seir, which means "hairy."

33:17. Succoth. A town situated east of the Jordan River near its confluence with the Jabbok River (Judg 8:5). A number of archaeologists have identified it with the site of Tell Deir 'Alla, based on Egyptian records (the stele of Shishak) and cultural remains which date from the *Chalcolithic to *Iron Age II. The name, which means "booths," would be appropriate for the temporary housing of this region's mixed population of pastoral nomads and miners (evidence of smelting has been found in Iron I levels).

33:18-19. Shechem. Identified with Tell Balata in the central highlands, about thirty-five miles north of Jerusalem, Shechem is known from many ancient sources, including the Egyptian records of Sen-Usert III (nineteenth century B.C.) and the *El Amarna tablets (fourteenth century B.C.). Nearly continuous occupation is evidenced through the second and first millennia, demonstrating the importance of this strategic city on the highway network running north from Egypt through Beersheba, Jerusalem and on to Damascus. It was Abram's first stop in Canaan (see comment on 12:6). The fertile soil in this area promoted agriculture as well as good grazing.

33:19. purchase of land. As in the case in Genesis 23, this land transaction includes an exact price (one hundred pieces of silver), thereby marking this as a deeded sale rather than a fee for usage of the property. Since he is settling within the landed territory of the town, Jacob must purchase the property he settles on. The amount he pays is uncertain because the value of the unit of money referred to here is unknown. As in Genesis 23 the eventual use of this land is for burial (see Josh 24:32).

33:20. altar significance. Altars function as sacrificial platforms. Their construction can also mark the introduction of the worship of a particular god in a new land. One tie between the generations of *covenantal leaders is their construction of altars in order to worship *Yahweh in the Promised Land (12:7-8; 13:18; 26:25). The name given to Jacob/Israel's altar, "El Elohe Israel," is an acknowledgment of his own name change and his acceptance of the role of covenantal heir that had been promised at Bethel (28:13-15). For another example of naming an altar, see Exodus 17:15.

34:1-31
Dinah and Shechem

34:2. Hivites. Based on their appearance in various narratives, the Hivites apparently inhabited an area in the central hill country of Canaan, ranging from Gibeon, near Jerusalem (Josh 9:1-7), to Shechem and on north to Mount Hermon (Josh 11:3; Judg 3:3). The origin of the Hivites is unknown (descendant of Ham in Gen 10:17), but it is possible that they are related to either *Hurrian or *Hittite peoples settling in Canaan during the period from the mid-second to early first millennium B.C.

34:2. ravishing women. Rape as a means of obtaining a marriage contract was apparently one stratagem used in the ancient Near East. Laws regulating this practice are found in Exodus 2:16-17, Deuteronomy 22:28-29, the Middle *Assyrian laws and the *Hittite laws. These often require the rapist to pay an especially high bride price and sometimes forbid any possibility of divorce. *Sumerian Law 7, like Genesis 34, deals with a case where a young, unbetrothed woman leaves her parents' home without permission and is raped. The result is an option by the parents to marry her

to the rapist without her consent.

34:7. concept of universal law. Ancient Near Eastern literature contains law collections of this time and earlier that make it clear that prohibitions concerning illicit and violent sexual behavior were not innovations at Sinai. The codes of conduct by which people lived in this time show great similarity to the laws enshrined at Sinai and demonstrate a common universal sense of morality and justice. Laws and less formal standards often sought to protect the honor and integrity of the family, the dignity of the individual and security within society.

34:11-12. bride price and gift. The bride price and gift paid by the groom's family was often dependent on the desirability of the marriage. A higher price could be expected if the bride's family was socially superior to that of the groom or there were other factors (such as the bride's beauty) which made her value rise. In the *Nuzi texts a typical bride price is thirty to forty shekels of silver.

34:13-17. circumcision. At the time that *circumcision was introduced (Gen 17), adult males as well as infants underwent this procedure as a mark of their membership in the community. Circumcision was practiced widely in the ancient Near East as a rite of puberty, fertility or marriage, but was not practiced by all peoples. The men of Shechem agree to submit to this in order to become acceptable as husbands to Jacob's daughters. The procedure performed on adults is quite painful and would have virtually debilitated the adult male population for several days.

34:20. gate of the city. The city gate was a place of assembly for legal and business transactions. It could also be used for public meetings that affected all of the city's citizens. In the small towns that were the ancient cities the houses were close together and the streets were narrow. The only open areas would be the market place (if the town had one) and the area of the gate. The former would have been unsuitable for matters of public business.

34:25-29. plundering the city. The negotiation between the parties had concerned appropriate recompense (bride price) for Dinah in the circumstances of her having been taken forcibly. As it turns out, the compensation that Dinah's brothers considered appropriate was the forfeiture of the life and goods of the entire city. Such was also attempted by the Greeks in the *Iliad* as they laid siege to Troy to recover Helen.

35:1-15
Jacob's Return to Bethel
35:1. building an altar. When Abram built altars during his journeys (12:6-8), it was not for the purpose of sacrifice but for calling on the name of the Lord. This also seems to be the case with Jacob, since no reference is made to offering sacrifices on the altar. Some have suggested that the altars served to mark the territory of the deity. Alternatively they were memorials to the name of the Lord.

35:2-5. ridding of foreign gods. The call to rid themselves of foreign gods is a call to commit themselves exclusively to *Yahweh. This does not mean that they understood or accepted philosophical monotheism, but that they accepted Yahweh as their family patron deity. The belief in a personal god who gave protection and provision to the family was common in early second-millennium Mesopotamia. This deity was not understood to replace the great cosmic gods but was the principal object of worship and religious devotion for the individual.

35:2. purification. Purification would have accompanied *ritual procedures but also may be a response to the bloodshed of chapter 34. It typically involved bathing and changing garments. Prepa-

ration for worship and *ritual also includes the disposal of any signs of loyalty to other gods. All of this took place at Shechem, where the events of chapter 34 took place, some twenty miles north of Bethel. The worship act is portrayed as a pilgrimage, as indicated by the terminology of verse 1. The relationship of earrings to worship of other gods is unclear. While the use of earrings to fashion idols is attested (Ex 32:2; Judg 8:24), and they are often part of the plunder of looted cities, neither of these appear to offer an explanation. It has been suggested that perhaps the earrings were *amulets of some sort, even stamped with an image of deity, though there is no evidence of earrings serving such a purpose. There is, however, an earring with an inscription of dedication to a goddess from the *Ur III period (about 2000 B.C.).

35:4. buried under the oak. The objects were buried under a special tree in Shechem, which possibly figures also in 12:6, Joshua 24:23-27 and Judges 9:6, 37. Sacred trees played a significant role in popular religion of the day, which would have viewed stone and tree as potential divine dwellings. In Canaanite religion they are believed to be symbols of *fertility (see Deut 12:2; Jer 3:9; Hos 4:13), though there is very little in the archaeological or literary remains of the Canaanites that would clarify the role of sacred trees.

35:14. anointed pillar. Just as Jacob had set up a stone at Bethel and anointed it in 28:18, so now another is set up and a libation (liquid offering) performed to commemorate the *theophany (God's appearance). It would not be unusual to have several standing stones erected in the same vicinity.

35:16-29
The Deaths of Rachel and Isaac
35:16-18. midwifing. Midwives, who

were generally older women, served as resources to teach young women about sexual activity and to aid in the birth of children. They were also a part of the naming *ritual and may have helped teach new mothers about nursing and child care.

35:16-18. death in childbirth. Death in childbirth was not an uncommon occurrence in the ancient world. The incantation literature of *Babylon contains a number of examples of spells to protect the mother and child in the birthing process; particularly incantations against Lamashtu, the demon who was believed to attack women and children.

35:18. naming children. Rachel names her child as she dies, giving a name that reflects her misery. It was customary for circumstances surrounding the birth to serve as the occasion for the name. In this case Jacob changes the name, as was the father's right. *Benjamin* can mean either son of the right (hand), signifying a place of protection, or son of the south (since Israelites oriented themselves toward the east, the south was on their right).

35:19-20. Rachel's tomb. Rachel's death in childbirth is placed on the way to Ephrath, north of Bethlehem, on the border of the later tribal territories of Judah and Benjamin (see 1 Sam 10:2), some twelve miles north of Bethlehem. Another example of raising a memorial pillar for the dead is found in 2 Samuel 18:18. The late mention of Rachel's tomb in Jeremiah 31 suggests that it was a well-known pilgrimage site down to the end of the monarchy period. More recent traditions demonstrate some confusion between a site for Rachel's tomb in Bethlehem and another north of Jerusalem.

35:21. Migdal Eder. The name of this place means "herding tower," a installation used by pastoralists to protect their animals from predators. Based on Jacob's itinerary, journeying south after burying Rachel, Migdal Eder would be near Jerusalem. This identification may be strengthened by mention in Micah 4:8 of "watchtower of the flock." Later traditions, however, place it closer to Bethlehem.

35:21-22. son with father's concubine. *Concubines are women without dowry who include among their duties providing children to the family. Childbearing was an important function in the ancient world, where survival of the family, and often survival at all, was tenuous at best. Since a concubine has been a sexual partner, a son who used his father's concubine was seen not only as incestuous but as attempting to usurp the authority of the family patriarch.

36:1-30
The Line of Esau

36:1-43. Esau's descendants. The genealogy of Esau unfolds in stages, beginning with his first three wives (two *Hittite and one the daughter of Ishmael). In the subsequent levels of the list twelve tribal names are identified (vv. 9-14, excluding Amalek, who is the son of a *concubine), which matches the genealogical lists of Nahor (22:20-24), Ishmael (25:13-16) and Israel. A third tier of descendants (vv. 15-19) appear to be clan names, with some repetition from the previous level. The final grouping contains the names of eight kings who reigned in Edom prior to the establishment of the Israelite monarchy (vv. 31-39). Among the best known of the names in the entire genealogy are Teman, identified with the southern region of Edom, and Uz, named as the homeland of Job.

36:12. Amalekite origins. The Amalekites wandered through vast stretches of land in the Negev, Transjordan and Sinai peninsula. They are unattested outside the Bible, and no archaeological remains can be positively linked to them. However, archaeological surveys of the region have turned up ample evidence of nomadic and semi-nomadic groups like the Amalekites during this period.

36:15-30. chiefs. The inclusion of many chiefs of different regions makes this list as much a king list as a genealogy in that these Bedouin groups had a chieftain form of government. The *Sumerian king list similarly features brief lines of kings connected to various geographical regions.

36:24. hot springs. One way of distinguishing persons with the same name in a genealogy is to provide a brief comment based on their career (see Lamech in 4:19-24; 5:25-31). Here Anah is distinguished from his uncle by the additional information that he discovered a "hot springs"—a natural phenomenon that could have benefited the clan. The translation here is based solely on the Vulgate. Jewish tradition translates it as "mules" and gives Anah credit for learning to crossbreed horses and donkeys.

37:1-11
Joseph's Dreams

37:3. Joseph's coat. The special coat provided to Joseph by his father signified a position of authority and favor. Though such coats may have been colorful, they were often distinguished by material, weave or length (of either hem or sleeve). Since the Hebrew word describing it is used only here, it is difficult to be certain which type of quality characterizes the coat. Egyptian paintings of this period depict well-dressed Canaanites as wearing long-sleeved, embroidered garments with a fringed scarf wrapped diagonally from waist to knee.

37:5-11. importance of dreams. Dreams in the ancient world were thought to offer information from the divine realm and were therefore taken very seriously. Some dreams, given to prophets and kings, were considered a means of divine revelation. Most dreams, however, even the ordinary dreams of common people, were believed to contain omens that communicated information about what the gods were doing. Those that were revelation usually identified the deity and often involved the deity. The dreams that were omens usually made no reference to deity. Dreams were often filled with symbolism necessitating an interpreter, though at times the symbols were reasonably self-evident. The information that came through dreams was not believed to be irreversible. Dreams of a rise to power like the ones Joseph had are known in the ancient Near East, notably one concerning Sargon, king of Akkad, half a millennium earlier than Joseph.

Joseph Sold into Slavery

37:12-13. shepherds grazing. The lush vegetation produced by the winter rains would have allowed shepherds to remain in pastures near their villages and camps. Once the rains ended, the herds would graze in harvested fields and then would be taken into the hill country, where vegetation remained through the summer months.

37:17. Dothan. Located at Tell Dothan, this is an imposing site covering twenty-five acres. It is situated fourteen miles north of Shechem, on the main route used by merchants and herdsmen going north to the Jezreel Valley. It developed into a major city site in the *Early Bronze Age (3200-2400 B.C.) and would have served as a natural landmark for travelers. The area around the city provided choice pasture land, thus explaining the presence of Joseph's brothers.

37:19-24. cisterns. Cisterns were hollowed out of the limestone bedrock or were dug and then lined with plaster to store rain water. They provided water for humans and animals through most of the dry months. When they were empty, they sometimes served as temporary cells for prisoners (see Jer 38:6).

37:25-28. slave trade. The slave trade existed from earliest times in the ancient Near East. Slaves were generally war captives or persons taken in raids. Traders often accepted slaves, whom they transported to new areas and sold. These persons seldom obtained their freedom.

37:25. spice trade and caravan routes. Caravans brought incense from south Arabia to Gaza on the Palestinian coast and to Egypt, using various routes through the Sinai Peninsula. It would have been along one of these northern Sinai routes that the Midianites met Joseph's brothers and purchased him for resale in Egypt along with the rest of their trade goods.

37:25-36. Midianite/Ishmaelite. The interchange of these two names in the story probably reflects a close affinity between the two groups. Some suggest that the Ishmaelites were considered a subtribe of the Midianites. Others suggest the Midianites simply purchased Joseph from the Ishmaelites. However, based on the intermingling of the names in Judges 8:24, it would appear that the biblical writer either assumed they were related or is reflecting a known kin tie between them.

37:28. twenty shekels. The twenty shekels paid for Joseph was about normal for a slave in this time period, as attested in other literature of this time (for instance, the laws of *Hammurabi). It would constitute approximately two years of wages.

37:34-35. mourning practices. Mourning practices generally included tearing one's robe, weeping, putting dust and ashes in the hair and wearing sackcloth. Sackcloth was made of goat or camel

hair and was coarse and uncomfortable. In many cases the sackcloth was only a loin covering. The official period of mourning was thirty days but could continue for as long as the mourner chose to continue to grieve.

38:1-30
Judah's Sons

38:1. Adullam. Located in the Shephelah, Adullam has been identified with Tell esh Sheikh Madhkur northwest of Hebron (see 1 Sam 22:1; Mic 1:15). It would have been at a lower elevation than Hebron (3,040 feet above sea level), and thus the statement that Judah "went down" is appropriate.

38:6-26. levirate marriage. One remedy for the disruption of inheritance caused by the premature death of a man before he had produced an heir was the custom of levirate marriage. As outlined in Genesis 38, the dead man's brother was required to impregnate the widow so that his brother's name (his inheritance share) would be passed on to the child born of this obligatory act. A similar statute is found in *Hittite Law 193 and some form of it may be represented in Ruth 4. The law is detailed in Deuteronomy 25:5-10, where the levir is allowed to refuse his obligation by participating in a public ceremony in which the widow shames him. This was probably made necessary by situations like the one Judah faces here, in which a greedy brother (Onan) refuses to impregnate Tamar because it would decrease his eventual inheritance share.

38:11. widows. In a society that is subject to disease and warfare, it is not uncommon to find widows. Ancient Israel dealt with this problem through levirate marriage (to insure an heir for the deceased husband) and remarriage of young widows as soon as possible after the mourning period. They wore special garments which designated them as widows.

Since a widow had no inheritance rights, special provisions were made for widows under the law allowing them to glean in harvested fields (Ruth 2) and protecting them from being oppressed (Deut 14:29; Ps 94:1-7). Only the widowed daughter of a priest could honorably return to her father's house (Lev 22:13).

38:13. Timnah. The exact location of the town in this narrative is uncertain. It is a fairly common place name in the allotment list and in the Samson epic (see Josh 15:10, 56; Judg 14:1-2; 2 Chron 28:18), with connections to the tribal territory of Judah in the southern hill country (possibly Tell el-Batashi, three and a half miles east of Tel Miqne-Ekron).

38:13-14. widow's clothes. A widow, like a married woman, did not wear a veil. She did wear a special garment which set her apart as a widow. These clothes entitled her to the privileges provided for widows in the law, such as gleaning and a portion of the tithe.

38:14, 21. Enaim. The two references to this place in the narrative argue for a place name rather than the more traditional translations of "an open place" (KJV) or "a fork in the road" (Vulgate, Targums). It may be the same as Enam (Josh 15:34) and may take its name from local springs. However, other than a general reference to the territory of Judah, its exact location is unknown.

38:15-23. prostitution. The Canaanite culture utilized *cult prostitution as a way of promoting *fertility. Devotees of the mother goddess *Ishtar or *Anat would reside at or near shrines and would dress in a veil, as the symbolic bride of the god *Baal or *El. Men would visit the shrine and use the services of the cult prostitutes prior to planting their fields or during other important seasons such as shearing or the period of lambing. In this way they gave honor to the gods and reenacted the divine marriage in an attempt to insure fertility and prosperity for their fields and herds.

Major Trade Routes in the Ancient Near East

Trade was the lifeblood of the major cultures of the ancient Near East. As early as 5000 B.C. there is evidence of trade in obsidian from northern Anatolia throughout the Near East. Although land travel was time consuming (fifteen or twenty miles a day) and dangerous, the desire for exotic as well as functional products was so great that merchants and governments were willing to take the risk in order to obtain the very high profits involved (a minimum of 100 percent). For instance, business documents from the Old Assyrian period (2100-1900 B.C.) and from the Mari archive (1800-1700 B.C.) mention commercial caravans of as many as two to three hundred donkeys traveling in Asia Minor and northern Syria. They followed the trade route from the Assyrian capital at Asshur on the Tigris River west to the Habur region and the Taurus Mountains, and on to the commercial center of Kanish in west central Asia Minor. The route then continued west through Cilicia to Antioch in Pisidia, Philadelphia, Sardis, Pergamum and Troy on the Ionian coast. Each city provided shelter, supplies and a ready market for these enterprising merchants.

The actual routes taken were dictated by the topography of the various regions (avoiding disease-infected swamps, uneven and deeply cut hill country) as well as political situations and potential markets. They radiated out from major population centers. Thus from Egypt the major trade route, known as the Great Trunk Road, started in Memphis on the Nile, crossed the northern Sinai peninsula, turned north up the coastal plain of Canaan, jogged east through the

38:18, 25. seal, cord and staff. One distinctive means of signing a document in the ancient Near East was to use a cylinder seal, which contained a mirror-image incision that could be rolled onto a clay tablet or pressed into sealing wax or clay bullae. Cylinder seals, many carved from precious and semiprecious stones, have been discovered from nearly every period post-*Early Bronze by archaeologists. The seal was often threaded onto a leather cord and worn around the neck of the owner. In Palestine it is more common to find stamp seals engraved on the flat side. Another form of identification mentioned here is the staff, an aid to walking as well as an animal goad and weapon. Since this was a personal item, it may well have been carved and polished, and thus known to belong to a particular person.

38:24. prostitution as capital crime. Prostitution or harlotry was generally punished by stoning to death (Deut 22:23-24). Tamar's sentence of death by fire is exceptional. This sentence is prescribed elsewhere only in cases where a daughter of a priest engages in harlotry and in cases of incest (Lev 20:14).

39:1-23
Joseph in Potiphar's House

39:1-20. Egyptian tale of two brothers. The Nineteenth Dynasty (c. 1225 B.C.) Egyptian tale of Anubis and Bata has many similarities to the story of Joseph and Potiphar's wife. In both cases a younger man is seduced by his master's wife and then falsely accused of rape when he refuses to give in to her desires. What may have made this Egyptian story so popular (the surviving papyrus is written in a cursive style [hieratic] rather than the more formal *hieroglyphic characters) is the common tale of rivalry between brothers (like Jacob and Esau), the high suspense and the use of folklore techniques (talking animals, intervention of the gods). Aside from the common general setting, the Joseph story has little else in

Valley of Jezreel at Megiddo and then turned north to Hazor. From there the route went northeast to Damascus, passed Ebla and Aleppo in Syria and came to the northwestern spur of the Euphrates River, which then served as a guide southward into the major cities of Mesopotamia. The other major route, known as the King's Highway, joined by the caravans coming north through Arabia, traversed the Transjordanian region from the Red Sea port of Ezion Geber north through Edom, Moab and Ammon and joining the Great Trunk Road at Damascus.

Since the northern and central deserts of Arabia were so inhospitable, trade routes skirted them to the north, traveling up the Tigris and Euphrates river valleys, west to Palmyra and Damascus, and then south along either the coastal highway through Palestine or down the King's Highway in Transjordan. Caravans transporting spices (myrrh, frankincense) and indigo traced the western coast of Arabia, transshipped to Ethiopia and further north to Egypt and traveled up the Nile. Eventually these merchants reached deep-water sea ports (ports used between 2500 and 100 B.C. include Byblos, Tyre, Sidon, Acco, Ugarit, Aqaba and Alexandria), which gave them access to markets and sources of natural resources (such as the copper mines of Cyprus) in the Mediterranean (Crete, Cyprus, the Aegean and Ionian islands, the coast of Turkey and North Africa) as well as along the Arabian peninsula and East Africa. The carrying trade was dominated by Ugarit (1600-1200 B.C.) and by the Phoenicians (1100-600 B.C.). The fleets would have hugged the coasts or navigated between islands in the Mediterranean or Red Sea, traveling at about forty miles a day.

common with this Egyptian tale.

39:16. keeping the cloak. Besides the interesting parallel to Joseph's brothers' taking his cloak, it should be noted that here again the cloak is to serve to identify Joseph. Garments often contained indications of status, rank or office and therefore could be used in such ways.

39:20. imprisoned with the king's prisoners. One indication of Potiphar's understanding of the affair between Joseph and his wife may be in the choice of prison. Rather than being executed for rape (as dictated in, for instance, the Middle *Assyrian laws), Joseph was put into a royal prison holding political prisoners. This may have been a bit more comfortable (as prisons go), but more importantly it will put him in contact with members of Pharaoh's court (Gen 40:1-23).

40:1-23
Pharaoh's Cupbearer and Baker

40:1-4. cupbearer's role. The cupbearer was a high-ranking member of a monarch's court (see Neh 1:11). He would have to be a trusted individual, since his primary responsibility was to taste all of his lord's food and drink and thus prevent his lord from being poisoned.

40:1-2. offenses against Pharaoh. Offenses against Pharaoh certainly could have taken many forms. Whether these officials were suspected of involvement in a conspiracy or just guilty of displeasing Pharaoh in the disposition of their duties is impossible to tell. It may be that they are under house arrest awaiting the investigation of charges against them.

40:5-18. interpretation of dreams. Dream interpretations were usually carried out by experts who had been trained in the available dream literature. More information is available from Mesopotamia than from Egypt. Both the Egyptians and the *Babylonians compiled what we call dream books, which contain sample dreams along with the key to their interpretation. Since dreams often depended on symbolism, the interpreter would have to have access to these documents preserving the empirical data concerning past dreams and interpretations. It was believed that the gods communicated through dreams, but not that they revealed the meanings of dreams. If they were going to reveal the meaning, why use a dream in the first place? But Joseph held a different view. He did not consult any "scientific" literature, but consulted God.

40:22. execution. Hanging was a way of dishonoring the corpse of an executed person (see Josh 8:29; 2 Sam 4:12). It may involve suspension from a rope by the neck or impalement on a stake. The actual form of execution may be stoning or beheading.

41:1-32
Joseph Interprets Pharaoh's Dreams

41:1-55. the identity of Pharaoh. The name of the Pharaoh of the Joseph story is unknown. Elements of the story have suggested to some a setting in either the *Hyksos period (1750-1550 B.C.) or the *Amarna Age (fourteenth century B.C.), when large numbers of Semites were either settled in Egypt or mentioned in Egyptian sources as serving in government positions. Our current knowledge of Egyptian history and practice would support this as the most logical and feasible choice. Biblical chronological information, however, suggests to some an earlier time in the Middle Kingdom Twelfth Dynasty (1963-1786). Without specific, historical references in the story it is impossible to associate the narrative with a particular reigning king. It is the practice of the author(s) of the book of Genesis to not mention any Pharaoh by name. This may have been intentional, since the Pharaoh

was considered by his people to be a god and the Israelites did not wish to invoke that name.

41:1-7. double dreams. In the ancient Near East, dreams were generally assumed to be communications from the gods. Some were quite simple and straightforward (see Jacob's dream at Bethel, 28:10-22), but in cases where the king or Pharaoh was involved special emphasis was sometimes added through the experience of a double dream. Thus here Pharaoh has two visions that warn of the coming famine in Egypt. Similarly, the *Sumerian king Gudea is said to have had a double dream in which he was instructed to build a temple. In both cases their dreams were interpreted by magicians or representatives of a god.

41:8-16. magicians and wise men. Egypt, as well as the Mesopotamian and *Hittite kingdoms, developed guilds of magicians whose task was to interpret signs and dreams and to concoct remedies for various types of medical problems through magical means. These specialists used *exorcism to frighten away demons and gods and incantations and curses to transmit evil into some one or some place (seen in the Egyptian *execration texts and Jer 19:10-13). Thousands of texts have been discovered throughout the ancient Near East which contain protection spells as well as recipes for the manufacture of *amulets to ward off evil and for the construction of dolls, incantation bowls and miniature figures designed to bring destruction on one's enemies. Mesopotamian magic distinguished between black and white magic, and thus practitioners were divided into sorcerers and magicians or wise men. Egypt, however, did not draw this distinction among its guild of magicians. Although their major task was medical, Egyptian magicians seemed to have employed a less

respectful manner toward the gods, including providing spells for souls to escape punishment in the underworld (Book of the Dead). It is very unusual in Egypt for the Pharaoh to be in need of an interpreter of his dreams. Since the Pharaoh was considered divine, the gods would communicate to him through dreams, and the meaning was typically presented as transparent to him. The Hebrew word used to describe the specialists Pharaoh sends for is from a technical Egyptian term sometimes thought to describe dream interpreters. It is used to describe the famous official Imhotep in a late inscription (second century B.C.) where he is portrayed giving advice to Pharaoh concerning a seven-year famine.

41:14. shaved. As a way of making himself more presentable to the Pharaoh, Joseph shaves. This may have involved shaving the head (Num 6:9) as well as the face (Jer 41:5). He would have thereby changed his appearance to look more like an Egyptian. Egyptian wall paintings demonstrate that the Egyptians were typically clean-shaven.

41:27-32. famine in Egypt. Although Egypt was one of the most consistent grain-producing areas in the ancient Near East because of the regularity of the Nile floods, it was occasionally plagued with famine. Such a disaster is mentioned in *Visions of Neferti,* an Egyptian document dating to the reign of Amenemhet I (1991-1962 B.C.). Here, as in Joseph's narration, a vision is interpreted and a national calamity predicted.

41:33-57
Joseph's Advice and Elevation

41:33-40. food rationing. In the face of the coming famine, Joseph's advice is to store one-fifth of the grain from each of the years of good harvest, which can then be distributed to the people when it becomes necessary. The building of

storehouses accompanies this sensible advice (see Ex 1:11; 1 Kings 9:19).

41:35. storage cities. Egypt's management of the Nile River and its predictability made that land a breadbasket for the rest of the ancient Near East. Storage cities were a hallmark of a prosperous people who thought in terms of the long run and realized that famine was always a possibility that needed to be planned for. There would typically be storage cities centrally located in each geographical region.

41:40. second to Pharaoh. Many Egyptian nobles could make the claim of being second only to Pharaoh, and several different titles imply this position: "Great Favorite of the Lord of the Two Lands," and "Foremost among his Courtiers" are two that have been identified from inscriptions.

41:41-45. Joseph's position. The job description and investiture ceremony detailed here give Joseph a position in Egyptian government comparable to "Grand Vizier" or "Overseer of the Royal Estates," both of which appear in Egyptian documents (see 1 Kings 16:9; Is 22:15, 19-21, for use of this latter title in Israel's bureaucracy). Such a position is detailed in Egyptian tomb paintings, showing the entire sequence of events from the granting of the title to the placing of robes and rings on the appointee by the Pharaoh. Joseph functions much the same as the "Overseer of the Granaries of Upper and Lower Egypt" would have done. Such a position for a non-Egyptian is uncommon prior to the *Hyksos period (1750-1550 B.C.), when a greater number of Semites served in Egypt. From the *El Amarna reign of Akhenaten comes a tomb of the Semitic official Tutu, who was appointed "highest mouth in the whole country," a position with powers comparable to Joseph's. Biographies in Egyptian tombs and literature from Egypt such as the

*Story of *Sinuhe* give us ample information about the details of the life of officials of Pharaoh. It is not unusual to find accounts of officials who were elevated from lowly status to high positions of authority. In Sinuhe's story he fled the royal court and lived in exile for many years, finally returning and being honored. As a result the description of Joseph's elevation and honors can be seen as typical against the Egyptian background of the time.

41:42. signet ring. Kings and royal administrators used a signet ring to seal official documents. This ring would have been distinctive and would have contained the name (cartouche in Egypt) of the king. Anyone using it thus acted in the name of the king (see Num 31:50; Esther 3:10; Tobit 1:20; 1 Maccabees 6:15). The chains and linen garment are given in a ceremony of investiture providing him with the accessories that will signify his status, rank and office.

41:43-44. Joseph's perquisites. Riding in a chariot with a set of guardsmen to clear his path and proclaim his position as "second in command" gave Joseph extremely high status (see 2 Sam 15:1; Esther 6:7-9). The title of second only to Pharaoh, or viceroy (*Akkadian *terdennu*; Is 20:1 *tartan*), gave Joseph extraordinary powers and would have required all but the king to bow to him. Furthermore, since Joseph had been given the king's favor or protection, no one was permitted to "raise a hand or foot" against him or oppose his orders (compare the powers granted in Ezra 7:21-26).

41:45. Egyptian name. The intent of giving Joseph an Egyptian name is to complete the transformation process of the investiture ceremony. Egyptianized, he is more likely to be accepted at court and by the Egyptian people (see the Egyptian tale of *Sinuhe's return to Egypt and his consignment of his barbarian clothing to the "sand crawlers"). This practice

of renaming a Semite official is also found in the reign of Pharaoh Merneptah (1224-1208 B.C.). The meaning of Joseph's Egyptian name is uncertain, but may be "the God has spoken and he will live" or "the one who knows."

41:45. priest of On. The marriage arranged for Joseph allied him with one of the most powerful priestly families in Egypt. During the period from 1600 to 1100 B.C., only the priests of Ptah of Memphis were more influential. The priest of On officiated at all major festivals and supervised lesser priests who served the sun god Re in the temple city of Heliopolis (ten miles northeast of Cairo).

42:1-38
The Brothers' First Encounter with Joseph

42:6-17. spying. Just as the Israelites later send out spies to reconnoiter the land of Canaan, so Joseph's brothers are accused of working on behalf of another country. Traders and merchants would have been commonly employed for such business, as they could move around the country unnoticed or unsuspected. Some governments are naturally suspicious of foreigners, and the charge of spying is always difficult to disprove.

42:25-28. trading of silver. Coined money was not invented and put into common use until the sixth century B.C. Thus precious metals, gems, spices, incense and other luxury items were bartered by weight. Their relative value would also depend on scarcity. Silver was used throughout antiquity as a common item of exchange. Since Egypt lacked native silver deposits, this metal was particularly desirable as a standard for business transactions

43:1-34
The Brothers' Second Encounter with Joseph

43:11. products of the land. The gifts that were sent by Jacob to Joseph represent the costliest and thus the most pleasing items available. Only the balm, honey/syrup and nuts would have been actual products of Canaan. The spices and myrrh were imported and thus were precious gifts intended to buy favorable treatment from Pharaoh's representative.

43:16. steward of the house. A high status and large household, such as Joseph's, would have required a staff of servants headed by a chief butler or steward. This person would have been in charge of the maintenance of the house, kept track of financial obligations and supervised the other servants. Joseph's use of this man as his confidant (see Gen 44:1, 4) suggests it was a position of high trust. Apparently, he was also a person to whom supplicants could go to intercede with his master (see Gen 43:19-23).

43:26. bowing to honor. The standard method of demonstrating obeisance in the ancient Near East was to bow to the ground. Egyptian tomb art is filled with examples of servants and royal officials prostrating themselves before the Pharaoh. In the *El Amarna tablets (fourteenth century B.C.), the format of each letter contains a greeting, followed by a set formula of honoring the Pharaoh by bowing seven times forward and backwards.

43:32. eating procedures. The Egyptians considered all other peoples barbarians. Thus they would not associate with them directly by eating at the same table. Joseph's meal was also separated from both the Egyptians and the sons of Jacob because of his high rank.

44:1-34
Joseph's Plot Is Hatched

44:5. divination cup. The cup that Joseph plants in Benjamin's sack is identified as being used for *divination. Just as tea leaves are read today, the ancients read omens by means of liquid in cups. One mechanism involved the pouring of oil onto water to see what shapes it would take (called lecanomancy). More popular methods of divination used everyday occurrences, configurations of the entrails of sacrificed animals or the movements of the heavenly bodies. Lecanomancy was used in the time of Joseph, as is attested by several *Old Babylonian omen texts concerned with the various possible configurations of the oil and their interpretations. Another technique, hydromancy, made its observations from the reflections in the water itself. Not enough is known about Egyptian divination techniques to offer more specific information, but in these early periods typically only people of status had access to divination procedures.

45:1-28
Joseph Reveals His Identity

45:8. titles of Joseph. The use of the title "father of Pharaoh" most likely is related to the Egyptian title *it-ntr*, "father of the god," used to refer to a variety of officials and priests who serve in the Pharaoh's court. "Father" represents an advisory relationship, perhaps to be equated with the role of the priest hired by Micah in Judges 17:10 or the role of Elisha as the king of Israel's counselor in 2 Kings 6:21.

45:10. Goshen. This Semitic place name most likely refers to the delta region of Lower Egypt in the area of the Wadi Tumeilat (from the eastern arm of the Nile River to the Great Bitter Lake). Egyptian texts from *Hyksos period make reference to Semites in this region, and it is an area which provides excellent pasturage for herds. Also arguing in favor of its location in Egypt proper is the use of the phrase "in the district of Rameses" (47:11) as an equation for Goshen.

45:19. carts. The provision of carts does not contrast Egyptian carts to Canaanite carts but is simply a thoughtful gesture so that the women and children will not have to walk, for seminomadic people would not usually keep carts.

45:22. provision for Benjamin. Joseph's role as administrator of Egypt was to ration out food and clothing to the people (a common feature in ancient Near Eastern texts from *Babylon and *Mari). He does this with his family as well (an ironic turn of events, since his story begins with his receiving a piece of clothing, 37:3). Just as Jacob has singled out Joseph for special favor, now Joseph shows his favor to his full brother Benjamin by giving him five times the amount as his other half brothers, as well as a large quantity of silver.

46:1-34
Jacob and His Family Travel to Egypt

46:1. sacrifice at Beersheba. Though the patriarchs build many altars, there is little reference to their offering sacrifices. The only previous one mentioned was connected to Jacob's agreement with Laban (31:54). Isaac had built an altar at Beersheba (26:25), but no record is made of his offering of sacrifices on that altar. Jacob is taking advantage of this trip to the south to make a pilgrimage to the place where he grew up and the shrine where his father worshiped.

46:29. chariots. Chariots in Egypt during this period were light, constructed of wooden frames and leather with two spoked wheels. The ornamental chariots of pharaohs (and undoubtedly their high officials) are often depicted in the art of the New Kingdom period.

46:34. shepherds in Egypt. It is unlikely that native Egyptian herdsmen would be detested by other Egyptians. Joseph's advice to his father is both a warning about Egyptian attitudes toward strangers and a piece of diplomacy in that they would claim independent status (they had their own herds to support them) and show they were not an ambitious group who wished to rise above their occupation as shepherds.

47:1-12
Jacob's Family Settles in Egypt

47:11. district of Rameses. An equation is made here between the "district of Rameses" and the land of Goshen (see 45:10). This northeastern section of the Delta region was known to be inhabited by Semites and it is the center of *Hyksos activity during the eighteenth to sixteenth centuries B.C. It will also be equated with the Tanis district, where the storehouse cities of Pithom and Rameses were said to be constructed by the Hebrew slaves (Ex 1:11). Pharaoh Rameses II, who did build and expand cities in this region during the mid-thirteenth century B.C., may be *anachronistically referred to in this phrase.

47:13-31
Joseph's Economic and Agrarian Strategies

47:16-17. bartering. Bartering has been a means of exchange from earliest times. The mutually beneficial exchange of property, goods or manufactured items was the basis of the ancient nonmonetary economy. In this case, livestock is used as payment for grain during the famine.

47:20-26. government ownership of land. Government acquires land through forfeiture of debt, through failure to pay taxes and because a family lacks an heir. When the Egyptian people have nothing else to pay for grain during the famine, they must sell their land to the government and become tenant farmers working for Pharaoh.

47:21-25. debt slavery. Debt slavery was fairly common throughout the ancient Near East. Peasants who had lost their land and possessed nothing but the clothing on their backs would sell themselves into short-term servitude to support themselves and their families. This might be only for a day (Ex 22:26-27) or for a period of years. In Israel the term of debt servitude could not exceed six years (Ex 21:2). The Egyptian example in this text, however, suggests perpetual servitude as tenant farmers for Pharaoh. Their rent was paid with one-fifth of the harvest.

47:22. priests' exemption. The observation that the priests had an allotment of food from Pharaoh and therefore did not have to sell their land reflects a common situation of priestly privileges in Egypt. The priesthood often accumulated significant political power to itself and used its sometimes extensive economic resources to wield that power. Many pharaohs found it advantageous to curry favor with them. In contrast, the Israelite system granted no land holdings to the tribe of Levi.

47:24. 20 percent to Pharaoh. Taxation of 20 percent would not be unusual in the ancient world, but too little is known of taxation in Egypt to shed specific light on the levy imposed by Joseph.

47:28-31. burials of ancestors. Once a family tomb was established, it would have become traditional for each family member to be entombed with all of the others. This tied the generations together and further strengthened a family's claim to the land where the tomb was located.

48:1-22
Jacob's Blessing on Ephraim and Manasseh

48:5-6. Ephraim and Manasseh as firstborn. While Jacob does not disinherit Reuben and Simeon, he adopts Joseph's sons, Ephraim and Manasseh, and gives them prioritized standing in inheritance. The adoption practice and formula here are very similar to those attested in the Code of *Hammurabi. Additionally, one *Ugaritic text features a grandfather adopting his grandson. In one sense this adoption could be seen as the means by which Joseph is given the double portion of the inheritance due to the firstborn, since two of his sons receive shares from Jacob's inheritance.

48:7. Rachel's tomb. Jacob's reminiscence about the death of his wife Rachel places her tomb in the vicinity of Bethlehem and Ephrath (see the discussion of this in 35:19-20).

48:12-19. reversed blessing. The younger son has received privileged treatment in each generation of the patriarchal narratives. Isaac received inheritance over Ishmael, and Jacob over Esau; Joseph was favored over his brothers, and now Ephraim is favored over Manasseh. In most ancient civilizations the firstborn had certain privileges in the division of the inheritance, and Israel was no different. Nevertheless, exceptions could be made for various reasons. For comments about deathbed pronouncements see 27:1-4.

48:22. the land of the Amorites. It appears that *Amorite is being used here as a generic term for all of the peoples of presettlement Canaan (see 15:19-21) and specifically those in the vicinity of Shechem where Jacob had purchased a piece of land (33:18-19). Although this does not detail the ethnic diversity of that region, certainly the Amorites, whose primary area of influence was in northern Mesopotamia and Syria, had a profound effect on the customs and religious practices of Canaan.

49:1-33
Jacob's Pronouncement
Concerning His Sons

49:1. patriarchal blessing. In the biblical material the patriarchal pronouncement generally concerns the destiny of the sons with regard to fertility of the ground, fertility of the family and relationships between family members. Blessings or curses pronounced by the patriarch of the family were always taken seriously and considered binding, even though they were not presented as prophetic messages from God.

49:8-12. hand on the neck. Jacob's blessing of his son Judah is reflective of the great importance attached to the tribe of Judah in later history. One sign of its power is found in the phrase "your hand will be on the neck of your enemies," which signifies control or subjugation of Judah's foes. The difficult term *Shiloh* in the third line of verse 10 (NIV: "to whom it belongs") has been most plausibly explained as reference to a gift offering (Hebrew *shay*) paid in tribute, thus "until one brings him tribute."

49:11. washing robes in wine. In this blessing of Judah, the future prosperity of that tribe is symbolized by abundant fertility. Wine will be so plentiful that they will be able to wash their clothes in it. It is also possible this is a reference to the dyeing industry, but that would figure into future economic prosperity.

49:13. haven for ships. As the coastline was lacking natural harbors, the sea was generally little more than a boundary to Israelites. Only in the northern coastal regions would there have been any inclination to develop seafaring skills.

49:14-15. donkey habits. The blessing of Issachar contains this characterization of a strong animal, which is sometimes stubborn and lazy and may sit down unexpectedly in an inconvenient place. The idea may also be suggestive of a tribe that allies itself with outsiders or is forced to serve others (contra Judg 5:15).

49:17. horse domestication. Reference to a rider on the horse assumes an advanced level of domestication of the horse. This was achieved in the third millennium. In Mesopotamia horseback riders are depicted in the middle of the third millennium, but in Egyptian materials not until a millennium later. Horses were usually used for pulling chariots, and horseback riding was not common.

50:1-14
Jacob's Burial

50:1-3. embalming. Although it was the usual practice in Egypt for everyone who could afford it, embalming of Israelites is found only in this passage. This was an elaborate and *ritual-filled procedure performed by a trained group of mortuary priests. It involved removing the internal organs and placing of the body in embalming fluids for forty days. The idea behind this is based on the Egyptian belief that the body had to be preserved as a repository for the soul after death. The bodies of Jacob and Joseph are embalmed, and while this may have been done to soothe the feelings of the Egyptians, it also served the purpose of preserving their bodies for later burial in Canaan.

50:3. mourning period. This period of mourning may include the forty days required to embalm the body plus the traditional thirty-day mourning period (see Deut 34:8). Since the Egyptians are also described as mourning Jacob's death, it would appear he was accorded royal honors as a visiting dignitary.

50:10-11. threshing floor of Atad. No exact location has been identified for this site, said to be east of the Jordan. It is strange that Jacob's remains would be taken east through Transjordan instead of on a more direct route to Hebron. Having the seven-day mourning ceremony on a threshing floor is quite appropriate. This is a place associated with business, law and life and thus suitable as a place for memorializing a tribal leader (see Num 15:20; Ruth 3; 2 Sam 24:16-24).

50:11. Abel-mizraim. The renaming of the threshing floor of Atad provides a lasting memorial to Jacob and the remarkable seven-day mourning ceremony conducted there. The name itself contains a familiar element: *abel* means "stream" and appears in several other place names (Num 33:49—Abel Shittim; Judg 11:33—Abel Keramim). Here, however, there is a pun on the Hebrew word *ebel*, "mourning."

50:15-26
The Last Years of Joseph

50:26. Joseph's age. Joseph dies at the age of 110, considered the ideal age for an Egyptian. Examination of mummies has demonstrated that the average life expectancy in Egypt was between forty and fifty years. The use of the coffin or sarcophagus in mummification was an Egyptian, not an Israelite, practice.

EXODUS

Introduction

The book of Exodus contains a virtual cornucopia of types of literature, from narrative to law to architectural instructions. All are skillfully woven together to narrate the sequence of events that led a people from feeling that God had abandoned them to understanding themselves to be God's elect people with his presence in their midst. As a result there are many different primary sources that may offer assistance.

As might be expected, Exodus has more connections to Egyptian sources than any other book. Unfortunately the uncertainty concerning the date of the events and the sparsity of materials from some of the related periods of Egyptian history leave many questions unanswered. As a result it is not so much the historical literature of Egypt that we depend on but all the sources that give information about geography or culture. Locating the cities and places mentioned in the biblical text is very difficult and many uncertainties remain, yet one by one some of the gaps are being closed as archaeology continues to investigate significant sites.

The legal passages of Exodus are comparable to a wide range of law collections from Mesopotamia. These include *Sumerian legal texts such as the reform of Uruinimgina (or Urukagina), the laws of *Ur-Nammu and the laws of *Lipit-Ishtar. These are fragmentary texts that date from the late third millennium and early second millennium B.C. The more extensive texts are the laws of *Eshnunna and *Hammurabi (from the *Old Babylonian period, eighteenth century B.C.), the *Hittite laws from the seventeenth century and the Middle Assyrian laws from the twelfth century. These law collections, as indicated by the paragraphs that surround them, are intended to testify to the gods how successful the king has been at establishing and maintaining justice in his kingdom. As such, the laws are designed to reflect the wisest and fairest decisions the king could imagine. Like the candidate making a campaign speech who seeks to find every possible piece of legislation that he can claim responsibility for, the king wanted to show himself in the best possible light.

These laws help us to see that the actual legislation that determined the shape of Israelite society was not all that different on the surface from the laws that would have characterized Assyrian or Babylonian society. What was different was that for Israel the law was part of God's revelation of what he was like. The Babylonians had just as strong prohibitions of murder as the Israelites had. But the Babylonians would have refrained from murder because murder was disruptive to the smooth ordering of society and the principles of civilization. Israelites would have refrained from murder because of who God was. The laws may look the same, but the foundation of the legal system was remarkably different. For the Israelites, *Yahweh their God was the source of all law and the foundation of all societal norms. In Mesopotamia the king was entrusted with the authority to perceive what the law ought to be and to establish the law. The gods were not moral, nor did they require moral behavior, but they did expect humans to preserve the values of civilization and therefore to act in orderly and civilized ways.

The point is, then, that the law given at Sinai does not necessarily prescribe *new* laws. Its actual legislation may be very much like the laws that Israel had been living under in Egypt and is clearly similar to the laws that governed other societies of the ancient Near East. What is new is the revelation of God that is accomplished through the institutionalization of the law as part of the *covenant between God and Israel. Comparing the law of the Bible to the ancient Near Eastern law collections can help us to understand both the concept of law and order as well as the philosophical and theological underpinnings of the law.

When we get to the section of Exodus that has to do with the construction of the tabernacle, we may be well served by understanding the use and construction of shrines (portable and otherwise) in the ancient Near East. The detailed description of the materials that were used in the construction of the tabernacle, can be understood as we become aware of the value that culture attached to those materials. For example, consider the value that our society places on a mink coat, an oak desk, a leather chair or a stone house. Alongside of materials, we also attach value to positioning, as in the penthouse apartment, the corner office or the house at the top of the hill. So as we become acquainted with the materials and positions that the ancient Israelites attached value to, we can appreciate the rationale behind certain details. Again, we will often find that the rationale is cultural rather than theological. Once we understand the cultural elements, we can avoid attaching a foreign theological significance to some of the features.

1:1-22
Israelite Slavery in Egypt

1:8-14. king who didn't know Joseph.
The book of Exodus maintains the anonymity of the Pharaohs who have dealings with the Israelites. Since Egyptian records have preserved no accounts of the Israelite presence, enslavement or exodus, identifying these Pharaohs can only be attempted by using the vague hints contained in the narrative. In the sixteenth and seventeenth centuries B.C. a group known as the Hyksos, who were not native Egyptians, ruled the land. It is usually thought that the Pharaoh referred to in this verse represents either the first of the *Hyksos rulers or the first of the native Egyptian rulers after the *Hyksos were driven out. The difference would be at least one hundred years (c. 1650 or 1550 B.C.), or up to two hundred years if some of the early *Hyksos rulers with only partial control subjected the Israelites to slavery.

1:10. reason for enslaving Israel. The argument for enslaving the Israelites is that if they are not enslaved they will join the enemy and leave the country. This would suggest the period when the *Hyksos are being driven from the land. The Egyptians would have wanted to keep the Israelite presence for economic reasons.

1:11. forced labor. The sheer number of man-hours needed for the massive engineering and construction projects undertaken in the ancient world made the use of forced labor not infrequent. It was used as a form of taxation (for instance, the common people might work one month out of the year without pay on government building projects). When the government projects proved too ambitious to staff with native people and prisoners of war, and too expensive to hire labor for, vulnerable groups of people would be targeted for forced labor.

1:11. Pithom. Pithom has been identified as the Egyptian Pi(r)-Atum, "real-estate of Atum," currently known as Tell el-Rataba, along the Ismalia Canal, approximately sixty miles northeast of Cairo. The text's identification of the building projects as store cities does not suggest they were only for storage of grain. The store cities were centrally located hubs in the region and could be capital cities.

1:11. Rameses. The location of the city of Rameses, disputed for many years, has now been positively identified as Tell ed-Dab'a, about twenty miles north of Pithom. The site has been extensively excavated by M. Bietak. It served as the *Hyksos capital, Avaris, and was rebuilt by Rameses II as his capital, Pi-Ramesse, in the thirteenth century. It was dismantled to build Tanis (about twelve miles to the north) as the Delta capital in the Twentieth Dynasty during the twelfth century B.C. (Judges period). Rameses II used various peoples as slave labor for building the city, including the Apiru (a term used in the second millennium to describe dispossessed peoples), a designation that would have been applied to the Hebrews as well as to other people.

1:14. brick making. The ancient records agree that brick makers had a filthy job. A work known as the *Satire on the Trades* attests to an existence that is perpetually muddy and miserable. Houses, public buildings, walls around cities and even pyramids were at times constructed of brick. Literally millions of bricks were needed, and daily individual quotas would vary depending on how many were assigned to a crew. Crews operated by division of labor, with tasks such as fetching and breaking up straw, hauling mud and water, shaping the bricks by hand or using molds, setting the bricks to dry in the sun and several days later hauling them to the building site. The bricks for a large building would be over a foot long and half as wide, and perhaps six inches thick.

1:15-22. delivery stools. In the ancient world women normally gave birth in a crouching or kneeling position. Small stools, stones or bricks could be used to support the mother's weight as she gave birth. Midwives did not just aid in parturition but were advisers through the whole process of conception, pregnancy, birth and child care.

2:1-10
The Birth of Moses

2:1-10. heroes spared at birth. In the ancient world there are other accounts of heroes being miraculously spared at birth or being raised in unlikely circumstances. The most intriguing such literary work is the *Legend of Sargon's Birth* (probably eighth century B.C.). Rather than sacrificing her child (as priestesses were supposed to do), Sargon's mother hid him in a reed basket by the bank of the Euphrates. After being carried down the river, he was found and raised by the royal gardener. He grew up to become the founder of the dynasty of *Akkad in the twenty-fourth century B.C. But there are important differences. Most of these stories feature a royal personage discarded to his fate and raised by commoners, while Moses, under careful supervision, is rescued by royalty and raised in privileged circumstances. There is no reason to assume that this daughter of Pharaoh would have been in a position of power or influence. Harem children by the score existed in every court, and daughters were considered less highly than sons.

2:3. reed basket coated with tar. The Hebrew word used for Moses' basket is the same as that used for Noah's ark. The papyrus used to make the floating cradle was also used in the construction of light boats in Egypt and Mesopotamia, a practice the biblical writers were aware of (Is 18:2). The reed bundles overlapped in three layers, and the pitch would make it watertight (Gen 6:14 uses a different word but shows the same concept).

2:8. wet nurse. Procurement of a wet nurse to nurse and care for the child until it was weaned was a normal procedure in wealthy or aristocratic households. Though Egyptian literature has provided little information, Mesopotamian legal texts speak of the adoption procedures for an abandoned child who has been found. The wet nurse serves as the paid legal guardian, with adoption taking place after weaning.

2:10. the name Moses. The name Moses is from the Egyptian *ms(w)*, meaning "to beget." It is a common element in names, often connected to a god's name, so Thutmosis ("Thoth begets" or "Thoth is born") or Rameses ("Ra begets" or "Ra is born"). Alternatively, since *ms* in Egyptian means "boy," Moses may simply have been called by a generic name. Wordplay occurs in that the closest Hebrew root means "to draw out."

2:10. growing up in Pharaoh's court. Growing up in the household of Pharaoh would have involved certain privileges in terms of education and training. This would have included training in literature and scribal arts as well as in warfare. Foreign languages would have been important for any work in diplomacy and probably were included. One of the qualities that Egyptians prized most was rhetoric (eloquence in speech and argumentation). Literary works such as *The Eloquent Peasant* show how impressed they were with someone who could speak well. Though Moses would have been trained in rhetoric, he did not consider himself skilled in this area (4:10-12).

2:11-25
Moses' Flight from Egypt to Midian

2:12-15. Moses' crime. Egyptians maintained a substantial sense of ethnic pride that caused them to consider foreigners inferior. For a foreigner to kill an Egyptian was a great crime.

2:15. flight from Egypt: Sinuhe. In one of the most well-known Egyptian tales, *The Story of *Sinuhe,* the main character fears disfavor from a new pharaoh early in the second millennium B.C. and flees through Canaan to Syria. There he marries the daughter of a Bedouin chieftain and becomes a powerful leader among those people.

2:15. Midian. The Midianites were a seminomadic people who are located in various regions in different stories and sources, from the Transjordan and the Negev in the region of Palestine to the northern Sinai. But the region east of the Gulf of Aqaba in northwest Arabia has the strongest claim to being the central location of the Midianite people.

2:16-19. shepherdesses. Normally women would have been shepherdesses only when there were no sons in the family. The disadvantages of this situation are highlighted in this account, where the other shepherds bully the girls.

2:23. Pharaoh's identity. Again the identity of this Pharaoh is not given. Most conclude that he is either Thutmose III or Rameses II.

3:1—4:17
The Burning Bush and the Call of Moses

3:1. name differences: Reuel (2:18); Jethro (3:1). In the previous chapter Moses' father-in-law was called Reuel, while here he is referred to as Jethro and in Numbers 10:29 as Hobab (see Judg 4:11). The difficulty can be resolved once the ambiguity of the terminology is recognized. The term designating male in-

laws is nonspecific. The term referred to a woman's male relatives and could be used for her father, brother or even grandfather. Most solutions take account of this. Perhaps Reuel is the grandfather head of the clan, Jethro is the father of Zipporah and technically the father-in-law of Moses, and Hobab is the brother-in-law of Moses, Jethro's son. Alternatively, Jethro and Hobab could both be brothers-in-law, and Reuel the father.

3:1. mountain of God. The mountain of God is here designated Horeb and elsewhere Sinai, though either one of those names could refer to the general area, a particular range or a single peak. Moses most likely calls it the mountain of God in recognition of the status it is going to achieve in the following chapters rather than because of any prior occurrences or superstitions. In the ancient and classical world deities normally were believed to have their dwelling places on mountains.

3:2-4. burning bush. Natural explanations for the burning bush have been plentiful, from bushes that exude flammable gas to those covered with brightly colored leaves or berries. In the late Egyptian Horus texts at the temple of Edfu the sky god is envisioned as a flame manifest in a particular type of bush, but this is a full millennium after Moses.

3:5-6. taking off sandals. It was common practice for priests to enter temples barefoot to prevent bringing in dust or impurities of any sort.

3:2-7. Yahweh, God of your father. God's identification of himself with the "God of your father" suggests that the concept of patron deity may still provide the most accurate understanding of how the Israelites thought about *Yahweh. This title ceases to be used once Yahweh becomes the national deity at Sinai. It also serves to identify him as the God of the *covenant.

3:7-10. land of milk and honey. The land of Canaan is described as a land "flowing with milk and honey." This refers to the bounty of the land for a pastoral lifestyle, but not necessarily in terms of agriculture. Milk is the product of herds, while honey represents a natural resource, probably the syrup of the date rather than bees' honey. A similar expression to this is found in the *Ugaritic epic of *Baal and Mot that describes the return of fertility to the land in terms of the wadis flowing with honey. Egyptian texts as early as the Story of *Sinuhe describe the land of Canaan as rich in natural resources as well as in cultivated produce.

3:8. peoples of Canaan. In the list of the six people groups that inhabited Canaan, the first three are well known while the latter three are barely known at all. Canaan is mentioned as early as the Ebla tablets (twenty-fourth century B.C.), and the Canaanite people were the principal inhabitants of the fortified cities of the land, though they do not seem to have been native to the land. The *Hittites were from Anatolia, modern Turkey, but groups had migrated south and occupied sections of Syria and Canaan. *Amorites (known in Mesopotamia as *Amurru* or *Martu)* are known from written documents as early as the middle third millennium B.C. Most scholars think that they occupied many areas in the Near East from their roots in Syria. There is still debate as to whether the term *Perizzites* is ethnic or sociological (those living in unwalled settlements). The Hivites are sometimes connected to the Horites, in which case they may be *Hurrians. The Jebusites occupied the region later associated with the tribe of Benjamin, notably the city of Jerusalem, and are often related to the Perizzites who were located in the same region. There is no mention of the Perizzites, Hivites or Jebusites outside the Bible.

3:11. Moses' objection. Moses' objection carried little persuasiveness, given the training provided for him in the household of Pharaoh (see comment on 2:10).

3:13-15. I AM. The personal name of Israel's God, *Yahweh (usually rendered LORD, v. 15), is built from the Hebrew verb "to be." Verse 14 uses an alternate form of the verb in the first person, "I am." The name Yahweh for the Israelite God is attested outside the Old Testament in the Mesha Inscription, the Arad Ostraca, the Lachish letters and inscriptions from Khirbet el-Qom and Kuntillat Ajrud, to name a few of the more prominent places. There are a number of possible occurrences of Yahweh or Yah as a deity's name outside of Israel, though all are debatable. One of the most intriguing is the reference to *"Yhw in the land of the Shasu,"* mentioned in some Egyptian inscriptions in Nubia (modern Sudan) from the mid-second millennium. The Shasu are Bedouins related in the same inscriptions to the area of Seir (see Deut 33:2; Judg 5:4). This might find confirmation in the biblical indication that Jethro the Midianite was a worshiper of Yahweh (chap. 18). We must remember, however, that Midian was also a descendant of Abraham (Gen 25:2-4), so this may not be unrelated to the Israelite God.

3:16-17. elders. The elders here are the clan leaders of Israel. Elders typically served as a ruling assembly overseeing the leadership of a village or community. The people would look for the endorsement of Moses by the elders before they would accept his leadership.

3:18-20. God of the Hebrews. "God of the Hebrews" is a title that is used only in the context of the exodus. Since the Israelites generally only refer to themselves as Hebrews to foreigners, some have related the term *Hebrew* to the Apiru/*Habiru known from ancient texts from this period. Apiru/Habiru is not an ethnic designation but a sociological one, referring to displaced peoples.

3:18. three-day journey to sacrifice. The request to Pharaoh is for a three-day religious pilgrimage into the wilderness. This would generally consist of one day for travel each way and one full day for the religious ceremonies. The refusal adds religious oppression to the crimes of Pharaoh.

3:19-20. mighty hand of God. The image of an outstretched or mighty hand or arm is common in Egyptian inscriptions to describe the power of Pharaoh. It is used throughout the exodus narratives to describe God's power over Pharaoh. See comment on Deuteronomy 26:8.

4:1-9. the three signs of Moses. The three signs the Lord gave to Moses each most likely had symbolic significance. The rod was the symbol of authority in Egypt, and Pharaoh was represented by the serpent figure, the uraeus, featured prominently on his crown. The first sign then suggests that Pharaoh and his authority are completely in the power of God. The second sign inflicts a skin disease, often translated "leprosy," on Moses' hand. In fact, however, the Hebrew term used describes many dermatological conditions, most far less severe than Hansen's disease (leprosy; see comment on Lev 13). Nonetheless, when inflicted in the Bible it is consistently a punishment for hubris—when an individual in pride presumptuously assumes a divinely appointed role (Num 12:1-12; 2 Kings 5:22-27; 2 Chron 26:16-21), thus demonstrating God's intention to punish Pharaoh. Its result is to drive the individual from God's presence, since it rendered the afflicted unclean. The third, turning water to blood, shows God's control of the prosperity of Egypt, which was entirely dependent on the waters of the Nile. It also anticipates the plagues that God will send.

4:17. Moses' staff. Moses' staff becomes the symbol of God's power and presence with Moses. It is carefully distinguished from instruments of magic in that Moses never uses it in connection with incantations or words of power. It is not used to manipulate God so, except in one unfortunate incident (Num 20), Moses does not wield it but only employs it as instructed.

4:18-26
Moses' Bloodguilt

4:19. Moses' standing. The fact that Egyptians are no longer seeking to kill Moses for his act of murder does not mean that he has been absolved of all guilt in the matter.

4:20-23. hardening Pharaoh's heart. This section contains the first reference to the hardening of Pharaoh's heart—a motif that occurs twenty times over the next ten chapters (during the plagues and up to the crossing of the sea). Several different verbs are used, and Pharaoh sometimes hardens his own heart, while other times it is hardened by the Lord. The concept has parallels to similar Egyptian expressions that convey perseverance, stubbornness, persistence and an unyielding nature. These can be good qualities or bad, depending on what type of behavior or attitude one is persisting in.

4:22. Israel, the firstborn of God. The passage artfully develops the issue of jeopardy to the firstborn: God's firstborn, Israel; Pharaoh's firstborn; and Moses' firstborn. Israel is God's firstborn in the sense that they are the first nation to enter into a relationship with him.

4:24-26. the Lord was about to kill him. The text has told us that there was no one in Egypt seeking to kill Moses (v. 19), but Moses still stood guilty of bloodshed before God. Later, cities of refuge were established to provide shelter for someone who felt there were mitigating circumstances in a homicide, but Moses had sought refuge in Midian. By leaving his place of refuge, Moses became vulnerable to being called to account for his crime. Others in the Old Testament whom the Lord called on to go somewhere but then accosted on the way include Jacob (Gen 31—32) and Balaam (Num 22). In each instance God did indeed want the individual to make the journey but had an issue to settle before he could proceed.

4:25. flint knife. A flint flake was used for to perform *circumcision in Israel and Egypt even after metal tools and weapons were readily available. They were very sharp, easily accessible and the traditional instrument for age-old *rituals.

4:25. bridegroom of blood. One recent study has plausibly suggested that *circumcision in many cultures was done by the man's in-laws and extended the protection of the family over the man and his children. If such was the Midianite practice, this could serve as an extension of the refuge that Moses had in Midian. From the Israelite side, the dabbing of the blood (v. 25) is seen also in the Passover *ritual (12:7) and offers protection from the slaughtering angel (12:44-48). Zipporah's comment that Moses was a bridegroom of bloodshed would indicate both his need for protection by the family and his need for expiating blood.

4:27-31
Moses' Return to Egypt
4:29. elders. The elders here are the clan leaders of Israel. Elders typically served as a ruling assembly overseeing the leadership of a village or community. The elders here accept the legitimacy of Moses' role and mission and acknowledge that he carries the authority of God.

5:1-21
Moses Confronts Pharaoh
5:1-5. festival in the desert. Festivals in the ancient world centered around cycles of nature (new year's or *fertility festivals), mythological events (enthronement or deity conquering chaos), agricultural events (harvest), or historical memorials (dedications or deliverances). They celebrate what deity has done and seek to perpetuate deity's action on their behalf. Often these elements were combined. They usually are celebrated at a holy place and therefore often require pilgrimage.

5:6-14. straw for bricks. Straw serves as a bonding agent in the brick as it is heated. Without sufficient straw or with poor-quality stubble, the bricks would not form as easily and a higher proportion would fall apart, thus making the quota harder to achieve. Quotas found in Egyptian literature often do not clarify the number in the crew or the time period involved, but we do know that the quotas were often not met.

5:22—6:12
God's Determination to Deliver
6:3-8. LORD. A casual reading of verse 3 might lead one to conclude that the name *Yahweh (LORD) was unfamiliar to the patriarchs, though Genesis 15:7 and 28:13 clearly suggest otherwise. It is true that El-Shaddai (God Almighty) was known to the patriarchs, and in Genesis 17:1 and 35:11 it is El-Shaddai who is connected to the aspects of the *covenant that were realized during the lifetimes of the patriarchs. In contrast, "Yahweh" is connected to the long-term promises, particularly that of the land, so it can rightfully be said that the patriarchs did not experience him (that is, he did not make himself known in that way). The patriarchs probably did not worship God by the name Yahweh, but the text does not require the conclusion

that the name was foreign to them.

6:6. outstretched arm. The Egyptians were used to hearing of the outstretched arm of Pharaoh accomplishing mighty deeds. Now Yahweh's outstretched arm is going to overwhelm Pharaoh. He is confirming this in fulfillment of the oath he made to Abraham, represented by the gesture of raising a hand (toward heaven). Here we can see that naming the gesture is simply another way of referring to the oath, for there is no higher power for God to swear by. See comment on Deuteronomy 26:8.

6:28—7:13
Moses and Aaron Before Pharaoh

7:9. serpent. The serpent was considered a wise and magical creature in Egypt. Wadjet, the patron goddess of lower Egypt, is represented as a snake (uraeus) on Pharaoh's crown. This came to symbolize the power of Pharaoh. But additionally Apopis, the enemy of the gods, in the form of a snake, represented the forces of chaos. It is therefore not arbitrary that the sign featured a serpent (whether cobra or crocodile, see below), for in Egyptian thinking there was no other creature so ominous.

7:11-13. magicians of Pharaoh. Pharaoh's magicians would have been specialists in spells and incantations as well as being familiar with the literature for omens and dreams. They would have practiced sympathetic magic (based on the idea that there is an association between an object and that which it symbolizes; for example, that what is done to a person's picture will happen to the person) and would have used their arts to command the gods and spirits. Magic was the thread that held creation together, and it was used both defensively and offensively by its practitioners, human or divine.

7:11-12. staffs turning into serpents.

Some have reported that there is a type of cobra that can be immobilized in rigid form if pressure is applied in a certain way to the neck, perhaps allowing the Egyptian magicians to appear to have rods that turned into snakes. This procedure is portrayed on Egyptian scarab *amulets and is practiced even today. It must be noted, though, that the word translated "serpent" in this section is not the same as the one used in 4:3-4. The creature referred to here is usually considered a sizable monster (see Gen 1:21), though it is used parallel to "cobra" in two places (Deut 32:33; Ps 91:13). This same creature is equated to Pharaoh in Ezekiel 29:3 and is thought by some to be a crocodile. There is no need to attribute a mere sleight of hand to Pharaoh's magicians—these were masters of the occult.

7:12. Aaron's staff swallowing magicians' staffs. When Aaron's serpent swallowed the magicians' serpents, the symbolism would clearly imply an Israelite triumph over Egypt. So, for instance, an Old Kingdom Pyramid Text uses the portrayal of one crown swallowing another to tell of Upper Egypt's conquest of Lower Egypt.

7:13. hardening of heart. This second mention of Pharaoh's hardened heart (see comment on 4:20-23) reflects his resolve to pursue the course he has chosen.

7:14—11:10
The Ten Plagues

7:14—11:10. plagues as attack on Egypt's gods and as natural occurrences. The plagues have been viewed by many as specific attacks on the gods of Egypt (see 12:12). This is certainly true in the sense that the Egyptians' gods were unable to protect them and that areas supposedly under the jurisdiction of their gods were used to attack them. Whether individual gods were being singled out is difficult to confirm. In another vein, some have suggested that a sequence of natural oc-currences can explain the plagues from a scientific point of view, all originating from an overflooding in the summer months and proceeding through a cause-and-effect process into March. Those who maintain such a position will still sometimes admit to the miraculous nature of the plagues in terms of timing, discrimination between Egyptians and Israelites, prior announcement and se-verity. For each plague we will cite the natural explanations that have been of-fered as well as indicating which gods have been considered targets of the plague. It will be for the reader to decide what role either of these explanations should play in the understanding of the text.

7:14-24. water to blood. The Nile was the lifeblood of Egypt. Agriculture and ultimately survival were dependent on the periodic flooding that deposited fer-tile soils along the river's 4,132 miles. The obese Hapi, one of the children of Horus, was technically not the god of the Nile but the personification of the inun-dation of the Nile. The blood-red color-ing has been attributed to an excess of both red earth and the bright red algae and its bacteria, both of which accom-pany a heavier than usual flooding. Rather than the abundant life usually brought by the river, this brought death to the fish and detriment to the soil. Such an occurrence is paralleled in an obser-vation in the *Admonitions of Ipuwer* (a few centuries before Moses) that the Nile had turned to blood and was un-drinkable. The biblical comment about the Egyptians digging down (v. 24) would be explained as an attempt to reach water that had been filtered through the soil.

7:19. buckets and jars. In verse 19 most translations make reference to wood and stone vessels, suggesting that water in such vessels was also changed. The Hebrew text says nothing of vessels. The combination of "sticks and stones" is used in *Ugaritic literature to refer to outlying, barren regions. The text also includes canals, which suggests the arti-ficial channels used for irrigation.

8:1-15. frog plague. It is natural that the frogs would desert the waters and banks clogged with decomposing fish. The goddess Heqet was envisioned as a frog and assisted with childbirth, but it is difficult to imagine how this was seen as a victory over her. The Egyptian magi-cians could not remove the plague, only make it worse.

8:16-19. gnat plague. The type of insect (NIV: "gnats") involved in this plague is not clear, since the Hebrew word is used only in this context. Most studies have favored either the mosquito or the tick as the likeliest identification. The former would breed in all the stagnant pools of water left from the flooding. "Finger of God" may be an Egyptian expression re-ferring to Aaron's rod. The failure of the magicians and their admission that God is at work begins to fulfill the Lord's pur-pose: They will know that I am *Yahweh.

8:20-32. land ruined by flies. The insect featured in the fourth plague is not named. Instead the text speaks of swarms, using a word known only in relation to this context. Flies are logical both to the climate and to the conditions that exist with rotting fish and frogs and decaying vegetation. Because it is a car-rier of skin anthrax (associated with later plagues), the species *Stomoxys cal-citrans* has been the most popular iden-tification. As both pests and carriers, these insects brought ruination on the land.

8:22. Goshen. This is the first plague that does not afflict the Israelites living in Goshen. The precise location of Goshen is still unknown, though it is certainly in the eastern part of the Delta region of the Nile.

8:26. sacrifice detestable to Egyptians. When Pharaoh offers to let them make their sacrifices in the land, Moses does not claim the need to conduct the *rituals at a holy site but objects that their rituals are unacceptable because they sacrifice that which is detestable to the Egyptians. Slaughter of animals to provide food for the gods was prevalent in Egyptian religious practice, as many reliefs portray, but blood sacrifices of animals played little role in the sun worship, king worship and *funerary observances that constituted much of Egyptian religion. Often the animal being slaughtered was considered to represent an enemy of the god.

9:1-7. livestock plague. The plague on the cattle is regularly identified as anthrax that was contracted from the bacteria that had come down the Nile and infected the fish, the frogs and the flies. The Egyptian goddess of love, Hathor, took the form of a cow, and the sacred Apis bull was so highly venerated that it was embalmed and buried in a necropolis with its own sarcophagus at death.

9:8-12. handful of soot. While some have concluded the ashes are taken from a brick kiln (symbolizing the labor of the Israelites), the Egyptians generally used sun-dried brick rather than kiln-fired. The furnace spoken of here is sizable and alternatively could be viewed as the place where the carcasses of the dead animals have been burned. The scattering of ashes is sometimes used as a magical *ritual in Egypt to bring an end to pestilence. Here it may bring an end to the cattle plague, but it translates into human misery.

9:10-12. boils plague. Skin anthrax would be carried by the bites of the flies which had had contact with the frogs and cattle, and would produce sores, particularly on the hands and feet.

9:13-35. effects of hail. Hail is destructive to crops as well as to humans and animals. The text's designation of which crops were affected (vv. 31-32) indicates that it was January or February.

10:1-20. locust plague. Locusts were all too common in the ancient Near East and were notorious for the devastation and havoc they brought. The locusts breed in the region of the Sudan and would have been more plentiful than usual in the wet climate that initiated the entire sequence. Their migration would strike in February or March and would follow the prevailing winds to either Egypt or Palestine. The east wind (v. 13) would bring them into Egypt. A locust will consume its own weight each day. Locust swarms have been known to cover as many as four hundred square miles, and even one square mile could teem with over one hundred million insects. Certainly anything that had survived the hail was now destroyed, and if they laid their eggs before being blown out to sea, the problem would recur in cycles. The economy in Egypt was destroyed, but the principal gods had yet to be humiliated.

10:19. west wind. The plague was ended by a "wind from the sea." In Israel this is a west wind, but in Egypt it would come from the north or northwest and therefore drive the locusts back to the sea.

10:21-29. darkness plague (that can be felt). The comment that it was darkness that could be felt (v. 21) suggests that the darkness was caused by something airborne, namely, the *khamsin* dust storms known in the region. There would be excessive dust from all of the red earth that had been brought down and deposited by the Nile, as well as from the barren earth left behind in the wake of the hail and locusts. The three-day duration is typical for this type of storm, which is most likely to occur between March and May. The fact that the text emphasizes the darkness rather than the dust storm may indicate that the sun god, Amon-Re, the national god of Egypt, the divine father of Pharaoh, is being specifically targeted.

11:1-10. tenth plague and Pharaoh. In Egypt Pharaoh was also considered a deity, and this last plague is directed at him. In the ninth plague his "father," the sun god, was defeated, and now his son, presumably the heir to the throne, will be slaughtered. This is a blow to Pharaoh's person, his kingship and his divinity.

11:4. the Lord going throughout Egypt. In Egypt the most notable and anticipated event of the major festivals was the god coming forth among the people. Here, however, the going forth of Israel's God throughout the land will be for the purposes of judgment.

11:2. ask for gold and silver. The instructions for the Israelites to ask for gold and silver articles and clothing (mentioned in other passages) from the Egyptians would most likely have correlated with the idea that the Israelites were going to have a feast for their God. Finery would be natural for such occasions, and it would not be odd to think that the Israelite slaves would not possess such luxuries. By now the people of Egypt would have been in despair from the plagues, and the thought that Israel's God might be appeased by a feast would make them very cooperative.

11:4. hand mill. The slave girl at her hand mill is portrayed as the lowest on the social ladder. The hand mill, or saddle-quern, was made up of two stones: a lower stone with a concave surface and a loaf-shaped upper stone. The daily chore of grinding grain into flour involved sliding the upper stone over the grain spread on the lower stone.

11:7. not a dog will bark. Dogs were not kept as pets but were considered undesirable and a general nuisance, perhaps as a rat would be viewed today. The statement that no dog would bark suggests unusual calm, for these roaming curs were easily antagonized by the slightest irregularity.

12:1-28
Passover

12:1-28. roots of Passover. According to the biblical account the Feast of Passover is instituted in association with the tenth plague, but that does not mean that its institution did not build on a previously existing festival of some sort. We should recall that God instituted *circumcision as a sign of the *covenant using a practice that previously existed with other purposes. Many elements of the Passover *ritual suggest that it may be adapted from a nomadic *ritual that sought to protect herdsmen from demonic attack and insure the *fertility of the herd. Even if this is so, each of the elements is suitably "converted" to the new context of the tenth plague and the exodus from Egypt. If such a conversion of a nomadic festival took place, it would be similar to the early western European Christians' superimposing Christmas on their pagan winter solstice festivals, with tokens such as holly, mistletoe and evergreen trees carried over.

12:1-11. calendar. This event established Abib (later called Nisan) as the first month in the religious calendar of Israel. By the civil calendar, Tishri, six months later, was the first month, and thus the month that "New Year's Day" was celebrated. The Israelite calendar was a lunar calendar with periodic adjustments to the solar year. Abib began with the first new moon after the spring equinox, generally mid-March, and went through mid-April.

12:5. year-old males without defect. As a yearling, the male would have survived the vulnerable period of early life (mortality rates were between 20 and 50 percent) and would be preparing to take on its role as a productive member of the flock. A flock needs fewer male members, however, and particularly among goats many of the males were slaughtered as yearlings for their coats and their meat. The females were kept until about age eight for bearing young and producing milk.

12:6. slaughtered at twilight. In Egypt's civil calendar each month was thirty days in length and divided into three periods of ten days each. The Egyptian religious calendar, including festivals, remained in a lunar sequence. The occurrence of the feast and the plague corresponded to the eve of what Egyptians called "half-month day." More importantly, since the month in lunar reckoning began at the new moon, the feast occurred at the time of the full moon, always the first after the spring equinox. The slaughter would take place at twilight, when the first full moon of the Israelite year rose.

12:7. function of blood. In primitive religions blood is often used to ward off evil powers, whereas in Israelite *ritual the blood served as a purifying element. While the former could certainly have been superstitiously believed by Israelites who retained these primitive elements in their religious thought and practice, the latter was the intended function.

12:8. menu. The menu for the Passover meal is one that would have been common in nomadic herding communities. The prohibition of yeast may additionally carry symbolic value. In later rabbinic literature and the New Testament it is associated with *impurity or *pollution. It is difficult to discern whether it carried such a connotation this early. The bitter herbs are identified in later rabbinic literature as lettuce, chicory, eryngo, horseradish and sow thistle, all easily prepared. It is uncertain, however, whether these are the ones included in

the biblical terminology. Lettuce is known to have been cultivated in Egypt, and the Hebrew word translated "bitter herbs" corresponds to an *Akkadian (Babylonian) word for lettuce. The command to roast avoids two other possibilities. On the one hand, it has been thought to contrast to pagan spring feasts that sometimes included raw meat. On the other hand, those in haste would not boil the meat, for that would necessitate greater preparation time to butcher, gut and dress the meat. Since this is a sacral meal, the meat, may not be eaten at any other time and must be properly disposed of.

12:11. Passover. The English translation "Passover" does not do justice to the Hebrew terminology *(pesah)*. That the verb has to do with protection can be seen in Isaiah 31:5, where it is parallel to shielding and delivering. The Lord is not portrayed as "passing over" the door but as protecting the entrance from the slaughtering angel (see 12:23). The blood on the doorposts and lintel can now be seen as purifying the doorway in preparation for the Lord's presence.

12:12-30
The Tenth Plague

12:12-13. Egyptian kingship festival. There may be some echo here of the famous Egyptian Sed festival, which represented a renewal of royal authority. Its celebration was intended for all the gods to affirm the kingship of Pharaoh, while here, as a result of the plagues, all the gods must acknowledge the kingship of *Yahweh—not a new enthronement, but a recognition of his ongoing power. In the Sed festival the king asserted his dominance of the land by going throughout the land (symbolically) as he desired. Pharaoh's kingship is being mocked even as Yahweh's is being asserted, for God goes throughout the land to establish his dominance by the plague.

12:14-20. Feast of Unleavened Bread. The Feast of Unleavened Bread is celebrated during the seven days after Passover. As a commemoration of the exodus from Egypt, it conveys that in their haste the Israelites were not able to bring any leaven and therefore had to bake their bread without it. Leaven was produced from the barley content of the dough that fermented and served as yeast. Small amounts would be kept from one batch, allowed to ferment, then used in another. With no "starter" set aside to ferment, the process would have to begin again, taking seven to twelve days to reach the necessary level of fermentation.

12:16. sacred assembly. Sacred assemblies or proclamations were an important part of most religious practice in the ancient world. They were local or national gatherings for public, corporate worship. The people were summoned together away from their normal occupations.

12:19. unleavened bread and barley harvest. The Feast of Unleavened Bread also coincided with the barley harvest and is the beginning of the harvest season. In this context the significance of the unleavened bread is that a new beginning is being made, and the first fruits of the barley harvest are eaten without waiting for fermentation.

12:21-28. see blood, "pass over." The blood is spread on the door frame with hyssop, a marjoram plant that came to be associated with purification, probably because of its use in *rituals such as these. Its consistency made it very adaptable for brushes and brooms.

12:23. the destroyer. The blood on the door frame would signal the Lord to protect those in that house from the destroyer. In Mesopotamia the demon Lamashtu (female) was seen as responsible for the death of children, while Namtaru (male) was responsible for plague. Egyptians likewise believed in a host of demons who threatened life and health at every level. In this passage, however, this is no demon operating independently of the gods, but a messenger of God's judgment. In Jeremiah the same term is used for a destroyer and plunderer of the nations (Jer 4:7).

12:29-30. firstborn. In Israel the dedica-

The Date of the Exodus

Assigning a date to the exodus has proven to be a difficult task. Since neither Pharaoh mentioned in the account is named, scholars have had to seek out more circumstantial pieces of data in order to make a case. These pieces of data can be divided into *internal* data (from the biblical text) and *external* data (pieced together from archaeological and historical research).

The internal evidence, composed primarily of genealogical or chronological time spans given in the biblical text (e.g., 1 Kings 6:1), suggests a date in the middle of the fifteenth century B.C. If this date is adopted as having the support of the biblical text, it can be defended in historical/archaeological terms but has to assume that a number of the conclusions that archaeologists have reached either suffer from lack of data or are the result of misinterpretation of the data. For instance, if the exodus took place around 1450, the conquest would be assigned to the Late *Bronze Age in Canaan. But archaeologists excavating the sites of the Israelite conquest have found no remains of walled cities in Late Bronze Age Canaan. Many of the sites show no evidence of occupation at all in the Late Bronze Age. In response it has been suggested that the destruction of the great fortified cities of Middle Bronze Age Canaan should be associated with

tion of the firstborn was a means of acknowledging the Lord as the provider of life, fertility and prosperity. By taking the firstborn of both man and beast, Yahweh is again asserting his rights to be viewed as the deity responsible for life in Egypt—a role usually attributed to Pharaoh.

12:31-42
Leaving Egypt

12:34. kneading troughs. The easiest way to transport the dough already mixed for the next day's bread was, as described, in the troughs used for kneading, covered with a cloth to keep the dust out.

12:37. route of journey. Rameses is Tell el-Dab'a in the eastern Delta (see comment on 1:8-14), where the Israelites were working to build a city for Pharaoh. Succoth has been identified as Tell el-Maskhuta toward the eastern end of the Wadi Tumilat. This would be a normal route to take to leave Egypt going east, as several Egyptian documents demonstrate. It is approximately one day's journey from Rameses to Succoth. (For the route of "The Exodus," see map 3 at the back of this book.)

12:37. number of Israelites. The size of the Israelite population has been considered problematic for several reasons. If there were six hundred thousand men, the total group would have numbered over two million. It is contended that the Delta region of Egypt could not have supported a population of that size (estimates suggest the entire population of Egypt at this time was only four or five million). The modern population of the area of the Wadi Tumilat is under twenty thousand. Egyptian armies of this time period comprised under twenty thousand. Indeed, for the battle of Qadesh (thirteenth century) the *Hittites amassed an army of thirty-seven thousand (thought to be exaggerated) that was believed to be one of the largest fighting forces ever assembled. Shamshi-Adad (1800 B.C. Assyria) claimed to have amassed an army of sixty thousand for the siege of Nurrugum. If Israel had a fighting forces of six hundred thousand, what would they have to fear?

As it traveled, the line of people would stretch for over two hundred miles. Even without animals, children and the

the conquest. However, archaeologists have usually dated the end of the Middle Bronze to about 1550, and it is quite complex to try to shift the whole system of dating by one hundred years.

The external evidence is usually considered to be more supportive of a thirteenth-century date, during the time of Rameses the Great. This view has to assume that some of the numbers given in the biblical text need to be read differently. For instance, the 480 years of 1 Kings 6:1 would have to be viewed as suggesting twelve generations (12 times 40), which may be significantly less than 480 years. Additionally, while it has been claimed that the historical/archaeological data of the thirteenth century fits better with the exodus, there are a number of difficulties that remain. Among them is the inscription of Pharaoh Merneptah toward the end of the thirteenth century that mentions Israel as a people group in Canaan.

Both dates have their difficulties, and it is likely that certain presuppositions we still hold are preventing us from seeing how all the pieces fit together. It is likely that historical and archaeological research will eventually be able to bring greater clarity to the issue. Until that time we will have to be content with our uncertainty.

elderly, travelers would not expect to make twenty miles a day (though caravans could make twenty to twenty-three). When families and animals move camp, the average would be only six miles per day. Whatever the case, the back of the line would be at least a couple of weeks behind the front of the line. This would create some difficulties in the crossing of the sea which seems to have been accomplished overnight, though certainly some have calculated how it could be done. The line, however, would be long enough to stretch from the crossing of the sea to Mount Sinai.

Furthermore, if a couple of million people lived in the wilderness for forty years and half of them died there, archaeologists expect they would find more trace of them—especially in places like Kadesh Barnea where they stayed for some time. When we turn our attention to their arrival in Canaan, the situation is no better. The population of Canaan during this period was far less than this Israelite force, and all archaeological evidence suggests there was a sharp decline in the population of the region in the *Late Bronze Age, when the Israelites took possession. Some estimates for the eighth century B.C. suggest there were still not a million people in the entire land of Israel even by that time. The modern population of Israel, even given the extensive metropolitan regions, is only about twice what the exodus population would have been. Yet the text is consistent in its reports of the size of the group (see Num 1:32; 11:21; 26:51). Many solutions have been offered, but all have problems. All of the above suggests that it is unlikely the numbers should be read the way that they traditionally have been.

12:40. 430 years. The chronology of this period is very difficult. First Kings 6:1 reports that 480 years separated the exodus from the dedication of the temple in 966. This would place the exodus in the mid-1400s. Adding the 430 years of this verse would suggest that the Israelites came to Egypt in the first half of the nineteenth century B.C. All sorts of variations exist, and several different options are defensible from both biblical and archaeological evidence. For a longer discussion see "The Date of the Exodus," pp. 96-97.

12:43-51
Passover Regulations

12:43. Passover regulations. Verse 38 mentions many non-Israelites who have joined the exodus, and so three additional regulations for the Passover are addressed in this section. First, only those who have been circumcised may participate. This indicates that it is a festival only for the community of Israel. Second is the command that none of the meat be taken outside the house, and third is that no bones be broken. Both of these concern ways that the meal might be shared with other noncommunity members, which is disallowed. The lamb must be cooked whole, in the house.

13:1-16
The Firstborn

13:1-3. consecration. The first male offspring born to any mother is considered as belonging to deity. In the ancient Near East this concept sometimes led to child sacrifice to insure *fertility. Alternatively, in ancestor worship the firstborn would have inherited the priestly function for the family. In Israel it leads to consecration—transferring the firstborn to the domain of deity for cultic service or to the temple for holy use. From that status the son may be redeemed, and Israelite law sees his place being taken by the Levites (Num 3:11-13).

13:4. Abib. The month of Abib spans our March and April. It is the ancient name for what was later called Nisan in the Israelite calendar.

13:5. peoples of Canaan and land of milk and honey. For the peoples of Canaan and the land flowing with milk and honey, see comments on 3:7-10 and 3:8.

13:6-10. Feast of Unleavened Bread. See comment on 12:14-20.

13:9. amulets. *Amulets were often worn in the ancient Near East as protection to ward off evil spirits. Precious metals and gems were considered particularly effective. At times amulets would include magical words or spells. Israelite practice disapproved of amulets, but the concept was converted to reminders of the law (such as this feast served), or at other places (see Deut 6:8) consisted of physical reminders that contained prayers or blessings such as the small silver scrolls that were found in a preexilic tomb just outside Jerusalem in 1979. These contain the blessing of Numbers 6:24-26 and represent the oldest copy of any biblical text now extant.

13:11-16. sacrifice of firstborn. Firstborn livestock were sacrificed in thanks to the Lord, but donkeys were not approved for sacrifice. In Canaanite practice donkeys were occasionally sacrificed and a covenant confirmation ceremony in the *Mari texts also features the sacrifice of a donkey. The importance of the donkey as a pack animal is probably responsible for this exclusion. Therefore donkeys, like sons, were to be redeemed —that is, another offering given in their place.

13:17—14:31
The Crossing of the Sea

13:17. road to the Philistines. The road through the Philistine country is a reference to the major route that ran through the Fertile Crescent from Egypt to Babylonia and is known as the Great Trunk road. It went along the coast of the Mediterranean, which took it through Philistine territory in southern Palestine before moving inland through the valley of Jezreel just south of the Carmel range. Along the north of the Sinai peninsula the Egyptians referred to it as the Way of Horus, and it was heavily defended since it was the route used by armies as well as trade caravans.

13:18. Red Sea. The body of water referred to in translations as the "Red Sea" is termed in Hebrew the "Reed Sea"—a term that can be used for a number of different bodies of water. The reeds it refers to are probably papyrus, which used to proliferate along the marshy section that extended from the Gulf of Suez to the Mediterranean, now largely obliterated by the Suez Canal. Such reeds grow only in fresh water. Proceeding north from the Gulf of Suez, one would have encountered the Bitter Lakes, Lake Timsah, Lake Balah and finally, right by the Mediterranean, Lake Menzaleh. The Wadi Tumilat through which Israel is traveling would have led to Lake Timsah, so that is often identified as the Sea of Reeds in this context, though each of the other lakes has its supporters. If the Israelites originally headed northwest, they may have turned back and found themselves by Lake Balah. If they were heading toward the region of Sinai, they certainly would not have gone down the west side of the Gulf of Suez, and, in any case, that is further away than the narrative suggests (about 120 miles from Succoth). So though the translation "Red Sea" has led to that being the popular identification, it is the least likely. An alternative to "Reed Sea" as a geographical distinction is the suggestion that the translation should be "Sea of Extinction." In this case the waters that are being parted are identified by imagery referring to a common ancient Near Eastern creation motif of the waters of chaos being harnessed and the enemies of God being overthrown.

13:20. Succoth. Succoth is generally identified as Tell el-Maskhuta toward the eastern end of the Wadi Tumilat. In Egyptian literature this is the area known as *Tjeku*, the Egyptian equivalent of Hebrew *succoth*. Etham is the equivalent of Egyptian *htm*, "fort" and could refer to any number of fortresses in this area. Since God turns them back in 14:2, they may still be following the way of the Philistines on this first leg. If so, Etham would most likely be Sile, modern Tell Abu Sefa, where the first fortress guarding the passage onto the frontier was located in ancient times. It was the normal point of departure for expeditions to Canaan. In this case, 13:17-18 is described in detail in 14:1-3. The problem is that this is some fifty miles from Succoth and would have taken several days to reach. There is also a fortress of Pharaoh Merneptah (end of thirteenth century) mentioned near Tjeku in Papyrus Anastasi VI. (For a possible route of the exodus, see map on p. 281.)

13:21-22. pillar of cloud/fire. Some have thought the pillar of cloud and fire is best explained as the result of volcanic activity. An eruption on the Island of Thera (six hundred miles northwest) in 1628 B.C. brought an end to Minoan civilization, and it is possible that its effects could have been seen in the delta. But the date is far too early (see "The Date of the Exodus," pp. 96-97), and this theory would offer no explanation of the movements of the pillar nor of the location described for it in the biblical account (they are moving southeast). The text does not suggest that the pillar was supernaturally generated, only that it was the means of supernatural guidance. For this reason some have suggested that it was the result of a brazier of some sort carried on a pole that would be used by the vanguard scouts. This was a method

often used by caravans. On the other hand, the pillar is always portrayed as acting (coming down, moving) rather than being operated (no human is ever said to move it), so the vanguard theory is difficult to support. In the ancient world a bright or flaming aura surrounding deity is the norm. In Egyptian literature it is depicted as the winged sun disk accompanied by storm clouds. *Akkadian uses the term *melammu* to describe this visible representation of the glory of deity, which in turn is enshrouded in smoke or cloud. In Canaanite mythology it has been suggested the *melammu* concept is expressed by the word *anan*, the same Hebrew word here translated "cloud," but the occurrences are too few and obscure for confidence. In any case, the pillar here would then be one: smoke being visible in the daytime, while the inner flame it covered would glow through at night.

14:1-4. Pi Hahiroth. Pi Hahiroth is not otherwise known, but many interpret it as meaning "mouth of the diggings," possibly referring to canal work. It is known that a north-south canal was being constructed during this period (Seti I) and that it passed through the region near Qantara, a few miles west of Sile.

14:2. Migdol. *Migdol* means "tower" or "fort" in Hebrew and was a term borrowed from Semitic languages into Egyptian. There were several locations so designated, and one is known near Succoth in this period.

14:2. Baal Zephon. Baal Zephon is connected to Tahpanhes in Jeremiah 44:1; 46:14, in turn identified as Tell Dafana, about twenty miles west of Sile. If they camped near here, Lake Balah would be the closest sea.

14:5-9. Egypt's army. Most chariot units of this period range between 10 and 150, so 600 is a large muster, and this represents only Pharaoh's unit. When Rameses II fought the *Hittites at the battle of

Qadesh, his enemy boasted 2,500 chariots.

14:19-20. hidden by cloud. Annals from the *Hittite king Murshili report that the storm god provided a cloud to hide them from their enemy, a claim also made by Priam, king of Troy, as well as others in Homer's *Iliad*.

14:21-22. sea driven back with east wind. Any sea shallow enough to be dried up by an east wind and shifting tides would not be sufficient to drown the Egyptians or to make walls of water. It is therefore difficult to devise any natural scenario to account for the facts reported by the text. This wind would not be the same as the *khamsin* (sirocco) that we associated with the ninth plague. That is a phenomenon drawn by a strong low-pressure system in North Africa, usually accompanied by thermal inversion. The east wind referred to here drives out of a high-pressure system over Mesopotamia and —opposite to a tornado, which rotates around a low-pressure system—features a sharp rise in barometric pressure.

14:23-25. the morning watch. The morning watch was from two to six a.m. The image of deity as flaming brilliance in the midst of a cloud is common throughout the Near East as well as in Greek mythology as early as Homer's *Iliad*, where Zeus sends forth lightning and causes horses to stumble and chariots to break. The Mesopotamian warrior god, Nergal, and the Canaanite *Baal each asserts his superiority in combat by means of his dazzling brilliance and fire.

15:1-21
The Song of Moses and Miriam

15:3. the Lord as warrior. The book of Exodus has been developing the idea of *Yahweh fighting for the Israelites against the Egyptians and their gods, so here the Lord is praised as a warrior. This is a concept that remains significant throughout the Old Testament and even into the New Testament. It is especially prominent in the books of Samuel, where the title "Yahweh of Armies" (Lord of Hosts) is common. Yahweh is the king and champion of the Israelites and will lead them forth victoriously in battle. Ancient mythologies often portrayed gods in battle, but these depictions generally concerned the harnessing and organizing of the cosmos. Both *Marduk (Babylonian) and *Baal (Canaanite) subdue the sea, which is personified in their divine foe (*Tiamat and Yamm respectively). In contrast, this hymn recognizes how Yahweh harnessed the natural sea (not representing a supernatural being) to overcome his historical, human foes. Nevertheless, bringing secure order out of conflict, being proclaimed king and establishing a dwelling are common themes both here and in the ancient Near Eastern literatures concerning cosmic battle.

15:4. Red Sea. Here the reference to the Reed Sea does not suggest further discussion of its identity (see comment on 13:18) but may well include a pun. The Hebrew word *suph* not only means "reed" but also means "end" as a noun and "swept away" as a verb (see Ps 73:19).

15:6-12. right hand. The right hand is the one that holds the weapon, so that it is the one that brings victory. In verse 12 the right hand is not seen as literally causing the earth to open up. In Hebrew the term for earth can occasionally also mean "netherworld," and that seems likely here. To say that the netherworld swallowed them is to say that they were sent to their graves. It should also be remembered that in Egyptian concepts of afterlife the wicked are devoured by the "Swallower" when they fail to convince the judges of their goodness.

15:13-16. terrified peoples. The terror of

the peoples becomes a standard theme in the account of the conquest. While the peoples of Canaan may have previously been terrified of the Egyptians (as the *Amarna correspondence from this period suggest some were), it is now not the arm of Pharaoh, but the arm of Yahweh, who has defeated Pharaoh, that poses a threat to them.

15:17-18. mountain of your inheritance. The combination of mountain, inheritance, dwelling and sanctuary suggests that Mount Zion (Jerusalem) is being referred to.

15:18. Yahweh as king. *Yahweh is not portrayed as a mythological king, a king of the gods who has subdued the cosmos and reigns over the subordinate gods of the pantheon. Rather he rules in the historical realm over his people, whom he has delivered by means of the forces of nature that he controls. This hymn does not exalt his defeat of other gods or of chaotic cosmic forces but his power over historical peoples.

15:20-21. prophetess. Miriam, here hailed as a prophetess and sister of Aaron (no mention of Moses), takes up the song. This is the only mention of Miriam by name in the book, and the only place she is referred to as a prophetess. The only other account that she is named in is the challenge to Moses' authority in Numbers 12. Other prominent prophetesses in the Old Testament include Deborah (Judg 4) and Huldah (2 Kings 22). There is no reason to think that it was odd for women to be found in this role. In fact, the prophetic texts from *Mari feature women in this role as often as men. It was also common for musical troupes to feature women. Music and prophecy also were associated, since music was commonly used to induce the trances from which prophetic utterances proceeded (1 Sam 10:5; 2 Kings 3:15).

15:22—17:7
God's Provision in the Wilderness

15:22-27. Desert of Shur. The wilderness of Shur is located in the northwest region of the Sinai peninsula. An east-west route runs through the region that connects Egypt to the King's Highway in Transjordan at Bozrah, or leads up into Palestine through Beersheba, but the Israelites did not take this route. *Shur* means "wall" in Hebrew, so it is possible that this term refers to the well-known Egyptian line of fortresses in this region. This is supported by Numbers 33:8, where it is called the wilderness of Etham (*etham* means "fort"). Built a few centuries earlier to protect the northeastern frontiers of Egypt, this series of garrisons was known as the Wall of the Ruler. This marked *Sinuhe's point of departure as he fled from Egypt in the *Story of Sinuhe.*

15:22. archaeological evidence in the Sinai. Although archaeological remains from the Bedouin population that has inhabited Sinai for ten thousand years have been found throughout the peninsula, archaeology has produced no evidence of the Israelites' passage through this region.

15:23. Marah. They traveled for three days before reaching Marah ("bitter"). If they crossed at Lake Balah, this would place them by what are well known today as the Bitter Lakes. If they crossed further south, Marah could be identified with an oasis called Bir Marah, where the water is saline with heavy mineral content.

15:25. wood turning water sweet. It is not uncommon for commentators to cite local traditions about a type of thorn bush native to the region that will absorb salinity, but no scientific investigation has provided identification or confirmed the existence of such a bush. In a later period Pliny reported that there was a type of barley that could neutralize saline content.

15:27. Elim oasis. The oasis at Elim with twelve springs and seventy palm trees is often identified as Wadi Gharandal, about sixty miles down the coast of the Gulf of Suez. It features tamarisks *(elim)* as well as palms and springs. It remains a major resting place for modern Bedouin. Closer to Marah is the site of Ayun Musa, just a few miles south of the tip of the Gulf of Suez. Besides having the appropriate groves of tamarisks and palms, it also features twelve springs and is probably to be preferred.

16:1-3. Desert of Sin. The Desert of Sin is an area in the west-central region of the peninsula. Here the main route moves inland five to ten miles for about the next seventy-five miles until it rejoins the coast at Abu Zenimah and the El Markha plain. This may be where they camped by the sea (Num 33:10-11). From there they moved east and northeast across the wilderness of Sin by way of the Wadi Ba'ba and Rod el 'Air to the region of Serabit el-Khadim, which is likely where Dophkah was (Num 33:11).

16:1. time of journey. Thus far the journey has taken about a month (the Israelites came out the fifteenth day of the first month).

16:3. pots of meat. In their exaggerated recollection of the situation in Egypt they refer to large pots filled with meat—we might say "meat by the bucketload."

16:4-9. bread from heaven/manna. The bread from heaven was called "manna" in verse 31, where it is described (see also Num 11:7). The fact that it came with the dew (v. 4) suggests that God's miraculous provision used a natural process. The most frequent identification is with the secretion of small aphids that feed on the sap of tamarisk trees. When it hardens and falls to the ground, it can be collected and used for a sweetener. The problem is that this occurs only during certain seasons (May to July) and only where there are tamarisk trees. A full season would normally produce only about five hundred pounds, in contrast to the biblical account that has the people gathering about half a pound per person per day. Alternatively, some would favor the sweet liquid of the hammada plant, common in southern Sinai, which is used to sweeten cakes. As with the plagues, it is not necessarily the occurrence of this phenomenon that is unnatural but the timing and magnitude. Nevertheless, these natural explanations seem to fall far short of the biblical data. The comparison to what most translations identify as the seed of the coriander (rarely found in the desert) is more likely to refer to a wider generic category of desert plants with white seeds.

16:10-11. glory of the Lord in the cloud. "The glory of the LORD" refers to the brightness that was evidence of his presence. The concept of deity appearing in this way was not limited to Israelite theology, for in Mesopotamia the gods displayed their power through their *melammu,* their divine brilliance.

16:13. quail. Small, plump migratory quail often come through the Sinai on their way north from the Sudan to Europe, generally in the months of March and April. They generally fly with the wind and are driven to ground (or water) if caught in a crosswind. In their exhaustion it is not unusual for them to fly so low that they can be easily caught. Quail looking for a place to land and rest have been known to sink small boats, and in the Sinai they have been noted to cover the ground so densely that some landed on the tops of others.

16:14-36. omer. An omer is a daily ration of bread or grain and represents about two quarts.

16:20. spoilage. If manna is the secretion

of aphids (see above on 16:4-9), ants are responsible for carrying it off each day once the temperature rises. They would also be the bugs that got into any additional manna the people tried to collect and save. The Hebrew word translated "maggots" can refer to any number of scale insects, but there is a different word for ants. Furthermore, the insect secretions are not subject to spoilage.

16:34. in front of the testimony. The testimony in verse 34 can only refer to the ark of the covenant, which has not been built at this point in the narrative. This appendix (vv. 31-36) is from the end of the wilderness wanderings (see v. 35), and therefore the manna sample was put in the ark later in the wilderness experience.

17:1. Rephidim. If the theory that Mount Sinai is toward the south of the peninsula is accepted, the journey to Rephidim begins the move inland to follow the most attractive route to the mountain. Wadi Refayid intersects Wadi Feiran a few miles north of the mountain and has been often identified as the site of Rephidim.

17:5-7. rock at Horeb. The location of this provision of water is identified with the rock at Horeb, but Horeb most likely refers to the region in the vicinity of Mount Sinai (Mount Horeb) rather than to a specific location.

17:6. water from rock. Sedimentary rock is known to feature pockets where water can collect just below the surface. If there is some seepage, one can see where these pockets exist and by breaking through the surface can release the collected water. Again, however, we are dealing with a quantity of water beyond what this explanation affords.

17:7. Massah and Meribah. Massah and Meribah do not represent new places but refer to this particular site at Rephidim.

17:8-15
The Attack of the Amalekites

17:8. Amalekites. The Amalekites, who were descended from Abraham through Esau (Gen 36:15), were a nomadic or seminomadic people who inhabited the general region of the Negev and the Sinai during the second half of the second millennium B.C.

17:11-12. battle signals. Signals were often used to deploy the various divisions in battle. It is possible that Moses used the staff in just such a way. When he was unable to relay divine guidance through the signals, the Israelites were not able to succeed. Alternatively, it has been noticed that Egyptian texts speak of the uplifted arms of Pharaoh to bring protection as well as to signal the attack.

17:15. altar: "Lord my banner." The altar Moses builds is one of commemoration of the victory. The name given it, "Yahweh is my standard," reflects the theology of Yahweh as the leader of the armies of Israel. In the Egyptian army the divisions were named for various gods (e.g., the division of Amun, division of Seth) and the standards would identify the division by means of some representation of the god.

18:1-27
Jethro and Moses

18:1-2. priest of what god? Jethro is identified as a priest of Midian rather than as a priest of a particular deity. Little is known of which god or gods the Midianites of this period worshiped. Priests were not necessarily affiliated to only one god, and therefore Jethro's recognition of *Yahweh's superiority does not suggest he was a priest or worshiper of Yahweh. Priests serving a sanctuary would be viewed as servants of the god of that sanctuary, but even these individuals were not monotheistic, so they would acknowledge the power of other deities when manifested.

18:5. mountain of God. "Mountain of God" is used to describe Mount Sinai. At Rephidim they are in the general vicinity of Sinai, but this chapter probably records events that took place after they had set up camp at the foot of the mountain itself.

18:7. respectful greeting. Moses' greeting of Jethro follows standard practice. Bowing down is a greeting to one who is of higher social standing and is an act of respect. The kiss on the cheek is the greeting of friendship. This is the only recorded incident where both are performed.

18:9-12. Yahweh and the gods. Jethro's acknowledgment of the superiority of *Yahweh does not suggest that he was a worshiper of Yahweh or that he became a worshiper of Yahweh. The polytheism of the ancient world allowed for the recognition of the relative strengths of various deities and would expect each deity to be praised in superlative terms when there was evidence of his activity or displays of his power. Regardless of Jethro's religious persuasions, Yahweh was accomplishing his purpose that through his mighty acts "all the world will know that I am Yahweh."

18:12. sacrificial meal. Sacrifices in the ancient world were often opportunities for communal meals. Though communal meals were used to ratify formal agreements, they were also a part of offerings of thanksgiving, more suitable to this context. This is like a banquet with *Yahweh as the guest of honor.

18:13-27. Moses' seat. The seat of the judge is a designated seat of authority when the judge's "court" was "in session." In cities this seat was usually at the entrance to the gate. Jethro advises Moses to establish a hierarchical judiciary with Moses at the top, as a king would have been in a monarchy, and as a priest or family patriarch would have been in tribal societies. In this structure it is recognized that some disputes can

be settled on point of law or by objective discretion (for information concerning the judiciary system in the ancient Near East, see comment on Deut 1:9-18). Such cases can be settled in the lower levels. In the absence of sufficient evidence in complex or serious cases, the matter was handled "prophetically"—that is, it was brought before God. This was where Moses' involvement was essential. It separates the "civil" aspects of the judiciary, in which Moses did not have to be involved, from the "religious" aspects. This system is not unlike that found in Egypt, where Pharaoh guaranteed justice but set up a system headed by the vizier, who was the "Prophet of Ma'at" (Ma'at is the goddess of truth and justice) and occupied the judgment chair. The establishment of this system formalized a sociological, if not political, role for Moses that moved Israel beyond being a purely tribal society to being a quasi-centralized government.

19:1-25
The Israelites at Mount Sinai

19:1-2. desert of Sinai. The Israelites reach the wilderness surrounding Sinai three months after leaving Egypt, though it is unclear whether "to the day" refers to the new moon or the full moon. Nevertheless, it is in the month of June. The location of Mount Sinai is far from certain, and at least a dozen different alternatives have been suggested. The three strongest contenders are Jebel Musa and Jebel Serbal in the south, and Jebel Sin Bishar in the north. Jebel Musa (7,486 feet) is in the cluster of mountains in central southern Sinai. As one of the highest peaks in the range it has enjoyed traditional support as far back as the fourth century A.D. It also features the er-Raha plain to its north that would have been suitable for the Israelite camp (providing about four hundred acres), though it lacks ready access to water.

Jebel Serbal (6,791 feet) is about twenty miles northwest of Jebel Musa and separated from the range so that it rises isolated above the Wadi Feiran. Its location near an oasis and on the main road passing through the region makes it an attractive choice, though the area available for the camp is much smaller than that at Jebel Musa. Some have favored a northern location, assuming that Moses' initial request of Pharaoh for a three-day pilgrimage (5:3) would take them to Mount Sinai. They also point out that a northern route is more directly linked to Kadesh Barnea and the vicinity of Moses' time in Midian.

19:4. carried on eagles' wings. Though the eagle cannot be ruled out, the bird named here is more usually taken to be the griffin vulture, with a wingspan of eight to ten feet. While Bible reference books often report how the eagle carries its young on its wings when they grow weary of flying, or catches them on their wings when they are fluttering in failure (see Deut 32:11), this behavior has been difficult for naturalists to confirm through observation. In fact most eagles and vultures do not take their first flight until they are three or four months old, at which time they are nearly full grown. Furthermore, observations by naturalists have consistently confirmed that the first flight is usually taken while the parents are away from the nest. Alternatively, if the metaphor here concerns a vulture, it may be political in nature. In Egypt the goddess Nekhbet is the vulture goddess who represented Upper Egypt and served as a protecting deity for Pharaoh and the land. Israel was protected in Egypt until Yahweh brought them to himself.

19:5-6. kingdom of priests. The phrase "treasured possession" uses a word common in other languages of the ancient Near East to describe accumulated assets, whether through division of spoils or inheritance from estate. That people can be so described is evident in a royal seal from *Alalakh, where the king identifies himself as the "treasured possession" of the god Hadad. Likewise in a *Ugaritic text the king of Ugarit's favored status as a vassal is noted by naming him a "treasured possession" of his *Hittite overlord. Additionally, the Israelites are identified as a "kingdom of priests," which identifies the nation as serving a priestly role among the nations, as intermediary between the peoples and God. Additionally there is a well-attested concept in the ancient Near East that a city or group of people may be freed from being subject to a king and placed in direct subjection to a deity. So Israel, freed from Egypt, is now given sacred status (see Is 61:5).

19:7. elders. The elders here are the clan leaders of Israel. Elders typically served as a ruling assembly overseeing the leadership of a village or community. They represent the people in accepting a *covenant arrangement, now a national agreement with commitment expected beyond the family covenant made with Abraham centuries earlier.

19:10-15. consecration. Consecration consisted of steps taken to make oneself ritually pure. This process primarily entailed washing and avoiding contact with objects that would render one unclean. The mountain was designated holy ground, so much so that even touching it would constitute desecration punishable by death. Stoning was the most common means of execution. In this way the entire community took responsibility for the penalty, though no single individual could be considered to have brought about the death of the criminal.

19:13. ram's horn. The ram's horn in verse 13 is referred to by a different word from that used for the shofar (trumpet) in verse 16, though it may be used for the same instrument. The shofar is capable of a variety of tones but cannot play a tune, so it is used primarily for signals either in worship or in warfare. The ram's horn was softened in hot water, bent and flattened to produce its distinctive shape.

20:1-17
The Ten Commandments

20:1-17. apodictic law. A number of collections of legal material have been found from ancient times, including *Sumerian, *Babylonian, *Hittite and *Assyrian collections. The most famous is the Code of *Hammurabi, dating from several hundred years earlier than Moses. These collections consist primarily of sample rulings in particular types of cases. As case law they present what penalties were assigned to a wide range of offenses, rather than indicating certain behavior to be right or wrong or telling people what they should or should not do. The type of law found in the Ten Commandments that prohibits or requires certain types of behavior is called *apodictic law and is rarely found in the legal collections of the ancient Near East.

20:1-17. Decalogue as covenant (not law). The Ten Commandments not only are connected to law but are also a part of the *covenant. The literary formulation of the covenant is quite similar to the formulations of international treaties in the ancient Near East. In the stipulations of these treaties, one often finds certain behavior either required or prohibited. In this sense it could be understood that the *apodictic form of the Ten Commandments puts them more in the category of covenant than in the category of law.

20:3. first commandment. When the text says that there should be no other god "before me," it does not refer to others having a higher position than *Yahweh.

The introduction in verse 2 has already indicated as a preexisting assumption that *Yahweh is their God. The phrase "before me" means "in my presence" and therefore prohibits other gods from being considered to be in the presence of Yahweh. This prohibits several concepts that were a standard part of ancient beliefs. Most religions of that day had a pantheon, a divine assembly that ruled the realm of the gods, the supernatural, and, ultimately, the human world. There would typically be a deity who was designated head of the pantheon, and he, like the other gods, would have at least one consort (female partner). This commandment forbids Israel to think in these terms. Yahweh is not the head of a pantheon, and he does not have a consort—there are no gods in his presence. The only divine assembly that is legitimate for their thinking is made up of angels (as in 1 Kings 22:19-20), not gods. This commandment also then effectively bans much mythology that deals with the interactions of the gods with one another.

20:4. second commandment. The second commandment concerns how *Yahweh is to be worshiped, for the idols that it prohibits are idols of him (the previous commandment already dismissed the thought of other gods). The commandment has nothing to do with art, though the graven images of the ancient world were indeed works of art. They were typically carved of wood and overlaid with hammered sheets of silver or gold, then clothed in the finest attire. But the prohibition is more concerned with how they are employed, and here the issue is power. Images of deity in the ancient Near East were where the deity became present in a special way, to the extent that the *cult statue became the god (when the god so favored his worshipers), even though it was not the only manifestation of the god. As a result of this linkage, spells, incantations and other magical acts could be performed on the image in order to threaten, bind or compel the deity. In contrast, other rites related to the image were intended to aid the deity or care for the deity. The images then represent a worldview, a concept of deity that was not consistent with how Yahweh had revealed himself.

20:5-6. punishing third and fourth generations. Punishment to the third or fourth generation is not granted to human judges but to God. It expresses the fact that *covenant violation brings guilt on the entire family. The third and fourth generation is then a way to refer to all living members of the family. But there is also a contrast here in the loyalty that extends over thousands of generations as over against the punishment that extends only three or four.

20:6. corporate solidarity. In the ancient Near East a person found his or her identity within a group such as the clan or family. Integration and interdependence were important values, and the group was bound together as a unit. As a result, individual behavior would not be viewed in isolation from the group. When there was sin in a family, all members shared the responsibility. This concept is known as *corporate identity.

20:7. third commandment. As the second commandment concerned the issue of exercising power over God, the third turns its attention to exercising God's power over others. This commandment does not refer to blasphemy or foul language. Rather it is intended to prevent the exploitation of the name of Yahweh for magical purposes or hexing. It also continues the concerns of the second commandment in that someone's name was believed to be intimately connected to that person's being and essence. The giving of one's name was an act of favor, trust and, in human terms, vulnerability. Israel was not to attempt to use Yah-

weh's name in magical ways to manipulate him. The commandment was also intended to insure that the use of Yahweh's name in oaths, vows and treaties was taken seriously.

20:8-11. fourth commandment. Sabbath observation has no known parallel in any of the cultures of the ancient Near East and is distinctive in that it is independent of any of the patterns or rhythms of nature. A similar term was used in *Babylonian texts as a full moon day when the king officiated at rites of reconciliation with deity, but it was not a work-free day and has little in common with the Israelite sabbath. The legislation does not require rest as much as it stipulates cessation, interrupting the normal activities of one's occupation.

20:12. fifth commandment. Honoring and respecting parents consists of respecting their instruction in the *covenant. This assumes that a religious heritage is being passed on. The home was seen as an important and necessary link for the covenant instruction of each successive generation. Honor is given to them as representatives of God's authority for the sake of covenant preservation. If parents are not heeded or their authority is repudiated, the covenant is in jeopardy. In this connection, notice that this commandment comes with covenant promise: living long in the land. In the ancient Near East it is not the religious heritage but the fabric of society that is threatened when there is no respect for parental authority and filial obligations are neglected. Violations would include striking parents, cursing parents, neglecting the care of elderly parents and failing to provide adequate burial.

20:13. sixth commandment. The word used here is not technically restricted to murder, but it does assume a person as both subject and object. It has been observed that it is used only in the context of homicide (whether accidental or intentional, premeditated or not, judicial, political or otherwise) within the *covenant community. Because of the nature of the term used, this verse cannot easily be brought into discussions of pacifism, capital punishments or vegetarianism. Some law collections of the ancient Near East do not treat murder, while in others the punishment only entails monetary compensation. Nevertheless the murderer still ran the risk of being targeted for execution by the victim's family in a blood feud.

20:14. seventh commandment. The purpose of the legislation was to protect the husband's name by assuring him that his children would be his own. The law does not insure marital fidelity; its focus is paternity, not sexual ethics. The integrity of the family is protected rather than the integrity of the marriage. If a married man had an affair with an unmarried woman, it was not considered adultery. The offender had to pay damages to the father (22:16-17). This is a natural result of a polygamous society. Promiscuous behavior is not acceptable (Deut 22:21; 23:2), but it is not called adultery if the woman is not married. In the Bible the wife is an extension of the husband, and his name is damaged through adultery. In other cultures the wife was considered property, and this would merely have been a case of damaged goods. Nonetheless, in Egypt (marriage contracts), Mesopotamia (hymns to Ninurta and Shamash) and Canaan (king of *Ugarit extradites and executes his wife), adultery was regularly referred to as "the great sin" and was considered extremely detrimental to society in that it was characteristic of anarchy. *Hittite laws, Middle *Assyrian laws and the Code of *Hammurabi all contain legislation against adultery. The protection of the integrity of the family unit was important because the family was the foundation of society. Compromise or col-

lapse of the family meant compromise or collapse of society.

20:15. eighth commandment. Property theft is prevented by the tenth commandment one step before the act. Though the verb used here in the eighth commandment can be used of stealing property, the command is much broader in its focus. Issues such as kidnapping (cf. Deut 24:7) as well as stealing intangibles (dignity, self-respect, freedom, rights) are all important. The word is also used for stealing in the sense of cheating—by cheating someone out of something, you are stealing from him.

20:16. ninth commandment. The terminology indicates the main focus is on formal slander and libel and is concerned primarily with the legal setting. The maintenance of justice was dependent on the reliability of the witness. Nevertheless, character assassination in any of its forms, legal or casual, would constitute false witness and would be a violation of this commandment.

20:12-17. commandments and community. Commandments five to nine all deal with issues of *covenant in community. They affect the transmission of the covenant in the community and the standing of individuals within the covenant community. Injunctions concern those things that would jeopardize the covenant's continuity from generation to generation or that would jeopardize the family line or reputation. The covenant must be passed on in the family, and the family must be preserved. In the ancient Near East the concerns were similar, but the focus on preservation of the community was viewed more in social and civil terms. Lists of ethical violations are found in Egypt in the Book of the Dead, where the individual denies that he has committed any of a long list of crimes. In Mesopotamia the incantation series known as *Shurpu* contains a list of crimes the individual confesses to in order to absolve himself of unknown offenses and thus appease an angry deity. But in neither of these works are these actions prohibited. They also include a wide range of other types of offenses.

20:17. tenth commandment. In the ancient Near East the concept of coveting occurs in expressions such as "to lift the eyes"—but it is a crime that can be detected and punished only when the desire is translated into action. Ancient Near Eastern literature shows that offenses such as theft and adultery can be described generally in terms of the desire that triggered the chain of events. Whatever action it spawns, this illegitimate desire for something that belongs to someone else is the core of the problem and a threat to the community; any action taken to fulfil such a desire is sin.

20:18. thunder and lightning. Thunder and lightning were considered to regularly accompany the presence of a deity in the ancient Near East, though that is often in a battle setting, not a revelation setting, since the gods of the ancient Near East were not accustomed to revealing themselves.

20:24-26
Altars

20:24. altar of earth. Some altars of this period were made of mud bricks, and that is perhaps what the text refers to when it speaks of altars of earth. Another possibility is that it refers to altars that had outer walls of stone but were filled with earth. No altars in the Bible are said to have been built of earth, and no altars of earth have been found by archaeologists.

20:25. altar of stones. Stones, if used, were not to be hewn. Unhewn stone was used for the Israelite altar uncovered by archaeologists at Arad, though altars at sites such as Dan and Beersheba feature ashlar masonry (a type of worked stone).

20:26. priestly modesty. Ritual nudity was widespread in the ancient Near East, whereas here every precaution is taken to assure modesty. Early Canaanite altars with steps are known from sites such as Megiddo. Israelite law also preserved modesty by legislating longer tunics and prescribing undergarments for the priests.

21:1—23:19
The Book of the Covenant

21:1—23:19. casuistic law. The principal form of law found throughout the ancient Near East was case or *casuistic law. It is characterized by an "if . . . then" clause, which is based on the idea of cause and effect. In the Israelite law codes, case law assumes the equality of all citizens, and thus punishment for crime is not hindered or magnified by class or wealth. This is not the case, however, in ancient Mesopotamia, where in *Hammurabi's code (c. 1750 B.C.) different degrees of punishments (from fines to execution) were prescribed for slaves, citizens and members of the nobility. Case law can be traced in its origins to *apodictic (command) laws, such as those found in the Ten Commandments. As persons committed crimes under varying circumstances, it became necessary to go beyond the simple statute "Do not steal" to take into account such things as time of day and the value of what had been stolen.

21:1—23:19. nature of the book of the covenant. The law code found in Exodus 21—23 is referred to as the "book of the *covenant" and is probably the oldest example of *casuistic law in the Bible. It deals with a wide variety of legal situations (slavery, theft, adultery) and tends to impose fairly harsh sentences (nine require execution), many of which are based on the principle of *lex talionis,* "an eye for an eye." The laws anticipate the range of life situations that would be faced in the village culture of the settlement and early monarchy period. They regulate business, marriage practice and personal responsibility. Their tone is less theological than the law collections in Leviticus and Deuteronomy.

21:2. Hebrew. The term *Hebrew* is used to designate an Israelite who has become landless and destitute. Although this person may be forced to sell himself and/or his family into debt slavery, he retains his rights as a member of the community and cannot be held in perpetual servitude. He is to be released, debt-free, after six years of labor.

21:2-6. debt slavery. Because of the fragile nature of the environment in much of the ancient Near East, farmers and small landowners often found themselves in debt. Their problems could magnify if a drought and resulting poor harvests continued over more than one year, and they could be forced to sell their land and property and eventually even their family and themselves. Israelite law takes this situation into account by providing a fair period of labor service to the creditor as well as a time limit on servitude for the debt slave. No one could serve more than six years, and when they were freed they went out debt-free. This would have been a good solution for some, but without their land to return to, many may have chosen to remain in the service of their creditor or to move to the cities to find jobs or join the military.

21:2-6. slave laws compared to ancient Near East. Israelite slave laws tend to be more humane than those found elsewhere in the ancient Near East. For instance, no slave could be kept in perpetual servitude without the permission of the slave. Escaped slaves did not have to be returned to their masters. In Mesopotamia a slave (generally obtained through warfare) could be freed by his master or he could purchase his

freedom. Hammurabi's laws set a time limit of three years on a debt slave, compared to six years in Exodus 21:2. Slaves were not given equal rights, and their punishment for injuring a free man was much more severe than if a free man injured him.

21:5-6. ear pierced on doorpost. Entrance ways are sacred and legally significant spots. When a slave chose to remain in slavery in order to preserve a family that he had established while in servitude, it would be appropriate to bring him to his master's doorway and then symbolically attach the slave to that place by driving an awl through his earlobe into the doorpost. It is possible that a ring was then placed on the ear to mark him as a perpetual slave.

21:7-11. sale of daughter into slavery. When a daughter was sold into slavery by her father, this was intended both as a payment of debt and as a way of obtaining a husband for her without a dowry. She has more rights than a male in the sense that she can be freed from slavery if her master does not provide her with food, clothing and marital rights. Selling children into slavery is attested across Mesopotamia in nearly every time period.

21:10. minimum provision. Since perpetual slavery was generally reserved for foreigners and prisoners of war, those persons who sold themselves into slavery because of debt were protected by law from being abused by their creditors. The law determines that six years is sufficient to pay off any debts and that the debt slave is to be released in the seventh year (a clear parallel with the seven-day creation cycle). *Hammurabi's law requires that a debt slave be released after three years of service, thus providing a Mesopotamian precedent for this procedure.

21:10-11. wife's provisions. Provision for a woman in one's charge throughout the ancient Near East consisted of food, clothing and oil. The third in the series here (NIV: "marital rights") is an attempt to translate a word that occurs only here in the Old Testament. The frequent occurrence of "oil" in that position in numerous ancient Near Eastern documents has led some to suspect that the word in the Hebrew text might also be an obscure term for oil (compare Hos 2:7; Eccles 9:7-9).

21:12. capital punishment. Capital punishment is required in those cases where the culprit is a threat to the well-being and the safety of the community. Thus murder, disrespect for parents (abuse), adultery and false worship are capital crimes, because they injure persons and corrupt the fabric of society. The principle involved assumes that leniency would encourage others to commit these crimes. Stoning is the usual form of execution. In this way no one person is responsible for the culprit's death, but the entire community has participated in the elimination of evil.

21:13. place of sanctuary. In those instances where unintentional homicide is committed, the person involved is given a chance to claim sanctuary in an appointed place, usually an altar or a shrine (see Num 35:12; Deut 4:41-43; 19:1-13; Josh 20). This protects him from the deceased's family and gives the authorities time to hear witnesses and make a judgment. The continued grant of sanctuary would then depend on whether the killing was judged a murder or an accidental death. Eventually, the number of places of sanctuary had to be increased as the size of the nation grew.

21:15, 17. cursing parents. Contrary to the NIV translation, studies have demonstrated that the infraction here is not cursing but treating with contempt. This is a more general category and would certainly include the prohibition of 21:15

that forbids striking a parent and would be the opposite of the fifth commandment to "honor your father and your mother" (20:12). Each injunction is designed to protect the cohesion of the family unit as well as insure that each subsequent generation provide their parents with the respect, food and protection they deserve (see Deut 21:18-21). Mesopotamian law codes and legal documents are also clear on the issue of treating parents with contempt. The *Sumerian laws allow a son who disowns his parents to be sold as a slave. *Hammurabi requires the amputation of the hand of a man who strikes his father. A will from *Ugarit describes a son's behavior using the same verb used in this verse and stipulates disinheritance.

21:16. kidnapping (slave trade). Kidnapping occasionally occurred because of the failure to pay a debt, but more often it was simply a part of the illicit slave trade. Mesopotamian and biblical law both require the death penalty for this crime. Such a harsh penalty reflects concern for individual freedom as well as protection against the raiding of weak households.

21:18-19. personal injury laws compared to ancient Near East. Liability for personal injury done as a result of a quarrel and not due to premeditated action is similar in the Bible and the codes of the ancient Near East. In both cases the injured party is entitled to compensation for medical expenses. There are some additions to this provision in each of the codes. The Exodus passage hinges on whether the injured person recovers enough to walk without a staff. *Hammurabi deals with the subsequent death of the injured person and the fine to be paid, based on social status. The *Hittite code requires that a man be sent to manage the injured person's house until he recovers.

21:20-21. human rights (slave as prop-

erty). The basic human right to life means that no death can go unpunished. Thus when a slave's owner beats him to death, an unspecified penalty is imposed. Such an assurance of punishment is designed to prevent such extreme abuse. However, there is no penalty if the slave recovers from his beating. The assumption is that the owner has the right to discipline his slaves, since they are his property. Their human rights are restricted, in this respect, because of their status.

21:22. miscarriage. Several ancient law codes include this statute penalizing a man for causing a woman to have a miscarriage. The variation between them generally depends on the status of the woman (*Hammurabi's laws indicate a small fine for injuring a slave woman; *Middle Assyrian laws specify a large fine, fifty lashes and a month's labor service for injuring a citizen's daughter), or the intent behind the injury (*Sumerian laws prescribe a fine for accidental injury and impose a much larger fine for deliberate injury). The Exodus law hinges on whether there is any further harm to the mother beyond the loss of the fetus and imposes a fine based on the claim of the husband and the pronouncement of the judges. The object of the fine is to compensate for the injury to the mother rather than the death of the fetus. However, Middle Assyrian law demands compensation for the death of the fetus with another life.

21:23-25. lex talionis. The legal principle of *lex talionis*, "an eye for an eye," is based on the idea of reciprocity and appropriate retaliation (see Lev 24:10-20). Ideally, when an injury is done to another person, the way to provide true justice is to cause an equal injury to the culprit. Although this may seem extreme, it in fact limits the punishment which can be inflicted on the person

accused of the injury. It cannot exceed the damage done. Since most personal liability laws involve the payment of a fine rather than a retaliatory body injury, it is most likely that the *talion* statement is a designated limit on compensation, with a value assigned to each item injured (see the laws of *Eshnunna, which set fines for the nose, finger, hand and foot). The *talion* is also found in its basic form in *Hammurabi's code 196-97, but the laws following that section contain variations based on the social status (free or slave or member of nobility) of the persons involved. In most cases the *talion* is applied when there is premeditated intent to do harm.

21:22-36. personal liability. There is a great emphasis placed on personal liability in the ancient Near East. In order to protect the person and that person's ability to work, very detailed statutes are written to deal with every conceivable injury done by human hand or by a person's property. The classic example is the case of the goring ox. In addition to Exodus, it is found in the laws of *Eshnunna and *Hammurabi, where the penalty for allowing a known gorer to run loose is a fine. The biblical example, however, requires that both the ox and his owner be stoned to death. Similar laws involving failure of an owner to deal with a known danger, include vicious dogs (Eshnunna), building code violations (Eshnunna; Ex 21:33-34), and injury to valuable animals by another animal or a human (*Lipit-Ishtar; Hammurabi—veterinary malpractice). Generally, these crimes are punishable by fines based on the degree of injury and the value of person or animal injured.

21:26-36. penalties for personal liability. The penalties imposed in cases of personal liability generally depend on who or what was injured. If a slave owner abuses his slaves to the point that he mutilates them—destroying an eye or knocking out a tooth—then the slave is freed in compensation. In cases where a death occurs, the circumstances decide the punishment. If an owner is aware of a dangerous situation and fails to do anything, then his life is forfeited if someone is killed due to his negligence. Similarly, if valuable animals are harmed or destroyed, then the owner who is responsible must provide equal compensation. There is latitude in the law, however, in cases where an owner is unaware of a potential danger and is thus not fully responsible for loss or injury.

22:1-4. theft in the ancient Near East. Theft can be defined as appropriation of goods or real property without legal consent. The number and specificity of the laws regarding theft in the ancient Near East suggest that it was a real problem. There are cases of burglary (22:2-3; *Hammurabi), robbery (Hammurabi), looting during a fire (Hammurabi), and use of property or natural resources without permission (e. g., illegal grazing in 22:5 and Hammurabi). The "paperwork-oriented" Mesopotamian culture placed a great deal of importance on contracts, bills of sale and the corroboration of witnesses to the sale (Hammurabi). These business practices, which were designed to prevent fraud, are also mentioned in the biblical text, but more often in narrative (Gen 23:16; Jer 32:8-15) than in the law codes. There are also instances where an oath is taken in cases where physical evidence is unavailable or responsibility for loss is uncertain (22:10-13; Hammurabi). In this way, God is solicited as a witness and the person taking the oath is laying himself open to divine justice.

22:1-4. penalties for theft. Prescribed punishments for theft vary based on the identity of the owner and the value of the property stolen. In *Hammurabi's laws the death penalty is required for

persons who steal from the temple or the palace. However, this is reduced to a fine of thirty times the value of the property stolen if the victim is a government or temple official and ten times the value for property of a citizen. This same law imposes the death penalty for a thief who fails to pay the fine. Exodus 22:3 tempers this by having the thief sold as a slave to compensate for the loss. These penalties, with their heavy fines or death sentences, suggest how seriously the society took this crime.

22:2-3. burglary. It is assumed that people have a right to defend themselves and their property from theft. Thus when a burglar enters a house at night and is killed by the homeowner, this is considered a case of self-defense (for instance in *Ur-Nammu's laws). That changes, however, if the break-in occurs during the day, because the homeowner could more clearly see the degree of threat and could call for help. *Hammurabi's laws add a symbolic deterrent to its burglary injunction by having the body of an executed burglar walled up in the hole he had dug in the mud-brick wall of his intended victim.

22:5-15. property liability. In most cases, liability for property damage or loss was based on circumstances or contracts. Restitution was generally based on the loss of real property (animals, grain, fruit) or the loss of productivity, if fields or orchards were damaged or taken out of production. There was also a clear sense of responsibility in cases based on negligence. Examples include the unchecked spread of fire, rampaging animals or the failure to maintain dams or irrigation systems. In each of these cases the person who allowed dangerous defects to persist or who did not keep a rein on the movement of his animals was required to pay restitution for any loses incurred (as in *Hammurabi and *Ur-Nammu). Not all loss was covered, however. In some cases, claims for loss were dismissed due to unforeseeable events or because they were included in rental agreements (22:13, 15).

22:5-15. penalties for property liability. Since loss of or damage to property can be computed in real terms, penalties in cases involving property liability were designed to provide just restitution of monetary value. According to the biblical statutes, this would sometimes be left up to the judges to determine. In other cases a set amount of double the value of the lost item is imposed. There is more specificity in the Mesopotamian codes, where the exact nature of the damage to a rental animal is listed with the appropriate compensation (as in *Lipit-Ishtar) and the exact amount of grain per acre in a flooded field is prescribed (*Hammurabi).

22:16. marriage pledge. Families negotiated marriage contracts that provided a bride price from the groom's family and a dowry from the bride's household. Once the couple was betrothed or pledged to each other, they were considered legally bound to the contract. Thus the penalty for rape depended on whether the woman was (1) a virgin and (2) pledged to be married.

22:16-17. bride price. The groom's household paid the bride price as part of the marriage agreement. This price would vary based on whether the woman was a virgin or had been married before. In this case the price for a virgin is required even though she has been raped.

22:16-17. premarital sex perspective. Premarital sex was discouraged for several reasons: (1) it usurped the authority of the father to arrange the marriage contract, (2) it diminished the potential value of the bride price, and (3) it prevented the husband from being assured that his first child was indeed his offspring. This law regulated illicit pre-

marital sex by imposing a forced marriage on the culprit and/or a fine equal to the bride price for a virgin. In this way the father would be spared the embarrassment and loss of revenue when negotiating a contract for a daughter who is no longer a virgin.

22:18. sorceress. Practitioners of magic were outlawed on pain of death within the Israelite community (see Lev 19:31; 20:27). Each law concerning them is in *apodictic or command form. This total intolerance may be due to their association with Canaanite religion or simply because their arts represented a challenge to God's supremacy over creation.

22:19. bestiality. Also written in command form are the laws forbidding sexual relations with animals (see Lev 21:15-16; Deut 17:21). Bestiality, like homosexuality, violates the basic injunction to be fruitful and multiply (Gen 1:28; 9:1). It also blurs the categories of creation by intermixing species. Such acts are also forbidden in the *Hittite laws.

22:21. vulnerability of aliens. The injunction to protect the "alien" is always based on the remembrance of the exodus and the alien status of the Israelites before they settled in Palestine (see Deut 24:17-22). It is also based on the image of God as the ultimate protector of the weak—whether that be the entire nation or the most vulnerable members of society. Humane treatment of aliens follows the spirit of the hospitality code, but it also recognizes a class of persons who are not citizens and who could be subject to discrimination or abuse if special provision were not made for them.

22:22-24. vulnerability of orphans. Orphans, aliens and widows formed the three classes of powerless persons in ancient society. God took special care of these people because of their basic vulnerability, requiring that they not be oppressed and cursing those who did oppress with the threat of becoming orphans themselves. The frequency of war, famine and disease insured that there would always be a large number of orphans. Although they could contribute to the general work force, they would have had to be adopted for them to inherit property or to learn a skill as an apprentice (as in *Hammurabi's laws).

22:22-24. vulnerability of widows. Like aliens and orphans, widows were often dependent on charity for survival. All three groups needed protection under the law because they were powerless to protect themselves. They were allowed to glean in fields, orchards and vineyards (Deut 24:19-21), and they retained their dignity as a protected class through divine statute. They could not inherit their husband's property, and their dowry would have been used to support their children (as in *Hammurabi's laws). In some cases they were owed levirate obligation by their deceased husband's family (see Deut 25:5-10; *Hittite laws), but otherwise they would be forced to seek employment or attempt to arrange a new marriage (see Ruth).

22:22-24. treatment of vulnerable classes. Based on the statements in the prologues of the *Ur-Nammu code and the Code of *Hammurabi, it is clear that kings considered it part of their role as "wise rulers" to protect the rights of the poor, the widow and the orphan. Similarly, in the Egyptian *Tale of the Eloquent Peasant*, the plaintiff begins by identifying his judge as "the father of the orphan, the husband of the widow." Individual statutes (seen in several Middle *Assyrian laws) protect a widow's right to remarry and provide for her when her husband is taken prisoner and presumed dead. In this way the vulnerable classes are provided for throughout the ancient Near East. Only the "alien" is not specifically mentioned outside the Bible. This is not to say that hospitality codes did not apply elsewhere, but this category is tied in the Bible to the unique exodus experience.

22:25. charging interest. Two principles are evident in the restriction on charging interest on loans: (1) a village-based, agricultural people realize they must depend on each other to survive, and (2) interest payments are a phenomenon of the city-based merchants with whom farmers sometimes had to deal and who were not concerned with the village community (see Hos 12:7-8). Thus to maintain their sense of the equality of all Israelites and to prevent growing antagonism between rural and urban citizens (see Neh 5:7, 10-11 and Ezek 22:12 for violations of the law), charging interest of Israelites had to be outlawed (see Lev 25:35-38; Deut 23:19). Only loans to non-Israelites could accrue interest (Deut 23:20). This stands in contrast to the more familiar business practices employed elsewhere and to the systematic listing of interest that can be charged on loans in the laws of *Eshnunna and *Hammurabi.

22:25. moneylending practices. Just as is the case today, farmers, craftsmen and businessmen borrowed amounts from moneylenders to finance the next year's planting, an expanded working area or a new business venture. All of these loans were made at interest, and, if the law codes are to be taken as community standards, the interest rates were set by law. The laws of *Eshnunna provide technical details on the rate of exchange on interest payments in either barley or silver. The produce of a field could be given as collateral on a loan (*Hammurabi), but if a natural disaster occurred, provision was made to cancel interest payments (Hammurabi). To prevent fraudulent practices, moneylenders were not allowed to harvest fields or orchards to claim what was owed to them. Instead the owner did the harvesting and thus insured that only the proper amount was paid; interest could not exceed 20 percent (Hammurabi).

22:26-27. cloak as pledge. Day laborers regularly pledged their garment as collateral against a full day's work. In many cases it was their only extra covering besides their loincloth. Thus the law requires it to be returned at the end of the day so that they are not left without protection against the night's chill (see Deut 24:12-13; Amos 2:8). If it were not returned to them, they would have to give up their free status and sell themselves as slaves. A late-seventh-century B.C. Hebrew inscription from Yavneh-Yam contains a plea by a field worker that his garment had been unjustly taken. He asks that his rights and his free status be returned to him along with the robe.

22:28. blasphemy of God or ruler. The Hebrew here allows for a translation of either "God" or "the judges," neither of whom should be ignored or slighted. Both judges and rulers (a chieftain was elected by the elders and certified in the position by God prior to the monarchy) were to be respected. Failure to do so cast doubt on the authority of the elders and God to chose a ruler and thus was punishable by death (see 2 Sam 19:9; 1 Kings 21:10). Blasphemy, the rejection of God's divine presence and power, is also a capital offense (Lev 24:15-16).

22:29. offerings from granaries. Cities stored the harvest in huge, stone-lined granary pits, and villagers had smaller versions cut out of the native limestone near their houses. A portion of every harvest was to be set aside as an offering to God. This injunction reminds the people to provide that offering before they filled and sealed their storage containers.

22:29. sacrifice of firstborn. The common belief was that fertility could be assured only if the firstborn of the flock and of every family was sacrificed to God (see 13:2; Lev 27:26). Israelite religion forbade human sacrifice, substituting an animal in place of the child (see Gen 22), and the service of the Levites in place of the dedicated firstborn (Num 3:12-13).

22:30. eighth day. The requirement that animals not be taken from their mothers and sacrificed until the eighth day after birth (see Lev 22:27) may be (1) a parallel with the *circumcision of sons on the eighth day (Gen 17:12), (2) a sign of humane treatment of animals or (3) an attempt to key sacrifice to the completion of a seven-day creation cycle.

22:31. meat from dead animal. As a sign that they are "set apart" as a people of God, the Israelites are restricted from eating food which may ritually contaminate them. Thus an animal that has been killed by other beasts may not be eaten because of the contact of the flesh with predators, which may be impure, and the uncertainty that its blood has been completely drained (see Lev 17:15).

22:31. dogs. Packs of feral dogs are often associated with eating carrion (Ps 59:6; 1 Kings 14:11). They scavenged in the streets and in the refuge piles on the outskirts of towns and villages. Dogs are often identified as impure, and the word is used in taunting an enemy or taking an oath (1 Sam 17:43; 2 Sam 16:9).

23:1-9. preserving integrity in justice system. Any justice system is subject to abuse when its officials are corrupt. To preserve the integrity of the legal process in Israel, judges are admonished to provide equal justice to all, not execute judgment on the guiltless and not take bribes. Witnesses are warned against giving false testimony and thus contributing to the conviction of the innocent. All Israelites are reminded of their responsibility to help their neighbor and to treat the alien with hospitality and fairness. In this way persons will feel confident in speaking to judges and can be assured of getting a fair hearing. Additionally everyone can rest easier knowing that their person and their property are the concern of all citizens.

23:1-9. vulnerability of the poor in ancient Near East. Because most cultures of the ancient Near East were class conscious, the poor were not always treated with the same equity as the rich and powerful. *Hammurabi did describe himself as a "devout, god-fearing prince" who brought justice to the land and protected the weak, but there are sufficient suggestions of abuse in the law codes and in wisdom literature to suggest that all was not well. The Egyptian *Teachings of Amenemope* includes admonitions against stealing from the poor, cheating the cripple and poaching on a widow's field. The speech of the "eloquent peasant" (Middle Kingdom Egypt, 2134-1786 B.C.) reminds a magistrate that he is to be a father to the orphan and a husband to the widow.

23:8. bribes in ancient world. Bribes include any income which is acquired by government officials and judges through illegal means. They are generally received in support of a legal claim and are designed to influence the decision on that claim. Because this is a subversion of justice, this practice is universally and officially condemned in the ancient world. The Code of *Hammurabi disbars a judge who changes a sealed judgment, and Hammurabi's royal correspondence refers to the punishment of an official who received a bribe. The biblical text includes legal prohibitions (23:8; Deut 16:19), and bribery of judges is condemned in the prophets (Is 1:23; Mic 3:11).

23:10-11. fallow year. Leaving the land fallow in the seventh year follows the pattern of the creation story and God's rest on the seventh day. It is likely that Israelite farmers set aside as fallow one-seventh of their fields each year rather than leaving all of their land fallow for an entire year. In Mesopotamia fields were left fallow even more frequently to limit the impact of the salt in the water used for irrigation. The practice also helps to prevent exhaustion of the nutrients in the soil. The social welfare aspect of the law (more directly explained in Lev 25:1-7, 18-22; see comments there) provides one more expression of concern for the poor.

23:13. invoking the names of other gods. In making sacrifices and participating in everyday activities like plowing or building a house, it was common practice in the ancient Near East to invoke the name of a god to bless their actions. To prevent the Israelites from practicing polytheism, it was necessary to ban the use of the names of other gods or to acknowledge their existence (see 20:3). Only Yahweh could be called upon for help and blessing.

23:15. Feast of Unleavened Bread. The Feast of Unleavened Bread signals the beginning of the barley harvest (March-April). Unleavened bread was made from the newly harvested grain and celebrated as the first sign of coming harvests that year. What was probably originally a Canaanite agricultural celebration was associated with the exodus and the Passover festival by the Israelites.

23:16. Feast of Harvest. This second of the three harvest festivals comes seven weeks after the harvest of the early grain (34:22; Deut 16:9-12) and is better known as the Feast of Weeks or Pentecost. In the agricultural cycle it marks the end of the wheat harvest season, and by tradition it is tied to the giving of the law on Mount Sinai. It is also associated with *covenant renewal and pilgrimage. Celebration includes the bringing of a "wave offering" of two loaves of bread and a basket of ripe fruit in thanksgiving for a good harvest.

23:16. Feast of Ingathering. The final harvest of the year occurred in the autumn prior to the onset of the rainy season and marked the beginning of a new agricultural year. At this time the last of the ripening grain and fruits were gathered and stored. The seven-day event is also known as the Feast of Tabernacles and is symbolized by the construction of booths for the harvesters. The festival was tied into Israelite tradition as a commemoration of the wilderness wanderings. It was also the occasion for the dedication of Solomon's temple in Jerusalem (1 Kings 8:65).

23:17. pilgrimage obligation. The requirement that all Israelite families (see Deut 16:11, 14) appear before God at the temple three times a year is tied to the agricultural calendar and the three major harvest festivals: Feast of Unleavened Bread, Feast of Harvest and Feast of Ingathering. This religious obligation would have been the occasion for fairs, the adjudication of legal disputes, the contracting of marriages and the rites of purification for those who had been physically or spiritually contaminated.

23:18. no yeast mixed in blood sacrifice. Yeast and leavened dough were strictly prohibited from use in animal sacrifice. This is based on the association of yeast with the process of corruption. Sacrificial blood, associated with life, might therefore be debased or corrupted if brought into contact with leaven.

23:18. handling of fat. The fatty portions of the animal sacrifice which were attached to the stomach and intestines were reserved for God's portion (29:12-13; Lev 3:16-17). They were not to be saved or put aside for the night, because they, like blood, contained the essence of life.

23:19. first fruits. The first produce of the harvest, associated with the Feast of Harvest, was to be brought to God as a sacrifice. This represented both thanksgiving as well as a symbolic portion of what was to come in the autumnal harvest (see Deut 26:2-11).

23:19. goat in mother's milk. The prohibition against cooking a young goat (perhaps symbolic of all young animals) in its mother's milk has been interpreted as a reaction against Canaanite or other foreign religious practices (see 34:26 and Deut 14:21). The regular birth of goats near the Feast of Ingathering and their inclusion in celebratory meals may be the basis of this law. It may also be based on an injunction to treat animals humanely, since an animal still nursing may have mother's milk in its stomach. There is also the consideration that mother's milk contains blood and would therefore corrupt either sacrificial meat or meals.

23:20-33
Bringing Israel to the Land

23:20. angel preparing way. The promise of an angel preparing the way for the people follows the narrative pattern of divine presence and guidance that is first set by the pillar of cloud and the pillar of fire in the exodus event (13:21-22).

23:21. my Name is in him. The "messenger" or angel sent by God is an extension of God himself, representing a continuous presence with the people of Israel. Since names and naming (see Gen 2:19; 17:5) were considered powerful in the ancient world (see 9:16; Lev 19:12), to say that Yahweh has invested his Name in this angel is to say that it is to be obeyed just as God is to be obeyed. All of God's presence and power is to be found in this messenger. He is to be trusted to do what God has promised.

23:23. peoples of Canaan. The list of peoples who inhabit Canaan is representative of the diverse ethnic character of that area. Because Canaan serves as a land bridge between Mesopotamia and Egypt, it has always attracted settlers from many different groups.

23:24. sacred stones. Among the objects that were erected at cultic sites in Canaan were altars, sacred poles and sacred stones. The latter were huge standing stones that represented the power of a local god. They occur alone as well as in groups.

23:28. hornet. The term which is translated "hornet" (see Deut 7:20; Josh 24:12) may be a form of divine "terror" like the plagues in Egypt. Egyptian and *Assyrian texts and reliefs portray the god as a winged disk terrifying the enemy before the arrival of their own armies. It may also be a pun based on its similarity to the word for Egypt (*zirah* and *mizraim*) and thus reflect Yahweh's use of Egyptian military campaigns in Canaan that weakened the area and made the Israelite settlement possible.

23:31. borders of the land. The limits of the Promised Land are set at the Red Sea (Gulf of Aqaba) or the border of Egypt to the southwest, the coast of the Mediterranean Sea on the west, and the Euphrates River and Mesopotamia on the east. At no time, even during Solomon's reign, did the nation actually include this much territory. However, given an ideal image, which includes all of the land between the two superpowers of the time, these borders are logical.

24:1-18
Ratification of Covenant

24:1. seventy elders. These men are the appointed representatives of the tribes. Their place here with Moses, Aaron and Aaron's sons is as *covenantal representatives. Their voice, like their number (seventy), stands for the nation as a whole accepting the covenant.

24:4. writing. Evidence of writing systems does not appear until about 3100 B.C. in the ancient Near East. Both Egyptian hieroglyphic and Mesopotamian *cuneiform scripts were syllabic and complex, thus creating the need for professional scribes who would read and write for the illiterate majority. The earliest examples of alphabetic script in the world are found in the region of Sinai (Serabit el-Khadim) during the mid-second millennium (these inscriptions are designated proto-Sinaitic; the Canaanite counterparts are called proto-Canaanite). Every alphabet in the world derives from this early script. The invention of alphabetic writing dramatically increased the literacy rate. Writing was used from its inception for business documents, treaties, histories, literature and religious works. The medium for writing was baked clay tablets in Mesopotamia and papyrus scrolls in Egypt. Monumental inscriptions were carved into stone in both areas. Unfortunately most of the documents written on papyrus or animal skins have decayed or been destroyed over the centuries. Writing something down was not only a way of preserving the memory of a transaction but also represented the conclusion of a treaty or *covenant (as in the case of this verse), and the act itself initiated the terms of the agreement.

24:4. altar and twelve pillars. The erection of an altar and pillars is part of the *covenant-making ceremony. They represent the presence of God and the twelve Israelite tribes who have come together to solemnly pledge their allegiance to each other through written treaty and sacrificial act (see Gen 31:45-54 and Josh 24:27 for similar commemorative pillars).

24:5. fellowship offering. This type of offering fits well into a *covenant ceremony, since it is designed to be shared with the participants. Only a portion was completely burned on the altar while the rest served as a meal consummating the treaty agreement between the people and God.

24:6. sprinkling blood on the altar. Blood, as the essence of the life force, belongs to God the Creator. Thus the blood drained from sacrificial animals was nearly always poured back on the altar. In this way the people were reminded of the sanctity of life and the giver of life.

24:7. book of the covenant. A public reading of the terms of the *covenant was a part of every covenant-renewal ceremony (see Josh 24:25-27; 2 Kings 23:2; Neh 8:5-9). In this way the law which had been given to them was recited, acknowledged and put into effect from that point on for the people of Israel. A number of *Hittite treaties from this time also stipulate that the agreement should be read aloud periodically.

24:8. sprinkling blood on the people. The use of sacrificial blood to sprinkle the people is unusual and occurs elsewhere only in the ordination ceremony of Aaron and his sons (Lev 8). A special bond is established through these symbolic acts marking the people as God's own. It may be that the twelve standing stones actually received the shower of blood, since they represented the people and could all be sprinkled at once.

24:10. saw the God of Israel. Seeing God face to face (a *theophany) is always described as dangerous (Gen 16:7-13; 28:16-17; 32:24-30; Judg 6:22-23). Here the representatives of the Israelites conclude the *covenant ceremony with a meal. God's presence, in this instance, however, raises no danger to them. They are there at God's bidding and under divine protection.

24:10. sapphire pavement. Since the blue gemstone sapphire was unknown in the ancient Near East, this richly decorated pavement was most likely studded with lapis lazuli (brought by traders from Afghanistan). It was used to trim royal audience chambers and thrones (see Ezek 1:26) and here marks the sovereignty of God in this treaty-making scene.

24:12. tablets of stone. It was common practice in the ancient Near East to record important documents, law codes and the heroic military campaign annals of kings on stone (see comment on 32:15-16 for more on stone tablets). The stone tablets given to Moses by God on Mount Sinai follow this pattern. Unfortunately, there is no certainty about what was written on them, although the tradition that it is the Ten Commandments is very old. The original tablets are destroyed (32:19) and then replaced by God (34:1). The second set were housed in the ark of the *covenant (Deut 10:5).

24:18. 40 as approximation? The number forty appears many times as a number of completion, signifying the passage of the appropriate amount of time: a generation (Gen 25:20), the age of a mature man (2:11), the period in the wilderness (16:35; Num 14:33), the rule of a judge or chief (Judg 3:11; 13:1). The regularity with which this symbolic number is used suggests it has both cultural and literary significance and is therefore not to be taken precisely in most instances.

25:1—27:21
The Tabernacle and Its Furniture

25:3. precious metals. Gold, silver and bronze represent the most important metals and alloys available to the Israelites in the premonarchic period. They were commodities of exchange and were used to fashion jewelry, cultic objects and incense altars. In this instance they represent the willingness of the people to contribute their most precious items to the construction and furnishing of the tabernacle.

25:4. colored yarns. Only the most precious items were to be used to decorate the tabernacle. Dyes, some made from the glandular fluid of sea mollusks and certain plants, were extremely expensive and were generally imported. The colors listed here are in descending order of expense and desirability: blue, purple, scarlet.

25:4. linen. Like other fabrics, the linen made from beaten flax was produced in various grades of fineness. Coarser linen was used for sailcloth, headgear and tunics. The term used here is for the "finest linen," which was used to garb Egyptian officials (Joseph in Gen 41:42) and in this case is to be used to furnish the tabernacle (see 26:31, 36; 38:9).

25:5. red dye. The tanning process is not often mentioned in the biblical text. It involved the use of lime, tree bark and plant juices, and required a ready water supply. In this case, it is possible that the ram skins were either tanned or dyed red or both through the manufacturing process.

25:5. sea cows (dolphins?). Both sea cows (a herbivorous mammal—dugong) and dolphins are found in the Red Sea, and their hides could have been tanned and used for decoration. These creatures had been hunted for their hides along the Arabian Gulf for millennia. This word may also be compared to an *Akkadian word which refers to a semiprecious yellow or orange stone and thus to the color of dye used.

25:5. acacia wood. A variety of desert tree found in the Sinai with extremely hard wood, suitable for use in the construction of the tabernacle and its furnishings. The word used here may be an Egyptian loan word, since acacia was widely used in Egypt.

25:6. anointing oil. The spices which were to be used for anointing purposes were myrrh, cinnamon, cane and cassia (see recipe in 30:23-25). Their purpose

was to remove all trace of secular odors and to transform the interior of the tabernacle into a sanctuary suitable for worship and God's presence.

25:7. onyx stones. Although translated "onyx" here, the exact identity of this precious gemstone is unknown. It is also mentioned in Genesis 2:12 as native to the land of Havilah near or in the Garden of Eden. Among the possibilities for this engravable stone are lapis lazuli and onyx, a chalcedony with milky-white bands alternating with black.

25:7. ephod. A priestly vestment reserved for the high priest (see chap. 28). It is constructed of gold and elaborately decorated with gemstones and is attached to the breastplate and one of the priest's outer garments (28:25, 31). It is associated with both the authority of the high priest and the presence of Yahweh.

25:10-22. the ark (size, design, function). The ark was a wooden box, open at the top, approximately 3¾ feet in length and 2½ feet in both width and height based on eighteen inches to the cubit. It was overlaid inside and out with sheets of the finest gold and had four rings (also gold-covered) attached to the sides for the insertion of two gold-encrusted poles, which were used to carry the ark and to protect it from the touch of all but the high priest. A golden cover, decorated with two winged cherubim, sealed the ark, securing the tablets of the law within it. Its primary function was to store the tablets and to serve as a "footstool" for God's throne, thereby providing an earthly link between God and the Israelites. In Egypt it was common for important documents that were confirmed by oath (e.g., international treaties) to be deposited beneath the feet of the deity. The Book of the Dead even speaks of a formula written on a metal brick by the hand of the god being deposited beneath the feet of the god. Therefore the footstool/receptacle combination follows known Egyptian practice. In Egyptian festivals the images of the gods were often carried in procession on portable barques. Paintings portray these as boxes about the size of the ark carried on poles and decorated with or flanked by guardian creatures. A similar-sized chest with rings (for carrying with poles) was found in Tutankhamen's tomb.

25:10. cubit. The standard dimension for the Israelite cubit was measured from the elbow to the tip of the middle finger. Using the measure of the Siloam tunnel, which is described as 1,200 cubits, and its actual length of 1,732.6 feet, this places the length of the cubit as between 17.5 and 18 inches. Since no cubit markers have been discovered by archaeologists, the actual length of a cubit is still uncertain.

25:16. the testimony. This term refers to the tablets of the law which were given to Moses. It was common practice in the ancient Near East to house law codes in specially constructed containers to represent their presentation before deity.

25:17. the kapporet (size, design, function). The kapporet, "atonement cover," is a sheet of solid gold which served as the lid of the ark (with the same dimensions specified in the text), but because it appears as a separate item from the ark, it has special significance. Decorating the kapporet were two facing cherubim, whose uplifted wings nearly met above the ark and served to symbolically uphold the invisible throne of God. Thus with the ark as the "footstool" and the kapporet as the support for the throne, God's presence is demonstrated to the people.

25:18-20. cherubim. Biblical descriptions as well as archaeological discoveries (including some fine ivory pieces from Nimrud in Mesopotamia, Arslan Tash in Syria and Samaria in Israel) suggest the cherubim are composite creatures (having features of a number of different creatures, like the Egyptian sphinx), often four-legged animal-bodies with wings. The cherubim appear in ancient art with some regularity flanking the thrones of kings and deities. The combination of cherubim as throne guardians, chests as footstools and statements in the Old Testament concerning Yahweh being enthroned on the cherubim (e.g., 1 Sam 4:4) supports the concept of the ark as representing the invisible throne of Yahweh. The use of empty thrones was widespread in the ancient world. They were provided for use by deities or royal personages when they were present.

25:23-30. table of bread of the Presence. The table of the Presence was a gold-encrusted, four-legged table, also carried by poles slipped through rings on each side. It held the twelve loaves of "show bread" (see Lev 24:5-9), which were perpetually displayed and replaced at the end of each week.

25:31-40. lampstand. The seven-branched golden menorah, or lampstand, stood in the outer sanctum of the tabernacle opposite the table of the Presence. Although its dimensions are not given, the lampstand was to be hammered from a single block of gold. Its function was to illumine the sacred precinct, and only Aaron and his sons were allowed to tend it. Numerous reliefs and even mosaics of menorahs have been found from New Testament times, when it had come to be used as a symbol for Judaism and for eternal life, but it is generally believed that these do not take the same form as the menorah of the Old Testament period. The earliest representation of the menorah is on a coin from the first century B.C., which depicts a very plain-looking seven-branched lampstand with a sloping base. Some believe that the lampstand represented the Tree of Life—a popular symbol in artistic work.

26:1-6. linen curtains with cherub design. Of the four layers which cover the tabernacle, this is the innermost. It consists of ten multicolored sheets of fine linen, decorated with a cherubim design. Each sheet measures twenty-eight cubits by four cubits (42 feet by 6 feet). They are sewn together in paired sets of five, producing two longer sheets, which are in turn clipped together with blue loops and gold clasps (total measurement, 60 feet by 42 feet).

26:7-13. goat-hair curtains. The layer of goat-hair curtains served as a protective covering over the linen curtains that cover the tabernacle. Like the linen curtains, they consisted of eleven separate sheets sewn together and then connected with loops and bronze clasps (measuring 66 feet by 45 feet).

26:14. ram-skin covering. No measurement is given for this third layer covering the top of the tabernacle, which was made of tanned ram's skin. These two middle layers may serve the dual purpose of protecting the tabernacle and of symbolizing the two animals most important to the economy (sheep and goats).

26:14. sea cow covering. The progression of coverings over the tabernacle is from finest fabric to strongest leather, thus providing an impermeable seal to the sacred precinct within. No measurements are given for the fourth layer of "sea cow" or dolphin hide (this would have served best as waterproofing; see 25:5).

26:15-30. the frame. The skeletal structure which held up the drapes screening the tabernacle was made of acacia wood. It consisted of three walls of upright planks connected by tenons and crossbars, which were inserted into gold or silver-lined slots. The entire structure measured thirty cubits (45 feet) in length and ten cubits (15 feet) in height and width.

26:31-35. the veil. The veil curtained off a cube-shaped section of the tabernacle, creating an inner sanctum known as the Holy of Holies where the ark of the covenant was housed. It measured ten cubits (15 feet) on each side, was hung from four gold-inlaid posts standing in silver bases and was made of multicolored yarns and fine linen. A cherubim design was stitched into it, as on the innermost hanging over the tabernacle.

26:1-36. design, size and layout of tabernacle. The tabernacle was a rectangular structure (50 cubits wide and 100 cubits long, or 75 feet by 150 feet) divided into two equal, sacred squares (75 feet by 75 feet), comprising three separate zones of holiness: the Holy of Holies containing the ark; the Holy Place, outside the veil, which housed the lampstand, the altar of incense, and the table of the bread of presence; and the outer court, where the sacrificial altar is placed. Both the ark and the sacrificial altar are located at the I-axis (exact center) of their respective sacred squares. The entrance to the outer court was located at the eastern end and was twenty cubits (35 feet) wide. The most sacred zones of the tabernacle (oriented on an east-west axis) could only be reached through the outer court. Portable structures of similar design (curtains hung over gold-gilded beams or poles) are found in Egypt as early as the mid-third millennium both in sacred and secular use. Egyptian royal tents of the nineteenth dynasty were a two-roomed tent with the outer chamber twice the length of the inner.

26:1-36. portable sanctuaries in ancient Near East. Although there is no evidence of a portable sanctuary quite as elaborate as the tabernacle, it is clear that Bedouin groups (both ancient and modern) do carry sacred objects and portable altars with them from one encampment to another. Ancient Near Eastern texts also describe the itineraries of priestly processions that took the images of gods, along with their various divine accoutrements, from one town to another within a kingdom. This allowed the god to visit shrines, make inspection tours of facilities owned by the principal temple community and participate in annual festivals outside the capital. Canaanite religious texts also speak of pavilions used for the dwelling of the gods. Archaeologists have found the remains of a Midianite tent shrine at Timnah that dates to the twelfth century B.C. It too was composed of curtains draped over poles, though it was not portable.

26:1-36. I-axis design of sanctuaries. The architectural symmetry of I-axis sanctuaries suggests the importance placed in antiquity on the geometry of sacred space. The divine being was considered the center of power in the universe. Therefore the sanctuary, at least symbolically, should reflect this central role by mapping the sacred precinct into zones of progressive holiness and placing the altar and the object associated with the god's presence at the exact center of the most holy spot within the sanctuary. In this way, a nexus of power and majesty was created that made the prayers, sacrifices and invocations of the god more effective.

27:1-8. altar. The altar was the place for the burning of sacrifices. Because it had to be portable, it was constructed as a hollow square (5 cubits by 5 cubits; 3 cubits high) made from acacia logs, with horns at each corner, and overlaid with a bronze sheath and a bronze grate. A variety of utensils (firepans, shovels, meat forks and sprinkling bowls) were used in dealing with sacrificial meat and ash. Like the ark it had attached rings and poles for easy transport. Although not as sacred as the ark, the altar also served as a touch point with God, placed at the I-axis of the outer court of the

tabernacle. Its service was restricted to Aaron's priestly family, and its function tied the people to the *covenant promise of fertility and the Promised Land. Through sacrifice the people acknowledged the bounty provided by God. Thus the altar brought them into communion with the power that protected and blessed them.

27:9-19. courtyard. Temple architecture demands that the most sacred precincts be separated from the profane world of everyday life by an area of enclosed space—in the case of the tabernacle, by the courtyard. This area was marked off by linen screen walls (7½ feet high), enclosing an area of approximately 11,250 square feet (100 cubits by 50 cubits). Since the inner portion of the tabernacle was fifteen feet high, these walls only screened the view from ground level and left the symbol of God's presence clearly visible. The draperies of the courtyard were held up by fifty-six columns placed in copper sockets. The use of these less valuable materials is reflective of the progression from precious to commonplace in the construction of the tabernacle.

27:21. the tent of meeting. Aaron and his sons are to place olive oil lamps before the "tent of meeting," which was the "holy place" immediately outside the veil separating that area from the Holy of Holies. Here God's presence was to be made manifest to Moses, and instruction was to be given to the people through these oracular messages (see 39:32; 40:2, 6, 29). The function of this space is therefore symbolic as well as utilitarian. The presence of God is acknowledged with the perpetually burning lamps. Aaron's servicing of the lamps provides a role for the priestly community here, and the assumption of guidance, first promised to Moses and thus to the people, is implicit in its name.

27:20-21. continually burning lamps.

The clearest refined olive oil was to be used to provide a perpetual light before the entrance to the Holy of Holies. These lamps, serviced by Aaron and his sons, symbolized the presence of God. The continuation of this priestly function is seen in 1 Samuel 3:3.

28:1-43
The Priests' Garments

28:1. priesthood. The creation of a professional priesthood is a mark of a maturing religious system. By singling out Aaron and his sons, God designates who is worthy to serve in the tabernacle and establishes a hereditary succession for future generations of high priests in Israel. Their lineage derives from the tribe of Levi and specifically through Aaron. Because their task will be to perform sacrifices for the people and officiate at major religious festivals, the priests have certain rights and responsibilities that no other Israelite will have. Special garments are worn only by priests. A portion of the sacrifice is set aside for them. They are not allowed to own land or to perform nonpriestly functions. They are held to a higher standard of obedience and are subject to swift punishment for failure to perform their duties or to provide the proper example to the people.

28:1. priests in ancient Near East. Every culture in the ancient Near East developed a priesthood. Only the Bedouin tribes did not set these individuals aside to perform priestly duties exclusively. Their role was to function as a part of a priestly community, serving temples, performing sacrifices, conducting religious services and staging festivals. Priests would have been educated within the temple from an early age, and their position in the priestly class was hereditary in some cases. They would have been among the few literate persons in their society and thus were relied upon to keep records of major events and tie them to the will of the gods. This process was known as *divination, and it, along with *ritual sacrifice, was the chief source of priestly power and authority. There was a distinctive hierarchy among priests—ranging from a chief priest, who sometimes rivaled the king in power, to midlevel individuals who performed daily *rituals and sacrifices, to musicians, and on down to temple servants, who performed the mundane housekeeping and custodial tasks necessary in any large community.

28:6-14. ephod. The most important of Aaron's priestly garments is the ephod, which was either a linen robe covering the upper body or a frontal piece attached to the shoulders and sashed at the waist. The use of all five colored yarns indicates its importance, as does the use of gold filigree and engraved stones. Placing the names of six tribes on each stone provided a continual reminder to all that he was representing the nation before God. The fact that the ephod is related to idols and false worship in later passages (Judg 17:5 and 8:24-27) suggests that it was a garment borrowed from Mesopotamian society—perhaps worn by priests or used to clothe idols. The breastpiece (28:15), the Urim and Thummim (28:30), and the ephod are used in *divination (1 Sam 23:9-11). Thus the high priest is clothed in garments that aid in the discernment of God's will.

28:15-30. breastpiece. Using a piece of the same multicolored linen as in the ephod, a nine-inch square pouch is created by doubling it over. This breastpiece is then securely attached to the ephod by means of gold braid and blue cords which attach to the rings on the breastpiece, the shoulder pieces of the ephod and the sash of the ephod. Embedded in gold settings on the breastpiece are twelve semiprecious stones in four rows of three stones (compare the list of precious stones in Ezek 28:13). Each stone is engraved with the name of one of the tribes of Israel and thus provides an additional reminder to all (including God) of the priest's responsibility as the people's representative. In the pouch, lying against the priest's heart, are placed the Urim and Thummim. Both these objects and the breastpiece itself are to be used as oracular devices to discern God's will. In the ancient Near East stones (including gemstones of various sorts) were believed to have *apotropaic value (offering protection from spirit forces). A seventh-century B.C. *Assyrian handbook preserves a list of various stones and what they "do"— possibilities range from appeasing divine anger to preventing migraine headaches. One ritual text lists twelve precious and semiprecious stones that are to be used to make a phylactery to be worn as a necklace.

28:30. Urim and Thummim. Unlike most of the other objects in this passage, there is no mention of "making" the Urim and Thummim. This suggests that they were already in use prior to this time and now were to be housed in the breastpiece and used by the high priest (see Lev 8:8 and Deut 33:8). No description of these objects is found in Scripture, although traditions from the Hellenistic and later periods suggest they were markers whose appearance and presentation when cast like lots would determine God's will (see Num 27:21; 1 Sam 14:37-41 and 28:6). There is no negative character attached to the Urim and Thummim as there are to other divinatory practices, and they are never mentioned in passages describing non-Israelite worship or *ritual. Nevertheless the practice of posing yes/no questions to the gods (asking *oracles) is known throughout the ancient Near East. Particularly of interest are the *Babylonian *tamitu* texts, which preserve the answers to many oracular questions. Positive and negative stones (thought to be bright stones and dark stones) were also used widely in Mesopotamia in a procedure called psephomancy. In one *Assyrian text alabaster and hematite are specifically mentioned. The yes/no question would be posed and then a stone drawn out. The same color stone would have to be drawn out three times consecutively for the answer to be confirmed. *Urim* is the Hebrew word for "lights" and therefore would logically be associated with bright or white stones. One recent study has pointed out that hematite, because of its use for weights and seals, was termed the "truth stone" in *Sumerian. The Hebrew word *Thummim* could have a similar meaning.

28:31-35. robe. Under the ephod, the high priest was to wear a loose-fitting, pullover blue robe that fell almost to the ankles. The collar was reinforced to prevent tearing, and there were only armholes, no sleeves. The hem was richly decorated with embroidered pomegranates, and bells were attached between the pomegranates.

28:33-34. pomegranates. Pomegranates were embroidered around the hem of the priest's robe in blue, purple and scarlet thread. This fruit is commonly mentioned in narrative and songs (Num 13:23, 20:5; Song 4:3, 6:7) and was used in decorating Solomon's temple (1 Kings 7:18). They generally are symbolic of the fertility of the Promised Land. Pomegranates were also used for decoration of ritual accessories in *Ugarit.

28:33-35. gold bells. Tiny gold bells were attached to the priest's robe between the embroidered pomegranates. Their function was to signal the high priest's movements within the Holy of Holies. They reminded the priest to perform his duties exactly according to the law and indicated to the people that he was within the holy precinct.

28:36-38. engraved plate. As a continuous reminder of his special role as priest, an engraved golden plate with the words "Holy to the LORD" is attached to his turban. It would parallel the diadem in the king's crown as symbolizing his authority. The plate of office also placed responsibility for infractions on the person in charge of all *rituals.

28:38. bearing guilt. As the person in charge of all religious *rituals, it was important that the high priest took his office seriously. Thus an engraved plate was attached to his turban as a sign of his authority and as a signal to him that he would bear the blame and the punishment for any failure to obey the laws of *ritual and sacrifice.

28:39-41. tunic. The standard garment worn by both men and women in the biblical period was a linen tunic. Worn next to the skin, ankle length, with long sleeves, it provided protection from the sun and sometimes was embroidered or given a fancy hem by the wealthy (Gen 37:3 and 2 Sam 13:18-19) or by priests.

28:39. turban. The turban was made of linen and, according to Josephus, was nonconical in shape (*Antiquities of the Jews* 3.7.6). It may be assumed that the turban of the high priest would have been more elaborate then that of ordinary priests (28:40). It had the engraved plate attached to it and would have been more colorful.

28:42-43. linen undergarments. Unlike the common people, the priests were required to wear linen undergarments beneath their tunics in order to cover their genitals. Thus they would not expose their nakedness when climbing the altar stairs or cleaning around it. Nudity, although common among Mesopotamian priests, was prohibited in Israelite practice.

29:1-44
Ordination Instructions

29:1-46. consecration ceremony. Having ordered the manufacture of the tabernacle, the ark, the altar and all the associated utensils and decorations, Moses now gives instruction about their consecration, and that of the priesthood, to the service of God. Moses functions as priest in orchestrating and performing the rituals of consecration, which will hereafter be handled by Aaron and his descendants. This is a seven-day *ritual designed to set precedents for the use of tabernacle and altar, the types of sacrifices that are to be made in these sacred precincts, and the role and privileges attached to the priests. One of the most significant items in the ritual is blood, which is the symbol of life and is sprinkled both on the altar and on the garments of the priests. Sacrificial items (wheat, cakes and oil) as well as animals are presented and burnt on the altar. In this way the tabernacle and altar are purified, preparing them for use. Some pieces of the meat are used for a wave offering and then set aside as the portion reserved for the priests. Throughout the ceremony the sense of continuity is drawn between the first consecration and all future priestly action.

29:2-3. fine wheat flour. The items used to consecrate the tabernacle, altar and priests are representative of the fertility of the land, the gifts of God to the people. The wheat flour used to make unleavened bread and cakes would be of finest quality and thus a fitting sacrifice by a people who were dependent on farming for most of their food.

29:2-3. cakes with oil. Wheat and olive oil were the chief cash crops of ancient Israel. By mixing them into a sacrificial cake, the people recognized the role of God in providing them with fertility each year. The sequence of offerings also signifies the seasonal events of planting and harvest and the agricultural festivals.

29:2-3. wafers spread with oil. The presentation of grain and meat offerings together signify the people's acceptance of the *covenant and the acknowledgment of God's role as the provider of fertility. While the significance of providing unleavened bread, cakes and wafers is not clear, it may represent either the standard baked goods of the time or items set aside for *ritual use.

29:4. wash with water. It would not be appropriate for the new priests to clothe themselves in their new sacral garments without first taking a ritual bath. They were to be fully immersed as a part of the consecration ceremony. After this only their hands and feet had to be washed before performing their duties (30:17-21).

29:5. waistband. Only the high priest has a specially designed and woven waistband to sash his garments. The lesser priests use ordinary sashes (29:9). This would be a mark of rank and would also serve the utilitarian function of keeping his robes bound when he had to bow or make sacrifices.

29:7. anointing. In this passage and in Leviticus 8:12, only the high priest was consecrated in his office by having his head anointed with oil. However, both Aaron and his sons are anointed in Exodus 30:30 and 40:15, suggesting varying traditions on this practice. Anointing the head with oil would compare with the anointing of kings in later periods (1 Sam 10:1; 16:13). In both cases the oil would symbolize the gifts of God to the people and the responsibilities now laid on their leaders through this ceremony. In Israelite practice anointing was a sign of election and was often closely related to endowment by the Spirit. See the comment on Leviticus 8:1-9.

29:8-9. tunics, headbands, sashes. Aaron's sons, who will serve as lesser priests under their father, have less elaborate priestly garments. They have distinctive clothing which sets them aside from other Israelites, but their consecration does not involve as much ceremony, just as their duties will be less important than those of the high priest.

29:10, 15, 19. laying hands on animals. As each sacrificial animal is brought to the altar, it is necessary for the priests to examine it to make sure it is suitable. Once that is done, a symbolic certification *ritual is performed in which the priests lay their hands on the animal, taking responsibility for its death and the purpose for which it is sacrificed. Some would also suggest that this constitutes an affirmation of ownership. See comment on Leviticus 1:3-4 for discussion of various possibilities.

29:12. blood on the horns of the altar. The horns of the altar are specifically symbolic of the presence of God in any sacrificial act. By placing the blood of the sacrificed bull on the horns, the priests are acknowledging that presence, the power of the God who gives life, and purifying themselves of their sin (see comment on Lev 4:7).

29:12. blood at the base of the altar. The altar is the focal point of animal sacrifice. It is the platform associated with giving God his due. For it to be fully consecrated to this service its very roots (base) must be purified with the blood of the sin offering (v. 14).

29:13. fat parts burned. No portion of the bull was to be saved, since this was a sin offering. Thus the fatty parts as well as the kidneys and liver, which might have been used for *divination (as was the practice in Mesopotamia) or given to the participants, were instead to be burned on the altar.

29:14. other parts outside the camp. Impurities and waste were to be disposed of outside of the camp (see Deut 23:12-

14). Since this bull had been used for a sin offering, its meat, hide and offal had become contaminated and thus could not be consumed or used in any way (see Lev 4:12).

29:14. sin offering. There are various kinds of sacrifices and offerings performed by the Israelites: generally for thanksgiving or expiation. A sin offering was designed to purify a person who had become unclean through contact with *impurity (physical or spiritual) or because of some event (nocturnal emission in Deut 23:10). It was also used in consecrating priests, since they were required to maintain an even higher standard of *purity than ordinary Israelites. The animals which were used in these *rituals received the sin and *impurity of the persons for whom they were sacrificed. Thus their entire substance was contaminated and could not be consumed or used to produce anything. Every portion of the sacrificed animal must be disposed of, with the organs and fat burnt on the altar and the flesh, hide and bones burned to ash outside the camp. This latter act prevented the people's habitation from becoming polluted. For more information see comment on Leviticus 4:1-3.

29:15-18. ram as a burnt offering. The first ram sacrificed in the *ritual of consecration is to be completely consumed by fire on the altar. Its carcass is cut up and washed so that it fits on top of the altar and retains no contaminating offal. Meat was precious to these pastoral people, but the ram and the bull, both symbols of fertility, must be totally destroyed so that the sacrificial offering to God is complete. There can be no holding back when the sacrifice is made in honor of God's power.

29:18. pleasing aroma. The gods of Mesopotamia could also be attracted to the smell of sacrifices (as in the *Gilgamesh flood story). However, addi-

tionally they had to consume the sacrifice to sustain themselves. In Israelite tradition, a "pleasing aroma" signified a proper sacrifice that would please God (see Gen 8:21). It becomes a technical term for a sacrifice acceptable to and accepted by God (compare Lev 26:31), not something he eats.

29:20. blood on earlobe, thumb, big toe. Just as blood is used to make the altar fit for service, so too it is used to designate the faculties of the priest: to hear the word of God, perform sacrifices with his hands and lead the people to worship with his feet. There is also an element of purification of each of these abilities through the blood of expiation (compare Lev 14:14).

29:20. blood on sides of altar. The blood of the three sacrificial animals is used to care for the sins of the newly consecrated priests. By sprinkling the first ram's blood on the altar, they also acknowledge God's power to grant life and the significance attached to their service as well as their commitment as God's servants (compare 24:5-6).

29:21. sprinkling priests with blood and oil. Blood and oil are the chief elements of the sacrificial process. By sprinkling the priests and their garments with these items, the ordination ceremony is completed, and the priests are physically marked for service (compare the marking of the people as guarantors of the *covenant in 24:8) as well as purified.

29:22-25. wave offering. In the third stage of sacrificial *ritual, portions from the basket of cereal offerings and the ram of ordination are to be elevated as a "wave offering." It is more likely that the ungainly pile of sacrificial gifts was elevated rather than actually waved, since that act would be less likely to unbalance and/or drop the sacred items. The terminology used in the text is more appropriately rendered "elevation offering" and such treatment of offerings is likewise depicted in Egyptian reliefs. This gesture physically signifies that all sacrificial items derive from and belong to God. In this case the cakes and wafers are elevated and then burnt on the altar. However, the meat from the ram will be used as the basis for a *covenantal feast that Aaron and his sons will consume, unlike the first ram, which was totally burned. A precedent is also set here regarding which portions of the sacrifice belong to the priests (note that Moses takes his share since he serves as the officiating priest—v. 26).

29:26-28. parts of sacrifice as food for priests. Since the priests were restricted entirely to religious duties and they did not own land, they were sustained through a portion of the sacrifices brought to the altar. Certain portions, the breast and the leg of the ram, were set aside specifically for the priests. Because this food had been presented for sacrifice and offered up to God, only the priests were allowed to consume it. What they did not consume was for the same reason to be destroyed.

29:29-30. priestly garments hereditary. In this section, which interrupts the discussion of sacrificial meat, provision is made for the ordination of future generations of priests. The original high priestly vestments created for Aaron were to be passed on to his successor at Aaron's death. Thus when Aaron dies Moses strips his body of all of his sacral garments and in a seven-day *ritual invests them on Aaron's son Eleazer (Num 20:22-29).

29:31. cooked in a sacred place. Since the meat of the wave offering and presentation offering was now sacred, it could not be prepared in ordinary precincts. Thus it is taken into the courtyard of the tabernacle to be cooked. In this way sacred items retain their power and authority by only being used or dealt with in similarly sacred areas.

29:34. burning leftovers. Because of its sacred nature, the sacrificial meat which has been set aside for the nourishment of priests cannot be used for any other purpose or consumed by ordinary individuals. Thus the portion which is not immediately consumed must be destroyed by fire to prevent any misuse of sacred substance.

29:36-37. making atonement. Basic to the transformation process that the sacrificial altar undergoes is the idea of purification. No item made by humans can, by definition, be pure enough to be used for God's service. Only through a lengthy (twice a day for seven days) and prescribed *ritual of daily sacrifices of valuable animals (bulls) can the altar be sufficiently purified to become holy and sacred itself. Through this process the inherent sin of the men who built the altar and the contaminated materials (in the sense that they are not holy) of which it is constructed become usable for God's service. Hereafter everything that comes in contact with the altar must be pure (both priests and sacrifices). If the level of *purity is maintained, then the sacrifices will be accepted and the people will benefit from their service. See comment on Leviticus 1:4.

29:37. whatever touches it will be holy. Because of the superior quality of the sacrificial altar's level of holiness (second only to the Holy of Holies in the tabernacle), anything that touches it becomes holy. Similarly, it is important that the altar be guarded from those persons or things which are impure so that the holiness is not lost or corrupted.

29:38. daily offerings. Caring for sin and the giving of thank offerings by the people are required daily, not just on special occasions (such as ordination). Thus the priests are to sacrifice two year-old lambs each day (known as the *tamid*, "perpetual" offering), one in the morning and the other in the evening. This daily *ritual signals to the people the continual presence of God among them as well as their constant obligation to obey the *covenant. The constant flow of movement to the sacrificial altar also maintains its holiness and reinforces the role of the priests as religious professionals.

29:40. tenth of an ephah. The principal dry measure in Israel was the homer, which equaled the load carried by a donkey. This weight varies in the sources from 3.8 bushels to 6.5 bushels. The ephah (an Egyptian loan word) equaled one-tenth of a homer (Ezek 45:11), or three-eighths to two-thirds of a bushel. One-tenth of an ephah (about 1.6 quarts) of fine flour was part of the daily sacrificial offering.

29:40. fourth of a hin. The hin (an Egyptian loan word) was a liquid measure equal to about a gallon. One-fourth of a hin (one quart) of olive oil was to be mixed with the flour as part of the daily sacrificial offering. In addition, a drink offering of a quart of wine was to be given daily.

29:40-41. drink offering. A libation or drink offering was part of the daily sacrifices in the tabernacle. They were presented with the lamb and the mixture of flour and oil in the morning and in the evening to signify God's protection and favor throughout the day. The pouring out of libations was a common household practice before meals, and that *ritual is carried over in the daily sacrifices as part of a communal, *covenant meal between God and the people.

30:1-38
Incense, Oil and Water

30:1-10. incense altar. Once the tabernacle was furnished and cleansed and the priesthood was ordained, the Presence of God entered the Holy of Holies to meet regularly with Moses (29:42-43). An additional object was therefore needed that would both represent the Presence and protect humans by veiling the Presence from their eyes. This was the incense altar, a small table (18 inches square and 3 feet high) constructed of acacia wood, with horns like the sacrificial altar, and covered with gold. It was placed in the area immediately outside the veil closing off the Holy of Holies. Like the ark, this inner altar had rings for carrying it with poles. A special blend of incense was burned on this altar every morning and evening. On the Day of Atonement blood from the sacrifice was to be daubed on each of its horns as a yearly repurification process.

30:7-8. burning of incense. The use of incense has been attested archaeologically from the earliest periods in Israelite history, although few incense altars have yet been excavated *in situ in Israelite shrines (Arad is the exception). The incense used probably consisted of a mixture of frankincense and other aromatic gums. The practice of burning incense has both practical and religious purposes. The smell of burning flesh from the sacrificial altar would have been unpleasant, and incense would have helped to mask that odor. The smoke from incense was also used to fumigate sacred precincts and to cast a veil of mystery within them to represent the presence of God or to mask God's presence from human eyes. It is also possible that the billowing of incense smoke signified the prayers of the people rising to God.

30:10. yearly atonement. The Day of Atonement was a special day set aside each year to remove the contamination from the sins of the past year. According to Leviticus 23:27-32 it fell ten days after the opening of the new year. On that day the high priest was to enter the inner precincts of the tabernacle and burn incense on the golden incense altar. Blood from the special sacrifice of the day was also to be daubed on the horns of the incense altar to tie this holiest of altars and its flow of incense to the need for cleansing of the nation's sins. A more elaborate description of this yearly *ritual, including the casting of the people's sins on the scapegoat, is found in Leviticus 16.

30:11-16. census temple tax. Every male aged twenty years and older was to pay a per capita tax of one-half shekel to help support the tabernacle. There is a sense of equality in this that no distinction is made between rich and poor—all pay the same amount. However, there is also a darker image here based on the threat of a plague and divine displeasure if they do not all submit to this census. Comparison with other such countings (Num 1 and 2 Sam 24) suggest that there is a real fear of taking a census because of its use for drafting men into the military and in the levying of taxes. However, in this case, at least, the "passing over" of the men as they paid their fee and were counted seemed to signify their acceptance of their responsibility to provide support for the construction and maintenance of the tabernacle.

30:11-16. census superstition. Taking a census was a practical measure utilized by governments in the ancient Near East as early as the Ebla tablets of around 2500 B.C. The benefits derived from this practice were not necessarily appreciated by the people since they led to increased tax levies as well as military or forced labor service. Viewed in this light, it is not surprising that popular notions existed that the census was a source of bad luck or the basis of divine displeasure. *Mari texts (eighteenth century B.C.) from Mesopotamia describe men fleeing to the mountains to avoid being counted. In 2 Samuel 24 God punishes David and Israel with a plague after a census is taken. The explanation for such a calamity could be that the census was motivated by human pride.

30:13. shekels. The half-shekel payment made by each Israelite male as temple tax, at least until the sixth century B.C., would have been made in a measure of precious metal, not coined money. The average shekel weighed 11.4 grams, although there are also references to a "heavy shekel," which may have weighed more. The sanctuary weight listed here may refer to a shekel with a more standard value and weight than the standard "marketplace" shekel.

30:13. gerah. The gerah (an *Akkadian loan word) is the smallest of the Israelite measures of weight. It weighed approximately half a gram and was equivalent to one-twentieth of a shekel.

30:17-21. bronze basin. A water-filled bronze basin was to be placed near the entrance to the courtyard between the sacrificial altar and the tabernacle proper. It was to be used by the priests to wash their hands and feet each time they entered this holy precinct, in preparation for their holy service. In this way they washed the impurities of the outside world from their hands before making sacrifices and cleaned their feet so that they did not track in the dust and grime of the street. This item is added to the list of tabernacle utensils after the ordination and consecration since it was to be used daily, not just on special occasions.

30:22-33. anointing oil. A special formula is prescribed for the mixture of precious spices (myrrh, cinnamon, cane, cassia) with olive oil into a substance for anointing the tabernacle and all of its furnishing as well as the priests. The process involved soaking the spices in water, boiling the water, then aging the concoction with the oil until the fragrance permeated the whole. To insure its exclusivity, the anointing oil is to be concocted by a professional perfumer and is designed to mark the sacred precincts and priests as holy.

30:23-24. spices. Since all of the spices listed in the anointing oil are imported products, they would have been expensive and extremely precious. They came from southern Arabia (myrrh), India or Sri Lanka (cinnamon), and other distant lands (see Jer 6:20 for fragrant cane) by sea and by way of the established caravan routes. They were mixed into aromatic oils by guilds of professional perfumers and were used for personal enhancement as well as to anoint priests and sacred places.

30:30-33. sacred recipe. The recipe for the anointing oil was reserved for sacred use. The special fragrance of the holy substance was only for the tabernacle and its personnel and was not to be used for secular purposes.

30:34-38. incense recipe. The incense burned on the golden incense altar in the tabernacle was mixed according to a special recipe that was not to be duplicated or used for other purposes. The recipe includes four specific items: gum or resin, perhaps from balsam trees; onycha from the glands of mollusks; galbanum, a resin native to Persia which adds pungency to other scents; and frankincense from southern Arabia.

31:1-18
Preparation for Construction of the Tabernacle and Its Furnishings

31:1-11. wood and metal craftsmanship. Having given instructions on how to construct the tabernacle and its furnishings, Moses now singles out craftsmen to carry out the task. Two men are named, Bezalel of Judah, who is said to have special God-given skill in metalworking, engraving and carpentry, and his skilled assistant, Oholiab of Dan. These two will then supervise the team of trained workers who will shape the various pieces of the tabernacle, cover many of its sacred objects with bronze and gold, stitch the fabrics used for the canopy, veil, and vestments of the priests, and engrave the stones for the ephah and breastplate.

31:12-17. sabbath as a sign of the covenant. While the individual's sign of participation in the *covenant is *circumcision, the sign of Israel's corporate participation in the covenant is the keeping of the sabbath. Like circumcision, the keeping of the sabbath is a continuous obligation required of each generation. Unlike circumcision, it is not a single act but an attitude to be consistently maintained and periodically expressed in action. With instruction given for construction of the tabernacle and workmen chosen to perform the task, it is now necessary to tie even this sacred work to the law of sabbath. Even this work must cease every seventh day as a sign of respect for God's role as the Creator and in acceptance of the covenantal promise to obey God's command (see 20:8-11). Although refraining from work may be an economic burden, this is counterbalanced by the rejuvenation of the spirit and the body through rest. The commandment to rest on the sabbath is so important that the death penalty is imposed on all violators.

31:14-15. work as criterion (profane vs. holy). The sign of obedience to the *covenant is the willingness to cease work on the sabbath. Neither profane nor holy work may be done on this day of total rest. No specific examples are given here, but the text cites both exclusion from the community and execution as punishment for violators. This may mean that each individual case would have to be examined to determine if the act performed was to be defined as "work" (see examples in Num 15:32-26 and Jer 17:21).

31:18. two tablets of the testimony. This statement in which God gives Moses the two stone tablets returns the narrative to the point where it was broken off at 24:18. It also provides the narrative indicator that the parenthetical material on the construction of the tabernacle and the consecration of the priesthood is at an end and that the storyteller is about to resume the narrative of the events on Mount Sinai. The term "tablets of the testimony" also appears in 32:15 and is the basis for the name "ark of the testimony" (25:16-22).

32:1-35
The Golden Calf

32:1. make us gods who will go before. Moses was the Israelites' sole contact with Yahweh and was the mediator of Yahweh's power and guidance, and, for all the people knew, he might be dead. With him gone it was believed that contact with Yahweh was lost and that they therefore needed a replacement mediator to serve the role of "going before them." This role is filled by an angel in 33:2. The calf is formed to likewise fill the role of Yahweh's representative.

32:2-4. calf idol. Bull or calf figurines, made either of bronze or of a combination of metals, have been found in several archaeological excavations (Mount Gilboa, Hazor and Ashkelon), but they are only three to seven inches long. The calf symbol was well known in the Canaanite context of the second millennium and represented fertility and strength. The gods were typically not depicted in the form of bulls or calves but portrayed standing on the back of the animal. Nevertheless worship of the animal image was not unknown, and there is little in the biblical text to suggest the Israelites understood the figure merely as a pedestal (not unlike the ark). The fact that the calf is worshiped in the context of a feast to Yahweh suggests that this may be a violation of the second commandment rather than the first.

32:4. manufacture of calf. When the heated gold was pliable enough, Aaron began to shape it, probably around a carved wooden figure.

32:4. these are your gods. The proclamation "These are your gods" implies that the calf is in some way representative of Yahweh—history is not being rewritten to suggest that a different deity was responsible for the deliverance.

32:5-6. altar for festival to Yahweh. Since the altar was built for the celebration of a sacred feast, it may be concluded that the altar was for sacrificial use, as verse 6 states. But just as the worship of Yahweh had been corrupted by introducing an image to represent him, so it was also corrupted in the conduct of the Israelites in worship. Their coarse and excessive carousing was a typical feature of pagan *fertility festivals.

32:9-14. anger of God. In ancient Near Eastern religions it was believed that gods habitually became angry with their worshipers (for both unknown and unknowable reasons) and lashed out at them. Moses' plea is thus focused on preserving the distinctiveness of Yahweh's reputation.

32:15-16. inscribed front and back. The use of two tablets probably indicates that Moses was given two copies, not that some of the commandments were on one tablet and some on the other. The fact that they were stone suggests a larger size than clay tablets would have been, though inscribed stone tablets such as the Gezer calendar were small enough to fit in the palm of the hand. The Egyptian practice of this period was to use flakes of stone chipped from rocks. Inscription on front and back was not unusual. When the writing reached the bottom of one side, the scribe would often continue around the bottom edge and move onto the second side. Even flakes that fit in the palm of the hand

135

could contain fifteen to twenty lines.

32:19-20. dancing. Dancing was often connected with cultic festivals in the ancient world and, especially in *fertility contexts, was often sensual in nature, though not necessarily so. Dancing is also known in the context of celebration of military victories, which would fit with this being a celebration of the deity who brought them out of Egypt.

32:19. breaking of tablets. The breaking of the tablets, though a result of Moses' anger, is not a fit of temper. The severance of a *covenant was typically symbolized by the breaking of the tablets on which the terms of the agreement were inscribed.

32:20. drinking idol-dust brew. The sequence of burn-grind-scatter-eat is also found in a *Ugaritic text to indicate total destruction of a deity. That gold does not burn is insignificant (the gold was probably shaped around a wooden figure; see comment on 32:4)—a very destructive action is being carried out. The forced drinking by the Israelites is not specified as punishment against them but represents the final, irreversible destruction of the calf.

32:30-35. the book. The concept of divine ledgers is well known from Mesopotamia, where the ledgers concern both the decrees of one's destiny and one's rewards and punishments.

30:35. the plague. Epidemic disease is known from numerous sources throughout the ancient Near East, but specific identification is impossible in the absence of symptoms.

33:1-6
Preparing to Leave Sinai

33:2. peoples of the land, flowing with milk and honey. For the peoples of the land see the comment on 3:8, and for the description of Canaan as "flowing with milk and honey" see the comment on 3:7-10.

33:7-23
Moses' Meeting with the Lord

33:7-10. tent of meeting. The system prescribed in the law (chaps. 25-30) was for a sanctuary to be built so that the Lord could dwell in their midst. Given the present situation, however, the Lord is not going to dwell in their midst, but the tent of meeting was to be set up outside the camp where Moses would receive guidance. Nothing is said to take place inside this tent, but the Lord meets with Moses at the door of the tent when the pillar of cloud descends. There are no sacrifices offered there, and it contains no altar. It is a place for prophetic, not priestly, activity. Once the tabernacle is constructed and takes its place in the middle of the camp, it also serves as a tent of meeting.

33:11. speaking face to face. Speaking face to face is an idiom suggesting an honest and open relationship. It does not contradict 33:20-23. Numbers 12:8 uses a different expression with the same meaning, "mouth to mouth."

33:18-23. God's glory, God's back, God's face. Moses' request to see the glory of God is not a request for God to do what he has never done before. In 16:7 the people were told they would see God's glory (see also Lev 9:23). Moses has negotiated for God's presence to accompany them (actually, to precede them). Moses requests that he might see the presence/glory of God taking his place in the lead. God agrees but warns that his face may not be seen. The concept of deity having an awesome, unapproachable appearance was not limited to Israelite theology, for in Mesopotamia the gods displayed their power through their *melammu,* their divine brilliance.

34:1-35
New Tablets and More Laws

**34:6-7. God's attributes and willingness to punish to third and fourth gen-

eration. Moses had asked to "know" God's ways (33:13), and this list of the thirteen attributes of God (according to Jewish tradition) serve as his answer. It is not unusual in the ancient world to find lists of various deities' attributes. While mercy and justice figure prominently among them, many lists are more interested in attributes of power, while this one focuses on the benevolent graciousness of God. This list is quoted many times in the Scriptures (Num 14:18; Neh 9:17; Pss 86:15; 103:8; 145:8; Joel 2:13; Jonah 4:2; Nah 1:3) and forms a sort of confessional statement. The litany of God's characteristics is still used in Jewish liturgy today and was probably an established part of the temple worship prior to the exile. Although compassion, constancy and the reliability of God's love are stressed, the consequences of failure to obey God's command are made perfectly clear by the magnification of punishment on future generations (see Deut 5:9). Punishment to the third or fourth generation expresses the fact that *covenant violation brings guilt on the entire family. "The third and fourth generation" thus refers to all living members of the family. This is a stark reminder of communal guilt after the incident of the golden calf (32:19-35).

34:12-13. destruction of pagan worship objects. In this section, which reiterates the importance of obedience to the commandments, special attention is given to the destruction of all forms of pagan worship, especially *cult objects and idols. This may be another response to the golden calf incident (32:19-35). It is clear that the inhabitants of the Promised Land will have other gods and other ways of worshiping them. The Israelites are warned not to be enticed into alliance with these people or into worshiping their gods. Thus they are not to leave any sign of foreign worship intact. Carrying out this command would be evidence of great faith, for the destruction of sacred objects was considered a grave offense to a deity and was believed to result in the severest of punishments. The obedience of the Israelites would be tangible expression of their confidence that God could protect them from reprisals.

34:13. Asherah poles. The goddess *Asherah (under various related names) appears to be the divine consort of the principal male deity in a number of Mesopotamian and Syro-Palestinian pantheons: the *Babylonian storm god Amurru; the *Ugaritic god *El; and perhaps even the Canaanite god *Baal. She was often represented in the Bible by sacred poles erected near an altar. Her popularity among Israelites still tainted by a polytheistic worldview may be suggested by the inscription from Kuntillet 'Ajrud in the northwest part of the Sinai, "Yahweh and his Asherah." The order to cut down these cultic poles signified the need to purify the nation of foreign influence. It also follows the theme in this section of obedience to the commandments of a "jealous God" who would not countenance the worship or the symbols of rival deities (20:4-5).

34:16. sacred prostitution. One can distinguish between several different categories. In "sacred" prostitution, the proceeds go to the temple. In "cultic" prostitution, the intent is to insure *fertility through sexual *ritual. We must also differentiate between occasional sacred/cultic prostitution (as in Gen 38) and professional sacred/cultic prostitution (as in 2 Kings 23:7). The evidence for cultic prostitution in ancient Israel or elsewhere in the ancient Near East is not conclusive. Canaanite texts list prostitutes among the temple personnel, and *Akkadian literature attests those who were dedicated for life to serve the temple in this way. Although the Hebrew word used here is related to an Akkadian word for prostitute, this does not prove that any religious ritual or cultic practice is involved. It is quite possible for prostitutes to be employed by temples as a means of raising funds without their having any official status as priestesses. Furthermore, since women often did not have personal assets, sometimes the only way of earning money by which to pay a vow appeared to be prostitution. The injunction against bringing the wages of a prostitute to the temple may, however, be a reaction against practices like that of the *Ishtar temple servants in the Neo-Babylonian period, who hired out female members of their community as prostitutes. Their wages would have been placed in the temple treasury. All of this demonstrates the existence of sacred prostitution, both occasional and professional, in Israel and the ancient Near East. But the existence of cultic prostitution on either level is more difficult to prove. Cultic prostitution is not easily confirmed in Mesopotamia, unless one includes the annual sacred marriage ritual. But it is hard to imagine that prostitutes serving at the temple of Ishtar (who personified sexual force) were not viewed as playing a sacred role in the fertility cult.

34:17. cast idols. It was a fairly common practice (attested by archaeological data) to mass produce images of many of the gods of the ancient Near East using cast molds. They could thus be manufactured in a variety of metals or clay and sold to individuals, who would in turn establish private shrines in their homes (see Judg 17:4-5). The prohibition here is a specific example further clarifying the commandment in 20:4 and speaks to the case of the casting of the golden calf in 32:2-4.

34:18. Feast of Unleavened Bread. This is a reiteration of the commandment in 23:15. It gains greater authority here by being included in the ritual version of the Ten Commandments (see 34:28).

34:19-20. first-born offerings. This commandment in the ritual version of the Ten Commandments is a repetition of the injunction given during the exodus narrative to redeem the first-born sons and the first-born of their livestock (13:11-13).

34:21. sabbath. This command to rest on the sabbath is a repetition of 20:9 (see comment there).

34:22. Feast of Weeks. This is the same wheat-harvest festival that is described as the Feast of Harvest in 23:16, one of the three major festivals of the agricultural year. It gains extra authority from its inclusion in the ritual version of the Ten Commandments.

34:22. Feast of Ingathering. This is the same spring-harvest festival that is described in 23:17. These major agricultural festivals are also mentioned in Deuteronomy 16:9-17. The additional promise to protect the harvesters from attack by neighboring peoples is a further incentive to the people to comply with the commandment to bring their harvest offerings three times a year.

34:23-24. pilgrimages. This is the same command to come with their harvest offerings that is set out in 23:17 and Deuteronomy 16:11, 14. Every male is required to appear before the Lord three times a year with the fruits of his labor in order to insure the future fertility of the land and to demonstrate compliance with the *covenant.

34:25. no blood with yeast. This command in the ritual version of the Ten Commandments is a repetition of the law in 23:18. Yeast allows bread to rise but is also associated with the corruption or spoiling of food and so must not be mixed with the blood, a symbol of life.

34:25. Passover leftovers. This command regarding the Passover meal first appears in 12:8-10 and is reiterated in 23:18. Its inclusion here follows the sequence established of laws concerning the major agricultural festivals and reinforces the tie between this group of laws and the exodus event. The prohibition of keeping leftovers is a sign of the sacred character of the feast.

34:26 first fruits. This command is a repetition of the law in 23:19. Just as the first-born son is redeemed through sacrifice, so too is the cereal and fruit harvest redeemed for the people's use by bringing the first of the harvest to God as a sacrifice.

34:26. kid in mother's milk. This command is a repetition of the law in 23:19. It is the basis for the prohibition against the mixture of milk and meat in cooking and in sacrifice. It may also reflect a reaction against such practices in Canaanite worship.

34:28. Ten Commandments, ritual version. The first set of Ten Commandments, which were written on two stone tablets by God, was destroyed by Moses in his disgust over the unfaithfulness of the people in the golden calf incident (32:19). Thus a second set of tablets is inscribed in 34:28, but the laws do not exactly correspond to those found in Exodus 20 and Deuteronomy 5. There is a greater emphasis on the exodus event in the laws included in this second list. It is also much more heavily balanced toward proper worship practices (including nearly verbatim sections from chap. 23) than the first set of the commandments.

34:29. Moses' "horns." The radiance of God is reflected in the shining texture of Moses' face when he returns with the tablets of the law. Although he is at first unaware of this phenomenon, Moses and the people recognize it as evidence that Moses has had direct contact with God. Subsequently, he wears a veil over his face to hide the radiance of his skin from the people. Jerome used the word *cornuta*, "horns," in translating Hebrew qaran, "radiant," in the Vulgate (c. A.D. 400) because the Hebrew term often refers to horns. Consequently tradition held that Moses grew horns as a result of this experience. The mistake is graphically portrayed in the horned statue of Moses sculpted by Michelangelo in the sixteenth century. The relatedness of horns and radiance can be seen in the ancient Near Eastern iconography that depicts rays or horns as symbols of power on the crowns of deities. These are related to the divine glory (Akkadiankadian *melammu*) that emanated from the gods, especially from their heads or crowns. So, for instance, the goddess Inanna in a *Sumerian hymn is portrayed as having a terrible countenance that glows radiantly and intimidates all those around her. A closer parallel may be found in the instance of Samsuiluna (son of *Hammurabi), who receives messengers from the god *Enlil whose faces are radiant.

35:1-4
Sabbath

35:2-3. lighting a fire on the sabbath. This command repeats the injunction against any form of sabbath labor found in 31:15, with the additional statement prohibiting the lighting of a fire on the sabbath. It is another expansion on the theme of those types of work that could not be performed on the sabbath (see 34:21). Later rabbinic pronouncement required the kindling of a light prior to the sabbath so that the house would not be left in darkness. However, no further fueling of the fire was allowed on the sabbath.

35:4—39:31
Carrying Out the Instructions

These chapters discuss the actual construction of the tabernacle. They include the gathering of the materials (35:4-29) and the introduction of Bezalel and Oholiab as the chief craftsmen and the selection of their crew (35:30—36:7; cf. 31:1-10). Exodus 36:8-38 describes the building of the tabernacle to the exact dimensions outlined in 26:1-36. This is followed by the construction of the ark (37:1-9; see 25:10-22), the lampstand (37:17-24; see 25:31-40), the altar of incense (37:25-29; see 30:1-10), the altar of burnt offering (38:1-8; see 27:1-8) and the courtyard (38:9-20; see 27:9-19), and a summary of the materials used by the craftsmen (38:21-31). The final section describes the creation of the vestments for the priests: the ephod (39:2-7; see 28:6-14), the breastpiece (39:8-21; see 28:15-30) and the other priestly garments (39:22-31; see 28:31-43). Moses then inspects everything, certifies it is correct and according to God's command, and gives it his blessing (39:32-43).

38:8. women who served at the entrance. In the ancient Near East there are many examples of women serving temples in various capacities. From menial tasks to priestly duties, from celibacy to prostitution, from short-term vows to lifelong dedication, examples of all sorts are available. It is therefore difficult to identify the nature of the service that the women mentioned here are performing. In 1 Samuel 2:22 the indictment of the sexual misconduct of Eli's sons suggests that the women either were involved in some duty of piety or were virgins. It must be noted, however, that there is no evidence of religiously motivated celibacy in Israel, and the text does not describe the women as virgins.

38:24. gold from the wave offering. The metals used in the construction of the tabernacle are listed in descending order of their value. As was done with the sacrificial meat set aside for the use of the priests (29:27), these materials were first presented as a wave offering to God as a way of consecrating them to their purpose.

38:24. 29 talents, 730 shekels of gold. The total amount of gold used in the decoration of the tabernacle's furnishings is described in talents (the largest unit of Israelite weight measure, equaling 3,000 shekels). The talent weighed 75.6 pounds, while the shekel weighed 0.4 ounces. Thus the total weight of gold used was 2,210.65 pounds.

38:25. 100 talents, 1775 shekels of silver. The total amount of silver given and used for the embellishment of the tabernacle's furnishings was 7,601 pounds (based on 3,000 shekels at 0.4 ounces equaling one talent and weighing 75.6 pounds). This amount is also linked to the total atonement tax (30:11-16) collected from each Israelite male.

38:26. beka. The beka is a weight of measure equal to one half of a shekel, that is, 0.2 ounces. This was the amount of the atonement tax exacted from every man twenty years old and above to provide funds for the construction and maintenance of the tabernacle (see 30:11-16).

38:26. number of Israelites. The number of men counted in the census and paying the atonement tax (see 30:11-16) of one-half shekel of silver is 603,550. This is the same number listed in the census in Numbers 1:46, which was used to determine the number of males who were twenty years old and thus able to serve in the military.

38:29-31. 70 talents, 2,400 shekels of bronze. With the equation of 3,000 shekels (0.4 ounces) per talent (75.6 pounds), the total amount of bronze presented as a wave offering and used in the construction of the tabernacle was 5,350 pounds. This more durable metal was used for the bases of the entranceway, the bronze altar and its grating, and the altar utensils, as well as the bases for each of the poles supporting the tent and the tent pegs.

39:32—40:38
Completion of the Tabernacle

40:17. timing. The tabernacle was erected on New Year's Day, two weeks short of the anniversary of the exodus event and exactly nine months after the people arrived at Mount Sinai. The construction process had been carried out with no deviation from the instructions given by God. It was only appropriate that a new era in the manner of worship should begin on New Year's Day.

LEVITICUS

Introduction

T he book of Leviticus is filled with instructions concerning how to
maintain the holy space that was set apart for God's presence. This
includes details of the sacrificial system, instructions for the priests and
laws concerning *purity. In the ancient world *impurity was believed to
create an environment for the demonic, so *purity needed to be maintained. This generally involved *rituals as well as incantations. For Israel
*purity was a positive value that included rules of ethical behavior as
well as issues of etiquette.

The ancient Near Eastern material that is most helpful for understanding the book of Leviticus is that which gives information about
sacrifices, rituals and instructions for priests and dealing with *impurity.
This information usually must be gleaned in bits and pieces from many
different sources. There are, however, a few major ritual texts available
that serve as significant sources of information. While *Hittite literature
contains many sorts of ritual texts, among the most helpful is the
Instructions for the Temple Officials from the mid-second millennium. This
text details the means that should be used to protect the sanctuary from
sacrilege and trespass. Mesopotamian sources are also plentiful.

The *maqlu* texts contain eight tablets of incantations as well as one tablet of rituals connected to the incantations. Most of these incantations are attempts to counter the powers of witchcraft. Other important series would include the *shurpu* texts, which concerned purification, the *bit rimki* texts concerning royal ablutions and the *namburbu* rituals of undoing.

Most of these texts assume a background of magic and divination where witchcraft, demonic forces and incantations represented powerful threats in society. Israelite beliefs ideally did not accept this worldview, and their concepts of *purity and *impurity had noticeable differences. Nevertheless, studying this material can expose many facets of the ancient worldview that the Israelites shared. Even though the biblical literature purged the rituals of the magical element, the institutionalized practices and the terminology describing them at times still contained the trappings or vestiges of the broader culture.

Certainly Israelite beliefs and practices were closer to the ancient Near East than they are to our own concepts of ritual, magic and *purity. Since we understand so little concerning these aspects of their worldview, we are often inclined to read very foreign theological concepts or symbolism into some of the practices and rules. This often creates an erroneous view of the nature and teaching of the book. By acquainting ourselves with the ancient Near Eastern worldview, we can avoid this type of error and understand the text a little more in the way that the Israelites would have understood it.

1:1-17
The Burnt Offering

1:1-2. tent of meeting. Prior to the construction of the tabernacle in Exodus the tent of meeting was outside the camp and served as a place of revelation (see the comment on Ex 33:7-10). However, now that the tabernacle is in operation, it also is referred to as the tent of meeting.

1:2. animal sacrifice. There have been many theories about what thinking was represented in the sacrificial system. In some cultures sacrifice was viewed as a means of caring for the deity by providing food. Others saw the sacrifice as a gift to please the god and request his aid. In other contexts the sacrifices have been viewed as a means of entering into relationship with deity or maintaining that relationship. These are only a few of over a dozen possibilities. The history of animal sacrifice is difficult to trace. Earliest *Sumerian literature, specifically the Lugalbanda Epic, attests that sacrifices (better considered "ritual slaughter") originated as a means of permitting meat consumption. Sharing the meat with the deity allowed people to slaughter the animal for their food. Earliest archaeological evidence for sacrifice comes from the altars of the Ubaid period in fourth millennium B.C. Mesopotamia. Through most of *Assyrian and *Babylonian history, *ritual slaughter was carried out in order to obtain the entrails, believed to provide omens.

1:3-4. burnt offering. The burnt offering is always a male animal that is completely burned on the altar, except for the skin. This is the type of sacrifice that was offered by Noah and the type that Isaac was supposed to be. Other peoples are portrayed in the Bible as making burnt offerings (e.g., Num 23:14-15), and texts from Syria (*Ugarit and *Alalakh) and Anatolia (the *Hittites) testify to the practice in Syro-Palestine. In contrast there is not yet any evidence of this type of sacrifice in Egypt or Mesopotamia. The burnt offering serves as a means to approach the Lord with a plea. The plea could concern victory, mercy, forgiveness, purification, favor or any number of other things. The purpose of the offering is to entreat the deity's response. At least one each day was offered up on behalf of the people of Israel. Special ceremonies and festival days also generally featured burnt offerings.

1:3. male. Male animals were both more valuable and more expendable. A herd could be sustained with only a few males in proportion to the many females needed to bear the young. This would mean that a large percentage of the males that were born could be used for food or sacrifice. On the other hand, the good strong males were desirable because their genetic traits would be reflected in a large portion of the herd.

1:4. laying hand on the head. The laying on of the hand is an important part of the sacrificial *ritual. It is not designed to transfer sin, for it is used in sacrifices that do not deal with sin. Other possibilities are that the offerer in some way identifies with the animal, perhaps as his substitute, or identifies the animal as belonging to him. Most occurrences of the ritual confirm that either transferring or designating is taking place (or both), but it is not always clear what is being transferred or designated, and it may vary from one situation to another.

1:4. atonement. The function of this sacrifice as well as others is "to make atonement" (NIV). Many scholars now agree, however, that "atonement" is not the best translation for the concept on either the *ritual or the theological level. Perhaps most convincing is the fact that in the ritual texts the object of "atonement" is neither the sin nor the person, but a holy object connected with God's presence, such as the ark or the altar. A second important observation is that in a number of cases this "atonement" is necessary even though no sin has been committed (for instance, the ritual *impurity of women each month). For these and other reasons recent scholars have preferred "purification" or, more technically, "purgation," as the translation. So the altar would be purged on behalf of the offerer whose sin or *impurity had ritually tarnished it. The purpose was to maintain the sanctity of God's presence in their midst. The ritual, like a disinfectant, is normally remedial, but it can be preventative. The agent is usually blood, but not always. This decontamination of the sanctuary renders the offerer clean and paves the way for his reconciliation with God. The purging of objects (including cities, houses, temples and persons) from ritual contamination or evil influence by wiping or rubbing on a substance is also known in ancient Near Eastern practice, though these are mainly magical rites.

1:5-9. role of priests. Some aspects of the *ritual were performed by the priests, because only the priests had access to the altar and the holy place. (See comment on Exodus 28:1 for general information.) The priests of the ancient Near East were involved not only in sacrificial rituals but also in *divination and other magical rites. Incantations and general advice concerning appeasement of the gods were also under the jurisdiction of the priests. Priests were expected to be skilled in the knowledge of which rituals were to be used for any desired results and in the appropriate performance of the rituals.

1:5. importance of blood. Blood serves as the mechanism for ritual cleansing in Israel—a concept not shared by its ancient Near Eastern neighbors. The blood represented the life or life force of the animal, so the animal had to be killed for the blood to have efficacy. See the comment on 17:11 for more information.

1:5. sprinkling on the altar. The sprinkling of the blood on all sides of the altar is the symbolic means of applying the death of the animal to the purging of any contamination that might interfere with the entreaty that is being made on the occasion of the sacrifice. The blood represents the life/death of the animal, and the altar represents the sanctuary (God's presence) and is specifically the place where a request before God would be made.

1:8-9. parts. The pieces include the head as well as the suet (the fat that surrounds the internal organs). The only parts washed are the entrails (intestines) and the legs, both so that no dung is present on the altar.

1:9. pleasing aroma. It is typical for sacrifices to yield what is identified as the pleasing aroma of roasting meat. While it is certainly anthropomorphic (picturing God in human terms) to phrase it this way, cooked meat would have generally been used only for communal meals and special occasions, so important concepts of community were associated with the scent (like the smell of a Thanksgiving meal). It would be no different from God's being pleased by a sight or sound. In surrounding ancient Near Eastern thought the anthropomorphism is much stronger, for there the gods need and receive sustenance from food, and the smell is associated with their anticipation of a meal.

1:10-13. north side of altar. The north side of the altar is indicated, most likely because that is where there was the most room for this work to be done.

1:14-17. birds as offering. Birds, mainly domesticated doves, were the offering used by those who were too poor to own or to give up one of the larger herd animals. Texts from *Alalakh and Anatolia show that birds were also suitable sacrifices in surrounding cultures. Recent study has suggested it is not the crop that was removed but the crissum, including the tail, anus and intestines. Again, then, this is a matter of cleaning the animal in preparation for sacrifice.

1:16. east side where the ashes are. As early as the rabbis, it was suggested that the ash heap was on the east side because that was farthest away from the sanctuary, but the text never offers a reason.

2:1-16
The Grain Offering

2:1-3. grain offering. The rabbis considered the grain offering to be a substitute for the burnt offering for poor people. Mesopotamian practice is known to have made similar provision for the poor. The word used to describe this offering means "gift" or tribute. The offering is used in situations where respect or honor are intended. The same term is used the same way in *Ugaritic and *Akkadian (Canaan and Mesopotamia). It is typically found on occasions of celebration rather than the context of sadness or mourning. Generally a small portion was burned on the altar as a token of the gift to the Lord, while the remainder was given to the officiating priest. Sometimes it was offered in conjunction with other offerings.

2:1. fine flour with oil and incense. The ingredients of this offering were grain, oil and incense. The grain was the grits or semolina left in the sieve after wheat was ground into flour. The oil was olive oil. The best-quality oil was extracted by crushing the olives. But for the grain offerings the lower quality was acceptable; this was extracted through pressing and grinding. Oil was used as shortening in cooking and was easily combustible. The incense was frankincense, which was made from the gum resin of a type of tree found only in southern Arabia and Somaliland, on either side of the Gulf of Aden. This *Boswellia* tree will grow only where there is a very particular combination of rainfall, temperature and soil condition. Its fragrant aroma made the demand for frankincense high throughout the Near East, where it was used widely in both Mesopotamia and Egypt (some was found in Tutankhamen's tomb). This demand, along with its rarity, made it very expensive and one of the staples of the camel caravan trade. The grain offerings used a small amount that was entirely burned in a slow smolder.

2:3. the portion of the priests. As was the case with many offerings, the priest received a portion of the grain offering to eat. This was a means of providing for the needs of the priesthood. For fuller discussion of this practice, see comment on 6:14-18.

2:4-10. baked grain offering; cakes, no yeast, with oil. The grain offering that is for the priests' consumption can be prepared in oven, griddle or pan. The same oil and semolina are used, but no incense. Here it is specified that no yeast is to be used. Sacred use typically prohibited yeast of any sort, perhaps because it introduced a principle of spoilage (fermentation).

2:11-13. honey. Honey represents a natural resource, probably the syrup of the date rather than bees' honey. There is no evidence of bee domestication in Israel, though the *Hittites had accomplished that and used bee honey in their sacrifices (as did the Canaanites). In the Bible honey occurs in lists with other agricultural products (see 2 Chron 31:5).

2:13. salt. Salt was used widely as symbolic of preservation. When treaties or alliances were made, salt was employed to symbolize that the terms would be preserved for a long time. *Babylonian, Persian, Arabic and Greek contexts all testify to this symbolic usage. In the Bible, likewise, the *covenant between the Lord and Israel is identified as a covenant of salt—a long-preserved covenant. Allies entering into such an agreement would generally share a communal meal where salted meat was featured. Thus the use of salt in the sacrifices was an appropriate reminder of the covenant relationship. Additionally, salt impedes the action of yeast (leaven), and since leaven was a symbol of rebellion, salt could easily represent that which inhibited rebellion.

2:14-16. first-fruits grain offering. Besides the grain offerings that substituted for burnt offerings and those that accompanied other sacrifices, some grain offerings were made in connection with the first fruits of the harvest. This grain has not undergone any processing but involves roasting from the sheaf in the green stage of ripening. It is likely that this offering used barley rather than wheat.

3:1-17
The Fellowship Offering

3:1-5. fellowship offering. The fellowship offering often accompanies the burnt offering and also involves an animal sacrifice. It is often present in conjunction with shared *covenantal meals (Ex 24:5; Josh 8:31) and, once kingship is instituted, often recognizes the role of the king in relation to either God or the people. A similar word referring to a gift between dignitaries also occurs in conjunction with festive meals from *Ugarit and *El Amarna (Canaanite). The three types of sacrifices in this category are the freewill offering, the vow offering and the thanksgiving offering. The common ground between them is that they provide the occasion for a meal with the offerer and his family and friends. The suet was burned on the altar, but all the meat became part of the meal.

3:4. fat covering the inner parts. The suet is the layer of fat around the internal organs, mainly the intestines, liver and kidneys. This can easily be peeled off and is inedible. Mesopotamians did not include the suet in their sacrifices, but many other cultures of the ancient Near East did. The description in the text is quite technical. J. Milgrom translates it in his commentary as follows: "The suet that covers the entrails and all the suet that is around the entrails; the two kidneys and the suet that is around them, that is on the sinews [not "loins" as in NIV]; and the caudate lobe of the liver, which he shall remove with the kidneys."

3:6-11. fat tail. When a flock animal is offered, the "fat tail" is included in the sacrifice. The sheep of this region had long tails, as long as four or five feet, weighing up to fifty pounds.

3:11. burned "as food." The language here again shows that the sacrificial terms used in Israel were influenced by non-Israelite notions of sacrifice. It is clear from passages such as Psalm 50:12-13 that the Israelites were not to consider sacrifices as food needed by God. Since the terminology is used only in this particular offering, perhaps it represents God's inclusion in the communal meal more than the meeting of any need for nourishment.

3:12-17. fat is the Lord's. The suet is grouped with the blood as the portion belonging to the Lord. Just as the blood is a token of the life of the animal, the suet is a token of the meat of the sacrifice.

4:1—5:13
The Purification Offering

4:1-3. sin offering. The purification offering has traditionally been called the "sin offering." The terminology has shifted as it has been recognized that the offering did not deal just with moral offenses but also with purification in cases of significant ritual uncleanness. In personal circumstances as well as in public services of consecration and in connection with certain festivals, the offering purified or purged the sanctuary (not the offerer) from the effects of the offense or condition. In the ancient Near East the purification of temples was a constant need, because the people felt that *impurity made the temple vulnerable to destructive demons. In Israel the preservation of the *purity of the sanctuary had to do with the holiness of God. If the Lord was to remain in their midst, the holiness of his sanctuary must be maintained.

4:4-12. laying on of the hands. The laying on of the hand is an important part of the sacrificial *ritual. It is not designed to transfer sin, for it is used in sacrifices that do not deal with sin. Other possibilities are that the offerer in some way identifies with the animal, perhaps as his substitute, or identifies the animal as belonging to him. Most occurrences of the ritual confirm that either transferring or designating is taking place (or both), but it is not always clear what is being transferred or designated, and it may vary from one situation to another.

4:6. sprinkling seven times. The sevenfold sprinkling is a means of purifying all the parts of the sanctuary without going to each one individually. The sprinkling is directed toward the veil that separated the outer sanctuary from the Holy of Holies.

4:7. horns of the altar. The horns at the four corners of the altar were part of altar design throughout the ancient Near East. Research has suggested that they are emblems of the gods, though their function is unknown. Both the incense altar inside the sanctuary and the altar for sacrifice outside the sanctuary had horns.

4:7. incense altar. In this sacrifice the blood is spread on the horns of the incense altar. Incense altars were a typical piece of furniture in both Israelite and Canaanite sanctuaries. The incense offered on these altars was a mixture of spices featuring most prominently frankincense, but also gum resin, onycha and galbanum. Later Jewish tradition included a dozen spices in the mixture. The smoke of the incense represented the prayers of the people going up to God.

4:12. burning of extra parts outside the camp. Once the blood and fat are offered, the rest of the animal (including the meat) is burned outside the camp, so that none of it benefits the human offerers. There is no meal connected to this sacrifice. The ash pile from the second-temple period was just north of the wall in Jerusalem. Analysis of its contents has confirmed that it contained animal remains.

4:13-32. forgiveness. Forgiveness is the intended result of the purification and reparation offerings. The verb *forgive* has only God as the subject, never humans, and does not rule out punishment (see Num 14:19-24). We must therefore conclude that the concept concerns relationship rather than the judicial issue of punishment. The one who is offering these sacrifices seeks reconciliation with God, not pardon from punishment.

5:1-4. public charge to testify. The first case concerns one who does not respond to a public proclamation requesting information concerning a court case. It was common in the ancient Near East for such public requests to be made. The second and third cases concern contact with *impurity. The fourth concerns an impulsive oath. *Hittite texts also connect oath breaking with *impurity.

5:5-10. actions classified as "sins." These cases constitute a separate category because they are neither inadvertent nor defiant. Whether through carelessness or weakness an offense has been committed, and time has passed either because of a memory lapse or perhaps unwillingness to pay the price. This offering is unlike that of chapter 4 in that it required confession but resembles it in that it results in purification of the sanctuary and reconciliation to God. **5:11-13. no oil or incense.** The offering to be brought was determined by the means one had. Even a grain offering could be used by the very poor. Oil and incense are omitted because they were associated with celebration, and this was not a festive occasion.

5:14—6:7
The Reparation Offering

5:14-16. reparation offering. The reparation offering was traditionally termed the guilt offering. Though the term that is used is often appropriately translated as guilt, the term serves a more technical function within the sacrificial system. This offering is designed to address a particular category of offense—understood to represent a breach of faith or an act of sacrilege. "Breach of faith" would appropriately describe the violation of a *covenant, while "sacrilege" refers generally to desecration of sacred areas or objects. Both of these crimes were well known in the ancient Near East, and examples can be found from the *Assyrians, *Babylonians, Egyptians, *Hittites and *Aramaeans. The Hittite *Instructions for Temple Officials* is particularly helpful in its identification of a number of categories of sacrilege, including (1) priests taking portions of sacrifices that do not belong to them, or taking valuables given to the temple for their families' use, and (2) laypeople failing to deliver offerings that belong to deity in a timely manner. The crime addressed by the purification offering (previous chapter) was contaminating the holy place with that which was unholy. The crime addressed by the reparation offering was appropriating that which was

holy into the realm of that which was profane. Neither of these offerings existed in the other sacrificial systems of the ancient Near East.

5:18. significance of ram. While the purification offering for a leader of Israel required a male goat, the male sheep (ram) of the reparation offering distinguishes this sacrifice from any that could be brought for purification. In addition to the ram the offender must pay in silver the value of what he has desecrated and add one fifth of the value for restitution. The sanctuary shekel used for the valuation is generally considered to be a fraction of the regular shekel, but precise information is not available.

6:1-7. comparison of crimes. In the cases listed here the innocence or guilt of the supposed offender can be determined only by resort to an oath, because in most cases the evidence is not available or identifiable. While the previous section of the text concerned sacrilege with regard to sacred objects, this section refers to the sacrilege committed by swearing falsely. Fines are imposed here to deal with the offense on the civil level, where it would be classified as a misdemeanor rather than as a felony. In many of the ancient law collections, however, monetary reimbursement was used even in felony cases.

6:8-13
The Burnt Offering

6:9. burnt offering kept burning through the night. This section begins the instructions to the priests concerning the sacrifices that have been described in the previous chapters. The burnt offering was the last sacrifice to be offered for the day, and the regulations here specify that it should burn all night, with cleaning of the altar to take place in the morning. In this way petition on behalf of Israel can continue throughout the nighttime hours.

6:10. linen garments. The linen for the clothing worn by the priests was imported from Egypt, where it was also distinctively used for priests' garments. Angels, too, are said to be dressed in linen (for example, Dan 10:5).

6:14-23
The Grain Offering

6:16. provision for the priests. Whether or not the worshiper ate a portion of the sacrifice, a number of the sacrifices provided an opportunity for the priests to eat. This was also true in *Babylonian practice, where the king, the priest and other temple personnel received portions of the sacrifices. As early as the *Sumerian period, texts show that it was considered a grievous crime to eat that which had been set apart as holy.

6:16. courtyard of the tent of meeting. The Israelite temple that was discovered at Arad has the courtyard divided into two, the area closer to the sanctuary being more private. Ezekiel's description of the temple features special rooms adjoining the temple for the priests to eat their portions. It is likely, then, that the courtyard mentioned here, whether a partitioned open-air section or adjoining rooms in an area still considered the courtyard, would have been a private area.

6:18. holiness by touch. There was a contagion to various of the sacred objects that could be transmitted directly, but not secondarily (Hag 2:12). Tortuous analysis has led some experts to conclude that only objects, not persons, became holy by contact with something holy, but not all are convinced that such a distinction existed. Mesopotamian regulations likewise forbade the touching of sacred objects, but there is no discussion of contagion. An object that "contracted" holiness was confiscated by the priests and thereafter restricted to sacred use.

6:20. tenth of an ephah. This is about five cups of flour for two offerings, each one making a flat cake of eight to ten inches in diameter.

6:24-30
The Purification Offering

6:27. laundering a blood-spattered garment. Since the blood in this sacrifice has absorbed *impurity, the garment is now rendered impure and must be washed.

6:28. treatment of pottery vessels and metal vessels. Earthenware vessels retain their porosity and therefore absorb the *impurity of what they contain. Bronze or copper containers, in contrast, can easily be rinsed and thereby be purified for further use.

7:1-10
The Reparation Offering

7:2. blood sprinkled on all sides. The sprinkling of the blood on all sides of the altar is the symbolic means of applying the death of the animal to the purging of any contamination that might interfere with the entreaty that is being made. The blood represents the life and death of the animal, and the altar represents the sanctuary (God's presence).

7:3. fat parts. The suet is the layer of fat around the internal organs, mainly the intestines, liver and kidneys. This can easily be peeled off and is inedible. See 3:1-5 for more information.

7:6. eaten in a holy place. There were areas in the tabernacle compound provided for such occasions. See 6:14-23.

7:6. priestly shares. The concept of priestly portions was discussed above in 6:14-23. Here the hide also belongs to the priest, a practice attested in *Babylon as well as in the larger Mediterranean context.

7:11-21
The Fellowship Offerings

7:12. preparation of thanksgiving offering. One each of four different breads are presented to the priest. The "cakes" are probably braided ring-bread perforated in the baking process, while the "wafers" are the thin disk-shaped variety, perhaps half an inch thick.

7:14. contribution. This term is traditionally rendered "heave offering" and refers to a dedicated gift. Cognate terms are attested in *Akkadian (Babylonian) and *Ugaritic. Being put in this category transfers ownership from the individual to the deity using informal procedures, generally not within the confines of the sanctuary.

7:15. difference between thanksgiving offering and other fellowship offerings. Unlike the other fellowship offerings, the thanksgiving offering was often made in places other than the sanctuary. As a result there is a stricter rule about eating it the day of the sacrifice, perhaps to avoid situations where *impurity could be contracted. This would not be as big a problem in the sanctuary precincts.

7:19-21. cutting off of those eating unclean food. The penalty cited here is not something that people carry out but refers to the action of God. Such a penalty is generally reserved for those encroaching on that which is sacred.

7:22-27
Eating of Fat (Suet) and Blood

7:22-27. prohibition against eating fat or blood. The suet is grouped with the blood as the portion belonging to the Lord. Just as the blood is a token of the life of the animal, the suet is a token of the meat of the sacrifice. The suet of nonsacrificial animals may be eaten, but the blood of any animal may not.

7:28-36
Priestly Portions

7:30-34. wave offering. Close textual analysis has demonstrated that nothing is "waved" in these offerings, though it is possible that the offering is lifted up before God in dedication (a practice attested in Egyptian "elevation offerings"). It is different from the "contribution" (v. 14) in that it is always in the presence of the Lord, that is, at the sanctuary. Most agree that it represents a special dedication ceremony. There are waving ceremonies attested in Mesopotamian and *Hittite rituals, but these are in quite different contexts from this Israelite ritual.

7:31-34. use of the breast and thigh. Since there is no mention of which breast, it is assumed that the animal is not quartered lengthwise but across the middle below the ribs, leaving the whole breast intact, a large piece of choice meat to be shared among the priests. The thigh is the choice individual portion and is reserved for the officiating priest.

8:1-36
The Consecration of Aaron and His Sons

8:1-9. anointing and anointing oil. The spices which were to be used for anointing purposes were myrrh, cinnamon, cane and cassia (see recipe in Ex 30:23-25). Oil symbolizes the gifts of God to the people and the responsibilities now laid on their leaders through this ceremony. In Israelite practice anointing was a sign of election and was often closely related to endowment by the spirit, though that is never implied concerning the priests. Among the Egyptians and *Hittites, anointing was believed to protect a person from the power of netherworld deities. They anointed both kings and priests. In the *Amarna texts there is reference to a king of Nuhasse being anointed by the Pharaoh. There is no evidence that kings in Mesopotamia were anointed, but some priests were. Additionally, throughout the ancient world anointing symbolized an advance of a person's legal status. Both concepts of protection and change of status may correlate to the priest's anointing, for it would offer him protection in handling sacred things and identify him with the divine realm.

8:5-30. consecration ceremony. Investiture and anointing would have been normal procedures for social occasions. In Mesopotamian literature examples would include preparing Enkidu for entrance into society in the *Gilgamesh Epic and the hospitality offered *Adapa when he is called before the high god Anu in the *Myth of Adapa*. In the Israelite consecration ceremony, preparation for entering the serving circle of deity simply accentuates the normal procedures by using the very finest clothing and the most expensive oil. Installation of priests in Egypt also included clothing and anointing rituals.

8:1-7. priests in the ancient world. Every culture in the ancient Near East developed a priesthood. Only the Bedouin tribes did not set these individuals aside to perform priestly duties exclusively. Their role was to function as a part of a priestly community, serving temples, performing sacrifices, conducting religious services and staging festivals. Priests would have been educated within the temple from an early age, and their position in the priestly class was hereditary in some cases. They would have been among the few literate persons in their society and thus were relied upon to keep records of major events and tie them to the will of the gods. This process was known as *divination, and it, along with *ritual sacrifice, was the chief source of priestly power and authority. There was a distinctive hierarchy among priests—ranging from a chief priest, who sometimes rivaled the king in power, to midlevel individuals who performed daily *rituals and sacrifices, to musicians, and on down to temple servants, who performed the mundane housekeeping and custodial tasks necessary in any large community.

8:7. ephod. The most important of Aaron's priestly garments is the ephod, which was either a linen robe covering the upper body or a frontal piece attached to the shoulders and sashed at the waist. The fact that the ephod is related to idols and false worship in later passages (Judg 17:5 and 8:24-27) suggests that it was a garment borrowed from Mesopotamian society—perhaps worn by priests or used to clothe idols. The breastpiece (Ex 28:15), the Urim and Thummim (Ex 28:30), and the ephod are used in *divination (1 Sam 23:9-11). Thus the high priest is clothed in garments which aid in the discernment of God's will. Discussion of the other items of the priests' garments can be found in the comments on Exodus 28.

8:8. Urim and Thummim. No description of these objects is found in Scripture, although traditions from the Hellenistic and later periods suggest they were markers whose appearance and presentation when cast like lots would determine God's will (see Num 27:21; 1 Sam 14:37-41; 28:6). There is no negative character attached to the Urim and Thummim as there are to other divinatory practices, and they are never mentioned in passages describing non-Israelite worship or *ritual. Nevertheless, the practice of posing yes/no questions to the gods (asking *oracles) is known throughout the ancient Near East. Particularly of interest are the *Babylonian *tamitu* texts, which preserve the answers to many oracular questions. Positive and negative stones (thought to be light stones and dark stones) were also used widely in Mesopotamia in a procedure called psephomancy. In one *Assyrian text, alabaster and hematite are specifically mentioned. The yes/no question would be posed and then a stone drawn out. The same color stone would have to be drawn out three times consecutively for the answer to be confirmed. *Urim* is the Hebrew word for "lights" and therefore would logically be associated with bright or white stones. One recent study has pointed out that hematite, because of its use for weights and seals, was termed the "truth stone" in *Sumerian. The Hebrew word *Thummim* could have a similar meaning.

8:9. the diadem. This refers to a symbol of authority worn on the forehead or on the front of a headpiece. Perhaps the best-known example of this in the ancient world is the serpent (uraeus) on the front of Pharaoh's crown, which was believed to be a protective device. In the descriptions of the high priest's garments the diadem is generally associated with a "gold plate" (NIV). Since the word translated "plate" here is also the word for flower, it is possible that the insignia was flower-shaped.

8:10-21. anointing the sancta. This is done to consecrate the tabernacle and its parts for sacred use. Egyptians regularly anointed the images of the gods, but this was part of the care procedures, not a consecration.

8:14. laying on the hand. See comment on 4:4-12.

8:22-30. ram for ordination. The idiom used here for ordination, the "filling of the hand," is known from *Akkadian contexts for both priests and kings. For *Assyrian king Adad-Nirari II it is specifically a scepter that is placed into his hand signifying the authority of his office. The idiom has wider use, however, and does not require an insignia. Here it is a sacrifice of a ram in addition to the purification offering (vv. 14-17) and the burnt offering (vv.18-21) that provides the authorization for their office.

8:23. right ear, right thumb, right big toe. It is uncertain which part of the ear is intended (lobe and antihelix are the most often suggested). The blood functions both to cleanse from *impurity and protect from "sacred contagion." Smearing or daubing *rituals in the ancient Near East generally focus on edges and entrances.

8:29. wave offering. See comment on 7:30-34. Discussion of the details of verses 25-29 can be found in comments on chapter 1.

8:30. sprinkling of oil and blood. Aaron has already been anointed with oil and daubed with blood, but the sprinkling here serves a different purpose, that of consecration.

8:31-36. atonement. The concept of "purification" is closer to the mark than "atonement." See the comment on 1:4.

8:35. staying for seven days. The high priest may not leave for any reason because this would expose him to uncleanness. In his duties he absorbs *impurity but remains immune to its effects as long as he is in the sanctuary complex. Leaving would make him vulnerable to the lethal jeopardy such *impurity creates. *Sumerian texts attest to the same concerns for *entu*-priestesses, who must not venture out of the temple while *Dumuzi, still in the realm of the dead, roams the streets (Dumuzi is a dying and rising god connected to the fertility cycle of the seasons). Seven-day dedication ceremonies were common, as in Gudea's dedication of the temple in *Lagash.

9:1-22
The Beginning of Priestly Service

9:1. eighth-day ceremony. Information concerning the details of this section may be found in the previous comments. With the seven-day initiation and dedication ceremony completed, the eighth day marks the inauguration of the system. This ceremony is to be punctuated with the appearance of the Lord

(vv. 4-6, 23-24). A similar initiation ceremony occurs when Solomon's temple is initiated (1 Kings 8:62-64), where the term *hanok* ("initiation") is used (cf. Hanukkah, though the present-day Jewish holiday is not related to this event but rather to the reinitiation of the altar and temple by the Maccabeans after they had been desecrated by Antiochus Epiphanes in the second century B.C.).

9:23—10:20
The Appearance of the Glory of the Lord and the Response

9:23. the glory of the Lord. Most temple dedications in the ancient Near East featured the deity being officially installed in the temple (generally by means of the image of the deity being taken in). Here there is no installation of *Yahweh, but his glory appears to emerge from the newly dedicated tabernacle, most likely in the form of the pillar of cloud and fire (see comment on Ex 13:21-22) that has represented the Lord's presence throughout the wilderness experience. Here the fire erupts from the pillar to consume the offerings.

10:1. censers. These are most likely long-handled pans that could also shovel up the hot coals. They served as portable altars because the incense was actually burned in them. Censers are also used for burning of incense in Egypt when people wanted to protect themselves from demonic forces. For a close parallel in the Bible, see Numbers 16:46-50.

10:1. unauthorized fire. Since access to the main altar (where coals for incense offerings were supposed to be obtained) was difficult given the consuming fire, and since Aaron's sons decided that incense was needed to shield the people from viewing the glory of the Lord (see 16:13), coals from another source (unauthorized fire) were used.

10:3. Aaron's silence. Aaron's silence is in contrast to the loud wailing that usually accompanied mourning. Rather than a stunned silence, it represents a determination to follow the procedure that officiating priests should not be in mourning.

10:4. relatives caring for the dead. One of the important roles for a family is to care for their dead. In this situation the brothers of the dead were not available in that they were still involved in officiating at the sacrifice. Therefore the cousins were instructed to perform the necessary duties.

10:6-7. mourning rites and anointing oil. Disheveled hair and torn clothing are two of the principal signs of mourning. Other signs would include shaving hair or beard, putting dust on the head, and even slashing oneself. The mourning period generally lasted seven days. Aaron was warned against doing this because it contradicted the priestly condition that he was required to maintain for the ceremony. It would cheapen the holiness of the sanctuary and God's presence to interrupt that which the anointing oil had put in motion. See 21:10-12.

10:8. wine and fermented drink. Dates, honey and grain products all could be fermented and used as beverages, but barley beer was probably the most common alcoholic beverage. There is some evidence of ritual intoxication in ancient Near Eastern literature and the Bible also attests the practice (Is 28:7).

10:10. the sacred compass. Verse 10 establishes several categories. Everything that was holy (consecrated to deity) was clean (ritually purified). That which was not holy (therefore profane or common) could be either clean or unclean. It was the duty of the priests to maintain the distinctions between these categories, and they did so by maintaining what is called the sacred compass. In this concept the center of sacred space was the Most Holy Place, where the ark was.

Radiating from that point out were concentric zones of holiness, each with its requirements of levels of *purity. The priests enforced the rules that would maintain the appropriate level of holiness and *purity for each zone.

10:11. priestly instruction. Instruction by the priests would have included ethical as well as *ritual matters, though here the emphasis is likely on the latter. Deuteronomy 24:8 offers an example of such priestly instruction. Priests in the ancient world were considered experts in ritual matters of the performance of the *cult and were regularly consulted about often complex procedures.

10:12-15. priestly portions. The details of verses 12-15 have been considered in comments on chapters 6 and 7.

10:16. the importance of eating the purification offering. The purification offering was believed to absorb the impurities that it was presented to remedy. This concept of ritual absorption is common in the ancient Near East. When a great amount is absorbed (as on the Day of Atonement), the entire offering is burned so as to dispose of the *impurity. But on most occasions the priest's eating of the prescribed parts plays a role in the purification process. Milgrom suggests that it symbolized holiness swallowing up *impurity. If this is so, Milgrom is right in understanding Aaron's explanation to Moses here as reflecting his fearful caution. The presence of his sons' corpses in the sanctuary area may have greatly increased the amount of *impurity absorbed by the purification offering, making it lethal to the priest.

11:1-46
Clean and Unclean Food

11:2. dietary restrictions. In Mesopotamia there were numerous occasions on which certain foods were prohibited for a short period. There is also evidence in *Babylonia that there were certain restrictions concerning animals that particular gods would accept for sacrifice. But there is no overriding system such as that found here. Yet though there is no known parallel in the ancient world to anything like the Israelite system of dietary restrictions, the permitted animals generally conform to the diet common in the ancient Near East.

11:3-7. criteria for classification of animals. The main criteria are (1) means of locomotion and (2) physical characteristics. Nothing is mentioned of their eating habits or the conditions of their habitat. Anthropologists have suggested that animals were considered clean or unclean depending on whether they possessed all the features that made them "normal" in their category. Other suggestions have concerned health and hygiene. The weakness of each of these is that there are too many examples that do not fit the explanation. A popular traditional explanation suggested that the animals prohibited had some connection to non-Israelite *rituals. In fact, however, the sacrificial practices of Israel's neighbors appear strikingly similar to Israel's. A recent promising suggestion is that the Israelite diet is modeled after God's "diet"—that is, if it could not be offered in sacrifice to God, then it was not suitable for human consumption either.

11:7. pigs. *Assyrian wisdom literature calls the pig unholy, unfit for the temple and an abomination to the gods. There is also one dream text in which eating pork is a bad omen. Yet it is clear that pork was a regular part of the diet in Mesopotamia. Some *Hittite *rituals require the sacrifice of a pig. Milgrom observes, however, that in such rituals the pig is not put on the altar as food for the god but absorbs *impurity and then is burned or buried as an offering to underworld deities. Likewise in Mesopotamia it was offered as a sacrifice to demons. There is evidence in Egypt of pigs used for food, and Herodotus claims they were used for sacrifice there as well. Egyptian sources speak of herds of swine being kept on temple property, and they were often included in donations to the temples. The pig was especially sacred to the god Seth. Most evidence for the sacrifice of pigs, however, comes from Greece and Rome, there also mostly to gods of the underworld. In urban settings pigs along with dogs often scavenged in the streets, making them additionally repulsive. The attitude toward the pig in Israel is very clear in Isaiah 65:4; 66:3, 17, the former showing close connection to worship of the dead. It is very possible then that sacrificing a pig was synonymous with sacrificing to demons or the dead.

11:8. transfer of *impurity. Objects that come into contact with a carcass absorb the uncleanness of the carcass unless they are imbedded in the ground. Springs and wells are therefore exempt, as is seed that is to be planted. The wet seed of verse 38 is being prepared to be used as food, and so it does become unclean. Any contact with a carcass made the individual unclean as well and required purification. Most eating of meat would have involved animals that had been ritually slaughtered and therefore would not transfer uncleanness.

12:1-8
Purification After Childbirth

12:2. ceremonial uncleanness. Not all uncleanness was avoidable, and the cause of uncleanness was often something that would in no way be considered sinful. There are several categories of uncleanness that could not be easily avoided, including sexual impurities, disease-related impurities and the uncleanness that came from contact with a corpse or carcass. Though it was a mat-

ter of etiquette rather than ethics, the sacred compass needed to be protected from that which was inappropriate. Additionally it was a common belief that demons inhabited menstrual blood. In Israel bodily emissions such as menstrual blood and semen were closely associated with life. When the potential for life that they represented went unfulfilled, they would represent death and therefore uncleanness. That the uncleanness from childbirth should be seen as similar to monthly uncleanness from the menstrual cycle was common in ancient cultures, including Egypt, *Babylonia and Persia.

12:3. circumcision. See comment on Genesis 17:9-14.

12:4-5. purification for 33/66 days. The initial seven-day period plus the thirty-three additional days brings the total to forty—the normal number for estimations. Postpartum blood flow can last anywhere from two to six weeks, so this would be a suitable approximation. Persians and Greeks had similar forty-day restrictions concerning entering sacred areas after giving birth, and many cultures require a longer purification time for girls. *Hittites considered the child unclean for three months (male) or four (female). There is no sure rationale for why the purification time differs depending on the gender of the child.

12:7. atonement. Cases like this make it clear that what has been called a "sin offering" is actually a purification offering (see the comments on chap. 4). There is no sin here that needs "atonement." Rather the *impurity is cleansed from the altar (see the comment on 1:4).

13:1-46
Skin Disease

13:2. varieties of skin disease. Those studying the language have concluded that the term often translated "leprosy" (NIV: "infectious skin disease") is more accurately rendered "lesion" or, less technical, "scaly skin." Such patches could be swollen or weeping, as well as flaking. Similar broad terminology also exists in *Akkadian, where the *Babylonians likewise considered it an unclean condition and the punishment of the gods. Clinical leprosy (Hansen's disease) has not been attested in the ancient Near East prior to the time of Alexander the Great. None of the most prominent characteristics of Hansen's disease are listed in the text, and the symptoms that are listed argue against a relationship to Hansen's disease. The condition discussed in the text is not presented as contagious. Descriptions suggest that modern diagnoses would include psoriasis, eczema, favus and seborrheic dermatitis, as well as a number of fungal-type infections. Comparison to "snow" most likely concerns the flakiness rather than the color ("white" is added in the translations that contain it). The great cultural aversion to skin diseases may be that in appearance, and sometimes odor, they resemble the rotting skin of the corpse and are therefore associated with death. This natural revulsion adds considerably to the victim's outcast status when combined with the quarantine that is ritually rather than medically motivated.

13:45. behavior of victim. The disheveled hair, torn clothing and covered face characterize the victim as a mourner. In the superstitions of the day the mourner would thus disguise himself from the evil forces hovering in the places of the dead. His cry would prevent someone from coming near, for popular belief held that even his breath could contaminate.

13:46. living outside the camp. Though the camp did not need to maintain the same level of *purity as the temple compound, there were restrictions. This restriction is also found in *Babylonian literature for victims of skin diseases forced to live in isolation. It is likely that they would have lived in the vicinity of the tombs.

13:47-59. contaminated cloth. This is a reference to various fungi and molds that can infect cloth or wood. Mesopotamian literature considers these growths to be associated with evil or the demonic, but they are not so personified in biblical text.

14:1-57
Purification of Scale Contamination

14:2. cleansing ritual. These *rituals are not concerned with dirt or bacteria but with ritual *impurity. Wild birds are used because the freed (contaminated) bird must never be inadvertently used for sacrifice. In Mesopotamian and *Hittite purification rituals birds are used because they are believed to carry the *impurity back to its source in the heavens. Cedar is apparently used for its red color, along with the yarn and the blood. This is not used magically by the Israelites (curing had already taken place) but symbolically. Many interpreters consider the red to represent life.

14:8. significance of shaving. Hair sometimes represents a person's life or identity, but here it has no symbolic value. It is shaved off so all may see the restored condition of the skin and so no residual *impurity could be harbored there.

14:10. three-tenths of an ephah. Three-tenths of an ephah is about six quarts, the equivalent of offering a grain offering for each of the three sheep offered.

14:10. log of oil. A log is a small amount, less than a pint, but it is difficult to be precise. The Bible uses the term only in this chapter, and the occurrences in other languages are equally vague.

14:12. guilt offering. This offering, better translated "reparation offering," is described in chapter 5. It is generally offered when the sanctuary has somehow suffered loss. It may be part of this *ritual to make amends for any offerings that had to be omitted by the individual during his quarantine. Another suggestion is that since skin affliction could at times be a punishment from God for an act of sacrilege, the reparation offering is made just in case there was some such offense that the victim was unaware of.

14:12. the wave offering. See comment on 7:30-34. This context is the only one in which the entire animal in included in the ceremony (see chaps. 7—8).

14:14. right ear, right thumb, right big toe. See comment on 8:23.

14:15. the use of the oil. Oil is used in the ancient Near East as a protective substance. Though that function may well have disappeared in Israel, oil was retained as an important ritual element (like mistletoe in homes today being no longer considered protection from demons but associated with the season). An Egyptian *ritual for preparing an idol for the day includes a similar procedure to that described here in verse 18.

14:18. atonement. The oil (or, more likely, the entire reparation *ritual), the purification offering, the burnt offering and the grain offering are each said to make atonement for the individual. For atonement as purgation see comments on chapter 1. Here it is used to describe the complex ritual process that provides the individual with a clean slate for being reinstated into full participation in the ritual system.

14:34. mildew. The reference here is to fungal infections, which were considered to be evil omens in the ancient world. Mesopotamian *rituals target fungus growths in a number of different contexts. The wall containing the fungus was believed to be the indicator of which member of the family would die. The fungus was an omen of the coming of demons and their troubles. There is no such element here, and only the house needs the ritual procedures, not the inhabitants.

14:48. purification ritual. This *rite shows some similarity to the fungus purification rites known from the rest of the ancient Near East. The *Hurrian ritual uses birds (two sacrificed, one released) and burns cedar just as the Israelites did. *Babylonians used a raven and a hawk. The latter was released into the wilderness. For the other details of this ritual, see the comment on the beginning of this chapter.

15:1-33
Discharges

15:1-15. discharges caused by disease. Described here is the discharge of mucus that is most frequently caused by gonorrhea (though only the more benign varieties were present in the ancient world). Alternatively it has been identified as infectious urinary bilharzia, a known scourge of the ancient world. This disease was caused by the parasite *Schistosoma* related to snails in the water system that have been detected in excavations. Such discharges were believed to be evidence of demonic presence in the person in the larger ancient Near East, but in Israel they required only washing of the individual and purification of the sanctuary, not *exorcism as in Mesopotamia.

15:16-18. seminal emissions. Among the *Hittites nocturnal emissions were considered to result from sexual intercourse with spirits. There is no such stigma here, and the purification requires only washing, not sacrifice. Any sexual activity would prevent one from entering the temple compound until evening. This was also true in Egyptian practice, though it is not in evidence in many other ancient Near Eastern cultures, presumably due to the prevalence of ritualized prostitution. In these cultures, illustrated by *Hittite practice, sexual intercourse required washing prior to participation in rituals but required no waiting period and was not explicitly prohibited on temple grounds. **15:19-24. menstruation.** Menstrual flow was considered a source of *impurity throughout the ancient world and in a few cultures represented danger of demonic influence. Again Israel treats it only as requiring washing, not sacrifice, and offers no protective rituals. A royal *Assyrian decree toward the end of the second millennium prohibited a menstruating woman from coming into the king's presence when sacrifices were being made.

15:25-33. irregular discharges. Menostaxis is the name for the principal cause of continued blood flow beyond the regular monthly period. This could result in nearly perpetual uncleanness and make it nearly impossible to have children, for sexual intercourse is prohibited when such a blood flow exists.

16:1-34
Day of Atonement (Purgation)

16:2. limited access to holy places. Temples in the ancient world were typically not houses of public worship. Access to sacred precincts was heavily restricted because they were considered holy ground. The more sacred the area, the more restricted the access, both to protect the human beings who would be taking their lives in their hands to trespass on sacred ground and to prevent desecration of the dwelling place of deity.

16:2. appearing in a cloud. *Akkadian uses the term *melammu* to describe the glowing, visible representation of the glory of deity, which in turn is enshrouded in smoke or cloud. In Canaanite mythology it has been suggested the *melammu* concept is expressed by the word *anan*, the same Hebrew word here

translated "cloud," but the occurrences are too few and obscure for confidence. **16:2. atonement cover.** Traditionally translated "mercy seat," though all translations are speculative. The term refers to the solid gold rectangular plate or sheet (made of one piece with the cherubim) that sat on top of the ark (see comment on Ex 25:17). One suggestion is that the word comes from Egyptian, where a similar-sounding word refers to a place to rest one's feet. Since the ark is at times viewed as a footstool for God, this would fit well.

16:4. Aaron's garments. See the comments on Exodus 28 for the description of the high priest's garments. Here he is not dressed in full regalia but, as an act of humility, in more simple linen clothing. The linen for the clothing worn by the priests was imported from Egypt, where it was also distinctively used for priests' garments. Angels, too, are said to be dressed in linen (for example, Dan 10:5). Later in the ceremony the high priest will change into the regular uniform (vv. 23-24).

16:6-10. purpose of the day. Though other cultures of the ancient Near East have *rituals to dispose of evil, in all of those the evil is of a ritual or demonic nature, while in Israel all of the sins of the people are included. The ceremony begins with purification offerings so that the priest can enter the holy place. Once inside, the blood ritual cleanses all the parts of the sanctuary from the impurities accumulated throughout the year. It works from the inside out until the sins are placed on the head of the "scapegoat," which carries them away. The goal of the regular purification offerings was forgiveness (see comment on 4:13-32). In contrast, this annual ritual is intended to dispose of the sins of the people.

16:8. Azazel. The Hebrew word translated "scapegoat" is *azazel*. This translation results in dividing the Hebrew word into two words—an unlikely solution. Since verse 8 identifies one goat as "for *Yahweh" and the other goat as "for Azazel," it is most consistent to consider Azazel a proper name, probably of a demon. Early Jewish interpreters had this understanding, as is demonstrated in the book of Enoch (second century B.C.). This goat is not sacrificed to Azazel (consistent with 17:7) but released "to Azazel" (v. 26). *Babylonians believed in *alu*-demons that lived in deserted waste land, and this may be a similar concept.

16:8. scapegoat concept in the ancient Near East. A number of *Hittite *rituals feature the transfer of evil to an animal that is then sent away. In some cases the animal is considered a gift to appease the gods or a type of sacrifice to the gods, but in others it is simply a means of disposing of the evil. Mesopotamian rituals that transfer *impurity often see the animal as a substitute for an individual—a substitute that will now become the object of demonic attack instead of the person. In the *Asakki Marsuti* ritual for fever, the goat that is the substitute for the sick man is sent out into the wilderness. All of these differ significantly from Israelite practice in that they are enacted by means of incantations (reciting words of power)—a concept totally absent in Israelite ritual. Additionally the Israelite practice shows no intention to appease the anger of deity or demon, whereas this is the most common motivation of the ancient Near Eastern rituals.

16:8. casting lots. Casting lots gives the Lord the opportunity to choose the goat for sacrifice.

16:12. function of the incense. Incense altars were typical of both Israelite and Canaanite sanctuaries. The incense offered on these altars was a mixture of spices featuring most prominently frankincense but also including gum resin, onycha and galbanum (see the comment on Ex 30:34-38). Later Jewish tradition included a dozen spices in the mixture. The smoke of the incense represented the prayers of the people going up to God.

16:29. tenth day of the seventh month. This would be in the fall, ten days after New Year's Day. In our calendar it falls toward the end of September.

16:34. atonement once a year. In the *Babylonian new year *ritual the priest slaughtered a ram to be used in purging the sanctuary. Incantations to exorcise demons were recited. The king declared himself free of a number of crimes concerning his office, and the body of the ram was thrown into the river.

17:1-18
Meat Consumption and Blood

17:4. guilty of bloodshed. Domestic animals suitable for sacrifice could not be ritually slaughtered for fellowship offerings except at the tabernacle/temple. This prohibition would help prevent the offering of these sacrifices to other gods or at unapproved shrines. It would also hinder the concept that the blood of an animal slaughtered away from the sanctuary could be considered as appeasing netherworld deities. It was this spilling of blood in illicit rituals that the individual would be guilty of.

17:7. goat idols. The term most likely refers to satyrlike demons who were believed to haunt the open fields and uninhabitable places.

17:9. cut off from his people. This terminology is generally accepted as reflecting a belief that God would carry out the appropriate punishment. It does not suggest any judicial or societal action against that person but awaits the action of God.

17:11. life in the blood. The idea that blood contained the essence of life is evident in the Mesopotamian belief that the first people were created from the blood of a slain deity. But there were no dietary restrictions regarding blood and nothing to suggest a ritual use of blood, either in terms of what was offered to deity or in purification rituals, anywhere else in the ancient Near East.

17:11. blood as atonement. It is because the blood was believed to contain the essence of life that it could serve as a purifying agent in the *rituals of the sacrificial system. For more discussion about the word translated "atonement," see the comment on 1:4.

17:12. prohibition against eating blood. Eating the blood could easily be viewed as one way of absorbing the life force of another creature. This type of thinking is forbidden, as is the idea that by ingesting it the individual has destroyed the life force by dissipation. Instead, the life is to be offered back to God, whence it came.

18:1-30
Sexual Prohibitions

18:1-29. sexual taboos. Every society develops sexual taboos to regulate marriage practices, adultery and unacceptable sexual practices. These restrictions vary from one culture to another, but they are all designed to reflect the economic and moral values of their society. The laws in chapter 18 are *apodictic (command) laws, which note only that these practices defile the people. The word used in verses 22-29 (NIV: "detestable") identifies the behavior as contrary to the character of God. A parallel term in *Sumerian and *Akkadian designates conduct as being despicable to deity. In the case of incest (vv. 6-18), the primary concern is over relations with immediate blood kin (father, mother, sister, brother, son, daughter) and affinal relations (wife, husband, uncle, aunt). The only exception is in the case of levirate obligation (Deut 25:5-10), when a man's

brother is required to have sexual relations with his sister-in-law. Incest was equally abhorrent in most other societies (e.g., the prohibitions in *Hittite laws). A Hittite treaty prohibits sexual relationships with sisters-in-law or cousins on pain of death. The exception is Egypt, where incest was a common practice in the royal family (but little attested elsewhere) as a means to strengthen or consolidate royal authority. This concept is also seen among *Elamite kings. Adultery (v. 20) violates the sanctity of the family and contaminates the inheritance process (see the comment on Ex 20:14).

18:21. children passed through the fire to Molech. Evidence of child sacrifice has been recovered from Phoenician sites in North Africa (Carthage) and Sardinia, and it was also practiced in Syria and Mesopotamia during the *Assyrian period (eighth and seventh centuries B.C.). Dedicating children to a god as a form of sacrifice is found in several biblical narratives. It can be explained as a means of promoting *fertility (Mic 6:6-7) or as a way of obtaining a military victory (Judg 11:30-40; 2 Kings 3:27). In no case, however, is this considered acceptable as a sacrifice to *Yahweh under biblical law (Deut 18:10). Many consider Molech to be a netherworld deity whose worship featured *rituals with Canaanite origins focusing on dead ancestors. An eighth-century B.C. Phoenician inscription speaks of sacrifices made to Molech before battle by the Cilicians and their enemies.

18:22-23. homosexuality and bestiality. Homosexuality (v. 22) and bestiality (v. 23) were both practiced in the context of *ritual or magic in the ancient Near East. The latter particularly occurs in the mythology of *Ugarit and is banned in legal materials (especially the *Hittite laws). The mixing of realms was contrary to concepts of *purity.

18:24-28. Canaanite sexual perversions.

These perversions should not be considered simply the result of human depravity. Sex had been ritually incorporated into worship in order to procure *fertility of the land, the herds and flocks, and the people. While the fertility aspect of Canaanite religion is well attested, little is known of specific details of ritualized sex. Temple personnel included male and female prostitutes, but their ritual role is still obscure. The implication of these verses is also that violation of the sexual code pollutes both the people and the land, requiring a cleansing process that will drive them out and allow resettlement by the Israelites. There is thus an understanding of an intimate relationship between land and people that would have been natural to a people who based their lives on agriculture and herding. Despite the assurance that the land would ultimately belong to them, however, caution is expressed that the Israelites not follow this same course of personal defilement and be exiled in turn.

19:1-37
Miscellaneous Laws

19:9-10. intentionally inefficient harvesting. In *fertility *cults, the portion left in the field would have served as an offering to the deities of the ground. Here it becomes a means to care for the poor. While no examples of this legislation survive in ancient Near Eastern law, texts from the town of *Nuzi suggest a similar practice.

19:11-19. social contract. This is another set of *apodictic (command) decrees similar to the Decalogue (Ten Commandments) of Exodus 20:1-17. It provides an even fuller concept of the social contract between God and the Israelites, as well as the rights and obligations of the Israelites among themselves. There are no other examples of such social contracts between people and their deity.

However the ancient Near Eastern gods were believed to be concerned about justice in society, and people considered themselves accountable to the gods, either to their personal/family gods or to Shamash, the god of justice. The gods were believed to judge people's conduct and were called upon to witness behavior in the human realm. Thus the social contracts that governed human behavior among Israel's neighbors were made between the human parties with the gods invoked by oath as protectors.

19:19. mixing animals, seeds, materials. Some mixtures were considered to be reserved for sacred use. The parallel passage in Deuteronomy 22:9-11 makes it clear that this is the issue in Israel as well. The mixture of wool and linen was used in the tabernacle and in the high priest's outer garments, and it was thus reserved for sacred use. This interpretation is also current in the Dead Sea Scrolls (4QMMT). Sowing of two types of seed is also prohibited in the *Hittite laws, with a death threat to violators.

19:20-22. status of slave girl. Standards of conduct and penalties vary for slaves. Ancient Near Eastern law contains several examples of punishment for the rape of a female slave. Both the Neo-Sumerian laws of *Ur-Nammu and the *Babylonian laws of *Eshnunna (both c. 2000 B.C.) prescribe fines for rape of a female slave. The Eshnunna law adds the further provision that the woman remains the property of her original owner, so that rape cannot become a predatory means of obtaining a slave. In the biblical example, the case is not considered adultery and therefore does not end in execution (see Deut 22:23-24), since she is still technically a slave, not a free woman (see Ex 22:15-17).

19:23-25. fruit tree husbandry. Orchards of fruit trees were of such great value that the law forbade cutting them during times of war (Deut 20:19). They usually contained more than one variety of tree (see Amos 9:14). Among the most common fruit trees were fig, olive, date and sycamore fig. Some orchards were irrigated (Num 24:6), but most appear to have been planted on terraced hillsides (Jer 31:5). Careful cultivation and pruning was necessary during the first three years in order to insure eventual good harvests and proper maturing of the trees. The fruit during this period could not be eaten and was declared unclean (literally, "uncircumcised"). In the fourth year the entire harvest was to be dedicated to God as an offering, and from the fifth year on the owner could eat the fruit.

19:26. divination. *Divination involves a variety of methods used by prophets (Mic 3:11), soothsayers, mediums and sorcerers to determine the will of the gods and to predict the future. These included the examination of the entrails of sacrificial animals, the analysis of omens of various types and the reading of the future in natural and unnatural phenomena (see Gen 44:5). The prohibition against eating meat with the "blood still in it" in this verse is tied to the injunction against participating in any form of divination or sorcery. Thus, rather than being a dietary law, this decree involves the practice of draining blood from a sacrificial animal into the ground or a sacred pit, which was designed to attract the spirits of the dead (see 1 Sam 28:7-19) or chthonic (underworld) deities in order to consult them about the future. Such practices are found in several *Hittite ritual texts and in Odysseus' visit to the underworld (*Odyssey* 11.23-29, 34-43). These practices were condemned (Deut 18:10-11) because they infringed on the idea of *Yahweh as an all-powerful God who was not controlled by fate.

19:27. significance of hair trimming. For men hair has symbolic value as a sign of manhood or virility (see 2 Sam 10:4). Women decorate their hair and groom it carefully as a sign of beauty. The prohibition against trimming the "sides of your head" or the "edges of your beard" uses the same terminology as in 19:9-10, which deals with the harvesting of fields. In both cases an offering is involved—one to the poor and the other to God. The law's placement here immediately after the prohibition against *divination suggests that the restriction on cutting the hair is based on the Canaanite practice of making an offering of hair to propitiate the spirits of the dead (see Deut 14:1). *Hammurabi's code penalizes false witnesses by having half the person's hair cut off. The Middle Assyrian code allows a debt-slave's master to pull out his/her hair as punishment (see Neh 13:25). Both laws suggest that shame is attached to the loss of hair. There is a Phoenician inscription from the ninth century B.C. reporting the dedication of shaven hair by an individual in fulfillment of a vow made to the goddess *Astarte. In ancient thinking hair (along with blood) was one of the main representatives of a person's life essence. As such it was often an ingredient in sympathetic magic. This is evident, for instance, in the practice of sending along a lock of a presumed prophet's hair when his prophecies were sent to the king of *Mari. The hair would be used in divination to determine whether the prophet's message would be accepted as valid.

19:28. cutting body for dead. Mourning and *cultic practices sometimes included lacerating oneself (see 1 Kings 18:28; Jer 16:6, 41:5). This may have been done to attract a god's attention, ward off the spirits of the dead or demonstrate greater grief then simply wailing. The prohibition may be due to its association with Canaanite religion. For instance, the *Ugaritic cycle of stories about the god *Baal (c. 1600-1200 B.C.) includes an example of mourning by the chief god *El over the death of Baal. His grief takes the ritual form of filling his hair with dirt, wearing sackcloth and cutting himself with a razor. The text reads that "he plowed his chest like a garden."

19:28. tattoo marks. The prohibition against marking the skin may involve either tattooing or painting the body as part of a religious *ritual. Such markings may have been designed to protect a person from the spirits of the dead or to demonstrate membership in a group. Some evidence for this has been found in the examination of human remains in Scythian tombs dating to the sixth century B.C. The Israelite law may prohibit this practice since it involves a self-imposed alteration of God's creation, unlike *circumcision, which is commanded by God.

19:29. prostitution. In line with the surrounding laws, which prohibit defiling either the people or the produce of the land, this law against selling a daughter into prostitution is designed to prevent defiling both her honor and that of the family. Financial problems might tempt a father to do this, but it is considered a moral pollution of both the people and of the land itself. As in 18:24-28, such a practice could result in eventual expulsion from the land. The extreme nature of this penalty may be based on the loss of honor of both the household and the community. However, it is also possible that this refers to *cultic prostitution and thus would mean the worship of gods other than *Yahweh.

19:31. mediums and spiritualists. The practitioners of spiritism and sorcery are condemned (Deut 18:10-11) because of their association with Canaanite religion and because their "art" attempted to circumvent *Yahweh by seeking knowledge and power from spirits. They represented a form of "popular religion"

that was closer to the folk practices of the common people and served as a form of "shadow religion" for many. Sometimes, because of its association with *divination, their *rituals and methods stood in direct opposition to "official religion" or as an alternative to be used in times of desperation (see Saul's use of the outlawed witch of Endor in 1 Sam 28). Sorcery and potions used in the practice of magic were also banned in *Hammurabi's code and the Middle Assyrian law, suggesting that the prohibition and fear of these practices was not unique to Israel.

19:35-36. honest measurements. The injunction to deal in honest weights and measures when doing business is directly related to the laws in 19:11-18, which require fair dealing and an internalized sense that your neighbor is to be treated as you would want to be treated. Standardization of weights and measures was required in *Hammurabi's code with regard to repayment of debts in grain or silver, and involving measuring out of grain to pay for wine. Penalties for violators ranged from forfeiture of property to execution.

20:1-27
Defiling Conduct

20:2-5. children of Molech. One of the major themes in this book equates idolatry with prostituting oneself after other gods. This in turn pollutes *Yahweh's sanctuary, the Israelites themselves and the land. The practice of sacrificing children to Molech (see comment on 18:21) is condemned, and the perpetrators are to be stoned (a form of communal execution which draws everyone into the act of purification). No violation of this command will be tolerated, even if God must mete out the punishment when the community chooses to turn a blind eye to sin. The idea of "cutting off" the sinner implies complete banishment from

God and the community and was generally a punishment that was seen as being carried out by God.

20:9. cursing parents. Contrary to the NIV translation, studies have demonstrated that the infraction here is not cursing but treating with contempt. This is a more general category and would certainly include the prohibition of Exodus 21:15, which forbids striking a parent, and would be the opposite of the fifth commandment to "honor your father and your mother" (Ex 20:12). Each injunction is designed to protect the cohesion of the family unit as well as insure that each subsequent generation provide their parents with the respect, food and protection they deserve (see Deut 21:18-21). Mesopotamian law codes and legal documents are also clear on the issue of treating parents with contempt. The *Sumerian laws allow a son who disowns his parents to be sold as a slave. *Hammurabi requires the amputation of the hand of a man who strikes his father. A will from *Ugarit describes a son's behavior using the same verb used in this verse and stipulates disinheritance.

20:10-16. capital punishment for sexual crimes. The violation of sexual codes (adultery, incest, homosexuality, bestiality) is placed on a par with idolatry in this law code and thus requires the sentence of death. Both defile persons and the land and cannot be tolerated. Crimes of this nature are also punishable in *Hammurabi's code (adultery requires trial by ordeal in laws 129 and 132; rape is a capital crime in law 130; incest is punished by exile in law 154), the *Middle Assyrian laws (homosexuality punished by castration in law 20) and the *Hittite laws (bestiality with pigs or dogs punished by death in law 199). These were all believed to undermine the family, the foundational element of Israelite society. To undermine the fam-

ily was to undermine the *covenant.

20:20-21. penalty of childlessness. Having children meant having someone to care for you in old age and give proper burial and the extension of the family into the next generation. Being childless represented the cutting off of the family and the risk of being neglected in old age and death.

20:27. medium or spiritist. See comment on 19:31.

21:1—22:32
Regulations for Priests

21:5. shaving practices of priests. Priests have the special injunction to keep themselves pure and holy because it is their responsibility to bring offerings to God. As a result, their skin and hair must remain intact, free of blemish or injury, as a testimony to that holiness. Thus they are prohibited from engaging in the mourning practices common in Canaan of gashing themselves, tearing their hair or shaving their beard. In fact it would be shameful for them to present themselves in any condition that was not holy (see Satan's accusation against the high priest Joshua in Zech 3:3).

21:7. marriage regulations for priests. There was a special regulation for priests against marrying a woman who was known to have engaged repeatedly in prostituting herself ("defiled by prostitution" implies flagrant abuse). Furthermore, he was also denied the right to marry a woman who was divorced. This is probably due to the fact that the principal charge made against a woman by her husband in a divorce proceeding was infidelity (see Num 5:11-31; Deut 22:13-14; 24:1).

21:10-14. special regulations for high priest. Even a higher standard of *purity was required for the high priest. He must avoid contaminating his person by coming into contact with the dead, even if this means absenting himself from his parents' funeral, and he cannot engage in the usual forms of mourning (see purification rituals for corpse contamination in Num 19). This restriction may also be an attempt to disassociate the priesthood from *cults of the dead. Furthermore, the priest's wife must be a virgin. She cannot have been married before, nor can she be either a divorcee or a prostitute. The high priest was anointed to represent the *purity of the nation in its dealings with God. Therefore he must avoid all contact with persons or objects that might defile him and through him the Holy of Holies.

21:16-23. prohibiting priests with defects. Just as animals with physical defects or blemishes may not be offered for sacrifice (22:19-22), priests who have a physical defect may not serve before the altar. Ritual *purity is required for the sacred precincts of the altar, the sacrifice and the religious practitioner officiating at the altar in every religion in the ancient Near East. Priests must therefore be in perfect health and in full command of their bodies and senses. Thus anyone who is "blind [even in one eye], lame, disfigured or deformed," is restricted from priestly service. The list is quite graphic and includes defects caused by accidents (broken bones, crushed testicles), birth defects (dwarfism, lameness, hunchback) or disease (skin afflictions, sores). Even though he may not approach the altar, the disabled priest is still entitled to his share of the priestly portion of the sacrifice.

21:21. food of his God. A portion of most sacrificial offerings was reserved for the nourishment of the priests (see 2:3, 10; 7:6, 31-34; 24:8-9; Num 18:12-13, 15, 26, for a description of the sacrifices and the priestly portion). Even if a priest is disqualified from taking part in the sacrificial *ritual, due to physical defect, he still has the right to eat from this divine meal, for he is still a priest. The sharing of the sacrificial repast by the deity and attending priests is also found in Egyptian and Mesopotamian texts, creating a special bond between servitor and deity. See comments on 1:1-2 and 3:6-11.

22:3-9. prohibiting priests with uncleanness. The altar and those who officiated at it were required to maintain strict *purity and cleanliness. This was the case among the Israelites as well as other peoples of the ancient Near East. Egyptian priests were required to undergo lengthy purification rites before approaching the altar. One *Hittite text contains a long list of instructions on maintaining the ritual *purity of priest and temple as well as the means to cleanse them in case of contamination, which is very similar to that found in chapter 22. Any source of contamination (improper or defective sacrifice or a defiled person or priest) would defile them and require lengthy purification rites before they could once again fulfill their function. The list in 22:4-5 provides a guide to persons who must be kept away from the sacred precincts and the priests, including those who have come in contact with the dead or an unclean animal or person or have eaten unclean food. *Hittite law, which prohibits persons who have had sexual relations with a horse or mule from becoming priests, provides another type of uncleanness which is not commensurate with serving as a priest.

22:8. carcasses. All animals found dead were unclean, so only those that had been ritually slaughtered with the blood properly drained were available for the priests.

22:10-16. eligibility for priestly portions. There are foods which are only to be consumed by the god(s) and their priests. A graphic example of this is found in the oath of a *Hittite prince, "Prayers of Kantuzilis," which certifies that he has never eaten "that which is holy to my god." At least in the Israelite law, the portion set aside for the priest may also be shared with members of his household, although not with guests or hired workers. The restrictions are based on the fact that this is sacred food, and it must not be given to persons outside his extended family (including his slaves). Even daughters who marry outside the priestly community are prohibited from eating this food. There is provision for her return to her father's household after the death of her husband, and in that case she will once again be allowed to eat from the sacrificial offering.

22:17-28. classes of unacceptable sacrifices. Just as the altar and the priests must be without defect and ritually pure, so too must the items brought for sacrifice. However, there are categories of acceptable offerings based on the type of sacrifice. For instance, when an animal is presented as a freewill offering or to fulfill a vow, it must be male and without defect. No beast which is blind, injured or maimed or which has skin disorders (warts or sores) will be accepted. But for lesser freewill offerings, a cow or sheep which is deformed or stunted will be accepted, although not one whose testicles are damaged. Similarly, in *Hittite *ritual, dogs, which were normally considered unclean, could be sacrificed to the gods of the underworld.

22:28. prohibition concerning slaughter of mother and young. The regulation that a mother and her young should not be offered the same day provided some protection to those with just a few animals who might otherwise have found themselves with ritual requirements that would decimate their small herd. There is nothing known of foreign *cultic practice that this would combat, though some have defended the alternative that the regulation had humanitarian concerns.

23:1-44
Religious Calendar

23:1-44. Israel's religious calendar. Versions of Israel's festal calendar are found in Exodus 23:12-19; 34:18-26; Leviticus 23; Deuteronomy 16:1-17; and Numbers 28—29. Each has its own characteristics and emphases. In Leviticus a list of the sacrifices required throughout the year is intertwined with the festivals of sabbath, Passover, the Feast of Unleavened Bread, the Feast of Weeks, the Feast of Trumpets, the Day of Atonement and the Feast of Tabernacles. These feasts mark the various stages in the agricultural year, celebrate harvests and give both credit and a sacrificial portion back to God, who has provided their bounty. Several also became related to historical events. Although the sabbath is not technically a feast day, it is appended here to mark its importance, and it provides a sense of how the ancients calculated time. Much of the rest of the ancient Near East had calendars more cognizant of the sun and moon, since these were manifestations of principal deities. While Israel's calendar did not neglect lunar and solar cycles, less attention was paid to equinoxes and solstices (sometimes viewed as times of conflict between sun and moon gods). Since the agricultural seasons ultimately link to the solar cycles, the lunar month/year system used throughout the ancient Near East had to be periodically adjusted to the solar cycle. This was done by adding a thirteenth month a few days in length when priests determined that an adjustment was called for.

23:3. sacred assembly on the sabbath. Sacred assemblies or proclamations were an important part of most religious practice in the ancient world. They refer to local or national gatherings for public, corporate worship. The people were summoned together away from their occupational work. Aside from performance of corporate *rituals, it is unclear what took place at these gatherings. In later times they were used for public readings, but evidence for this on all such occasions in the early periods is lacking (see Deut 31:10-13). This passage is the only reference to these gatherings in association with the sabbath.

23:5. Passover. This celebration refers to the Passover sacrifice commemorating the departure from Egypt (detailed in Ex 12—13). It is to begin at twilight on the fourteenth day of the first month (March-April). Since the sacrifice is to be a year-old lamb, some speculate that the origin of this event is found among the pastoral nomadic groups of the land and was at this time appended to the agriculturally based Feast of Unleavened Bread. Eventually, Passover became a pilgrimage festival when worship was centralized in Jerusalem, but it returned to home celebration after the destruction of the temple in A.D. 70.

23:6-8. Feast of Unleavened Bread. The Feast of Unleavened Bread signals the beginning of the barley harvest (March-April). Unleavened bread was made from the newly harvested grain without adding yeast and was celebrated as the first sign of coming harvests that year. The seven days of celebration and burnt offering are enclosed by days at the beginning and the end when no work is allowed (see comment on Ex 12:14-20).

23:10-14. wave offering for harvest. As a part of the harvest festival, the "first fruits" are brought to the priest. He in turn waves the sheaf of grain or elevates it before the altar of the Lord. This gesture physically draws God's attention to the sacrifice and signifies that all gifts and sacrificial items derive from and belong to God. It also releases the remainder of the harvest for the people's use (see comment on 7:28-38).

23:12-13. burnt, grain and drink offering. The burnt offering of the year-old lamb, a quantity twice the usual amount of grain, and a libation of wine constituted the three major products of Israel (sometimes with olive oil replacing or supplementing wine—see 2:1; Num 15:4-7). By combining them, the fertility provided by God will be directed toward all of their efforts in animal husbandry and farming. The pleasing odor draws *Yahweh's attention to the sacrifice (see Noah's sacrifice in Gen 8:20-21) and marks it as the properly prescribed thanksgiving *ritual—not the feeding of a god as in Mesopotamian and Egyptian religions.

23:15-22. Feast of Weeks. This second of the three major harvest festivals comes seven weeks after the harvest of the early grain (Ex 34:22; Deut 16:9-12) and is also known as the Feast of Harvest or Pentecost (Ex 23:16). In the agricultural cycle it marks the end of the wheat harvest season, and by tradition it is tied to the giving of the law on Mount Sinai. It is also associated with *covenant renewal and pilgrimage. Celebration includes the bringing of a "wave offering" of two loaves of bread, animal sacrifices (seven year-old lambs, one bull and two rams) and a drink offering in thanksgiving for a good harvest. A goat is also to be sacrificed as a sin offering for the people.

23:16-20. offerings. The Feast of Weeks requires a variety of offerings from the people. The "new grain" offering is distinct from the regular grain offering (see 2:13). The two loaves are made with yeast, but they will not actually be taken up on the altar (see regulations in 7:13). The animals that serve as burnt offerings (seven year-old lambs, a young bull and two rams) demonstrate the mixed character of the Israelite economy. The reason for the inclusion of a sin offering of a goat is unclear beyond the idea that the people must be restored to *cultic *purity prior to consuming their harvest.

23:23-25. Feast of Trumpets. The first day of the seventh month (the most sacred month in the Israelite calendar) was to be marked with the blowing of ram's horn (shofar), commemorating the *covenantal agreement and gifts of God to the people. No work is allowed, and burnt offerings are presented (see Num 29:2-6 for items sacrificed). The festival would continue until the tenth day of the month when the Day of Atonement would be observed (see 16:29-34 for details). In later times the Feast of Trumpets would become the New Year's festival, but that occurred in late postexilic times.

23:26-32. Day of Atonement. For information on the Day of Atonement, see the comments on chapter 16.

23:33-43. Feast of Tabernacles. The final harvest of the year occurred in the autumn prior to the onset of the rainy season and marked the beginning of a new agricultural year (fifteenth day of the seventh month). At this time the last of the ripening grain and fruits were gathered and stored. The seven-day event was also known as the Feast of Ingathering (Ex 23:16) and was symbolized by the construction of booths decorated with greenery for the harvesters. The festival was tied into Israelite tradition as a commemoration of the wilderness wanderings. It was also the occasion for the dedication of Solomon's temple in Jerusalem (1 Kings 8:65).

23:40. fruit, leaves and branches. To represent the abundance and lushness of the land, Israelites were instructed to celebrate, decorating their booths with fruit (citron) as well as leaves and branches from willow and palm trees. The festal occasion probably included dancing and processions carrying bundles of the leafy branches. In this way, the people acknowledge the abundance provided by God and communally celebrate the visible fulfillment of the *covenant.

23:42-43. live in booths. As a way of commemorating their life in the wilderness, the Israelites are told to construct booths and live in them during the seven days of the Feast of Tabernacles. The more practical application of these temporary shelters would be to serve as housing for workers who would protect the harvest until its distribution after the festival.

24:1-9
Maintaining the Holy Place

24:2-4. oil lamps. Only the highest quality olive oil was to be used in the sacred oil lamps that illuminated the sacred precincts of the tabernacle. They were placed on golden lampstands (see Ex 25:31-39), which stood just outside the curtain of the testimony in the tent of meeting (see Ex 27:20-21). They were to burn from evening until morning, and Aaron and his descendants were given a sacred trust to keep them lit for all time to come. Like many of the *cultic items associated with the tent of meeting, the oil lamps symbolized the presence and protection of *Yahweh as well as the perpetual service of the priests.

24:4. significance of the menorah. The familiar image of the menorah, with its six branches and center lamp, comes from the description in Exodus 25:31-40 and may be symbolic of the tree of life in the Garden of Eden. However, the description of the lampstand in 24:4 only includes the fact that it is made of gold. The number of lamps is also not specified here.

24:5-9. setting out of the bread and incense. The twelve loaves of the bread of the Presence (Ex 25:23-30) represented the twelve tribes of Israel. These loaves were consumed by the priests every sabbath, and new loaves were put in their place. The burning of frankincense provided the "sacrificial aroma," substituted for burning the flour on the altar.

Because the loaves were sacred, they were reserved for the priests (although see 1 Sam 21:4-6).

24:10-23
The Case of the Blasphemer

24:10-16. nature of blasphemy. The name of God is holy. Just as the people are warned not to misuse the name of God (Ex 20:7), to pronounce a curse using God's name without authorization or to curse God by name (Ex 22:28) is considered blasphemy. This is a capital offense, punishable by stoning. The *Assyrian texts condemn blasphemers to having their tongues cut out and to being skinned alive.

24:14-16. stoning as means of execution. Stoning is a communal form of execution and the most commonly mentioned form of execution in the Bible. It is used to punish crimes against the entire community (apostasy in 20:2; sorcery in 20:27), and it requires all those persons who have been offended to participate. Because it cannot be determined whose individual stone caused the death of the condemned, no one person need bear the guilt for the death. Mesopotamian texts do not mention stoning, but employ drowning, impalement, beheading and burning as forms of execution.

24:17-22. lex talionis. The legal concept of equal retribution or "an eye for an eye," is found in biblical (Ex 21:23-25; Deut 19:21) and Mesopotamian law codes. It has variations in *Hammurabi's code (eighteenth-century B.C. *Babylonia) based on the social status (nobility, citizen, slave) of the accused and the person harmed. It is possible that a price was set to redeem a life in capital cases or to replace the necessity of inflicting matching harm (broken arm, gouged eye, etc.). The basis for such laws was to insure legal restitution and thereby avoid the culturally disruptive necessity of seeking private revenge. Ideally, when an injury is done to another person, the way to provide true justice is to cause an equal injury to the culprit. Although this may seem extreme, it in fact limits the punishment that can be inflicted on the person accused of the injury.

25:1-55
Sabbatical Year and Jubilee

25:2-7. sabbatical rest for land. This set of laws requiring that the land lie fallow every seventh year parallels that found in Exodus 23:10-11. However only here is the term *sabbatical* applied to the seventh year. The benefit derived from resting the land is to retard the rate of salinization (sodium content in the soil) caused by irrigation. Large areas in Mesopotamia were actually left abandoned due to exhaustion of the soil and a disastrously high salt content. During the seventh year no cultivation of the soil is allowed. *Ugaritic texts likewise feature seven-year agricultural cycles, and some would contend that a fallow-year concept is also included. However, all of the people, as well as hired laborers and the farm animals, are allowed to eat the produce of the land that grows on its own. Such a policy may actually have been enforced on portions of each field every year, so that eventually it was all allowed to rest.

25:8-55. Jubilee year. Every fiftieth year (seven sabbaths of years plus one year) was marked by a general release from debt, servitude and a return of all land that had been mortgaged or sold to the rightful owner. Such concerns for the perpetual ownership of the land are also evident in *Ugaritic real estate documents. Declarations that returned land to its original owners and freed debt slaves were periodically made among the *Hittites and in Mesopotamia (often in the first year of a new king's reign) and are attested in proclamations by early kings such as Uruinimgina and Ammisaduqa. At the heart of the Israelite laws is the idea of the inalienable right of the people to their land. The land could be used to redeem a debt but must be released at the Jubilee in much the same way that debt slaves were to be released in the seventh year of their servitude (Ex 23:10-11; Deut 15:1-11). This could, of course, serve as the basis for the returned exiles' claim to their former lands, but this does not exclude the practice from previous historical periods.

25:23. God as owner of land compared to temple economy. All of the land occupied by the Israelites was the property of *Yahweh. It was granted to them as tenants, and as such they could not sell it outright to anyone. In the Jubilee year (every fiftieth year), all land that had been consigned for payment of debts was to be returned to its owners. If a man died, it was the responsibility of his nearest kin to redeem the land so that it would remain in the family (25:24-25; Jer 32:6-15). This concept is similar to that found in Egypt, where the "divine" Pharaoh owned the land and granted it to his subjects. However, it stands in contrast with the temple economy that existed in Mesopotamia. There land was owned by individual citizens, the king and the temples of the various gods. The laws of *Hammurabi speak of the king's land grants, which could revert to him upon the death of the vassal. The land owned by the temples was granted to tenants, who paid a portion of their harvest for the right to work the land. This patchwork of ownership, while depending in many cases on tenants who could not sell the land, did not provide the sense of unity implied in the biblical concept.

25:24-25. kinsman redeemer. Since *Yahweh has granted the land to the Israelites as tenants, they cannot sell it,

and if they mortgage a portion of it to pay debts, it is the obligation of their kinsman to "redeem" the land by paying off the mortgage. This demonstrates both the sense of obligation and the solidarity that are the hallmarks of ancient Israel's communally based society. Evidence of this legislation's being put into practice is found in Jeremiah's redeeming of his kinsman's land during the siege of Jerusalem (Jer 32:6-15) and in the legal background to Ruth 4:1-12. In this way the land remained within the extended family as a sign of their membership in the *covenantal community. The importance of this inalienable right to land can be seen in Naboth's refusal to relinquish the "inheritance of my fathers" when King Ahab offers to buy his vineyard (1 Kings 21:2-3). In Mesopotamia (especially the earlier periods) land was often privately owned by families rather than individuals.

25:29-31. difference between houses in walled cities and houses in villages. There is a different legal classification for dwellings in walled towns and those in unwalled villages. In the towns, inhabited by Levites, artisans and government officials, a house could only be redeemed from its buyer within one year. After that the sale was final. Similarly, the Law of *Eshnunna allows a debtor who has sold his house first claim to repurchase it when it comes up for sale again. However, Israelite village dwellings (literally, "encampments") adjacent to fields and pasture lands fell within the same legal category as arable land and could not be sold in perpetuity and were to be released in the Jubilee year. Such legislation is based on the different social conditions in these two settings and indicates an awareness that property in urban centers produced no harvest. It merely provided shelter and business space.

25:38. prohibition against taking inter-

est. Like the other prohibitions against charging interest on loans to fellow Israelites (Ex 22:25; Deut 23:19, see comments there), this legislation is designed to help a person to escape his insolvent condition and to prevent him from falling into debt servitude due to default on a loan. This applies to loans of money as well as grain, which would ordinarily be paid back at the end of the harvest. These laws are also a way to allow the debtor to retain a measure of personal dignity and honor by being treated on a level higher than a slave or a foreigner (see Deut 23:20). Both the laws of *Eshnunna and *Hammurabi's code contain set rates of interest on loans (20 percent to 33.3 percent was not uncommon and was considered fair). However, it was understood that "acts of god," such as a flood, require compassion on the debtor and a cancellation of interest payments.

25:39-55. slavery in Israel. Ancient Israel considered permanent slavery the most inhumane condition possible. The laws dealing with slavery reflect an understanding of the reasons for poverty and try to deal with its victims nonviolently. They also do not account for the principal cause of slavery in Mesopotamia—warfare. One sign of Israelite concern may be seen in the practice of allowing a household to pledge the work of its members as collateral when it borrowed goods or services from another household. To avoid confiscation of their land and children, the members of a household in default would work off their debt one day at a time. As a state, Israel tried to prevent debt from accumulating to the point where slavery was the only option. Thus the laws against charging interest on loans worked in most cases to aid the poor (Ex 22:24; Deut 23:19-20; Lev 25:35-37; Ezek 18:3). In these cases a household could become destitute and at the insistence of its creditors sell members of the house-

hold into slavery to pay debts (2 Kings 4:1; Neh 5:1-5). Slavery in this case is defined as temporary debt slavery, since the law restricts the number of years a man may be held to six (Ex 21:2-11; Deut 15:12-18). Regulations also restrict the sale or the enslavement of Israelites by other Israelites (Lev 25:35-42). In this case the Israelite who is in financial difficulties would be reduced to the status of a hired hand or indentured servant rather than a slave, even if his owner is a non-Israelite (25:47-55). Verse 48 refers to the redemption of slaves, a practice also attested in a number of Mesopotamian sources.

26:1-46
Obedience and Disobedience

26:1. sacred stone. Like idols (19:4), sacred standing stones are also prohibited as foreign *cult objects. They may have been huge monoliths representing a god or a set of pillars arranged around an altar or shrine. Some of those found in excavations at Gezer and Hazor were decorated with carvings such as raised hands or symbols associated with a particular deity.

26:1. nature and forms of idols. Idols came in a variety of shapes and sizes in the ancient Near East. They were carved from stone and wood and were cast in molds using gold, silver and bronze (see Is 40:19-20). Basically human in appearance (except those from Egypt, which combined human and animal characteristics), they had distinctive, even formalized, poises, clothing and hairstyles. The image was not the deity, but the deity was thought to inhabit the image and manifest its presence and will through the image. Archaeologists have found very few life-sized images that the texts describe, but there are renderings of them that allow accurate knowledge of details.

26:3-45. blessings and curses in treaty

formulae. It is typical of ancient Near Eastern legal codes and treaties to append a section of divine blessings and curses (see Deut 28; Code of *Hammurabi [eighteenth century B.C.]; Esarhaddon Treaty [680-669 B.C.]; thirteenth-century B.C. treaty between Rameses II of Egypt and *Hittite king Hattusilis III). Characteristically, the curses far outweigh the blessings and, as in this case, are generally arranged in order of increasing severity. The principle behind these statements is the need to insure compliance with law or with treaties by bringing in divine goodwill and sanction. In this way the parties will feel more obligated than if they were to simply depend on the conscientiousness of their people or neighbors.

26:4-5. importance of fertility. Without continuous yield from the land, the people could not survive. Thus fertility, in the form of regular rainfall and abundant harvest from fields and vines, was a constant concern. As a result many of the gods of the ancient Near East were concerned with rain and storm, *fertility and the growing seasons. The inclusion of fertility in the set of blessings here is a reiteration of *Yahweh's *covenant promise to give the people land and children (i.e., a country of their own and fertility to insure life to each successive generation).

26:5. agricultural calendar. As noted in the Gezer calendar, a tenth-century B.C. schoolboy exercise on a fragment of limestone, the Israelite year was divided into agricultural seasons. Thus the "rain in season" would come in the fall (October-November) to moisten the newly planted fields and in early spring (March-April) to complete the ripening process before harvest (Deut 11:14).

26:8. five will chase a hundred. A sign of the promised blessing of peace is that *Yahweh, the "Divine Warrior," will fight for them and give them the victory over their enemies, no matter how great the odds against them. Thus five can rout a hundred. This underdog-turned-conqueror theme is also found in Deuteronomy 32:30, Joshua 23:10 and Isaiah 30:17. Similar assurance of the aid of a "Divine Warrior" is found in the Moabite inscription of King Mesha (c. 830 B.C.).

26:13. bars of the yoke. Yokes, usually made of wood, consisted of a bar across the nape of the animals' necks. The bar had pegs placed down through it on either side of each animal's head. The pegs were then tied together under the chin. As slaves in Egypt, the people were burdened with work like oxen bound to a yoke (see Jer 28:10-14). God has broken this yoke of bondage, freeing them of their heavy burdens and allowing them to stand upright like free men and women. Their freedom and their human dignity have thus been restored.

26:16. nature of the illnesses. The diseases promised in this curse include a "wasting disease," a fever, an illness that damages the sufferer's eyesight and causes loss of appetite. These may all be explained by the "terror"—depression and anxiety caused by God's wrath and the incursions of their enemies. Although there have been clinical diagnostic texts discovered from Mesopotamia, it is impossible to attach a specific diagnosis to the diseases mentioned here.

26:19. iron sky, bronze ground. The sense of this metaphoric curse is also found in the execration (curse) of Deuteronomy 28 and in the Treaty of Esarhaddon (seventh century B.C.). It implies that the land itself will turn against the people, becoming hard as bronze because the iron gates of heaven will have closed and no rain will fall on it.

26:26. ten women baking with one oven. The picture of so little grain that numerous women can all bake their bread in the same oven is also found on the *Aramaic statue found at Tell Fekherye, where one hundred women cannot fill up an oven with their bread.

26:29. cannibalism in ancient Near East. Only ultimate desperation and immanent starvation would cause the people of the ancient Near East to resort to cannibalism (see 2 Kings 6:24-30). It is included as part of the curses section here and in Deuteronomy 28:53-57 and in the *Assyrian treaties of the seventh century B.C. to demonstrate just how horrible God's punishment will be on the disobedient.

27:1-34
Vows

27:2-13. nature of vows. Information concerning vows can be found in most of the cultures of the ancient Near East, including *Hittite, *Ugaritic, Mesopotamian and, less often, Egyptian. Vows are voluntary agreements made with deity. In this case the vow involves pledging the value of a person dedicated to temple service (see 1 Sam 1:11). This may relate back to the redemption of the firstborn in Exodus 13:13; 34:20 and Numbers 18:15-16, but it does not involve human sacrifice. The table of equivalences defines the value of the person to be redeemed based on gender, age and ability to work. In this way the temple received sufficient funds to make needed repairs and purchase equipment (see 2 Kings 12:5-6). As is the case in all vows, God is invoked (note the seriousness of this act in Ex 20:7), and both parties are expected to act according to the terms of the vow. The vows would typically be conditional and accompany a petition made to deity. The items that are given to redeem the person become sacred and cannot be redeemed themselves unless, by their nature, they are unacceptable for dedication (i.e., unclean or unfit). The huge amounts involved (up to fifty shekels) make it unlikely this vow was common.

27:2-8. dedication of persons. The concept of dedicating a person to temple service may be based on the idea that a family must sacrifice (i.e., give up their labor) to God's service. Thus Samuel was dedicated to the shrine at Shiloh by Hannah prior to his birth (1 Sam 1:11). However, in the labor-poor region of Israel, this would have been impractical. Thus a system was created whereby the obligation was fulfilled by redemption of the person through a set table of equivalencies based on age, gender, ability to work and ability to pay. This might be compared to the laws of bodily injury in the *Ur-Nammu code, the Laws of *Eshnunna and the laws of *Hammurabi, which set a specific monetary fine based on the type of injury, age, social status and gender of the victim.

27:3-8. relative values. The set of relative values established for redemption of persons dedicated to temple service is based on four criteria: age, gender, ability to work and ability to pay. The assumption is that the value of the labor service of an adult male between age twenty and sixty is fifty silver shekels. Even though they may serve longer than an adult, the value set for children is only a fraction of this amount (based on gender). However, for persons over sixty, the amount, understandably, is less than for those of standard working age. The amount set for the poor is based on a priest's determination of their ability to pay. Although these amounts may reflect the value of slaves, this amount fluctuates too much over time to be a reliable indicator.

27:3-7. amounts of money. The amounts of money specified for redemption of persons dedicated to temple service are all in silver. The largest, fifty shekels, based on the silver content of twenty gerahs/shekels (27:25), was many times the annual wage for a laborer. This makes it unlikely that many persons would have made this type of vow, knowing it must be paid once the vow is made. They simply could not have paid this sum and therefore the redemption of a dedicated person may have been a rare occasion.

27:3. sanctuary shekel. The price in silver to be paid was based on the "standard" sanctuary shekel (11-13 grams), as opposed to the royal (2 Sam 14:26) and common shekel weights, which were generally in the ten-gram range.

27:9-13. redeeming animals. If a person wished to use an animal as payment of the vow, then the determination of its value and its acceptability would be based on priestly inspection for blemish or other imperfection, and on whether the animal was clean (i.e., acceptable for sacrifice). If an animal was ceremonially unclean, it could still be offered, but it in turn would be redeemed with an extra payment of one-fifth of its value. If it was the intent of the donor to give the animal up for sacrifice, it could not under any circumstances be redeemed (see 22:21-25). Such care over the ritual *purity of sacrificial animals was also common in *Hittite and Mesopotamian rituals.

27:14-25. dedication of house or land. The consecration of a dwelling or of fields, whether owned by a person or held as collateral for a debt, may be made, but they must be inspected and valued by the priest. This allows for a set amount should the owner wish to redeem them, plus one-fifth of their value. It also could involve a purification *ritual of the property, as is also evident in *Hittite texts. The basis for this practice might involve a vow to make special provision, beyond normal sacrifices or tithes, for God's sanctuary or priesthood, and it may result from the lack of an heir. Thus the produce of land or the use of the house (for storage or rents) would belong to God. The Year of Jubilee is also a factor which must be taken into

account in this valuation and assignment of property. Only land which was owned and not redeemed may ultimately become the permanent property of the priests (27:20-21).

27:21. priest property. We know from *Hittite, Egyptian and Mesopotamian texts that temple communities owned land and benefited from its produce. Although the practice of deeding over property to the temple is not mentioned outside the Bible, it seems likely that the priestly community throughout the ancient Near East could acquire ownership of land that was consecrated to the use of the god(s). This is made possible if the owner of the land fails to redeem it. At that point, the land becomes "holy" and like sacrificial animals may not be redeemed in the future. Thus in the Israelite Jubilee year celebration, instead of the land reverting to its original owner, it becomes the permanent property of the priests.

27:25. twenty gerahs to the shekel. The sanctuary shekel (weighing 11-13 grams) was to have a silver content of twenty gerahs (0.571 grams or 8.71 grains). This established the weight as acceptable payment for dedicated persons or property.

27:29. person dedicated to destruction. There are some acts which cannot be expiated through sacrifice or redemption. Persons who have been condemned for false worship (Ex 22:19) or for violating the ban (Josh 7:13-26) or for murder (Num 35:31-34) or willful violations of ritual *purity (as in the *Hittite texts) may not be redeemed. In some cases their families and their property were also destroyed in a general purging of evil. They have committed acts that violate God's holiness and contaminate the community. Therefore their sentence must be carried out without exception. Only in this way can God's name be restored to its proper sanctity and the people be cleansed of their *impurity.

27:31-33. redeeming the tithe. Since all of the produce of the land (grain and fruit) belongs to God, a tithe must be made on it (Deut 14:22-26). Those items set aside for the tithe could not be considered part of the "freewill" offerings, since the tithe is considered the unrestricted property of *Yahweh. The amount of the tithe may be redeemed by a payment of its value plus one-fifth of that value. Note that this payment can be made only for farm produce (compare Num 18:14-19). Animals not only cannot be redeemed, but any attempt to do so results in the loss of both the animal originally chosen for the tithe and the one substituted.

NUMBERS

Introduction

T he book of Numbers contains instructions for travel and setting up the camp, as well as records of the events that took place during the nearly forty years the Israelites spent in the wilderness. It also includes a number of ritual and legal passages. Many of the sources that contribute to an understanding of the books of Exodus and Leviticus also provide background for the book of Numbers. In addition, itineraries from Egyptian sources can help in locating various places listed in the Israelites' travels. These itineraries come from a number of different sources, including the *Execration Texts (where the names of certain cities were written on bowls and then shattered in connection with cursing rituals; Twelfth Dynasty, *Middle Bronze period) and the topographical lists carved on the walls of temples such as those at Karnak and Medinet Habu (*Late Bronze period). They preserve maps in a list form as they name each of the cities that would be encountered traveling along certain routes. It is interesting that some biblical sites, which archaeologists have considered suspect because no remains from a given period have been found there, are attested in the Egyptian itineraries for the same period.

Numbers, like several of the other books of the Pentateuch, contains information concerning Israel's ritual calendar. Information about feast days and ritual calendars is abundant in the ancient Near East because calendars were generally regulated by the priesthood. Nevertheless, it is difficult to ferret out many of the critical details of observances and especially to discover what is behind the formation of the traditions that are institutionalized in these calendars. It is a treacherous path that seeks to identify the links between the festivals of differing cultures even though there may be evidence of many areas of cultural exchange or dependence.

1:1-46
Census

1:1. Desert of Sinai. "Desert of Sinai" refers to the wilderness area surrounding the mountain where the Israelites were camped (see comment on Ex 19:1-2).

1:1. chronology. By comparing this to Exodus 40:17 it can be seen that the tabernacle has now been set up for one month and the people have been camped at Sinai for nearly a year.

1:2. purpose of census. Censuses in the ancient world were used as a means of conscripting men for either military service or government building projects. They also were often accompanied or even motivated by the collection of a head tax. This census is for conscription into the army, but it cannot easily be separated from the one in Exodus 30:11-16 (see comment) where a temple tax is collected.

1:46. size of the population. For some of the problems see the comment on Exodus 12:37.

1:47—2:34
The Arrangement of the Camp

1:52. grouping of the tribes. The camp of the priests and Levites surrounded the sanctuary, while the other tribal camps formed an outer rectangle with three camps on each side. Rectangular military encampments were the norm in Egyptian practice of this time and are portrayed in ninth-century *Assyrian art with the king protected in the center. Judah leads the prominent eastern camp (the tabernacle entrance faced east) as the leader among the tribes. Reuben, the tribe of the eldest son, leads the southern group, while Dan, the tribe of the eldest of the *concubines' sons, leads the northern group. The tribes from Rachel's sons are on the west side, led by Ephraim, the son of Joseph with firstborn rights.

1:52. standards. In Egypt each army division was named after a deity, and the standard for that division bore a representation of that deity. It would therefore be reasonable to assume that the standard of each tribe displayed a symbol of the tribe. On the other hand, some interpreters have interpreted this word to refer to a military unit rather than a standard.

3:1—4:49
The Levite Clans

3:7-10. Levites as sanctuary guards. Encamped around the sanctuary and instructed to put to death any trespasser, the Levites restricted the access to the tabernacle. Ancient sanctuaries were not public places for gathering but were the divine residences. The priests are seen as guards in *Hittite texts as well as in texts from *Mari on the upper Euphrates. In *Babylonian beliefs there were also demons or protective spirits who guarded temple entrances.

3:12-13. Levites in the place of the firstborn. In the ancient world many cultures featured an ancestor *cult in which libations were poured out on behalf of the dead ancestors, whose spirits would then offer protection and help to those still living. In *Babylon the disembodied spirit (*utukki*) or the ghost (*etemmu*) could become very dangerous if not cared for and often were the objects of incantations. Care for the dead would begin with proper burial and would continue with ongoing gifts and honor of the memory and name of the deceased. The firstborn was responsible for maintaining this ancestor worship and therefore inherited the family gods (often images of deceased ancestors). While ancestor worship or *funerary cult were not approved for Israelites, the indictments of the prophets make it clear that it was one of the deviant practices of the common people. The transfer of the status of the firstborn to the Levites therefore implies that rather than a family-level ancestor worship maintained by the firstborn, Israel would have a national-level religious practice maintained and regulated by the Levites (see also the comments at Ex 13:1-3; Deut 14:1-2; 26:14).

3:47-51. redemption money. The concept of ransom or redemption money occurs both in *Akkadian (Babylonian) and *Ugaritic (Canaanite) texts, though not in this same function. The nation here bought back its first-born from God by "trading" the Levites, and the remainder of the firstborn had to be bought back with money according to the value set in 27:6. Normally about two and a half shekels would weigh about one ounce, although there are also references to a "heavy shekel," which may have weighed more. The sanctuary weight listed here may refer to a shekel which has a more standard value and weight than the standard "marketplace" shekel. Five shekels would have represented about half a year's wages.

4:6. hide of sea cows. Both sea cows (a herbivorous mammal, the dugong) and dolphins are found in the Red Sea, and their hides could have been tanned and used for decoration. These creatures had been hunted for their hides along the Arabian Gulf for millennia. Alternatively, this word may be compared to an *Akkadian word which refers to a semiprecious yellow or orange stone, and thus to the color of dye used rather than to an animal.

4:6. blue cloth. This has more recently been interpreted as a blue-purple or violet color. The dye for this color was one of the major exports of Phoenicia, where it was extracted from the murex snail (*Murex trunculus*), which inhabited shallow coastal waters of the Mediterranean. An ancient refinery has also been found at Dor along the northern coast of Israel. One chemist estimated that a quarter of a million snails would be needed to produce one ounce of pure dye. This dye was used in the manufacture of the most sacred objects such as the veil of the Holy of Holies and the high priestly garments.

4:46-48. number of the Levites. Here the number of Levite men aged thirty to fifty is 8,580, while in 3:30 the total number of males over a month old was 22,000. This would imply that there were 13420 males younger than thirty and older than fifty. This is a reasonable distribution and argues that the number should be understood at face value.

5:1-4
Persons Sent Outside the Camp

5:2. infectious skin diseases. For the nature of these diseases see comment on Leviticus 13:2.

5:2. discharges. For discussion of the various classes of discharges, see the comments on Leviticus 15.

5:2. ceremonial uncleanness. Not all uncleanness was avoidable, and the cause of uncleanness was often something that would in no way be considered sinful. There are several categories of uncleanness that could not be easily avoided, including sexual impurities, disease-related impurities and the uncleanness that came from contact with corpse or carcass. Though it was a matter of etiquette rather than ethics, the sacred compass needed to be protected from that which was inappropriate. Additionally it was a common belief that demons inhabited menstrual blood. That the uncleanness from childbirth should be seen as similar to monthly uncleanness is common in ancient cultures, including Egypt, *Babylonia and Persia.

5:3. living outside the camp. Though the camp did not need to maintain the same level of *purity as the temple compound, there were restrictions. This restriction is also found in *Babylonian literature for victims of skin diseases forced to live in isolation. It is likely that they would have lived in the vicinity of the tombs.

5:5-10
Restitution in Fraud Cases

5:6-7. nature of the legislation. This section concerns a case where someone has used a formal oath to defraud someone else in court and later feels guilty about having done so. Giving restitution plus 20 percent to the defrauded individual, his next of kin or to the priest, plus the appropriate reparation offering, is commanded. In *Hammurabi's laws one-sixth is typically added to restitution amounts in the form of interest payments.

5:11-31
The Case of the Jealous Husband

5:14. basis for legal action. The only basis for this action is the jealousy of the woman's husband. The word used to describe the nature of the crime in verse 12 usually refers to a breach of faith or an act of sacrilege (see the comment on Lev 5:14-16). It is therefore likely that the woman has previously been asked to swear an oath to her innocence and is now being accused of swearing falsely. Such an accusation may come about if the woman is now found to be pregnant and the husband contends that the child is not his.

5:15. the husband's actions. It is unclear why the husband brings the particular offering that he does. Unlike the regular meal offering, it is barley (as offered by the poor) instead of wheat, and it omits the oil and incense as meal offerings associated with potential offenses do. Generally oil and incense were associated with celebration, and this was not a festive occasion.

5:16-17. the priest's actions. A text from *Mari (northwest Mesopotamia) speaks of a trial by ordeal where the gods are asked to drink water which contains dirt taken from the city gate. This bound the gods to their oath to protect the city. Here the ingredients are sacred (water from the laver, dirt from the sanctuary floor) and mixed with the inscribed curses that concern the woman's obligation to preserve the *purity of the sanctuary.

5:18. loosening the hair. This is elsewhere connected to mourning and may suggest that the woman is to adopt a posture of mourning until the Lord's verdict is clarified.

5:23-24. trial by ordeal in the ancient Near East. "Ordeal" describes a judicial situation in which the accused is placed in the hand of God using some mechanism, generally one that will put the accused in jeopardy. If the deity intervenes to protect the accused from harm, the verdict is innocent. Most trials by ordeal in the ancient Near East involved dangers such as water, fire or poison. The accused who is exposed to these threats is in effect being assumed guilty until the deity declares otherwise by action on her behalf. In contrast, the procedure in this text invokes neither magic nor danger but simply creates a situation for God to respond to. Thus the woman here is presumed innocent until circumstances (directed by the Lord) show otherwise. *Hammurabi's laws contain similar cases in which the woman undergoes a river ordeal to determine her guilt or innocence.

5:27. the negative potential results. Suggestions have ranged from a flooded uterus to false pregnancy to pelvic prolapse to atrophied genitalia. Whatever the actual physical manifestations might be, the text clearly indicates that the result is sterility. If the woman has been brought into this process because of pregnancy, it may be that the potion would be expected to induce a miscarriage in the case that the pregnancy came about through illicit behavior.

6:1-21
The Nazirite Vow

6:3. abstinence from drinks. There are a number of different words used to describe fermented drinks made from grapes used here. While some of the terms could at times refer to intoxicants made from other ingredients (e.g., grain), only those that can refer to grape products are used here. That suggests that only grape intoxicants are prohibited to the *Nazirite. It is not drunkenness that is the issue here, but grape drinks of any sort.

6:3-4. abstinence from grape products. Prohibition of grape products has suggested to some interpreters that a nomadic lifestyle is being elevated, but it is very difficult to see that as a biblical or priestly agenda. Alternatively one must notice that the grape is one of the principal, one could say characteristic, staples of Canaan and therefore symbolically connected to the issue of fertility (note that the spies bring back a huge cluster of grapes [13:24] as evidence of the fertility of the land). The use of raisins in raisin cakes for the *fertility *cult can be seen in Hosea 3:1.

6:5. significance of hair. There is a Phoenician inscription from the ninth century B.C. reporting the dedication of shaven hair by an individual in fulfillment of a vow made to the goddess *Astarte. It is of importance that in the biblical text there is no discussion of what should be done with the hair that is cut. It is neither dedicated as in the above inscription, nor is it deposited in the temple as in some cultures. The dedicated hair is uncut (v. 9), not cut. For men hair has symbolic value as a sign of manhood or virility (see 2 Sam 10:4). Women decorate their hair and groom it care-

fully as a sign of beauty. The prohibition against trimming the "sides of your head" or the "edges of your beard" uses the same terminology as in Leviticus 19:9-10, which deals with the harvesting of fields. In both cases an offering is involved—one to the poor and the other to God. *Hammurabi's code penalizes false witnesses by having half the person's hair cut off. The Middle Assyrian code allows a debt-slave's master to pull out his/her hair as punishment (see Neh 13:25). Both laws suggest that shame is attached to the loss of hair. In ancient thinking hair (along with blood) was one of the main representatives of a person's life essence. As such it was often an ingredient in sympathetic magic. This is evident, for instance, in the practice of sending along a lock of a presumed prophet's hair when his prophecies were sent to the king of *Mari. The hair would be used in divination to determine whether the prophet's message would be accepted as valid. (See Lev 19:27.)

6:6-7. corpse prohibition. Corpse contamination was one of the most common and unavoidable causes of ritual uncleanness (see comment on 19:11). Some have further speculated that ritual uncleanness from corpse contamination may also represent a statement against the always prevalent *cult of the dead (see comment on 3:1, Levites in the place of the first-born).

6:8. Nazirite background. It may be no coincidence that the three prohibited areas for the *Nazirite represent fertility (grape products), sympathetic magic (hair) and the *cult of the dead (corpse contamination). These are the three principal popular religious practices that *Yahweh worship sought to eliminate. It is difficult to reconstruct, however, why these elements were chosen, or what the original thinking behind the vow was.

6:9-12. ritual procedure in case of violation. Ritual violation of the vow required the purging of the altar but only included the least expensive offerings (pigeons). It was also necessary to offer a lamb for a reparation offering because the violation involved a breach of faith (see comment on Lev 5:14-16).

6:13-20. conclusion of the vow. A whole series of offerings (see the comments on the early chapters of Leviticus for more information on each) concludes the vow, followed by the cutting and burning of the hair. Most vows in the ancient Near East were conditional vows attached to some past or present entreaty (see comment on Lev 27), and there is no reason to assume that the *Nazirite vow is any different. It is not surprising, then, that the vow culminates in offertory gifts. What is unusual, against the background of ancient Near Eastern vows, is the ritualized period of abstinence that precedes the offerings.

6:22-27
The Priestly Blessing

6:24-26. ancient Near Eastern blessings. In the ancient world blessings and curses were believed to have a power all their own that would result in their fulfillment. This blessing is probably one that the priests were to give to someone leaving the sanctuary after participating in some *ritual. Two small silver scrolls (about one inch long) have been found in the area known as Keteph Hinnom in Jerusalem. They were *amulets in a burial cave from the sixth or seventh century B.C., and they contained this benediction. At present they represent the oldest example of any text of Scripture. The concept of the shining face of the deity resulting in mercy is found in Mesopotamian documents and inscriptions from as early as the twelfth century B.C. as well as in a letter from *Ugarit. Additionally a phrase invoking the gods

to grant watch-care and well-being is used regularly in *Ugaritic and *Akkadian salutations. Finally, the phrase "the Lord bless you and keep you" is also included in the words (Hebrew) painted on a large storage jar from the ninth century B.C. found at Kuntillet Ajrud in the northern Sinai.

7:1-89
Offerings for the Tabernacle

7:1. function of anointing sacred objects. Anointing is an act of dedication. It is unclear whether here the anointing is with oil or blood—the former is usually deemed more likely.

7:13. silver plate. The two silver objects named here are more bowl-shaped, the former almost twice the size of the latter and probably deeper. They weigh about three pounds and one and a half pounds respectively.

7:13. fine flour. The flour here was the grits or semolina left in the sieve after wheat was ground into flour. It is the same as was used for the grain offerings (see comment on Lev 2:1).

7:14. gold ladle. These ladles weighed about four ounces. The word translated "ladle" is simply the word for "hand." There are tongs found at *Amarna whose ends are shaped like hands, but the fact that these implements could be filled with incense suggests ladles rather than tongs. Though they were relatively small, the incense they held was valuable so even this small amount was a substantial gift, in addition to the value of the gold.

7:84-88. function of the offerings brought. The text does not speak of the animals actually being sacrificed, and the word translated "offerings" does not refer to sacrifices. The animals were dedicated for tabernacle use for particular offerings (as indicated in the lists), but they became part of the sanctuary livestock to be used as the need arose. In providing basic supplies for operation, this resembled a housewarming party.

8:1-4
The Lampstand

8:2. lampstand. The design of three branches on either side of a central axis is common in the *Late Bronze Age cultures of the Mediterranean. See comment on Exodus 25:31-40.

8:5-26
The Levites

8:7. shaving the body for purification. Egyptian priests were also required to shave their heads and bodies as part of their purification process. Razors were often bronze, either knife-shaped with rounded handles or blades with a thin handle attached perpendicular to the flat.

8:10. laying on of hands. This is the same procedure that the Israelites used when presenting a sacrifice (see comment below). It is symbolic of designating the Levites to serve on behalf of the Israelites.

8:11. Levites as a wave offering. The wave offering (better: elevation offering) is a rite of dedication (see comment on Lev 8:27).

8:12. Levites laying hands on the bulls. See comment on Leviticus 1:4.

8:12. making atonement for Levites. For the word here translated "atonement" as a purifying consequence of sacrifice, see comment on Lev 1:3-4. But there is no sacrifice being offered here, only sacrificial symbolism being used. The Levites do not perform purification rites on behalf of the Israelites—that is the task of the priests. Instead the Levites protect against divine wrath by providing a ransom. This is a common concept in *Babylonian and *Hittite appeasement *rituals.

9:1-14
The Passover

9:1. Desert of Sinai. This is the wilderness area around Mount Sinai (see comment on 1:1).

9:2. Passover. This is the first celebration of Passover since its inception a year earlier in Egypt. For the meaning of the Hebrew term see comment on Exodus 12:11. For further discussion about Passover see the comments on Exodus 12:1-23.

9:15-23
The Guidance of the Cloud

9:15. the function and nature of the cloud. Some have thought the pillar of cloud and fire could be best explained as the result of volcanic activity. An eruption on the Island of Thera (six hundred miles northwest) in 1628 B.C. brought an end to Minoan civilization, and it is possible that its effects could have been seen in the Delta. But the date is far too early (see "The Date of the Exodus," pp.96-97), and this theory would offer no explanation of the movements of the pillar, nor of the location described for it in the biblical account (they are moving southeast). The text does not suggest that the pillar was supernaturally generated, only that it was the means of supernatural guidance. For this reason some have suggested that it was the result of a brazier of some sort carried on a pole that would be used by the vanguard scouts. This was a method often used by caravans. On the other hand, the pillar is always portrayed as acting (coming down, moving) rather than being operated (no human is ever said to move it), so the vanguard theory is difficult to support. In the ancient world a bright or flaming aura surrounding deity is the norm. In Egyptian literature it is depicted as the winged sun disk accompanied by storm clouds. *Akkadian uses the term *melammu* to describe this visible representation of the glory of deity, which in turn is enshrouded in smoke or cloud. In Canaanite mythology it has been suggested the *melammu* concept is expressed by the word *anan,* the same Hebrew word here translated "cloud," but the occurrences are too few and obscure for confidence. In any case, the pillar here would then be one; smoke being visible in the daytime, while the inner flame it covered would glow through at night. (See Ex 13:21-22.)

10:1-10
The Trumpets

10:2. silver trumpets. As is obvious from the materials they are made of, these are not the ram's horn trumpets that are referred to in other contexts. Tubular flared trumpets were used in this period in military as well as ritual contexts. This is depicted on Egyptian reliefs as well as evidenced by actual instruments found, for example, in the tomb of King Tut (a silver trumpet nearly two feet long).

10:2. silver work. The techniques of silver mining were known as early as the mid-third millennium. A process called cupellation using a crucible was used to extract silver from lead and refine it through several stages of purification. In *Ur silversmith artisans were producing musical instruments as well as jewelry and other items in the third millennium.

10:3-7. trumpet signaling. In warfare signaling was done in various ways. Fire signals were common both along garrison lines as well as in the open field. Basic commands were at times communicated by upraised staff or javelin. Trumpet signals are attested in Egypt in the *Late Bronze Age (this time period) in both military and religious contexts. A preset code would include some combination of long and short blasts.

10:11-36
Leaving Sinai

10:11. chronology. At this point the Isra-

elites are still at Sinai having left Egypt only thirteen months earlier. In our calendar it would be early May.

10:12. itinerary. If the Wilderness of Sinai is in the southern section of the Sinai peninsula, as we have suggested, this is a march toward the northeast. The Wilderness of Paran includes Kadesh Barnea and is generally located in the northeast corner of the Sinai peninsula. Several of the sites they stop at on the way are mentioned at the end of chapter 11. The Israelites spend the bulk of their forty years of wandering in the Wilderness of Paran.

10:29. Hobab, son of Reuel. In Exodus 2 Moses' father-in-law was called Reuel, in Exodus 3 he is referred to as Jethro, and here he appears to be named Hobab (see Judg 4:11). The difficulty can be resolved once the ambiguity of the terminology is recognized. The term designating male in-laws is nonspecific. Referring to a male near-relative of the bride, the term could be used for her father, brother, or even grandfather. Most solutions take account of this. Perhaps Reuel is the grandfather head of the clan, Jethro is the father of Zipporah and technically the father-in-law of Moses, and Hobab is the brother-in-law of Moses, Jethro's son. Alternatively, Jethro and Hobab could both be brothers-in-law, and Reuel the father. (See Ex 3:1.)

11:1—12:16
A Rebellious and Quarrelsome People

11:3. Taberah. There is good reason to associate Taberah with Kibroth Hattaavah (v. 34), since there is no record of travel between these two accounts. Each name reflects an incident that occurred there. No firm identification of these sites is possible.

11:4. meat. The meat they are craving is not beef, lamb or venison. The Israelites had livestock with them but would have been reluctant to slaughter them and thus deplete their herds and flocks. Furthermore, these meats were not part of their normal diet but were eaten only on special occasions. Life by the river in Egypt had accustomed them to a regular diet of fish, however, and the next verse clarifies that this is the meat referred to.

11:5. diet in Egypt. Five types of produce are mentioned here as staples of the Israelite diet in Egypt. Several of them arc known from Egyptian texts and wall paintings. The melons are either watermelons or muskmelons.

11:7-9. manna. The bread from heaven was called manna in Exodus 16:31, where it is described. The fact that it came with the dew (Ex 16:4) suggests that God's miraculous provision used a natural process. The most frequent identification is with the secretion of small aphids that feed on the sap of tamarisk trees. When it hardens and falls to the ground, it can be collected and used for a sweetener. The problem is that this only occurs during certain seasons (May to July) and only where there are tamarisk trees. A full season would normally produce only about five hundred pounds, in contrast to the biblical account that has the people gathering about half a pound per person per day. Alternatively, some would favor the sweet liquid of the hammada plant, common in southern Sinai, that is used to sweeten cakes. As with the plagues, it is not necessarily the occurrence of this phenomenon that is unnatural but the timing and magnitude. Nevertheless, these natural explanations seem to fall far short of the biblical data. The comparison to what most translations identify as the seed of the coriander (rarely found in the desert) is more likely to refer to a wider generic category of desert plants with white seeds. (See Ex 16:4-9.)

11:25. the Spirit and prophesying. Ecstatic prophecy, or prophecy that appears to proceed from someone in a "possessed" or trancelike state, is known in Israel as well as in the ancient Near East. In Mesopotamia the ecstatic prophet's title was *muhhu,* and in Israel the ecstasies often resulted in the prophets being thought of as madmen (see, for example, 1 Sam 19:19-24; Jer 29:26). Here the phenomenon does not result in prophetic messages from the Lord but serves as a sign of the power of God on the elders. In that sense it could be compared to the tongues of fire in the upper room in Acts 2.

11:31. quail. Small, plump migratory quail often come through the Sinai on their way north from the Sudan to Europe, usually in the months of March and April. They generally fly with the wind and are driven to ground (or water) if caught in a crosswind. In their exhaustion it is not unusual for them to fly so low that they can be easily caught. Quail looking for a place to land and rest have been known to sink small boats, and in the Sinai they have been noted to cover the ground so densely that some landed on the tops of others. (See Ex 16:13.)

11:32. 10 homers. A homer is a donkey load. It certainly became a more precise dry measure in time, but it is not always used with precision. Estimates of ten homers would run anywhere from forty to sixty bushels. By any estimate the Israelites were overcome with greed. Normally the quails would have been preserved with salt before being laid out to dry. Since this step is not mentioned by the text, it may have been omitted. This suggests that the plague was food poisoning.

11:34. Kibroth Hattaavah. This location cannot be identified with any degree of confidence.

11:35. Hazeroth. Tentatively identified by some as Ain el-Khadra.

12:1. Cushite wife of Moses. "Cush" can refer to several different places in the Old Testament, though it most frequently is the designation for the area translations usually render "Ethiopia." This is misleading, for the area Cush refers to is not modern Ethiopia (Abyssinia) but the area along the Nile just south of Egypt, ancient Nubia (in modern Sudan). The boundary between Egypt and Nubia in ancient times was usually either at the first or second cataract of the Nile. It is unlikely that Nubia ever extended much beyond the sixth cataract at Khartoum. Another possibility connects Cush here with Cushan, identified in Habakkuk 3:7 with Midian. This has been attractive to some because of Moses' known marriage to a Midianite woman, Zipporah (see Ex 2—4). While the objection of Miriam and Aaron appears to have been ethnic, there is little evidence to clarify what the woman's ethnic background was. Nubians are depicted with dark skin pigmentation in Egyptian paintings but are generally lacking other negroid features.

12:5. pillar of cloud. For a general discussion of the pillar of cloud, see the comment on Exodus 13:21-22. For the pillar as a means of God meeting with Moses, see comment on Exodus 33:10. Here they come to the tent of meeting for judgment of a case. In Canaanite literature the chief deity *El also dwells in a tent and from that tent (where the divine assembly is thought to meet) come forth decrees and judgments. For another example of judgment proceeding from the tent in terms of punishment, see the comment on Leviticus 9:23.

12:6. prophets. By this date there was already a well-established prophetic institution in the ancient Near East. As this text indicates, the usual modes of revelation were dreams and visions. In over fifty texts from the town of *Mari (several centuries earlier than Moses) local officials report prophetic utterances to the king of Mari, Zimri-Lim. Yahweh could choose to speak through anyone, but Moses' status and experience go beyond that of other prophets. Both dreams and visions often used symbolism that required interpretation (often through use of *divination or by an expert in the dream books; see comment on Gen 40:5-18), but there were no such riddles to solve in order to understand God's revelation to Moses.

12:10. Miriam's disease. Hansen's disease (the modern term for leprosy) is unattested in the ancient Near East prior to the time of Alexander the Great (see comment on Lev 13:1-46). The skin diseases described here and elsewhere in the Old Testament are more along the line of psoriasis and eczema. The analogy to a stillborn in verse 12 further confirms this type of diagnosis in that it describes exfoliation (peeling of the skin, not associated with Hansen's disease), not necrosis (destruction of body tissue, including bones and nerves). A stillborn progresses from reddish coloring to a brownish gray and then begins to lose its skin.

12:16. Desert of Paran. See comment on 10:12.

13:1-33
The Reconnaissance of the Land

13:21-22. scope of the exploration. The Wilderness of Zin is the area going south from an imaginary line drawn between the southern tip of the Dead Sea and the Mediterranean, an area also referred to as the Negev. It constitutes the southern border of Canaan. Rehob has often been identified with Tell el-Balat Beth-rehob, almost halfway from the Mediterranean to Hazor. Lebo Hamath is most likely modern Lebweh on one of the sources of the Orontes. This was the southern border of the land of Hamath and therefore the northern border of Canaan. These reference points suggest the scouts explored the land between the Jordan River and the Mediterranean up and down its full 350-mile length.

13:22. Anakites. The descendants of Anak are specifically mentioned in verses 22 and 28. When names are given, they are *Hurrian (biblical Horites; see comment on Deut 2). The descendants of Anak are generally considered "giants" (v. 33; Deut 2:10-11; 2 Sam 21:18-22), though the description "gigantic" may be more appropriate. There is no mention of the Anakites in other sources, but the Egyptian letter on Papyrus Anastasi I (thirteenth century B.C.) describes fierce warriors in Canaan that are seven to nine feet tall. Two female skeletons about seven feet tall from the twelfth century have been found at Tell es-Sa'ideyeh in Transjordan.

13:22. the building of Hebron. Hebron was built seven years before Zoan. Zoan refers to the Egyptian city of Dja'net, which the Greeks called Tanis. It became the capital city of the Delta region in the Twenty-first Dynasty (twelfth century B.C.). The earliest major builder identified by the archaeological finds is Psusennes I in the middle of the eleventh century. The archaeology of Hebron is very complex. The site was occupied in the *Early Bronze Age (third millennium), and there was a fortified city on the site in the Middle Bronze Age II (up to the middle of the second millennium). There is evidence of a tribal population during the period of the conquest and then a permanent settlement again in the *Iron Age (from 1200 on). It is difficult to be certain which building of Hebron this verse refers to.

13:24. the Valley of Eshcol. There are many wadis in this general area, and there is no way of telling which one may have been referred to here. Around Hebron today, Ramet el-'Amleh is known for its grape produce and is near a wadi.

13:26. Kadesh. Kadesh Barnea is usually identified as 'Ain el-Qudeirat, about fifty miles south of Beersheba, which has the most plentiful water supply in the region. There are no archaeological remains on this site from this period, but the site has long been a stopping place for nomads and Bedouin, and the abundance of "Negev" ware (pottery dated to this period) suggests that was true during the time of the Israelite wanderings as well.

13:27. land flowing with milk and honey. The land of Canaan is described as a land "flowing with milk and honey." This refers to the bounty of the land for a pastoral lifestyle, but not necessarily in terms of agriculture. Milk is the product of herds, while honey represents a natural resource, probably the syrup of the date rather than bees' honey. A similar expression to this is found in the *Ugaritic epic of *Baal and Mot, which describes the return of fertility to the land in terms of the wadis flowing with honey. Egyptian texts as early as the *Story of *Sinuhe* describe the land of Canaan as rich in natural resources as well as in cultivated produce. (See Ex 3:7-10.)

13:29. inhabitants of the land. The people groups inhabiting the land are identified in verse 29 as the Amalekites, *Hittites, Jebusites, *Amorites and Canaanites. The Amalekites, who were descended from Abraham through Esau (Gen 36:15), were a nomadic or semi-nomadic people who inhabited the general region of the Negev and the Sinai during the second half of the second millennium B.C. The well-known Hittites were from Anatolia, modern Turkey, but groups occupying sections of Syria and Canaan were also called Hittites and may or may not be related. The Hittites in Canaan have Semitic names, while the Hittites of Anatolia were Indo-European. Jebusites inhabited the area around Jerusalem and are known only from the Old Testament, which tells us very little about them. *Amorites (known in Mesopotamia as *Amurru* or *Martu*) are known from written documents as early as the middle third millennium B.C. Most scholars think that their roots were in Syria but that they came to occupy many areas in the Near East. The term can be used to refer to a geographical area ("westerners") or to an ethnic group. Some Amorites were nomadic, but there were Amorite city-states in Syria as early as the end of the third millennium. The Canaanites were the principle inhabitants of the fortified cities of the land, though they do not seem to have been native to the land. The kings of this area refer to themselves in the *Amarna letters (mid-second millennium) as *Kinanu*, a term also used in Egyptian inscriptions of this period. There are also records from Egypt concerning the population of Canaan. A prisoner list from a campaign of Amenhotep II (fifteenth century) lists numbers of Canaanites, *Apiru* (unlanded or dispossessed peoples), *Shasu* (nomadic peoples sometimes connected with biblical groups like the Midianites or Amalekites) and *Hurru* (Hurrians).

13:33. like grasshoppers. It is not unusual to use an animal metaphor to describe relative size in exaggerated comparison (cf. English "shrimp"). Grasshoppers were edible, so this invites the additional frightening prospect that "we wouldn't have even made a mouthful to them." In the *Ugaritic Epic of *Keret an army is compared to grasshoppers to indicate the vast number of soldiers.

13:33. Nephilim. The only other sure reference to the Nephilim is in Genesis 6:4, which offers little information in terms of identification. Some have also seen the word in Ezekiel 32:27 (with a slight text variation), where it would re-

fer to warriors. Earliest interpretation (intertestamental) is divided between considering them giants, heroes and fallen angels.

14:1-45
The People Decide Not to Enter the Land

14:6. tearing clothes. Along with placing ashes in the hair, the tearing of clothing was a common form of mourning in the ancient Near East. One example outside the Bible is found in the *Ugaritic Epic of *Aqhat (c. 1600 B.C.) in which the sister of the hero tears her father's garment as she foretells a coming drought. Such an act often implied grief over the death of a relative, friend or prominent individual (2 Sam 3:31). However, it also was a sign of shame (as in this case) or loss of honor or status (2 Sam 13:19).

14:8. flowing with milk and honey. See comment on 13:27.

14:13-16. divine sponsorship and its implications. All of the peoples of the ancient Near East believed in the patronage of the gods. Each city had a patron deity (e.g., *Marduk in *Babylon), and many professions also had particular gods to whom they looked for special aid. Such associations, however, meant that when a city or a group of people warred with another, their gods also joined in the battle. The god/gods of the losing side were discredited and often abandoned by their worshipers. Thus Moses' prayer to Yahweh involves the knowledge of God's sponsorship of the Israelites and the promise of land and children. If Yahweh should destroy the Israelites in the wilderness for their disobedience, it could be construed as failure on God's part to fulfill these promises.

14:25. geographical information. These instructions require the Israelites, who fear moving directly north into Canaan, to proceed south from Kadesh in the

Wilderness of Paran to the area of Elath on the Gulf of Aqaba. *Yam Suph* in this verse is therefore not the Red Sea but, as in Numbers 21:4 and Deuteronomy 1:40; 2:1, refers to the Gulf of Aqaba on the eastern coast of the Sinai peninsula.

14:36-38. fate of the spies. Initially God was so angry at the Israelites' grumbling that they were all condemned to die of a plague (v. 12). However, after Moses asked Yahweh to have mercy, this sentence is changed to the death of all these unfaithful people in the wilderness without seeing the Promised Land. Only the spies who had brought a report questioning God's power died immediately of a plague. The term translated "plague" is too vague to identify a particular disease, although some consider it to represent bubonic plague. In the Old Testament it is generally a punishment from God for serious desecration or blasphemy.

14:45. Hormah. "Hormah" has a double meaning here. In the Hebrew it means "destruction," and this is what happened to the invading Israelites. It is also a geographic term for a site seven and a half miles east of Beersheba, tentatively identified with Tell Masos (Khirbet el-Meshash).

15:1-31
Sacrifice Regulations in the Land

15:1-31. general elements of the sacrificial system. Within the Israelite sacrificial system there were both obligatory and voluntary offerings, and they applied to the entire Israelite community as well as to resident aliens. The obligatory sacrifices, brought to a shrine or temple and burnt on the altar by priests, included portions of the harvest (grain, fruits, oil, wine) as well as from the flocks and herds. A portion of each offering was then designated for the use and maintenance of the priestly community.

Some sacrifices were expiatory and designed to mitigate specific sins or infractions of the law as well as to serve as part of the *ritual of purification after a person came in contact with unclean items (corpses, diseased persons, body fluids). Voluntary sacrifices were offered as evidence of generosity or in thanksgiving for a particular joy (marriage, birth of a son, a particularly good harvest). Unlike sacrificial offerings in the rest of the ancient Near East, however, those to *Yahweh were not designed to nourish the god (see the famished gods at the end of the flood story in the *Babylonian *Gilgamesh Epic). They only were presented in a ritually correct manner ("an aroma pleasing to the Lord") in order to obtain God's blessing or forgiveness. For further information see the comments on the early part of Leviticus.

15:22-26. community culpability. Inadvertent violations of the law also require purification. For example, in *Hammurabi's code, an unknowing violator of the slave laws must take an oath before the god to clear himself. In the Israelite context, the entire community is held responsible for sins committed unknowingly and for sins of omission (usually involving *ritual or matters of law). The community is defined as both Israelites and resident aliens. The infraction may involve commission of an act without knowledge that it is a violation of the law or confusion over the consumption of some portion of the sacrificial meat or fat. Unlike in Leviticus 4:13-21, however, the expiatory sacrifice of a young bull is not called a "sin" (purification) offering. Instead it is referred to here as a "burnt offering," and a male goat is also to be sacrificed as the purification offering (see comment on Lev 4:1-3).

15:30. defiant sin. Providing contrast to inadvertent sin, this offense is committed with full knowledge of one's actions and premeditated defiance of God and community. For instance, in *Sumerian law a son who publicly denounces his father is disinherited and can be sold as a slave. Similarly, according to Israelite law deliberate criminal acts cannot be allowed to go unpunished, since they violate not only God's laws but the community's collective *covenant to obey these statutes. The sentence "to be cut off from his people," implies punishment by both human and divine agencies—perhaps capital punishment by the authorities and extinction of his family line by God.

15:30. blasphemy. The verb "to blaspheme" is used only here in the Old Testament and means to taunt or revile God so as to deny the authority of God. Such an act demonstrates total defiance of the law, and, because of its danger to the community, the violator must be "cut off from his people." This may involve capital punishment, but it also probably implies punishment by God through the elimination of the person's entire family line. One example of the extreme nature of this offense can be found in the Cyrus Cylinder (c. 540 B.C.), which charges the *Babylonian king Nabonidus with failing to recognize *Marduk's authority as the city god and explains that the god has abandoned him and allowed the Persians to capture the city unmolested.

15:32-36
The Sabbath Breaker

15:32-36. gathering wood on the sabbath. This story provides a legal *etiology explaining the seriousness of violating the sabbath (gathering wood, presumably to cook with, violates Ex 35:3) and provides a precedent for future violations of the sabbath (see Nehemiah's civil reforms in Neh 13:15-22). Detention of the culprit is only until God provides the proper form of punishment, which in this case is stoning. Communal and other forms of execution must be performed outside the camp in order to prevent contamination from contact with the corpse.

15:37-41
Tassel Regulation

15:37-41. tassels on the garments. All adult male Israelites were commanded to sew blue cords into the four quarters of the hem of their robes as a perpetual reminder of God's commandments. The blue dye was extracted from the gland of the *Murex trunculus* snail and was very costly (see comment on 4:6). Decorative hems are common in ancient Near Eastern fashion as many reliefs, paintings and texts attest. Hem design was often an indication of a person's status or office. The tassels are symbolic and are designed to promote right action, not to serve as an *amulet to ward off danger or temptation. The blue cord may signify the status of each Israelite as a member of a kingdom of priests (see comment on Ex 19:5-6).

16:1—17:13
Korah's Revolt and Aaron's Rod

16:1-3. clan and tribal political structure. Each person within the Israelite community was identified as a member of a particular household, clan and tribe. This not only set them into particular kinship groups (the Reubenites claiming ascendancy here over Moses) but also served as the basis on which they could be appointed elders and members of council—so many from each tribe and clan to aid in maintaining order and assisting Moses in the administration of justice. Rivalries between the kinship groups are typical of tribal confederations. In this type of loose political structure, loyalties to the smaller kin affiliations often supersede ties of loyalty to the overall group. Even during the monarchy period, the kings will be faced with this type of mixed loyalty (2 Sam 20:1-2; 1 Kings 12:16-17).

16:6-7. the function of incense censers. The censers are most likely long-handled pans that could also shovel up the hot coals. They served as portable altars, because the incense was actually burned in them. Censers were also used for burning of incense in Egypt when people wanted to protect themselves from demonic forces. Burning incense purifies the area of the altar and signifies God's presence (see comments on Ex 30:7-8, 34-38). Moses proposes a test, ordering the followers of the rebellious Korah to offer incense in a censer before God. This was the exclusive prerogative of priests and could be very dangerous for anyone, priest or nonpriests, who might do it incorrectly (Lev 10:1-2).

16:10. distinction between Levites and priests. The Levites were given custody of the tabernacle and the sacred precincts around the altar. It was their responsibility to monitor Israelites who brought their offerings to be sacrificed and prevent them from violating any statute or encroaching on sacred areas reserved for the priests. Priests actually performed the *ritual and the sacrifices on the altar. Although both groups belonged to the priestly community and received a share of the sacrificial offerings, priests had the greatest responsibility and power over *ritual acts. Differentiation of task and authority were also common in Mesopotamian temple communities.

16:13-14. land flowing with milk and honey. The phrase "flowing with milk and honey" becomes synonymous with the Promised Land. It occurs as part of the *covenant promise and is used here in contrast to the harshness of life in the wilderness. This would also relate the lush grazing that would insure good milk production in sheep, goats and cattle. See also comment on Exodus 3:7-10.

16:14. gouging out the eyes. This is an idiom meaning to trick or "pull the wool over one's eyes." Korah's followers refuse to participate in any test suggested by Moses, calling him a charlatan who has already hoodwinked the people into following him.

16:28-30. curse pronouncement. To demonstrate his authority from God, Moses calls for a demonstration of power similar to the plagues in Egypt. The rebel leaders Dathan and Abiram stand in defiance, along with their households, and Moses must curse them so thoroughly that no doubt is left about God's choice of leader. Therefore he asks God to open the earth and take these men and their families down to Sheol alive. The underworld in ancient Near Eastern tradition (Ugaritic and Mesopotamian epics) is often portrayed as a gaping mouth. Thus no one can claim a natural event like an earthquake killed them. Their fate was predicted, and Moses proves to be a true prophet when it occurs.

16:31-35. earthquake and fire as judgment. Both earthquake and fire cause the death of many people. However in this case the men opposing Moses and Aaron are consumed, along with their households, by the earth and by a divine fire (God's *kabod* "glory"). The entire community witnesses the event, which demonstrates God's choice of Moses as leader. The "Lament for the Destruction of Ur" in Mesopotamian literature provides a similar manifestation of divine wrath through firestorm and earthquake.

16:47. incense as atonement. In this instance, God's wrath over the people's rebellion against Moses had "broken out" in the form of a plague. Moses has Aaron burn incense as a type of *apotropaic remedy (similar to the blood painted on their door frames during the Passover in Ex 12:7). The burning of the incense by an authorized priest was designed to provide expiation for the people's sins and guard them from God's anger. However, the more common means of expiation was blood sacrifice (see Lev 17:11). Egyptian use of incense to ward off hostile supernatural powers is well attested. To that end censers were carried in cultic processions. They are depicted in the *rituals performed when a city was under siege.

16:47-50. nature of the plague. The plague, which kills 14,700 people, takes the form of the "Angel Destroyer" who had cut down the firstborn in Egypt. So devastating is its power that Moses orders Aaron to carry a burning censer in among the dead and dying in order to ward off any further destruction. This is extraordinary, since priests normally were not to come in contact with the dead. Apparently this was the only way to hold the plague in check. An exact diagnosis of the plague is not possible from the text (see comment on 25:8).

17:2-7. staff as insignia of tribal leadership. The staff was used by shepherds to guide their flocks. In the hands of an elder or tribal leader, the staff (probably distinctively carved and known to belong to that man) symbolized his authority (see Gen 38:18). By writing the name of each of the twelve tribal leaders on the staffs and placing them before the tent of meeting, there would be no question whose flowered at God's command and who was therefore the designated priest. This public pattern of discernment is also found in Joshua 7:14-15 and 1 Samuel 10:20-21.

17:4-11. divination by wooden objects. The method of determining who is God's chosen priestly leader involves a form of *divination (using objects to ascertain God's will). This method is not to be confused with the divination practices condemned in Hosea 4:12, which involve either a wooden idol or an *Asherah pole. Here each tribal leader, plus Aaron, is commanded to place his staff in the tent of meeting. The text contains a pun on the word for staff, which also means "tribe" in Hebrew, signifying God's intention to differentiate between the leaders of the tribes. This event is never repeated and thus is not a part of a cultic *ritual. When Aaron's blooms, his authority is certified and no further argument is allowed on this matter. Association of divination practices in proximity to a tree may be found in the references to the soothsayer's tree in Judges 9:37 and to Deborah's palm tree in Judges 4:4-5. *Ugaritic texts also mention the use of trees in ritual contexts.

17:8. significance of almonds. Aaron's staff sprouts, blossoms and flowers as an almond branch. This whole creative process signifies God's power over creation, the fruitfulness of the Promised Land (see Gen 43:11) and the "diligence" (Hebrew meaning for *saqed* "almond") expected of Aaron's priesthood. In Jeremiah 1:11-12 the sprouting almond branch symbolizes God's watching over Israel. The almond was recognized as the earliest of the blossoming plants of the region (e.g., in the Egyptian Wisdom of *Ahiqar) and may therefore also signify the priority of Aaron's office.

18:1-32
Priestly Duties and Prerogatives

18:1-7. concept and care of the sacred compass. The center of the sacred space was the Most Holy Place where the ark was. Radiating from that point out were concentric zones of holiness, each with its requirements of levels of *purity. One of the principal tasks of the priests was to enforce the rules that would maintain the appropriate level of holiness for each zone. Since the entire tribe of Levi had been singled out to serve as priests, it was necessary to assign duties and responsibilities and to create a hierarchy within the group headed by Aaron and his sons. All of the Levites were put in the charge of Aaron's household. They were to perform the mundane tasks necessary to maintain the tent of meeting, guard its precincts and assist worshipers who brought offerings for sacrifice. However, no one other than Aaron and his sons and their descendants was to be allowed to actually perform the sacrifices or to minister before the ark of the testimony. Any violation by a Levite of these restrictions would result in the death of both the Levite and Aaron. Any non-Levite who entered the forbidden precincts of the sanctuary was condemned to death. Through these restrictions on the community and the placing of such heavy responsibilities on Aaron's family, the mystery and power associated with God's service and the items tied to it are magnified and protected.

18:8-10. sacrificial portions. The most sacred sacrificial portions are designated to be consumed by Aaron and his sons as a reward for their heavy responsibilities. This consists of those items which are brought into the most sacred precincts of the tent of meeting (see Lev 6:1-7:10). They may not be shared, as are other portions, with their families but must be eaten by priests who are ritually pure and therefore holy enough to consume sacred gifts. This includes grain, sin and guilt offerings, some of which is to be burnt on the altar while the remainder becomes the holy food of the priests. Hittite sacred texts also express concern over the consumption of the "god's food" by princes and other secular officials. The seriousness of sacred property is also found in Mesopotamian law, where strict penalties (heavy fines or capital punishment) are prescribed for theft of temple property.

18:11. wave offerings. Continuing the list of sacrificial portions set aside for the priests and their families are the wave offerings. These consist of items brought to the sanctuary and given a special distinction through an elevation *ritual before the altar (see comment on Lev 8:22-30). This does not include all wave offerings, since some are totally consumed by fire (Ex 29:22-25) and some are reserved solely for male priests (Lev 14:12-14).

18:12-19. priestly prerogatives. Completing the list of items perpetually set aside for the priests and their families (excluding daughters-in-law and laborers) are the first fruits of the harvest (grain, oil and wine) and the meat of first-born animals. Some regulations are imposed. Unclean animals may be redeemed for a set price by their owners, and human babies must be redeemed by their parents (see Ex 13:12-13; 34:19-20). All blood, fat and certain internal organs are to be burnt on the altar as a well-being offering (see Lev 3:9; 7:3). Since these animal products contain the symbolic essence of life, it is proper that they be given entirely to God rather than set aside for priestly consumption.

18:16. sanctuary shekel. The shekel weight used for the redemption of children and unclean animals is equivalent to twenty gerahs of silver (50 gerahs = 1 oz.). It will not be in the form of coined money until the fourth century B.C.

18:19. covenant of salt. Salt was used widely as symbolic of preservation. When treaties or alliances were made, salt was employed to symbolize that the terms would be preserved for a long time. *Babylonian, Persian, Arabic and Greek contexts all testify to this symbolic usage. In the Bible, likewise, the *covenant between the Lord and Israel is identified as a covenant of salt—a long-preserved covenant. Allies entering into such an agreement would generally share a communal meal where salted meat was featured. Thus the use of salt in the sacrifices was an appropriate reminder of the covenant relationship.

Additionally, salt impedes the action of yeast (leaven), and since leaven was a symbol of rebellion, salt could easily represent that which inhibited rebellion. (See Lev 2:13.)

18:21-32. tithing as priests' wages in the ancient Near East. Apparently, the practice of designating one-tenth of all produce (cereal, fruit and animal) as wages for the priesthood was unique to the Israelites. Although Mesopotamian temples did exact rents from tenant farmers on their lands, they were not able to tax the entire population. As a result, the revenues needed to maintain the temple and the priesthood came from their own lands and from gifts from individuals and royalty. Kings also had lands from which they derived revenue in Egypt and Mesopotamia, but this did not have the same significance as a tithe. In Canaanite culture the tithe was very similar to that in Israel but went to the king and his administration rather than to the priesthood, though priests were sometimes included among the administrative personnel. Since the Levites were not given land in the distribution after the conquest, they were to be supported by all of the people through the tithe. It should be noted, however, that the Levites also paid a tithe of what they received to Aaron and his family, thereby providing a clear distinction between Levites and priests.

19:1-22
The Ceremony of the Red Heifer

19:2-10. significance of the red heifer. The animal designated for sacrifice and whose blood will be mixed with ashes to serve as a means of purifying persons who have come in contact with the dead is a young cow. The color red may symbolize blood, but that is uncertain. The exact age of the animal is not made clear by the Hebrew, but the fact that it was not to be allowed to pull the plow or do any other type of work suggests it may have just reached maturity. One example of this may be the cows hitched to the wagon bearing the ark by the Philistines in 1 Samuel 6:7. They were suitable for sacrifice and thus could be used in this test of divine intention. The case of an unknown homicide in Deuteronomy 21:1-9 also requires the sacrifice of a heifer and the use of its blood for a purification *ritual. The blood and the innocence of the animal are the keys to purification.

19:2-10. ritual of the red heifer. In order to create the mixture needed to cleanse a person who has become contaminated through contact with a corpse, the law requires that a red heifer without blemish that has never been yoked for labor be taken outside the camp and slaughtered by Eleazar, Aaron's son. Eleazar does this because Aaron, the high priest, would have been contaminated by the carcass of the animal. Eleazar sprinkles some of its blood seven times on the tent of meeting and then supervises the burning of the carcass, while throwing cedar wood, hyssop and scarlet wool on the fire. The ashes are kept outside the camp for later use in purification *rituals. These actions cause participants in the sacrifice to become unclean until evening, even though they bathe and wash their clothes. Comparison with *Hittite ritual corroborates that it is the ritual act, plus the ingredients concocted to purify persons, that causes a temporary *impurity by the priest.

19:11. ritual contamination from a corpse. There was a widespread *cult of the dead in the ancient Near East. Although there was no well-defined concept of afterlife in Mesopotamia or ancient Israel, it was still believed that the spirits of the dead could effect the living. For instance, in Hittite texts the terror of the dead seems to come from the fear of being "unclean before" the spirits of the dead, just as one would be before a god. Thus offerings were made in tombs to the ancestors, but actual contamination by corpses does not appear to be a concern for the *Hittites. In contrast the Mesopotamian *namburbi* *ritual evidences a significant fear of corpse contamination. What may have been of concern was a mixing of the two spheres of existence, the living and the dead. When a person came in contact with the dead, whether human or animal, contamination occurred. Purification was necessary so that that person did not infect others or the entire community with his *impurity. The biblical purification rituals are perhaps the most detailed of any developed in the ancient Near East, although those employed by the Hittites also involved bathing, sacrifices and a period of exclusion.

19:17-19. cleansing ritual. To cleanse a person contaminated by a corpse, a ceremonially clean man takes the ashes of the red heifer, mixes them with water from a spring or running stream, and sprinkles the unclean person using a hyssop branch. The hyssop is used because its hairy branches can absorb liquid. Sprinkling takes place on the third and seventh days (both of these prime numbers are often used in *rituals and stories). Then, on the seventh day, the unclean person purifies him- or herself by bathing and washing clothing. That evening he or she will be ritually pure again. In this way there is no mixing of clean and unclean within the community itself, and the ideal is maintained of a community worthy to serve their God.

19:20-21. water of cleansing. The mixture of ashes from the sacrificed heifer and water from a spring or running stream is called the "water of cleansing." It is sprinkled on an unclean person as part of the cleansing *ritual. Hittite ritual

texts also include water as a means of removing actual or suspected *impurity. However, the mixture described in Numbers also makes the person who sprinkles the water unclean until evening. This is based on association with the mixture's purpose and the assumed contamination created by the sacrificial ingredients themselves.

20:1-13
Water from the Rock

20:1. chronological note. At this point the forty years of wandering in the wilderness are coming to an end, and the remaining survivors of the exodus must leave the scene, since they are not allowed to enter the Promised Land. Thus in the first month of the fortieth year Miriam, Moses' sister, dies, marking the transition of leadership that will culminate in Aaron's death in the fifth month (Num 33:38).

20:1. Wilderness of Zin. The Wilderness of Zin lies north of the Wilderness of Paran. Although its exact location is unknown, it is referred to as the southern boundary of the Promised Land (Num 34:3-4; Josh 15:1, 3). Kadesh, the oasis where the Israelites spend a considerable time, is in the Desert of Zin (see chaps. 13—14).

20:6. appearance of the glory of the Lord. During times of crisis Moses and Aaron turn to God for guidance and assistance. They go to the entrance of the tent of meeting and as supplicants they bow to the ground. Because of their humble submission of their plea, God's "glory" (*kabod*) appears and provides a solution (see similar instances in Num 14:5-12; 16:19-22). A physical manifestation of a god's aura or power is common in Mesopotamian epics, where it is referred to as the god's *melammu*, and it can be used as a means of defeating an enemy (as in *Marduk's struggle with *Tiamat in the *Enuma Elish).

20:1-13. water from the rock. Sedimentary rock is known to feature pockets where water can collect just below the surface. If there is some seepage, one can see where these pockets exist and by breaking through the surface can release the collected water. Again, however, we are dealing with a quantity of water beyond what this explanation affords.

20:13. waters of Meribah. The location of the waters of Meribah in Exodus 17 had been in the vicinity of Sinai, specifically at Rephidim. Now they are at Kadesh, about 150 air miles north-northeast of Rephidim. Nevertheless, these are waters of quarreling *(meribah)*, just as those had been.

20:14-21
Request to the Edomites

20:14-21. Late Bronze Age Edom. Edom was the territory ranging south from the Dead Sea to the Gulf of Aqaba. Recently archaeologists have found small amounts of pottery from the *Late Bronze period at a number of settlements in this region, but no architectural remains or written records. The Egyptians referred to the nomadic population there as the Shosu, though that term may refer to social class rather than to ethnic origin.

20:22-29
The Death of Aaron

20:22-26. Mount Hor. The death site for Aaron (although Deut 10:6 identifies his death with Moseroth). The traditional location is near Petra at Jebal Nabi Harun, but this is not "on the border of Edom." Another possibility is Jebal Madrah, west of Kadesh and near the Edomite border, but it lacks sufficient water sources.

20:29. 30 days of mourning. The normal mourning period is seven days (Gen 50:10; 1 Sam 31:13). However, to demonstrate their importance, both Moses (Deut 34:8) and Aaron are mourned for

thirty days. The occasion is also marked by transition of leadership, with Eleazar succeeding his father as high priest and wearing his vestments (Num 20:26). Similarly, Joshua succeeds Moses (Deut 34:9).

21:1-3
The Destruction of Arad

21:1-3. Arad. The site identified as Arad was a walled city in the *Early Bronze period (first half of the third millennium), well before the time of Abraham. It had a major role in the copper industry that thrived in the Sinai peninsula. The next occupation detected by archaeologists is connected with the Early *Iron Age (Judges period), and there was a series of citadels and even a temple on the site about the time of Solomon. Since there is no sign of occupation during the period of the exodus and conquest, some archaeologists have suggested that the Arad of the Canaanite period is the site now identified as Tell Malhata, about seven or eight miles southwest of the site now known as Arad. Egyptian inscriptions of the tenth century identify two Arads.

21:1. Atharim. This word is obscure and may be either a place name or a profession (KJV and LXX translate it "spies"). Most likely it is to be identified with the area just south of the Dead Sea, possibly with the site of Tamar. Here the Israelites were attacked by the army of the king of Arad.

21:3. Hormah. The Hebrew word means "destruction." It is applied as a place name here to commemorate the Israelite victory. They had vowed to totally destroy the cities of the Canaanites in that area and dedicate the spoil to the sanctuary if God gave them the victory. This is similar to the *herem, "holy war," declared against Jericho (Josh 6:17-19, 24). As a geographical name it refers to a site seven and a half miles east of Beersheba tentatively identified with Tell Masos (Khirbet el-Meshash).

21:4-9
The Bronze Serpent

21:4. itinerary. The Israelites marched south from Mount Hor on the border of Edom toward Elath at the northern end of the Gulf of Aqabah. Archaeological survey of the area suggests that the Edomites did not extend this far until the time of Solomon (tenth century B.C.).

21:6-7. snakes. The snakes are not clearly identified but may be a species of desert viper. Their "fiery" or "winged" character may have to do with their association with the cobra or their quick spring as they strike (Deut 8:15). For general information see the comment on Genesis 3:1.

21:8-9. bronze snake on a pole. The Hebrew here is actually "copper" snake. Bronze, an alloy of copper and tin, was smelted in the Timnah region where this event occurred, and thus the translation here has a physical background. Excavations in that area have unearthed an Egyptian temple to the god Hathor. During the period of the Judges this temple was adopted by Midianites in the area, who made it into a shrine draped with curtains. In the inner chamber of this shrine was found a five-inch long copper image of a snake. It was common in the ancient Near East to believe that the image of something could protect against the thing itself. As a result Egyptians (living as well as dead) sometimes wore snake-shaped *amulets to protect them from serpents. Finally it is of interest that a well-known bronze bowl from *Nineveh with Hebrew names on it depicts a winged snake on a pole of some sort.

21:10-20
Journey Through Moab

21:10-20. itinerary. A fuller list of stops

on this journey is given in Numbers 33:41-48. A number of the towns are unknown, making it difficult to offer archaeological evidence. Nevertheless, a number of the stops also occur on Egyptian maps and itineraries from this period. The Zered Valley is today the Wadi el-Hesa, and the Arnon River flows through the Wadi el-Mojib. Both flow from east to west, the former into the southern end of the Dead Sea and the latter into a midpoint on the east side.

21:14. book of the wars of the Lord. In compiling the history and traditions of the conquest, the biblical writers drew on a variety of sources, both written and oral. Among the written sources was the Book of Jashar (see Josh 10:13; 2 Sam 1:18) and the Book of the Wars of the Lord. Based on the three fragments of these documents that appear in the Bible, they were composed primarily of victory songs and tales of the mighty acts of God and the leaders of the Israelites during this formative period. Unfortunately, neither book has survived, but their mention in the biblical text indicates that the narrative was based, at least in part, on cultural memories.

21:21-35
Sihon and Og

21:21. Amorites. The *Amurru or Amorites of Mesopotamia formed a significant ethnic group after 2000 B.C. and are mentioned in the *Mari texts and the administrative documents of *Hammurabi of *Babylon during the eighteenth century B.C. Egyptian records list them as one of several kingdoms during the fourteenth century B.C. in the area south of the Orontes River and into Transjordan. Their effective control of Transjordan may be associated with the conflict between Egypt and the Hittite Empire. The indecisive battle of Kadesh (c. 1290 B.C.) between these two powers opened a temporary political opportunity for

Amorite control, but the coming of the *Sea Peoples in 1200 B.C. further disrupted the region. In the Bible, *Amorites* is used as an ethnic term for the kingdoms of Sihon and Og (Num 21:21, 33) as well as for the inhabitants of Canaan (Gen 15:16; Deut 1:7).

21:23. Jahaz. The site of the battle with the forces of the *Amorite king Sihon is given as Jahaz. Its probable location, based on the church historian Eusebius (fourth century A.D.) and the Mesha inscription (ninth century B.C.), is between the territories of Madaba and Dibon, at Khirbet Medeiniyeh at the eastern edge of Moab by the Wadi al-Themed. The battle is also mentioned in Deuteronomy 2:33 and Judges 11:20.

21:24-30. captured land. The area of central Transjordan which is here described as the kingdoms of Sihon and Og stretches from the Arnon River valley in the south to the Jabbok River in the north. It would include Moab but not Ammon. It seems likely that these "kingdoms" were not organized states in this period and that their conquest provided passage for the Israelites without the tribes actually taking control of and settling this region.

21:25-28. Heshbon. The modern site of Tell-Heshban is located nearly fifty miles directly east of Jerusalem. However, archaeologists have not been able to detect any evidence that this site was settled prior to 1200 B.C. Some have suspected that the *Late Bronze city of Heshbon may have been at a different site, with Tell Jalul named as one possibility. Recent surveys and excavations in this region have turned up more and more *Late Bronze pottery, but it remains difficult to assess the nature of the occupation during this period.

21:29. Chemosh. The Moabite god *Chemosh, mentioned here in Israel's "taunt song" marking their victory over the Transjordanian kingdoms of Sihon and Og, is also mentioned in the ninth-century B.C. Moabite inscription of King Mesha (see also Judg 11:24; 1 Kings 11:7). As the national god of Moab, Chemosh stood in opposition to *Yahweh, just as Moab did to Israel. His *cult has similarities to Yahweh worship, and his attributes (giving of land to his people and victory in battle) are also similar. This may simply be an indication that the expectations placed on their gods by the people of the ancient Near East were very much the same from one nation to another. Chemosh first appears in the list of gods from ancient Ebla in northern Syria (c. 2600-2250 B.C.) and may have also been worshiped in Mesopotamia and *Ugarit as an elemental deity associated with clay or mud bricks.

21:30. area of destruction. Heshbon and Dibon are the major cities in the north and south respectively in the northern section of Moab (north of the Arnon). For Heshbon see the comment earlier in this chapter. Dibon is modern Dhiban, just a mile or two north of the Arnon (Wadi al-Mujib). In the ninth century B.C. it served as one of Mesha's royal cities and is prominent in the Mesha inscription that was found there. The lack of *Late Bronze finds at the site raises questions about whether the ancient city was at Dhiban or somewhere else nearby. The fact that Rameses II also lists Dibon on his itinerary shows that there was a Late Bronze city of that name. Nophah has not been identified, and even the reading of the name is uncertain. Medeba is the principal city in the central region of north Moab and is identified with the modern city of the same name. There has been limited excavation on the site because of the modern town.

21:32. Jazer. This geographical name is associated with both a city as well as the surrounding region, including small villages or "daughters." Although its location is disputed, the most likely site is

Khirbet Jazzir, twelve miles south of the Jabbok River. It served as an outpost on the border with Ammon and represented the eastward thrust of the Israelite forces.

21:33. Bashan. After defeating Sihon, the Israelites travel northward to the region of Bashan in the area (known today as the Golan Heights) bordered by Mount Hermon to the north, Jebel Druze to the east and the Sea of Galilee to the west, where they defeated King Og at Edrei (modern Der'a, thirty miles east of the Sea of Galilee). It is a broad, fertile plateau region noted for its grazing (Ps 22:12; Amos 4:1-3). See the comment on Deuteronomy 3 for more detail.

21:33. Edrei. The Israelites defeat the *Amorite king Og at Edrei on the southeastern border of Bashan. The site is identified as modern Der'a in Syria, about sixty miles south of Damascus and thirty miles east of the Sea of Galilee near the Yarmuk River. Though no excavations have been conducted there, the town is also mentioned in ancient texts from Egypt and *Ugarit.

21:33. Og. The *Amorite king of Bashan, Og, is mentioned as the last of the Rephaim or giants, whose "bed was made of iron and was more than thirteen feet long and six feet wide" (see comment on Deut 3:11). There is no historical information that sheds light on this individual. The victory was celebrated many times in Israelite tradition and is recorded in Deuteronomy 1:4; 3:1-13; 4:47; 29:7; 31:4; Joshua 2:10; 9:10; and 1 Kings 4:19.

22:1—24:25
Balaam and Balak

22:1. plains of Moab. This is the broad plain or steppe region immediately north of the Dead Sea and east of the Jordan River, just opposite the "plains of Jericho" (Josh 4:13). Its location serves as the jumping-off point for entrance into Canaan.

22:2. Balak of Moab. Balak, the king of Moab, is unknown in other historical sources. In fact, there is very little of Moab's history that has been recovered aside from the information given in the Mesha Inscription concerning the ninth century. It must be remembered that the title *king* could be used for rulers of vast empires or, as most likely in this case, petty rulers or tribal leaders.

22:4-7. Midianites. The Midianites are a people living in the southern portions of the Transjordan region. They are described as the descendants of Abraham and Keturah (Gen 25:106) and operate as traders and caravaneers in the Joseph narrative (Gen 37:25-36). Moses joins the Midianite clan of Jethro after fleeing Egypt (see comment on Ex 2:15), but the Midianites do not join the Israelites in the conquest of Canaan. In the Balaam narrative, the Midianite elders are allied with the Moabites and participate in the hiring of the prophet to curse Israel.

22:4-20. Balaam at Deir Allah. In 1967 a Dutch archaeological expedition led by H. J. Franken discovered some inscribed pieces of plaster at a site in Jordan known as Deir 'Allah. The fragments are apparently written in *Aramaic and date to about 850 B.C. They mention Balaam son of Beor, the same figure described as a "seer" in Numbers 22—24. Although the text is very fragmentary, with many breaks and uncertain words, it can be established that Balaam was a seer who received a divine message during the night and that his message was not what his neighbors expected to hear. Whether this text refers to the events described in the Bible is questionable, but it does establish a nonbiblical tradition current in the ninth century of a prophet named Balaam. It may be that Balaam's notoriety was such that he remained an important prophetic figure for centuries and could thus be identified with the earlier Israelite narratives of the conquest.

22:5. Pethor. This is probably to be identified with Pitru on the Sajur River, a tributary of the upper Euphrates, located about twelve miles from Carchemish in northern Syria. Since Balaam is said to have been brought from *Aram in Numbers 23:7, this identification seems appropriate. However, the distance involved (about four hundred miles) has caused some to look closer to Moab for the site of Pethor.

22:6. prophetic status of Balaam. In Joshua 13:22, Balaam is described as a "soothsayer," while in Numbers 22:6 he is said to be a man whose blessings and curses are effective. He is from the region of upper Mesopotamia, near Carchemish, and has an international reputation as a true prophet. Throughout the narrative in Numbers 22—24, Balaam continually reminds Balak that he can speak only the words which God gives him to speak (Num 22:18, 38; 23:12, 26; 24:13). Although Balaam uses sacrificial rituals to obtain God's answer, he is not to be considered simply a diviner. *Divination, while sometimes used by Mesopotamian prophets, is more often associated with *cultic personnel who examine sacrificial animals or natural conditions (flights of birds, etc.). In each case, Balaam seems to have direct communication with God and then speaks God's word in the form of *oracles to Balak. This is the typical form of prophetic address found in the books of Isaiah, Jeremiah and other Israelite prophets. Spoken oracles are also recorded in over fifty *Mari texts (a few centuries earlier than Balaam, about 250 miles downstream from Carchemish). Through either lay people or temple personnel, various messages are offered to Zimri-Lim, king of Mari, from various deities. Therefore it is clear that prophetic activity in the ancient Near East during this general time period was not uncommon.

22:6. power of a curse. Curses draw the wrath of the deity on persons, groups, cities or places. They may be composed and spoken by anyone, with an intent to bring death, destruction, disease and defeat. Ritual performance was also employed, as in a Hittite text that requires water to be poured and a curse spoken against anyone who gave the king "polluted" water to drink. Curses often accompanied *covenant or treaty agreements to involve the power of the gods as cosigners and to put treaty breakers on notice of their peril. However, cursing can have negative effects on the one who curses as well. The death penalty was imposed on those who curse their parents (Ex 21:17) or God (Lev 24:11-24). In the Israelite tradition expressed in the Balaam narrative, Yahweh alone was capable of carrying out a curse, and no prophet acting on his own could effectively curse anyone. Yet Balak describes Balaam as one so attuned to the gods that both his blessings and his curses are always effective. In effect, the prophet, as a god's intermediary or representative, is believed to be capable of interceding for good or ill with the god(s). Balaam discounts this, however, saying he can only speak what God gives him to speak.

22:7. fee for *divination. It is to be expected that a fee or reward would be paid for vital information (see 2 Sam 4:10). Diviners, as religious practitioners, would be paid for their services (1 Sam 9:8). However, Balaam is not to be paid until after he curses the Israelites (Num 24:11). Thus this may simply be an offer rather than a retainer for services.

22:18. Balaam and Yahweh. If Balaam is truly a Mesopotamian prophet who has spoken in the name of many gods, it seems unusual that he would refer to *Yahweh as "the LORD my God." It is perfectly possible that Balaam was familiar with the Israelite God, at least by reputation (see Rahab's speech in Josh 2:9-11). Or he may always refer to each god he is dealing with in these intimate terms to demonstrate his prophetic authority. Balak's interest in Balaam seems to be based on his ability to invoke blessings or curses—no matter which god he calls upon. There is little reason to maintain that Balaam served Yahweh exclusively.

22:21-35. God opposing after sending. There are times when there seems to be a strange change of mind by God. The Lord called on Jacob (Gen 31—32) and Moses to go somewhere but then accosted each on the way. In each instance God did indeed want the individual to make the journey but had an issue to settle first.

22:22-35. angel of the Lord. In the ancient world direct communication between heads of state was a rarity. Diplomatic and political exchange normally required the use of an intermediary. The messenger who served as the intermediary was a fully vested representative of the party he represented. He spoke for that party and with the authority of that party. He was accorded the same treatment as that party would enjoy were he there in person. While this was standard protocol, there was no confusion about the person's identity. All of this treatment simply served as appropriate recognition of the individual that he represented. Gifts given were understood to belong to the represented party, not the representative. Words spoken to the representative were expected to be reported back in accurate detail and were understood as having been spoken directly to the represented individual. When official words were spoken by the representative, everyone understood that he was not speaking for himself but was merely conveying the words, opinions, policies and decisions of his liege. In the same way the Angel of the Lord serves as the messenger, the royal envoy endowed with the authority of the sender of the message. The word in Hebrew describing what the angel of the Lord does here is *satan*. This being is not the personified "accuser" or "adversary" found in Job 1—2 and Zechariah 3:1. The term is used only to explain the adversarial role played by the angel.

22:28-30. speaking animals. The only other instance in the Bible of a talking animal is the dialogue between Eve and the serpent in Genesis 3:1-5. In that case the serpent is described as the most cunning of the animals, and it is possible that it was the only animal that could speak. In the Balaam narrative the donkey is able to speak only after God gives it that ability. Such stories are commonly identified as fables, and they are quite popular in ancient as well as more recent literature. They generally have a wisdom theme and are designed to establish or question basic truths. Among the ancient Near Eastern examples are the talking cattle in the Egyptian *Tale of Two Brothers* and the dialogue between the leopard and the gazelle in the *Assyrian Teachings of *Ahiqar*. The effect of the speaking animal in this story is to make it clear to Balaam that God can speak through any creature he chooses, with no credit to the creature.

22:36-41. geography. From the city of Ar-Moab (NIV: "the Moabite town") near the northern border of Moab, the two proceed north to Kiriath Huzoth and Bamoth Baal. Ar-Moab (see 21:15) has not been identified with certainty, but is usually connected with modern Balu'a along the southern tributary that the King's Highway followed to the Arnon. The location of Kiriath Huzoth is unknown, as is Bamoth Baal. Some place the latter some twenty-five to thirty miles north of Ar along the King's Highway, though some would place it farther north, in closer proximity to where the Israelites were camped.

23:1. seven altars. The number seven is often attested in the Bible and may be associated with the days of creation or the fact that it is a prime number (see 1 Kings 18:43; 2 Kings 5:10). Nowhere else in the Bible are seven altars constructed for sacrifice. This may relate to a non-Israelite *ritual in which each of the altars is dedicated to a different god. It is conceivable that when an international treaty was concluded and the gods were called to witness the agreement (as in the treaty between the *Assyrian king Esarhaddon and Baal of Tyre, which calls on the "seven gods"), altars to each god would be erected and sacrifices made before them (see Gen 31:44-54). But nontreaty contexts in Mesopotamia also attest the practice of using seven altars in order to offer seven sacrifices simultaneously before the high gods.

23:1. sacrifice of bulls and rams. These were the most prized and valuable stock animals in the ancient Near East, and thus their sacrifice would have signified a supreme effort on the part of the worshipers to please the god(s) and gain their aid. The sacrifice of seven of these animals is also found in Job's sin offering for his three friends (Job 42:8).

23:3. barren height for revelation. The translation "barren height" is contested, and the meaning of the Hebrew word questionable. It seems clear from the context that Balaam separated himself from the Moabites to practice his *divination alone. This may have been required by the *ritual or perhaps by God's desire to only communicate directly with Balaam. In any case, high places are often associated with gods and their revelations (Mounts Sinai, Zaphon, Olympus).

23:4. meeting with *Elohim. In the ancient world messages from deity were generally conveyed through dreams, communications from the dead or temple personnel in prophetic trances. The language here suggests none of those options, though the nature of Balaam's encounter with God is not described.

23:14. Zophim/Pisgah. *Zophim* means "watchmen" or "lookout." Used in relation to Pisgah, the generic term for the promontories of the Moabite plateau looking west toward Canaan (see Num 21:20), *Zophim* simply means that Balaam went to a known observation point to watch for a sign from God. It is possible that he intended to observe the flight of birds in order to receive an omen. This is not only a common *divination practice in Mesopotamia but one that the Deir Allah inscription (see comment on 22:4) appears to relate to Balaam.

24:1-2. difference in Balaam's method and role of the Spirit of God. As a Mesopotamian prophet, Balaam's usual procedures when invoking a god or seeking an omen would have been to engage in some form of *divination. Having now perceived that Yahweh's intent is to bless the Israelites, Balaam dispenses with these mechanical methods and leaves himself open to direct revelation from God. At that point he turns toward the Israelites and is empowered by God's Spirit. He speaks the divine blessing, probably in a trance. It is his willingness to become vulnerable in the sight of the Moabite king that demonstrates the truth of his message and provides an example of ecstatic prophecy (see 1 Sam 10:5-6, 10-11).

24:5-7. metaphors. Balaam's *oracle contains a promise of abundance and prosperity for Israel. Looking down on their tents, he likens them to a forest containing aromatic aloe and cedars. Aloes are not native to Canaan, but the metaphor may refer to the immigrant Israelites "planted" in the Promised Land by God. Cedars do not grow near streams, and this may simply refer to any coniferous tree. The image of abundant waters and seed refer to the richness of the land of Canaan and the *covenantal promise of children. By referring to a king, the author speaks of the future nation's triumph over its enemies, the Amalekites, whose king, Agag, will be defeated by Saul (1 Sam 15:7-8).

24:7. Agag. Agag was the mighty king of the Amalekites in the time of Saul (1 Sam 15:7-8). Although Saul defeats them, the Amalekites continue to be a thorn in Israel's side (1 Sam 27:8; 30:1; 2 Sam 1:1). Agag's name appears again in the book of Esther as the ethnic name for the villain Haman the Agagite. Some have suggested that Agag should be understood as a title (like Pharaoh), but evidence is unavailable.

24:17. star and scepter metaphors. While a star is a common metaphor for kings in the ancient Near East, it is seldom used in the Bible (Is 14:12; Ezek 32:7). Its association here with a scepter, the symbol of royal power (Ps 45:6), however, makes this identification more certain. Balaam's *oracle thus predicts the rise of the monarchy in Israel and the extension of its power (like the waving of the scepter) over the lands of Transjordan. As in the Egyptian inscription of Tuthmoses III (c. 1504-1450 B.C.), the scepter is also used as a mace to crush the heads of enemy nations.

24:20. Amalekites. The Amalekites were a confederation of tribes living primarily in the steppe area southeast of Canaan (Ex 17; Judg 6—7). There may have also been groups of Amalekites in the hill country west of Samaria. They are always portrayed as Israel's rival for territory. The title of "first among the nations" may refer to what they called themselves or perhaps to their distinction as the first people to challenge the Israelites (Ex 17:8-15).

24:21-22. Kenites. Although the Kenites are described as friendly prior to this *oracle (Moses' father-in-law, Ex 2:16-22), they are condemned here with the Amalekites. They were nomadic tribes living around Kadesh in the northern Sinai peninsula and in the region of Galilee and may have been itinerant metalworkers (there were copper mines nearby in Sinai) as well as shepherds. Balaam mocks their mountain settlements, saying that they cannot prevent their eventual fall to Asshur.

24:22-24. Asshur. It is unlikely that this reference is to the Neo-Assyrian empire, which dominated the entire ancient Near East during the eighth and seventh centuries B.C. That would place the focus (and, some would say, composition) of this *oracle very late. However, the Asshurim, a tribe descended from Abraham and Keturah (Gen 25:3) does not seem significant enough to defeat the Kenites. The *Assyrians of the fourteenth century were sufficiently militaristic to contribute to the fall of the *Hurrian kingdom of Mitanni, but there is no evidence of military activity further west. This most likely should be identified as the Asshur mentioned in connection with the Ishmaelites in Genesis 25:18.

24:24. Kittim. This is the ancient name for the island of Cyprus (Gen 10:4) and derives from the name of the city Kition. In later texts (Qumran), Kittim is used as a generic for maritime nations (Dan 11:30) or for the Romans. Here some have suggested that it may refer to the "Sea Peoples"—the amalgamation of tribes (including the Philistines) that invaded the Near East around 1200 B.C.

24:24. Eber. Eber is identified as the ancestor of the Hebrews in Genesis 10:21 and 11:14. That cannot fit the context of this *oracle, however, since it would be a curse on Israel. Possible solutions may be a reference to an attack by the Kittim on "Heber," either one of the clans of the

Kenites or of the Israelite tribe of Asher. No really satisfactory explanation has been put forward for this name.

25:1-18
The Incident at Baal-Peor

25:1. Shittim. The full name of this site was Abel-shittim (Num 33:49), and it is the jumping-off point for Joshua's spies and for the Israelite's entrance into Canaan (Josh 2:1; 3:1; Mic 6:5). Josephus places it seven miles from the Jordan River. Its actual location is uncertain, but it may be Tell el-Hammam on the Wadi Kefrein.

25:3. Baal of Peor. It is not uncommon for the god *Baal to be identified with different mountains (Zaphon) or city sites in the region of Canaan (see Num 32:38; 33:7; 2 Kings 1:2). In this case, the Israelites are influenced by the Moabite women to worship the city god of Peor (see Deut 3:29 for Beth Peor). This is apparently their first contact with Baal, the Canaanite god of *fertility and rain, since the name does not appear in Genesis. The result is disastrous and sets a precedent for God's reaction to idolatry.

25:4. corpse exposure. Although the form of execution is unclear here (see 2 Sam 21:9 for a similar use of words), there is a purpose in placing the bodies of these unfaithful leaders on public display. It may be an attempt to propitiate God's anger or a warning to others that idolatry will not be tolerated. Legal tradition forbade leaving bodies exposed or impaled overnight (Deut 21:22-23). Impalement and public display of corpses was common punishment by the *Assyrians (referred to in the annals of Sennacherib and Ashurbanipal).

25:6. brought to his family. The unnamed Israelite may simply be introducing this Midianite woman to his family as his wife. But many have believed that the cause of distress here is the practice of ritual intercourse. By bringing a Midi-anite woman to his family, this man was encouraging all of his male kin to participate in this forbidden *ritual—even though the people were supposed to be repenting for their previous idolatry. The "chamber" (v. 8) into which they enter appears to be in the sacred enclosure and therefore suggests ritual intercourse. Though the ritual may have been *fertility-oriented, the Israelites are not engaging in agriculture, so it is difficult to imagine what connection that might have here. Alternatively, Psalm 106:28 links Baal-Peor to sacrifices for the dead (NIV: "lifeless gods"). The plague of verse 3 may have been attributed to ancestral spirits who could be appeased by ritual intercourse. In this case the "family" the woman was brought to may be the ancestral spirits.

25:8. the plague. Since no symptoms are given, the nature of the plague afflicting the Israelites is unclear. Diagnostic texts from Mesopotamia often sought to identify a causal relationship between certain symptoms or illnesses and the presumed sins that caused them. Israel had no such hierarchy of diseases, but they would interpret major or sudden outbreak of serious disease as punishment from God. Endemic and epidemic diseases in the ancient world included typhoid, malaria, cholera, tuberculosis, anthrax, bubonic plague, diphtheria and more. Yahweh's use of plague is similar to that associated with plague deities in the ancient Near East. In Mesopotamian mythology, Nergal (or, Erra) is the god of plague and king of the netherworld. The comparable Canaanite deity is Resheph, and the Hittite, Irshappa. Mur-shilish, a Hittite king of this general period, complains in one prayer about a plague that has lasted twenty years. He sees it as a punishment for his father's sins.

25:13. covenant of priesthood. Like the *covenant made with David (2 Sam 7:8-

16; Ps 89:29), this is an "everlasting" covenant. Again, this language and the concept of a perpetual treaty agreement is not unique. It is common in Mesopotamian treaty texts (see the *Assyrian Vassal Treaties of Esarhaddon). In this instance, Phineas's act of piety is the basis for marking his particular branch of Aaron's family as the group with the sole right to officiate in the temple (see the genealogy in 1 Chron 6:3-14, which traces Phineas's lineage and not that of his brothers).

26:1-65
The Second Census
26:55. distribution by lot. By employing lots to determine the distribution of the land, the decision is left to God's judgment. This process was also employed at *Mari in Mesopotamia to allocate fiefs by the king to vassals and military retirees.

27:1-11
The Case of Zelophehad's Daughters
27:1-11. daughters' inheritance rights. Land is generally redeemed by a male relative if a man dies without a male heir (for the levirate obligation see comment on Deut 25:5-10; for the Jubilee year see comment on Lev 25:8-55; for the relative's claim see Lev 25:25-28). The separate question of a daughter's right to inherit requires, in this case, an *oracle and a divine decision, since it cannot be dealt with under existing legislation. Levirate rights (Deut 25:5-10) apparently do not apply here, since no male heirs (sons or paternal brothers) are mentioned. In this situation, therefore, the decision is made and laws are enacted giving daughters the right to inherit in the absence of any male heirs, as well as establishing a law of procedure in cases of inheritance. Some precedent seems to exist for this in Mesopotamian

legal documents (Sumerian text Gudea statute B [c. 2150 B.C.]; *Alalakh [eighteenth century B.C.]; *Nuzi; and *Emar). The law in Numbers 27, however, has to be modified later due to the problem of the potential loss of a family's land if the daughter marries out of her tribe. Thus Numbers 36:6-9 adds the further stipulation that daughters who inherit land from their father must marry within their own tribal clans.

27:12-23
Joshua Commissioned
27:12. Abarim range. This is a range of mountains extending east of the mouth of the Jordan River and on around the northern end of the Dead Sea (see Deut 32:49). It forms the northwestern rim of the Moabite plateau. The specific peak in this range from which Moses will view the Promised Land is Mount Nebo, 2,740 feet in height.

27:14. geography. The parenthetical note that retells the story of Moses' and Aaron's sin at Meribah is based on the version in Numbers 20:1-13. This places the events near the oasis of Kadesh Barnea, probably 'Ein Qudeirat in the wadi el'Ain, the largest oasis in the northern Sinai. The Wilderness of Zin is the barren region in the Negev south of Canaan that extends toward the Sinai.

27:18. the spirit. As Moses' chosen successor, Joshua's qualification for this position is based on the authority of God with which he has been endowed. He has shown this trait in military campaigns (Ex 17:9-13) as well as in his courage in standing up to the people and the elders (Num 14:6-10; 26:65). Eventually he will be invested with the spirit of wisdom (Deut 34:9), but here it is his God-given skills as a leader that stand out as the basis of his elevation to command. There is no established political authority over all the tribes except that designated by the

Lord. The recognition of the empowerment by the spirit of God becomes the criterion by which political authority is granted by the tribes.

27:18. laying on of hands. Part of the process of investing a person with authority and signifying the transferral of power from one leader to another involves the laying on of hands (see Num 8:10; Lev 16:21). For instance, the paintings found in the *El Amarna rock tombs (c. 1400-1350 B.C.) portray the investiture of officials by Pharaoh. They are given special garments, and Pharaoh is pictured extending his arms over them as a sign of their new authority.

27:21. priest and the Urim. One sign of Joshua's new leadership role as Moses' successor is his use of the oracular office of the High Priest. By using the Urim and Thummim, the high priest could consult God and obtain a yes or no answer to questions (see this practice by David and Abiathar in 1 Sam 23:9-12; 30:7-8). While it is uncertain what the Urim and Thummim actually looked like, their use is similar to the oracular questions and answers found in *Babylonian omen texts. They were kept in a pocket inside the high priest's "breastplate" and next to his heart (Ex 28:16; Lev 8:8). For further information, see the comment on Exodus 28:30.

28:1-15
Offerings

28:1-30. festivals and holy days. The major religious festivals and holy days celebrated throughout the ancient Near East were for the most part agriculturally based. While daily offerings were made to the gods, there were "patron days" in specific towns and villages for locally honored deities, as well as occasions when the national god(s) were paraded from one town to another, "visiting" shrines and promoting the general *fertility and well-being of the

land. The single most important of the Mesopotamian festivals was the *Akitu* or new year's celebration. The monarch assumed the role of the chief god, while the high priestess served as his consort and represented the chief goddess. Their performance of a series of intricate sacred *rituals and sacrifices was designed to please the gods and thus insure a prosperous and fertile year ahead. During the year, based on a lunar calendar, "new moon" festivals were celebrated, as were the events of the agricultural calendar (the coming of the rains or annual flood waters, plowing and harvesting). Some rituals grew out of the changing of the seasons, such as the mourning for the "dying god" Tammuz (or *Dumuzi), who could be released from the underworld only through the tears of devotees (see Ezek 8:14).

28:1-8. daily offerings: who makes them and why. The heart of the sacrificial system in ancient Israel was the daily offering made for the people by the priests. This was a communal offering made on behalf of the people rather than an offering that each person made. Although the actual content of the sacrifice apparently differed from one time period to another (compare morning and evening animal sacrifice here with a morning animal sacrifice and an evening grain offering in 2 Kings 16:15), its intent was to provide continuous thanksgiving to God and signify daily compliance with the *covenant (see the comment on burnt offerings at Lev 1:1). The belief is quite clear that any interruption in this pattern would have resulted in dire consequences for the people (see Dan 8:11-14).

28:9-10. sabbath offering: who and why. The injunction to observe the sabbath each seventh day by ceasing work and by offering an additional burnt offering marks the weekly commemoration of the release from Egyptian bondage (Ex 20:11). Every Israelite, as well as their animals, servants and visitors, is required by this statute to observe the sabbath (Ex 31:12-17). This offering is not made by each family or clan but is made on behalf of the people as a whole. There is little evidence that the sabbath was used as a time for worship gatherings in ancient Israel. The sabbath is not tied to any other calendar event during the year and only has parallels in the celebration of the sabbatical and Jubilee years (Lev 25). Because the exodus event is unique to the Israelites, no similar, weekly holy day is observed by the peoples of the ancient Near East.

28:11-15. new moon offering: who and why. The lunar calendar was used throughout the ancient Near East and the worship of the moon god Sin was quite common, especially in northern Mesopotamia. Each new month began the first day of the new moon and signified the moon god's continuing dominion. The inclusion of a new moon offering in the liturgical calendar only appears in Numbers 28, although its celebration is known elsewhere (1 Sam 20:5; 2 Kings 4:23). Like the sabbath offering, the sacrifice marking the new moon is in addition to the daily offering. It is placed on a par with other major festivals with its sacrifice of a larger number of valuable animals (two bulls, a ram and seven sheep) and the addition of a sacrificial goat as a sin offering.

28:16—29:40
The Festival Calendar

28:16-25. Feast of Unleavened Bread. The Feast of Unleavened Bread signals the beginning of the barley harvest (March-April). Unleavened bread was made from the newly harvested grain without adding yeast and was eaten with joy as the first sign of coming har-

vests that year. For further information see the comments on Exodus 12:14-20.

28:26-31. Feast of Weeks. This second of the three major harvest festivals comes seven weeks after the harvest of the early grain (Ex 34:22; Deut 16:9-12) and is also known as the Feast of Harvest or Pentecost (Ex 23:16). Like the sabbath celebration, the Feast of Weeks is not tied to the lunar calendar (in this case because of the inaccuracy of a calendar based solely on the phases of the moon). In the agricultural cycle it marks the end of the wheat harvest season, and by tradition it is tied to the giving of the law on Mount Sinai. It is also associated with *covenant renewal and pilgrimage. Celebration includes the bringing of a "wave offering" (see comment on Lev 8:27) of two loaves of bread, animal sacrifices (seven year-old lambs, one bull and two rams) and a drink offering in thanksgiving for a good harvest (see Lev 23:15-22). Like the other major feasts, a goat is also to be sacrificed as a sin offering for the people (Num 28:30).

29:1-6. Feast of Trumpets. The first day of the seventh month (the most sacred month in the Israelite calendar) was to be marked with the blowing of ram's horns (shofar) by the priests, commemorating the *covenantal agreement and gifts of God to the people. Its significance may partially derive from its being the seventh new moon of the seventh month of the year (compare this to the sabbatical cycle). No work is allowed, and burnt offerings are presented in addition to the daily offerings. The festival would continue until the tenth day of the month when the Day of Atonement would be observed (see Lev 16:29-34 for details). In later times the Feast of Trumpets would become the new year's festival, but that occurs in late postexilic times (see Lev 23:23-25).

29:7-11. Day of Atonement. The Day of Atonement was a special day set aside each year to deal with the people's sins. The seriousness of this occasion is demonstrated by the fact that all of the *rituals had to be performed inside the sanctuary by the high priest. According to Leviticus 23:27-32 the Day of Atonement fell ten days after the opening of the civil new year (during the seventh month). On that day the people remained home in prayer and fasting while the high priest entered the inner precincts of the tabernacle and burned incense on the golden incense altar. Blood from this special sacrifice was also to be daubed on the horns of the incense altar to tie this holiest of altars and its flow of incense to the need for getting rid of the nation's sins. A more elaborate description of this yearly ritual, including the casting of the people's sins on the scapegoat, is found in Leviticus 16. See comments there for further information.

29:12-39. Feast of Tabernacles. The final harvest of the year occurred in the autumn prior to the onset of the rainy season and marked the beginning of a new agricultural year (fifteenth day of the seventh month). At this time the last of the ripening grain and fruits were gathered and stored, allowing time afterwards for pilgrimage to Jerusalem. The seven-day event is also known as the Feast of Ingathering (Ex 23:16) and is symbolized by the construction of booths decorated with greenery for the harvesters. The festival was tied into Israelite tradition as a commemoration of the wilderness wanderings (see Lev 23:33-43). It was also the occasion for the dedication of Solomon's temple in Jerusalem (1 Kings 8:65) and was such a popular festival that the prophet Zechariah described it as the eschatological feast celebrated by the nations following Yahweh's ultimate triumph (Zech 14:16).

29:13-38. number of animals. There are more animals sacrificed during the eight days of the Feast of Tabernacles than any other annual festival. A total of 71 bulls, 15 rams, 105 lambs and 8 goats are sacrificed, with accompanying cereal and drink offerings (compare the much smaller number prescribed in Ezek 45:13-25 for holy days). The number of bulls offered diminishes during the days of the festival, perhaps as a way of denoting the passage of time or possibly as a means of sparing the nation some of its most valuable livestock. The very large number of animals involved, however, speaks both to the joy associated with the harvest (a sign of the *covenant's fulfillment) and to the need to feed the large number of persons who have made the pilgrimage to Jerusalem.

30:1-16
Regulations Concerning Vows

30:2-15. importance and role of vows. The taking of a vow magnifies the devotion of an individual in performing a specific task (sacrifice—see Lev 27; transport of the ark to Jerusalem by David—Ps 132:2-5) or serves as a form of bargaining with the deity to obtain a goal (Jephthah's vow to gain a victory—Judg 11:30-31). Thus a vow differs from an oath in that it is generally conditional rather than just promissory. It can also be used to initiate a special dedicatory period, as was the case with the *Nazirite vows (Num 6), or, during war, as a form of abstinence sacrifice, which devotes all of the spoils to God (Num 21:1-3; Josh 6:18-19). Since this is a religious act, drawing the deity into a pact with the worshiper, it may not be broken under penalty of God's displeasure (see Ex 20:7 and the injunction not to "misuse" God's name). For more information, see the comment on Leviticus 27:2-13.

30:3-15. women and vows. According to the injunction in this passage, young women and wives may not pledge themselves to a vow without the consent of their father or husband. The father or husband, as head of a household, has the right to annul any such vow. However, if he first approves of the vow and later attempts to obstruct a woman from carrying it out, he bears the punishment for its nonfulfillment (vv. 14-15). In the first case (vv. 3-5) unmarried women are considered wards of their father and thus do not own property and may not, without prior consent, obstruct their father's ability to arrange their marriage or to utilize their person to benefit the family. Married women are similarly bound to their husband's household and may not make decisions without consulting their husband that might affect the functioning or economic viability of the household (vv. 6-8, 10-13). Only in the case of Hannah (1 Sam 1) does a wife on her own initiative make a vow, dedicating her child to temple service at Shiloh.

30:3-15. the subordinate role of women. Although women often had great influence over their husbands (especially royal women), only widows and elderly women appear to have been able to act on their own in Israelite society. Young women still living with their parents and wives were under the legal control of their fathers and husbands. They could not own property, start a business, initiate a lawsuit or arrange their own marriage. All of these acts were reserved for the male. There do seem to have been instances in which married women functioned more freely in the community (as in Prov 31), but the implication is always that this was done with the consent of their husbands. Their primary responsibility, in the biblical context as well as in the wider ancient Near Eastern context, was to maintain the home, provide heirs for their husbands and, when possible, assist with the economic assets of the household (farming, herding, manufacturing). In *Hammurabi's laws a woman who neglected her household duties in preferring business pursuits could be divorced by her husband. Older women beyond childbearing years may have moved into a different social category, functioning as female elders (see Deborah [Judg 4—5] and the wise women of Tekoa and Abel [2 Sam 14:2-20; 20:15-22]).

31:1-54
Battle with the Midianites

31:1-12. Midianites. Midianite territory centered in the region east of the Gulf of Aqaba in northwest Arabia, but the Midianites ranged west into the Sinai peninsula as well as north into Transjordan in various periods. Though their early history appears to be seminomadic or Bedouin in nature, archaeological study has revealed villages, walled cities and extensive irrigation in this region, beginning as early as the *Late Bronze period (the time of the exodus and early judges). There is, so far, no reference to the Midianites in ancient texts.

31:6. articles from the sanctuary. Nearly every army in the ancient Near East included priests and diviners (as seen in the *Mari texts), prophets (2 Kings 3) and portable sacred objects (Assyrian Annals of Shalmaneser III [858-824 B.C.]). In this way, the god(s) could be consulted on the battlefield or invoked to lead the soldiers to victory. Phineas, Aaron's son and a high-ranking priest himself, thus helps build the confidence of the army with his presence. Exactly which items are included here is uncertain but may have included the ark of the covenant, the breastplate of the priest and the Urim and Thummim (see the carrying of the ark into battle elsewhere—Josh 6:4-7; 1 Sam 4:3-8).

31:6. trumpets for signaling. When large numbers of troops are deployed over a fairly wide area, the piercing notes of the trumpets could serve a dual purpose, symbolizing the voice of God to frighten the enemy (see Judg 7:17-22) and giving signals to the various detachments of the army (see 2 Chron 13:2). While the shofar or horn trumpet is used elsewhere as a signaling device (Judg 3:27; 6:34; Neh 4:18-20), the Hebrew word here is for a metal trumpet, probably made of bronze or silver and capable of producing four or five tones. Tubular flared trumpets were used in this period in military as well as ritual contexts. This is depicted on Egyptian reliefs as well as evidenced by actual instruments found, for example, in the tomb of King Tut (a silver trumpet nearly two feet long). Trumpet signals are attested in Egypt in the *Late Bronze Age (this time period) in both military and religious contexts. A preset code would include some combination of long and short blasts.

31:17-18. rationale for who is put to death. The criteria used to determine who would be executed were two: (1) all the boys must be killed to prevent them from presenting a military threat in the future, and (2) all nonvirgins must die since they have already been contaminated by sexual contact with a proscribed people. Virgins represent an "unplowed field" and may be adopted through marriage into the Israelite tribes (see Judg 21:11-12). It is also possible that they were enslaved or used as *concubines. These young women were presumably innocent of the seduction of the Israelites by Midianite women at Baal-Peor (Num 25).

31:19-24. purification. The soldiers required purification because of their contact with the dead. The seven-day purification *ritual for the soldiers and for the plunder taken in war had to be performed outside the camp (compare Deut 23:10-15) in order to prevent contamination of the rest of the people (see Num 19:11-13, 16-22). Purification included bathing (Num 19:18-19) and

laundering by the soldiers (see Lev 11:25, 28 and the *War Scroll* from Qumran for similar injunctions). The spoils are purified by means of fire and water. Bathing metals in fire is also found in *Hittite birth rituals.

31:25-50. conventions for distribution of plunder. Soldiers until very recently were paid in plunder. This became a sacred right in the ancient Near East. In the *Mari texts officers took oaths that they would not infringe on the booty due to their men. Normally, the god(s) also received a share, which was collected on the battlefield by the accompanying priests. In this case the convention set for distribution provides the soldiers with a share ten times that of the civilians, while one-five-hundredth of the army's share was set aside for Eleazar (and the maintenance of the sanctuary) and one-fiftieth of the civilians' share was given to support the Levites. This could be compared to the tithe given by Abraham to Melchizedek of Salem in Genesis 14:20 and David's equal distribution to soldiers and civilians in 1 Samuel 30:24-25.

31:50. gold for ransom. Counting people in the ancient world was particularly unpopular (see comment on Ex 30:11-16) and could be subject to divine displeasure, since it might suggest distrust of the god(s) as well as a concern with personal power (see the plague which results from David's census in 2 Sam 24:1-17). According to the law in Exodus 30:12, whenever a census is taken a ransom must be paid for the life of each man counted. Thus after counting the army of Israel and determining that not a single casualty had been inflicted by the Midianites, the officers paid this ransom with the golden objects they had stripped from the bodies of the dead. This ransom (NIV: "atonement") is made to prevent a plague (see Num 8:19), and the golden jewelry is melted into sacred vessels that will serve the needs of the sanctuary as an eternal memorial to the victory and the people's willingness to submit to God's law. The amount of gold given is about six hundred pounds.

32:1-42
The Tribes Who Inherited Transjordan

32:1. Jazer and Gilead. The Transjordanian region in the area of the Jabbok River provided suitable grazing and was an attractive place for the tribes of Reuben and Gad to settle. Jazer is probably Khirbet Jazzir, twelve miles south of the Jabbok, on the border with Ammon (see Num 21:32). The region of Gilead (mentioned in *Ugaritic texts) extends from the Arnon River in the south to Bashan and the Transjordanian side of the Galilee in the north.

32:3. cities list. This same list of cities also appears in Numbers 32:34-38. Ataroth is identified with Khirbet 'Attarus, eight miles northwest of Dibon and eight miles east of the Dead Sea. It is also mentioned in the Mesha stele inscription (c. 830 B.C.) as a site built by the Israelites and inhabited by the tribe of Gad. Dibon (=Diban), the Moabite capital, is approximately four miles north of the Arnon River and twelve miles east of the Dead Sea. Nimrah, near modern Tell Nimrin, is in the northern sector of Transjordan along with Jazer. Heshbon (=Hesban), on the northwest corner of the Madaba plain (three miles northeast of Mount Nebo), is said to be the capital of the *Amorite king Sihon, but there is no archaeological evidence for permanent occupation prior to 1200 B.C. (see comment on Num 21:25-28). Elealeh (= el-'Al) is located northeast of Heshbon (see Is 15:4; 16:9; Jer 48:34). Sebam is an unknown site. Nebo has also not been located, but it is mentioned in the Mesha stele. Beon (=Ma'in, Baal Meon in Num

32:38) is ten miles southwest of Heshbon. In his victory stele Mesha (ninth-century king of Moab) claims to have built it.

32:1-37. Transjordan topography. A wide range of topography characterizes Transjordan, which included the areas of Bashan, Gilead, Ammon, Moab and Edom. In the north this includes the Mount Hermon range (highest peak at 9,230 feet above sea level) and a portion of the rift valley between the Huleh basin (230 feet above sea level) and the Sea of Galilee (695 feet below sea level). The southern limit of the region is at the Gulf of Aqaba. The rift valley extends south following the Jordan River to the Dead Sea (2,550 feet below sea level at its deepest point). East of the Jordan, the hills of Gilead rise to 3,500 feet above sea level and in the south the mountains of Edom stand 5,700 feet near the region of Petra. Most north-south travel followed the "King's Highway," starting at Damascus, cutting across the major wadis and skirting the desert to the east. East-west travel followed the Yabis, Jabbok, Nimrin and Abu Gharaba wadis. The generally dry climate necessitates irrigation farming but supplies sufficient pasturage for pastoral nomadic groups.

32:34-42. geography of tribal settlements in Transjordan. Based on the locations of the cities in this list (see Num 32:3 for locations of most of them), the tribe of Gad built cities in the southern, northern and northwestern sectors of the region of Transjordan (principally Gilead and Bashan). The Reubenites focused on the city of Heshbon, along with its surrounding villages. Joshua 13:15-31 presents the final distribution of cities, which yields to Reuben certain of the cities that the Gadites had built. Locations which can be posited for cities not discussed in Numbers 32:3 include Aroer, three miles south of Diban on the Arnon River; Jogbehah (=Jubeihat), five miles northwest of Rabbah; Beth Haran (=either Tell er-Rame or Tell Iktanu), south of Tell Nimrim; Kiriathaim (=Khirbet el-Qureiyat), six miles northwest of Diban. Archaeological attention to this area has increased in the last couple of decades, but many of these sites have yet to be excavated.

33:1-56
The Wilderness Itinerary

33:1-49. the itinerary of the journey. The itinerary form is common in ancient Near Eastern annals, including those of the ninth century B.C. *Assyrian kings, who described their campaigns in terms of stopping points and cities conquered. Closer to this period are the Egyptian itineraries preserved in the records of their various excursions into the Syro-Palestine region. This list provides a fairly complete chronicle of the journey from Rameses in Egypt to the Jordan crossing prior to the conquest. However, the omission of some important sites (Massah, Meribah) suggests that it is not comprehensive. The stages of the journey include (1) Egypt to the wilderness of Sinai (vv. 5-15; many of these sites are discussed specifically in the comments on Ex 13—17); (2) from the wilderness to Ezion Geber (vv. 16-35); (3) Ezion Geber to Kadesh in the wilderness of Zin (v. 36); and (4) Kadesh to Moab (vv. 37-49). Many of the names are obscure, occurring only here in the biblical record and unknown from ancient records or modern geographical and archaeological studies. Among those place names that can be at least tentatively identified are Rameses (=Tell el-Dab'a, see comment on Ex 1:8-14); Ezion Geber, a port city located at the head of the Gulf of Aqaba (1 Kings 9:26), either Tell el-Kheleifeh or on the island of Jezirat Far'on (the only site in the region with evidence of a substantial harbor area); Punon (=Khirbet Feinan), thirty miles south of the Dead

Sea; mountains of Abarim, near Mount Nebo, just east of the Dead Sea (see comment on Num 27:12); and Abel-shittim (Shittim, see comment on Num 25:1), which is either Tell el-Hammam on the Wadi Kefrein (runs east-west into the Jordan across from Jericho) or just east of that site at Tell Kefrein.

34:1-29
The Land to Be Assigned

34:1-12. trace the boundaries. The boundaries of the Promised Land are laid out here as a logical sequel to the order to displace the present inhabitants of the area (Num 33:50-56). Although these are not the actual borders of the nation of Israel at any point in its history, they are a close approximation of the territory claimed by Egypt in Canaan during the fifteenth to thirteenth centuries B.C. (see 2 Sam 3:10 for the realized dimensions: "from Dan to Beersheba") and are also approached by the description of the territory controlled by David and Solomon. The boundaries are outlined, using a set of then-known border points (see Josh 15—19 for the tribal divisions). The most obvious limits are those to the east and west—the Jordan River and the Mediterranean Sea respectively. The northern border reaches to the mountains of Lebanon as far as Mount Hor (unknown peak, probably in the Lebanese range) and Lebo (=Lebo Hamath, most likely modern Lebweh on one of the sources of the Orontes). This was the southern border of the land of Hamath and therefore the northern border of Canaan, including the Damascus area and Bashan (roughly equated to the modern Golan Heights). Zedad is likely modern Sedad, about thirty-five miles northeast of Lebweh, while Ziphron and Hazar Enan are commonly identified as the two oases to the southeast of Zedad. Moving south, the territory passes through the Galilee to the Yarmuk valley (the sites mentioned in v. 11 are unknown) where it moves west to the Jordan valley and from there south to Kadesh Barnea (see the comment on Num 13) in the Wilderness of Zin (see comment on Num 20:1) before swinging west to the Mediterranean at El-'Arish. It is common to identify Hazar Addar and Azmon with two of the other springs in the vicinity of Kadesh, namely, 'Ain Qedeis and 'Ain Muweilih. The location of Scorpion Pass *(akrabim)* is unknown, though it is usually identified with a narrow passage along the Wadi Marra headed northeast toward the south end of the Dead Sea.

35:1-34
Cities of Refuge

35:1-5. Levitical cities. Since their primary responsibility is as sacrificial priests and religious officials, the Levites are not given a portion of the Promised Land to farm (see Num 18:23-24). However, they do receive forty-eight towns, with their surrounding area as pasturage for their flocks and herds (see Lev 25:32-34 for their property rights in these towns). The precedent of assigning towns to priestly control can be seen in the practice of Egypt's rule in Canaan (and also in Hittite practice), where some cities were set aside as royal estates and placed in the hands of the priesthood, which administered that territory. These Egyptian administrative centers were typically fortified and collected the tribute or tax money from that region. Likewise in Mesopotamian and Syrian practice, designated cities had royal pasturelands connected to them. While a secular administrative role is not evident for the Levitical cities, they may well have been centers for religious instruction and collection of sanctuary revenues. Since pastureland is specified, it may also be that livestock collected for ritual use was provided for in this way.

35:6-34. cities of refuge and the judicial system. Six of the Levitical cities were to serve as places of refuge for persons who had committed an unintentional homicide (see also Deut 4:41-43). This solution, which provides asylum to the accused and prevents the "blood avenger" from killing him, may be an extension or alternative to the use of asylum altars mentioned in Exodus 21:12-14. The priestly community would have been concerned about polluting the altar and the sanctuary when a lawbreaker grasped the horns of the altar. Thus by extending the asylum zone to the entire city of refuge, this *pollution would not happen, and the person accused would also have better accommodations until the trial was completed. Sacred cities or royal cities with privileged status are evidenced throughout the ancient Near East, but the protection they offer is often in terms of freedom from certain government imposed obligations, though one text speaks of a prohibition against shedding the blood of anyone under such protection. The concept of asylum is also found in classical sources and suggests an attempt on the part of the government to tighten control over the judicial system, removing the rights of revenge from families, and insuring due process.

35:9-34. family responsibility for vengeance. While the biblical law clearly indicates the responsibility of the "blood avenger" to avenge the death of a kinsman, this practice of blood feud could be disruptive to the administration of justice, and thus the six cities of refuge were established to provide a "cooling off" phase as well as due process for the accused. Two witnesses were necessary to convict (Num 35:30), and then it became the responsibility of the "blood avenger" to execute the felon (Num 35:19-21; Deut 19:12). No ransom for the convicted murderer was possible

(Num 35:31-32). This contrasts with laws formulated elsewhere in the ancient Near East. Both the Hittite laws and the Middle *Assyrian laws provide for the payment of a ransom to buy back the life of the murderer. The Assyrian law reflects a middle ground, giving the deceased's next-of-kin the option of executing the murderer or accepting a ransom.

35:25, 28. death of the high priest. It is not the period of exile within the city of refuge that absolves a person of unintentional homicide (see Josh 20:2-6). The blood of the slain can only be expiated by another death, for bloodguilt accompanies every human slaying. However, since the accused has not been judged a murderer, he must remain in refuge until the death of the high priest. It is thus the high priest's death that eliminates the bloodguilt attached to the homicide. In this way even the death of the high priest continues his *cultic service to the people by removing bloodguilt and disposing of their sins (see Ex 28:36-38; Lev 16:16).

35:33. bloodshed polluting the land. The Promised Land, as a gift of the *covenant, is sacred and can be polluted by bloodshed and idolatry (see Ezek 36:17-18). Since blood is the source of life and a gift of God, the *pollution caused by shedding blood can be wiped away only by the shedding of blood. Thus even the blood of animals must be poured on the altar as a ransom for the person who slaughtered them (see Lev

17:11). That is why the convicted murderer must be executed and why the death of the high priest wipes away the pollution of the unintentional homicide. Failure to obey this command corrupts the land. If the land and its people become polluted, God can no longer dwell in their midst. And if he abandons the land, it will no longer yield its covenantal bounty (see Gen 4:10-12).

36:1-13
Case of Inheritance Law

36:1-13. tribal retention of land inherited by daughters. In the law established in Numbers 27:1-11, Zelophehad's daughters were given the right to inherit land since there was no male heir (the apocryphal book Tobit [6:13] shows an application of the law). A loophole was inadvertently created here which would have allowed for the transference of property to another tribe through marriage. Thus this codicil was added, restricting women who had inherited land from marrying outside their tribe so that the original tribal allotment would remain intact. Here it becomes clear that the preservation of family property holdings was one of the highest values in Israelite society. That is because the land was the gift of the *covenant, so each family's allotment was its share in the covenant. While land ownership was important in the rest of the ancient Near East, no other country had such strong religious overtones connected to the land.

Deuteronomy

Introduction

The book of Deuteronomy follows the format of agreements between nations, as described in the sidebar "The Covenant and Ancient Treaties." In these ancient covenants, the largest section was usually the stipulations section, which detailed the obligations of the vassal. These would include general expectations, such as loyalty, as well as specifics, such as paying tribute and housing garrison troops. There would also be prohibitions against harboring fugitives and making alliances with other nations. There were obligations to contribute to the defense of the suzerain nation and to treat envoys with respect.

In Deuteronomy the stipulations are in the form of laws that detail expectations and prohibitions. Some interpreters believe that the laws in chapters 6—26 (or 12—26) are arranged according to the Ten Commandments. Just as the ancient law collections have a prologue and an epilogue to give them a literary framework (see the introduction to Exodus), it is the covenant that provides the literary framework for the law. The literary framework of *Hammurabi's laws helps us to understand that the collection of laws was not for framing legislation but for demonstrating how just Hammurabi's reign was. Likewise the literary framework of Deuteronomy gives us an idea of why these laws were collected. Deuteronomy is framing these laws not as legislation but as *covenant.

When the people of the ancient Near East agreed to a treaty and its stipulations, they were obliged to abide by the terms of the treaty. It is the same level of obligation that would be connected to the laws of the land, but it operates differently, not within a legal system. For example, in today's world each country has its own laws, enacted by its legislative bodies, that are binding on its citizens. But there is also international law, which in part has been established by multinational bodies, often by treaty-type agreements. This international law is binding on all of the parties involved in the agreement. The binding nature of Deuteronomy is tied to treaty rather than to law (that is, to the covenant rather than to legislation). What that means is that Israel's obligations were connected to sustaining the relationship outlined in the covenant. If they were to be God's people (covenant), they were expected to conduct themselves in the described ways (stipulations). We should therefore not look at the laws as laws of the land (though they may well have been). The Israelites were not supposed to keep the law because it was the law; they were to keep the law because it reflected something of the nature of God and of what he wanted them to be like in order to remain in relationship with him.

An additional characteristic of Deuteronomy is that it is presented as the exhortations of Moses to the people. In this way Moses is seen as the mediator of the covenant because as God's messenger or envoy he is establishing the terms of the treaty. The *Hittite treaties preserve only the treaties themselves and offer no insight into the envoy who delivered the treaty. Other texts, however, allow us to gain some insight into the role of the envoy. He often presented his message verbally but had a written copy for the documentation and for the records. The words of Moses admonishing the people to be loyal to the terms of the covenant are very much in line with what any royal envoy would have been expected to say. The vassal would have been reminded that it was a privilege to be brought into this agreement and that it would be prudent to refrain from any action that would jeopardize those privileges.

1:1-8
Introduction

1:1-2. geography. The Arabah is the area of the Jordan rift, sometimes limited to the section between the Dead Sea and the Gulf of Aqaba. The list of locations looks more like an itinerary than a description of the Israelites' present location (thus the comment concerning the trip along the Mount Seir road). The sites are difficult to identify with any certainty. Mount Seir is another name for Edom, and the Mount Seir road takes one from the Sinai peninsula into Edom. For details on Kadesh Barnea see the comment on Numbers 13:26, and the for location of Sinai/Horeb see the comment on Exodus 19:1-2. The eleven-day journey (140 miles) mentioned here is consistent with a southern location for Mount Sinai.

1:3. chronology. The eleventh month is Tebet, and it spans our December-January. In Israel it is the middle of the rainy season, but in the southern region where the Israelites still are there is very little rainfall (an average of two inches per year), and though it is winter, the average daytime temperature would still be about sixty-five degrees Fahrenheit. It is difficult to assign a number to this fortieth year since the text has offered us no anchor to absolute chronology. In the ancient world chronology was only noted in relative terms ("the fifth year of king X"), and the biblical text does the same (here, the fortieth year since the exodus). There was no absolute chronology system ("the year 1385"). See "The Date of the Exodus," pp. 96-97.

1:4. history. The account of these battles is found in Numbers 21:21-35. Of the three sites mentioned here, only Heshbon has been excavated, and it has been controversial (see comment on Num 21:25-28). Ashtaroth is identified here as the capital city of Bashan. It is men-tioned in Egyptian and *Assyrian texts and the *Amarna letters, and some think it occurs in a text from *Ugarit as a place where the god *El reigns. It is known today as Tell 'Ashtarah and is located on the Yarmuk River about twenty-five miles east of the Sea of Galilee. Neither Sihon nor Og is known from any extrabiblical records.

1:6. Horeb. Horeb is another name for Mount Sinai, most likely located in the southern section of the Sinai peninsula. For more detailed discussion see the comment on Exodus 19:1-2.

1:7. geography. The description in this verse is largely by topographical areas. The hill country of the *Amorites may refer to the entire southern region, in contrast to the land of the Canaanites, which would be the northern region. The Arabah refers to the Jordan rift valley from the Gulf of Aqaba north, while the hill country extends north and south along the west side of the Jordan River, interrupted by the valley of Jezreel. The Shephelah (NIV: "western foothills") descend from the mountains to the coast in the southern section. The Negev is the wilderness in the triangle formed by the Dead Sea, the Mediterranean Sea and the Gulf of Aqaba. The Lebanon is the northern mountain range, and the northwestern spur of the Euphrates marks the northeastern border.

1:9-18
Judiciary System

1:16. judicial structures in the ancient Near East. Egyptian and *Hittite records of this general period likewise evidence a judicial system set up in tiers, and the Hittite *Instructions to Officers and Commanders* even has military leaders in the position of judge, as verse 13 here does. This suggests the close relationship between military activity and the activity of judging that the book of Judges implies. In most other systems difficult cases were referred to the king, whereas here Moses serves as the final adjudicator. Thus in the ancient Near East, leaders, whether tribal, military, city, provincial or national, had the obligation of judging the cases under their jurisdiction. There was no trial by jury, though at times a group of elders may have been involved in judging a case together. When only one individual judge was involved, the danger of favoring the powerful or the wealthy was very real. In both ancient Near Eastern documents and the Bible impartiality is valued, along with discernment. There were no lawyers, so most people represented themselves in court. Witnesses could be called, and oaths played a very significant role since most of our scientific means of gathering evidence were not available.

1:19-25
The Commission and Report of the Spies

1:19. Amorites. The *Amorites were also known as the Amurru (in *Akkadian) and the Martu (in *Sumerian). The term *Amorites* ("westerners"), like the term *Canaanites,* can be used to describe the general population of the land of Canaan. As an ethnic group, Amorites are known from written sources as early as the middle third millennium B.C. Most scholars think that their homeland was in Syria, from where they came to occupy many areas in the Near East.

1:24. the valley of Eshcol. There are many wadis in this general area, and there is no way of telling which one may be referred to here. Around Hebron today, Ramet el-'Amleh is known for its grape production and is near a wadi.

1:26-46
The Rebellion of the People

1:28. Anakites. The descendants of Anak are specifically mentioned in Numbers 13:22, 28. When names are given, they are *Hurrian (biblical Horites; see comment on Deut 2). The descendants of Anak are generally considered "giants" (Num 13:33; Deut 2:10-11; 2 Sam 21:18-22), though the description "gigantic" may be more appropriate. There is no mention of the Anakites in other sources, but the Egyptian letter on Papyrus Anastasi I (thirteenth century B.C.) describes fierce warriors in Canaan that are seven to nine feet tall. Two female skeletons about seven feet tall from the twelfth century have been found at Tell es-Sa'ideyeh in Transjordan.

1:44. Seir to Hormah. Seir is generally considered the mountainous central region of Edom (with elevations generally over five thousand feet) between Wadi al-Ghuwayr on the north and Ras en-Naqb on the south. Hormah is a site seven and a half miles east of Beersheba, tentatively identified with Tell Masos (Khirbet el-Meshash). Seir to Hormah is about fifty miles along a route to the northwest.

1:46. Kadesh Barnea. Kadesh Barnea is usually identified as 'Ain el-Qudeirat, about fifty miles south of Beersheba, which has the most plentiful water supply in the region. There are no archaeological remains on this site from this period, but the site has long been a stopping place for nomads and Bedouin, and the abundance of "Negev" ware (pottery dated to this period) suggests that was true during the time of the Israelite wanderings as well.

2:1-25
Wandering in the Wilderness

2:1. geography. Traveling the road to the Red Sea took the Israelites south along the Arabah, but probably not as far south as Elath at the tip of the Gulf of Aqaba. Instead it appears they turned north at one of the east-west wadis in the southern region of Seir to arrive at the route north that would take them to the plains of Moab.

2:8. Arabah road. The Arabah road runs north-south from the Gulf of Aqaba to the Dead Sea through the rift valley.

2:8. Elath and Ezion Geber. Elath is near the modern city of Aqaba at the tip of the Gulf of Aqaba. Ezion Geber was a port city located at the head of the Gulf of Aqaba (1 Kings 9:26) and may be either Tell el-Kheleifeh (which some identify as Elath) or on the island of Jezirat Far'on (the only site in the region with evidence of a substantial harbor area).

2:9. Ar. "Ar" is sometimes seen as a variant of Aroer. While some consider it a regional name, others have suggested it be identified with Khirbet Balu along one of the tributaries of the Arnon on the King's Highway, the major north-south route running on the east side of the Jordan.

2:10. Emites. These people are also referred to in Genesis 14:6, but nothing else is known of them.

2:10. Anakites. See comment on 1:26-46.

2:11. Rephaites. The Rephaites are mentioned as one of the ethnic groups inhabiting the land of Canaan in Genesis 15:20, but nothing else is known of them either inside or outside the Bible. The *Ugaritic texts speak of the Rephaim, whom some scholars consider to be the shades of dead heroes and kings. There is no cause, however, to think of this biblical group in those terms, though the Rephaim referred to in poetic texts such as Isaiah 14:9 (as well as in Job and Psalms) may be spirits.

2:12. Horites. The Horites are known throughout ancient Near Eastern literature as the *Hurrians. They were an Indo-European ethnic group centered along the Euphrates River in the third and second millennia. They established a political empire known as *Mitanni in the mid-second millennium, but it was breaking up around the time of the events of this book. Many Hurrian groups therefore ended up as displaced people and wandered into Syria and Palestine. The Hurrians were the dominant ethnic group in *Nuzi, and Hurrian groups are known from *Alalakh, *Mari, *Ugarit and the *Amarna texts as well. The Egyptians often referred to Canaan as Khurri land.

2:13. Zered Valley. The Zered Valley is the border between Edom and Moab. It is probably the wadi known today as Wadi al-Hesa, which runs east from the southern tip of the Dead Sea for about thirty miles.

2:19. Ammonites. The Ammonites lived north of the Moabites in the region around the Jabbok River. They are known from *Assyrian records as Bit-

The Covenant and Ancient Near Eastern Treaties

Archaeologists have recovered many treaties from the second and first millennia between nations and their vassals. The second-millennium treaties are mostly made between the Hittites and others, while the first-millennium examples come during the time of Assyrian kings Esarhaddon and Assurbanipal in the seventh century B.C. The format followed in these treaties shows striking similarity to the format of a number of *covenant documents in the Bible, most notably Deuteronomy. The treaties begin with a preamble that identifies the suzerain who is making the treaty. Besides giving his titles and attributes, it emphasizes his greatness and his right to proclaim the treaty. In Deuteronomy this occupies the first five verses of chapter 1. Next the treaties offer a historical prologue in which the relationship between the parties is reviewed. Priority is given to the kindness and power of the suzerain. In Deuteronomy this section

Ammon and as the land of Benammanu. They were settling this territory just around the time of the Israelite wanderings.

2:20. Zamzummites. The Zamzummites are known as the Zuzim in Genesis 14:5, but aside from their association with the Rephaites, nothing more is known about them.

2:22. Edomites and Horites. Nothing is known of this historic warfare between Esau's descendants and the *Hurrians. There have so far been no positive archaeological evidences of a Hurrian presence in Edom.

2:23. Avvites and Caphtorites. Caphtor is identified as Crete and is often associated with the homeland of the Philistines (Gen 10:14; Amos 9:7). Gaza was one of the five cities of the Philistines in the coastal plain. The Avvites are unknown outside the few obscure references to them in the Bible.

2:24. Arnon Gorge. The Arnon is today identified as the Wadi al-Mawjib, which flows about thirty miles northwest and west through Transjordan before emptying into the Dead Sea at its midpoint. The Arnon was often the northern border of Moab, though at times the Moabites extended their control north to Heshbon.

2:25. divine terror. The dread of a deity as a divine warrior was often believed to precede a powerful, successful army into battle. Egyptian texts attribute this terror to Amun-Re in the inscriptions of Thutmose III, and *Hittite, *Assyrian and *Babylonian texts all have their divine warriors who strike terror into the hearts of the enemy.

2:26-37
Battle Against Sihon the Amorite

2:26. Sihon the *Amorite. This battle is initially recorded in Numbers 21. Sihon is known only from the biblical records, and archaeology has little information to offer regarding his capital city or his kingdom.

2:26. Heshbon. The modern site of Tell-Heshban is located nearly fifty miles directly east of Jerusalem. However, archaeologists have not been able to detect any evidence that this site was settled prior to 1200 B.C. Some have suspected that the *Late Bronze city of Heshbon that was Sihon's capital was at a different site, with Tell Jalul named as one possibility. Recent surveys and excavations in this region have turned up more and more Late Bronze pottery, but it remains difficult to assess the nature of the occupation during this period.

2:26. Desert of Kedemoth. This refers to the wilderness region beyond the eastern border of Moab. The city of Kede-

comprises 1:6—3:29 (and some would extend it through the end of chap. 11). The core of the treaty is the stipulations section, which details the obligations of each party. Deuteronomy accomplishes the same thing by its presentation of the law in chapters 4—26. The treaties are concluded by three sections of legal material, including instructions concerning the document, witnesses to the agreement and the blessings or curses that will result from honoring or violating it. Deuteronomy addresses such issues in chapters 28 and 31.

As a result of the recognition of this format, it becomes evident that God used a very familiar literary form to communicate his covenant to Israel. Israelites would have realized that the Lord was putting himself in the place of the suzerain and that they should respond as a vassal would. It was a relationship bringing support and protection to the vassal as he was loyal to the suzerain.

moth is identified tentatively as Saliya at the southern corner.

2:32. Jahaz. The site of the battle with the forces of the *Amorite king Sihon is given as Jahaz. Its probable location, based on the church historian Eusebius (fourth century A.D.) and the Mesha inscription (ninth century B.C.), is between the territories of Madaba and Dibon, at Khirbet Medeiniyeh at the eastern edge of Moab by the Wadi al-Themed. The battle is also mentioned in Deuteronomy 2:33 and Judges 11:20.

21:24-30. captured land. The area of central Transjordan, which is here described as the kingdoms of Sihon and Og, stretches from the Arnon River valley in the south to the Jabbok River in the north. It would include Moab but not Ammon. It seems likely that these "kingdoms" were not organized states in this period and that their conquest provided passage for the Israelites without the tribes' actually taking control of and settling this region.

2:34. complete destruction. See comment on the "ban" in 7:2.

2:36-37. geography. Aroer was a border fortress, identified as modern 'Ara'ir just north of the Arnon gorge, where it turns south. *Late Bronze remains have been found at the site. The Israelites are victorious throughout the Transjordan territories from the Arnon (north boundary of Moab) up to the Jabbok (the territory of the Ammonites), about fifty miles north to south and twenty to twenty-five miles east to west.

3:1-11
The Battle Against Og
of Bashan

3:1. Bashan. After defeating Sihon, the Israelites traveled northward to Og's kingdom in the area known today as the Golan Heights. It was bordered by Mount Hermon to the north, Jebel Druze (Mount Hauran) to the east, the Sea of Galilee to the west and the Yarmuk region to the south. They defeated King Og at Edrei (modern Der'a, thirty miles east of the Sea of Galilee). Bashan proper, more limited to the region of the (upper?) Yarmuk, is a broad, fertile plateau region noted for its grazing (Ps 22:12; Amos 4:1-3).

3:1. Og. There is no extrabiblical information either from historical sources or from archaeology to shed light on Og.

3:4. Argob. From the description here it is obvious that the region of Argob is heavily populated. It is sometimes equated with Bashan, and one possibility is that it refers to the area just south of the Yarmuk and half encircled by it. The *Assyrian kings of the ninth century also found and conquered many cities in this region in the vicinity of Mount Hauran.

3:5. fortified cities in Transjordan. There has been little excavation in this region, but sites such as Tel Soreg may be characteristic of the unwalled farming communities in the area. Seven cities in the area east of the Sea of Galilee are mentioned in the *Amarna texts of the fourteenth century in an area they identify as Garu (=Geshur?). Archaeological surveys in the Golan Heights have located twenty-seven cities occupied at the end of the *Middle Bronze period and eight in the *Late Bronze.

3:5. gates and bars. Gateways were often multichambered (featuring inner and outer gates) and sometimes included a turn of some sort within the gateway. The *Iron Age outer gate at Tell en-Nasebeh has slots in the stone beside the gate where bars would have been placed. The inhabitants would lock the gates by sliding the bars into sockets in the wall.

3:9. Hermon/Sirion/Senir. Hermon is in the Anti-Lebanon range. Its highest peak, Jabal ash-Shaykh, has an elevation of 9,232 feet and is usually snowcapped.

The term *Sirion* is used in Egyptian, *Hittite and *Ugaritic materials. *Assyrian records of the ninth century refer to it as Saniru.

3:10. Salecah and Edrei. Edrei is identified as modern Der'a in Syria, about sixty miles south of Damascus and thirty miles east of the Sea of Galilee near the Yarmuk River. No excavations have been conducted here. The town is also mentioned in ancient texts from Egypt and *Ugarit. Salecah, modern Salhad, is another twenty-five miles east of Edrei.

3:11. Og's iron bed. Though many commentators and even some translations have identified this as a basalt sarcophagus, the language is clear enough and "iron bed" should be retained. Just as many objects described as gold, silver or ivory are not made of those but are decorated, overlaid or gilded with them, so we need not imagine a bed of solid iron. This account is still in the *Bronze Age, when iron was considered precious, so it would not be strange for this to be noted as a remarkable piece. The bed is about thirteen feet long and six feet wide. Beds were not just for sleeping but were often used for reclining on during feasts and celebrations. Some reliefs picture kings reclining on magnificent couches.

3:11. Rephaim. See comment on 2:11.

3:12-20
The Division of Transjordan

3:12-17. geography. Gilead is the hilly section of Transjordan between the Jabbok on the south almost to the Yarmuk on the north. The southern half of this, as well as the territory taken from Sihon south to the Arnon (northern border of Moab), was given to the tribes of Reuben and Gad. The section of Gilead that extends into the curve of the Yarmuk (the region of Argob?) as well as some territory north of the Yarmuk (all taken from Og) was assigned to Manasseh. Geshur and Maacah are excepted, though apparently part of Og's kingdom. Geshur is a small area just east of the Sea of Galilee. Maacah is just north of Geshur and stretches to Hermon. It is referred to in the Egyptian *Execration Texts.

3:17. Pisgah. Pisgah is the designation of one of the peaks of the Abarim range (Num 27:12) paired with Mount Nebo, which is slightly higher. They are identified as the two peaks of Jebel Shayhan, about five miles northwest of Medeba and about a mile and a half apart. They stand about ten miles from the Jordan River.

3:21-29
Moses Views the Land

3:27. view from Pisgah. Though Pisgah is about four hundred feet lower than Nebo in elevation, it is farther north and west and affords a better view of the Jordan Valley and the land opposite. At this point the Mediterranean is about sixty miles west, but it cannot be seen because the hills on the west side of the Jordan obscure the view. On a clear day one can see Mount Hermon, about a hundred miles to the north, the mountains to the northwest that flank the Jezreel Valley (Tabor and Gilboa), the mountains of the central hill country (Ebal and Gerizim) and to the southwest as far as Engedi.

3:29. valley near Beth Peor. The Wadi Ayun Musa at the foot of Mount Nebo is generally considered to be the Valley of Beth Peor, with the site Khirbet Ayun Musa as probably the town.

4:1-40
Call to Obedience to the Law

4:3. Baal Peor. *Baal Peor is the god who was worshiped at Beth Peor. This refers back to the incident in Numbers 25, when the Israelites were drawn into idolatrous worship by the Moabite women. It was perhaps their first exposure to the *fertility worship of Canaan. Fertility *cults are common in agrarian societies where the populace is dependent on rainfall and the fertility of the soil for survival. These cults often featured a "dying and rising" god in the pattern of the change of the seasons. The association of human fertility with the earth's fertility led to the development of sexual elements in the religious *rituals.

4:6-8. result of the laws. The laws are presented here as an evidence of wisdom and righteousness that will distinguish Israel from the other nations. In a number of the collections of laws known from the ancient Near East there is a prologue and epilogue explaining that the collection of laws will demonstrate how wise and just the king is. Likewise Solomon's wisdom was evidenced by how he was able to make just decrees and rulings. The kings of the ancient Near East usually counted on their collections of laws to convince the gods that they were wise and just rulers. Here the Lord is revealing his own wisdom and justice to his people and the world.

4:7. nearness of god. In Mesopotamia the laws were presented to the god of justice (Shamash) by the king as evidence that he was a just king. The king had been given the authority to make laws by the gods, the guardians of cosmic law. Law was seen as something inherent in the universe, and laws were supposed to somehow reflect that impersonal cosmic law. In Israelite thinking, however, law emanated from the character of God and he was seen as the source of the laws. Moses was not the lawmaker, *Yahweh was. By proclaiming laws, the Lord is therefore revealing himself in an act that distinguished him from the other gods of the ancient world. This is the "nearness" that the text remarks on.

4:10. Horeb. Horeb is another name for Mount Sinai, most likely located in the southern section of the Sinai peninsula. See the comment on Exodus 19:1-2.

4:13. two stone tablets. See the comments on Exodus 24:12; 32:15-16.

4:15-18. prohibition of images. The second commandment concerns how *Yahweh is to be worshiped, for the idols that it prohibits are idols of him (the previous commandment already dismissed the thought of other gods). The commandment has nothing to do with art, though the graven images of the ancient world were indeed works of art. They were typically carved of wood and overlaid with hammered sheets of silver or gold, then clothed in the finest attire. But the prohibition is more concerned with how they are employed, and here the issue is power. Images of deity in the ancient Near East were where the deity became present in a special way, to the extent that the *cult statue became the god (when the god so favored his worshipers), even though it was not the only manifestation of the god. As a result of this linkage, spells, incantations and other magical acts could be performed on the image in order to threaten, bind or compel the deity. In contrast, other rites related to the image were intended to aid the deity or care for the deity. The images then represent a worldview, a concept of deity that was not consistent with how Yahweh had revealed himself.

4:19. astral worship in the ancient Near East. The celestial gods (sun god, moon god and Venus particularly; in *Babylonia, Shamash, Sin and *Ishtar respectively) were primary in most ancient religions. Controlling calendar and time, seasons and weather, they were viewed as the most powerful of the gods. They provided signs by which omens were read, and they looked down on all. *Yahweh has now warned the Israelites against *fertility worship (v. 3), magic and manipulation (idolatry, vv. 16-18), and omens and linking deities to cosmic phenomena (v. 19), all the major characteristics of the pagan polytheism of the ancient world.

4:20. iron-smelting furnace. The ancient world did not have the blast furnace, which is used today to produce cast iron. Iron has a melting point of 1,537 degrees C., a temperature that could not be consistently achieved with ancient technology. But once the iron is heated beyond 1,100 degrees C., it takes a spongy, semi-solid form that can be forged. The furnace was usually fueled by charcoal to provide the carbon necessary for the chemical process. The strength of the steel is dependent on the amount of carbon it is able to absorb. The lower the temperature, the more often the process has to be repeated in order to get rid of enough slag to achieve a usable product. While a furnace can certainly be a metaphor of oppression, the fire of the smelting furnace is not destructive but constructive. It is the furnace that transforms the malleable ore to the durable iron product. The exodus experience transformed Israel into the *covenant people of God.

4:26. heaven and earth as witnesses. In ancient Near Eastern treaties the gods are typically called to witness as ones who would be able to adjudicate any failures to adhere to the terms. Here heaven and earth are not understood as deified, but, representing the entire created universe, they signify that the agreement is intended to endure long beyond human life spans. A clearer indication of the implications can be seen in the fuller wording of Psalm 89:28-29, 34-37 (see also Jer 33:20-21).

4:28. view of idols. Other passages that articulate this view are Isaiah 44; Jeremiah 10; and Psalm 115:4-8. On the beliefs about idols in ancient Near Eastern religious practice, see the comment on 4:15-18. It has long been of interest to scholars that the text does not refute mythology or the existence of the pagan gods but attacks their understanding of idols. In the end, however, it is very difficult to prove to someone that his gods do not exist. But it can be shown that the gods do not operate in the way they are believed to. To the biblical authors the "idol as fetish" aspect of pagan belief was the most vulnerable and the most ridiculous. If the gods were not manifest in their images, then many of the other aspects of the common worldview were also in jeopardy.

4:32-34. Israel's unique experience with deity. The two aspects the text highlights as unique are the two major features of the *covenant: election (vv. 34,37) and revelation (vv. 33, 35). *Yahweh distinguished himself from the gods of the ancient Near East by these actions. The gods of the ancient Near East were sometimes believed to have chosen an individual or a family to favor with their blessing. Usually this would be a king who claimed a particular deity as his sponsor. But without revelation, such "election" is only inference or propaganda. The gods of the ancient Near East did not reveal their long-term plans and were not necessarily considered to have any. They did not reveal what they were like or what pleased or displeased them. All of this had to be inferred or deduced by those who worshiped them. But *Yahweh has chosen to reveal himself both through the law ("I am holy, so you are to be holy") and through his actions (covenant with forefathers, plagues, exodus, bringing them to the land, etc.).

4:41-43
Cities of Refuge

4:42. cities of refuge. For more information on the cities of refuge, see the comments on Numbers 35. Bezer is in the region around Medeba. It is known from the Mesha inscription (ninth century B.C.), but its archaeological identification is uncertain. The principal candidates are Umm al-Amad (about seven miles northeast of Medeba) and Tell Jalul (three or four miles directly east of Medeba). Ramoth Gilead is generally identified as Tell er-Rumeith near modern Ramtha south of Edrei along the King's Highway. Excavations at the site, however, have turned up nothing earlier than Solomon. Golan, the modern Sahm al-Joulan, is at the eastern boundary of the Golan Heights on the east side of the river el-Allan.

4:44-49
Territorial Description
4:48. borders. Finally the whole Transjordan territory is circumscribed, from the Arnon River in the south (the north border of Moab proper) to Mount Hermon in the north. The Jordan rift valley is included and the Dead Sea (Sea of Arabah).

5:1-33
The Ten Commandments
5:2. Horeb. Horeb is another name for Mount Sinai, most likely located in the southern section of the Sinai peninsula. For more detailed discussion see the comment on Exodus 19:1-2.
5:6-21. the Ten Commandments. See the comments on Exodus 20.
5:22. two stone tablets. The use of two tablets probably indicates that Moses was given two copies, not that some of the commandments were on one tablet and some on the other. The fact that they were stone suggests a larger size than clay tablets would have been, though inscribed stone tablets such as the Gezer calendar were small enough to fit in the palm of the hand. The Egyptian practice of this period was to use flakes of stone chipped from rocks. Inscription on front and back was not unusual. When the writing reached the bottom of one side, the scribe would often continue around the bottom edge and move onto the second side. Even flakes that fit in the palm of the hand could contain fifteen to twenty lines.

6:1-25
The Importance of the Law
6:3. milk and honey. The land of Canaan is described as a land "flowing with milk and honey." This refers to the bounty of the land for a pastoral lifestyle, but not necessarily in terms of agriculture. Milk is the product of herds, while honey represents a natural resource, probably the syrup of the date rather than bees' honey. A similar expression to this is found in the *Ugaritic epic of *Baal and Mot that describes the return of fertility to the land in terms of the wadis flowing with honey. Egyptian texts as early as the *Story of *Sinuhe describe the land of Canaan as rich in natural resources as well as in cultivated produce.
6:4. categories of monotheism. There are several levels of monotheism that can be identified and that may have characterized the beliefs of various Israelites in various periods. The ultimate monotheism could be called *philosophical monotheism:* there has only ever been one God in existence. *Henotheism* acknowledges the existence of other gods but often insists on the supremacy of one's own god. Similarly, *monolatry* describes a situation where a person or group has determined to worship only one God, regardless of whether other gods, exist or not. Finally, a *practical monotheist* may acknowledge a number of gods, but most of his religious and worship activity is focused on one particular deity. The material in Deuteronomy does not allow for practical monotheism but does allow for henotheism and monolatry at the very least.
6:4. Yahweh is one. The claim that a deity is one, or alone, in other ancient

Near Eastern texts (made, for instance, by *Enlil [Sumerian] and *Baal [Canaanite]) generally relates to the supremacy of their rule. Another possibility is that the statement insists on a unified view of *Yahweh. Since a major god in the ancient Near East may have a number of different shrines, each shrine would come to emphasize a different perspective on the god. In Mesopotamia they may consider *Ishtar of Arbela quite differently from Ishtar of *Uruk. Inscriptions in Palestine do in fact indicate that this was true in Israel as well, as reference is made to Yahweh of Samaria and Yahweh of Teman.

6:4. monotheism in the ancient Near East. There were two movements interpreted as monotheistic in the ancient Near East of the Old Testament period. The first was by the Egyptian pharaoh Akhenaten in the general time period of the Pentateuch; the second by the *Babylonian king Nabonidus in the years just before the fall of Babylon to the Persian king Cyrus. Neither movement lasted more than twenty years. Akhenaten attempted to establish the sole worship of the sun disk, Aten, a god with no mythology, portrayed with no human form. It was a worship without image and had little use for temple or *ritual. Every attempt was made to eradicate the worship of Amun-Re, previously the major deity of the land, and the sun disk was proclaimed the sole god (though there was no apparent attempt to eradicate many other gods). Though Akhenaten may have intended this to be philosophical monotheism (some have even tried to identify it as trinitarian), it does not appear that many of his subjects adopted his beliefs. Nabonidus embarked on an official sponsorship of the moon god Sin by restoring his temple in Harran. For ten years he then stayed in Teima in northwest Arabia, apparently (according to some interpretations) devoted to establishing the *cult of Sin. There is little evidence, however, that this was done to the exclusion of other deities. Though he favored Sin, he continued to make requisite appearances at and donations to other temples. His time in Teima may have been the result of a falling out with the priestly powers in Babylon, or may have had trade policies or other political ends motivating it, but there is no reason to attribute monotheistic reform to it. Whether Israelite belief at this stage is labeled monotheism or henotheism, there is thus little to compare it with in the rest of the ancient world.

6:6. anatomical metaphors. Like English, Hebrew used parts of the body metaphorically to refer to different aspects of the person. "Hand" can refer to power or authority; "arm" to strength; "head" to leadership, and so on. Many of these metaphors have carried into English either because of their inherent logic or because of the role of the Bible in the English-speaking world. Not all anatomical metaphors, however, carry the same significance in the two languages. For instance, the kidneys were considered the seat of the conscience in Hebrew, and the throat was connected with life and essence of personhood. In English, "heart" is used metaphorically for the seat of emotions, in contrast to logic and reason. Hebrew uses it as the center of both emotions and reason/intellect. This usage is also true of the related Semitic languages, such as *Ugaritic, *Aramaic and *Akkadian.

6:8. symbols on hands and forehead. Headbands and armbands were common accessories in Syro-Palestine, though there is no graphic evidence proving Israelites wore them. *Amulets were often worn in the ancient Near East as protection from evil spirits. Precious metals and gems were considered particularly effective. At times amulets would include magical words or spells. Israelite practice disapproved of amulets, but if used here they are converted to reminders of the law or, in other places, may contain prayers or blessings, such as the small silver scrolls that were found in a preexilic tomb just outside Jerusalem in 1979. These miniature scrolls contain the blessing of Numbers 6:24-26 and represent the oldest extant copy of any biblical text. There is also evidence that symbols worn on the forehead or arm were used as indicators of loyalty to a particular deity.

6:9. inscription on door frames and gates. Aside from doorways as entrances representing the house itself and needing special protection, there is evidence from Egypt of sacred inscriptions on doorposts. Requirements of this sort could function either to *preserve* the continuity of life in positive ways and a mutually beneficial relationship with deity; or to *prevent* negative consequences of dangerous situations. While Passover blood on the doorposts functioned in the latter way, the law on the doorposts is an example of the former. The idea that written texts provided protection is found in the Mesopotamian *Erra Epic,* where the invasion by the god of plague can be prevented as long as a copy of the text of this work is kept in the house.

6:10-11. cities of Canaan in the Late Bronze Age. *Late Bronze Age Canaan (1550-1200 B.C.) was characterized by declining population and fewer fortified cities than the *Middle Bronze period. Even the villages and rural settlements show significant decline. In the *Amarna letters (fourteenth-century correspondence between Canaan and Egypt), Hazor and Megiddo were two of the most important and powerful city states in the north, Shechem in the central region, and Jerusalem and Gezer in the south. Archaeology has found that the cities' wealthier inhabitants had comfortable houses, usually with center courtyards. Most cities were surrounded by arable land farmed by the majority of the population. The work of digging wells and hewing out stone cisterns, preparing the soil and setting up irrigation had all been part of the agricultural lifestyle in Canaan. Groves and vineyards usually took many years to develop and be productive, but all of this groundwork was already done.

6:13. oaths in Yahweh's name. Since oaths were considered powerful and effective, the utterance of oaths would demonstrate which deity was truly considered powerful. Though inheriting the cities, homes and farms of the Canaanites, the Israelites are not to inherit the gods that had been associated with protecting these cities and providing fertility to this land. One of the ways to demonstrate their rejection of those gods is to refuse to attribute power to them through oaths.

6:16. Massah. Massah is the name given to the place at Rephidim near Sinai where water came out of the rock (see Ex 17:7).

7:1-26
Promises and Policies Concerning the Nations

7:1. peoples of Canaan. The *Hittites were from Anatolia, modern Turkey, but groups occupying sections of Syria and Canaan were also called Hittites and may or may not have been related. The Hittites in Canaan have Semitic names, while the Hittites of Anatolia were Indo-European. Girgashites are little known, though they are attested in the *Ugaritic texts. *Amorites (known in Mesopotamia as Amurru or Martu) are known from written documents as early as the middle third millennium B.C.. Most scholars think that they came to occupy many areas in the Near East from their roots in Syria. The term can be used to refer to a geographical area ("westerners") or to an ethnic group. Some Amorites were nomadic, but there were Amorite city-states in Syria as early as the end of the third millennium. Canaan is mentioned as early as the Ebla tablets (twenty-fourth century B.C.), and the Canaanite people were the principal inhabitants of the fortified cities of the land, though they do not seem to have been native to the land. The kings of this area refer to themselves in the *Amarna letters (mid-second millennium) as *Kinanu*, a term also used in Egyptian inscriptions of this period. There is still debate as to whether the term *Perizzites* is ethnic or sociological (those living in unwalled settlements). The Hivites are sometimes connected to the Horites, in which case they may be *Hurrians. The Jebusites occupied the region later associated with the tribe of Benjamin, notably the city of Jerusalem, and are often related to the Perizzites who were located in the same region. There is no mention of the Perizzites, Hivites or Jebusites outside the Bible.

7:2. the ban *(herem)*. "Ban" is sometimes chosen as the English word to represent the concept of total destruction that is commanded here in verse 2 and elaborated in verses 5-6. Just as there were some types of sacrifices that belonged entirely to the Lord, while others were shared by priest and offerer, so some plunder was set aside as belonging solely to the Lord. Just as the whole burnt offering was entirely consumed on the altar, so the ban mandated total destruction. Since the warfare was commanded by Yahweh and represented his judgment on the Canaanites, the Israelites were on a divine mission with Yahweh as their commander. Since it was his war, not theirs, and he was the victor, the spoil belonged to him. Although the divine warrior motif occurs throughout

the ancient Near East, the *herem* concept is more limited—the only other occurrence of the term is in the Moabite Mesha inscription, but the idea of total destruction is also in the *Hittite material. Some sites, such as Gezer, feature a distinct burn layer in association with the *Late Bronze period. Under siege conditions sanitation is at its worst and disease is often rampant. The practice of burning everything after the defeat of a city thus had an element of health connected to it.

7:3. command not to intermarry. In *Hittite documents of this period certain cities are designated temple cities and accorded special privileges. In order to protect those privileges, the inhabitants are prohibited from marrying outside the community. In a similar way the entire land of Israel has been designated "God's land," and the Israelites are a kingdom of priests. The prohibition against intermarriage therefore protects the privileges of the *covenant as well as the *purity of their religious ideals.

7:5. sacred stones. Standing stones or *masseboth* were apparently a common feature of Canaanite religion and also appear as memorials in a number of Israelite *covenantal contexts (see Ex 24:3-8; Josh 24:25-27). Their association with *Asherah, *Baal and other Canaanite deities is the basis for their being condemned as rivals and a threat to *Yahweh worship. Archaeologists have discovered sacred stones at Gezer, Shechem, Hazor and Arad. In the latter three cases, they are clearly within a sacred precinct and part of the *cultic practices at these sites. The Hazor stones include incised representations of upraised arms and a sun disk.

7:5. Asherah poles. *Asherah can be either the name of a *fertility goddess or the name of a *cult object (as here). The goddess was popular in the pagan deviations in Israel and was sometimes considered to be a consort of *Yahweh.

An indication of this belief is found in the inscriptions from Kuntillet Ajrud and Khirbet el-Qom. In Canaanite mythology she was the consort of the chief god, *El. She appears in Mesopotamian literature as early as the eighteenth century, where she is the consort of the *Amorite god Amurru. The *cult symbol may or may not have borne a representation of the deity on it. The pole may represent an artificial tree, since Asherah is often associated with sacred groves. Sometimes the cult object can be made or built, while on other occasions it is planted. We have little information on the function of these poles in *ritual practice.

7:6-11. the *covenant relationship. The terminology used here of love, loyalty and obedience are common to the international treaties of this time. *Hittite, *Akkadian, *Ugaritic and *Aramaic examples all show that the positive action of the suzerain toward the vassal is expressed as love, kindness and graciousness, and in return the vassal is expected to respond with obedience and loyalty.

7:15. diseases of Egypt. Some consider this to be a reference to the plagues, while others associate it with diseases indigenous to Egypt. If the latter is intended, it is difficult to be more specific, though examination of mummies has suggested the prevalence of smallpox, malaria and polio. Emphysema and tuberculosis are also evidenced. Egyptian medicine was well known for its treatment of eye diseases and diseases of the digestive and excretory/urinary systems. This might suggest that that was where persistent disease was encountered. All of these were worsened by the very primitive sanitation conditions archaeologists have identified even around the estates of the wealthy. The dry season in Egypt is known for its proliferation of diseases, usually brought to an end by the annual flooding of the Nile.

7:20. the hornet. Insects are often used as metaphors for armies, for instance, bees and flies (Is 7:18-19) and locusts (Joel 1—2). However, some interpreters see this as a wordplay on *Egypt* (see comment on Ex 23:28) or a reference to Egypt by means of an insect that was used to symbolize Lower Egypt. Other interpreters have translated the word as "plague" or "terror."

8:1-19
Remembering What God Had Done

8:3. manna. The food that nourished the Israelites in the wilderness is not easily identified. For possibilities see the comment on Exodus 16:4-9.

8:4. clothes not wearing out. In the Gilgamesh Epic, *Utnapishtim instructs that *Gilgamesh be clothed with garments that do not wear out for his return journey. Job 13:28 describes the "wearing out" of clothes as being "motheaten" or perhaps moldy. This verse suggests a supernatural protection from decay.

8:7. water sources. The text mentions streams, pools and springs. The first is the result of runoff from precipitation at high elevations, and the other two represent subterranean water sources. In a land where rainfall is seasonal and, in some areas, limited, irrigation is necessary to sustain agriculture, and water sources are important both for animal herds and for human settlements. While there are few streams west of the Jordan, there are many springs that were used to sustain cities and villages.

8:8. staples of agriculture. Seven agricultural products are mentioned here that are the staple products of the region. The Egyptian *Story of *Sinuhe* describes the land of Canaan and lists six of the seven named here (pomegranates are omitted). Wine and olive oil were two of the principal exports of the region, while the other products provided a significant portion of their diet. The honey referred to here is the product of the date palm, not bees' honey.

8:9. iron and copper. The text also identifies the natural resources of the land from the mining perspective. There are numerous deposits of poor-quality iron ore in Palestine, but few of high quality. The only major deposits of iron ore known in Palestine today are at Mugharat el-Wardeh in the Ajlun hills by the Jabbok River. Copper mining sites are mostly in Transjordan. While iron can be mined on the surface, copper mining requires shafts.

9:1-6
Conquest as Punishment

9:1. walled cities. City defenses were of most concern in troubled, insecure times. The latter part of the *Middle Bronze Age in Canaan (eighteenth-sixteenth centuries) was one such time, and many fortified cities were built. The end of that period brought the destruction of many of these cities, and many were not rebuilt during the *Late Bronze Age (1550-1200). It is generally assumed that this was because Egypt controlled the region and offered security to it. There were, however, still a number of fortified cities that served as administrative centers for Egyptian control. The fortification techniques developed in the Middle Bronze period included steep earthen slopes (some reaching fifty feet) at the foundation of the walls and a ditch around the outside dug to bedrock. These features would both hamper the approach of siege machines and prevent tunneling. The stone walls were twenty-five to thirty feet wide and perhaps thirty feet high.

9:2. Anakites. See comment on 1:28.

9:7—10:11
Remembering the Events at Sinai

9:8. Horeb. Horeb is another name for Mount Sinai, most likely located in the southern section of the Sinai peninsula. See comment on Exodus 19:1-2.

9:9. stone tablets. See comment on 5:22.

9:16. golden calf. Bull or calf figurines, made either of bronze or a combination of metals, have been found in several archaeological excavations (Mount Gilboa, Hazor and Ashkelon), but they are only three to seven inches long. The calf symbol was well known in the Canaanite context of the second millennium and represented fertility and strength. The gods were typically not depicted in the form of bulls or calves, but portrayed standing on the back of the animal. Nevertheless worship of the animal image was not unknown, and there is little in the biblical text to suggest the Israelites understood the figure merely as a pedestal (not unlike the ark). The fact that the calf is worshiped in the context of a feast to Yahweh suggests that this may be a violation of the second commandment rather than the first.

9:22. Taberah, Massah, Kibroth Hattaavah. These are all places where the Israelites experienced God's judgment. Taberah and Kibroth Hattaavah are in Numbers 11 in connection with the plague from eating quail, and Massah is associated with the incident in Exodus 16 where the people challenged the Lord to provide water.

9:23. Kadesh Barnea. Kadesh Barnea was the main camping place during the wilderness wandering. See comment on 1:46.

9:28. belligerent deities. Though the claim made in verse 28 might seem a preposterous way to think, it would not have been an unusual view in the religious world of the ancient Near East. In a polytheistic system gods could not be omnipotent, so they might fail to accomplish something they set out to do. Additionally they were not considered to be friendly, forthright or predictable. Examples would include the Mesopotamian god *Ea telling his "favorite" *Adapa that the food he would be offered was "bread of death" when in reality it would have procured eternal life for him. In the *Gilgamesh Epic, Ea advises deceiving the people into thinking that blessings cannot rain down on them unless *Utnapishtim leaves in his boat. After they send him off, they are rained on in a totally unexpected way when the flood comes and destroys them. Around 1200 B.C. the Libyans complain that the gods gave them initial success against Egypt with the intent to eventually destroy them. In Egypt the mortuary texts (Pyramid Texts and Coffin Texts) are targeted against hostile deities.

10:6. wells of the Jaakanites, Moserah, Gudgodah, Jotbathah. These sites are also in the itinerary of Numbers 33:30-34. Most of them are unidentified, but Jotbathah has been associated with Tabeh, an oasis along the western shore of the Gulf of Aqaba.

10:12—11:32
Covenant Response to Yahweh

10:17. divine titles. The enumeration of divine names and attributes is a common form of praise in the ancient Near East. Perhaps most notable is the *Babylonian creation epic, *Enuma Elish, that proclaims the fifty names of *Marduk, chief god of Babylon.

10:17. gods accepting bribes. In the religious beliefs of the ancient Near East the gods could be manipulated because they were believed to have needs. Sacrifice and temple upkeep were part of a program of taking care of them and feeding them. By providing the food, clothing and shelter that the gods needed, an individual could win the favor of the deity. This text makes it clear that *Yahweh is not to be thought of in the same way as the gods of Israel's neighbors. This also reflects the picture of Yahweh as a just judge who refuses to distort justice for personal gain.

11:1. loving deity in ancient Near East. In the *Amarna letters (from vassal kings of Canaan to their Egyptian overlord) "love" is used as a characterization of friendly and loyal international relationships. It expresses the vassal's intentions to be loyal and to honor the terms of the treaty agreement between the parties. The biblical text shows a clear example of this usage in 1 Kings 5:15. There are rare instances in Mesopotamian literature where an individual is admonished to love a deity, but in general the gods of the ancient Near East neither sought love from their worshipers nor entered into *covenant relationships with them.

11:2. outstretched arm. The "outstretched arm" is a metaphor that was used by the Egyptian Pharaohs for the extension of their power and authority. It was *Yahweh's outstretched arm that extended his power over Egypt to bring deliverance to his people. See comment on Deuteronomy 26:8.

11:4. Red Sea/Reed Sea. There have been many different suggestions concerning the identification of this body of water. Lake Balah or Lake Timsah are the most common. See comment on Exodus 13:18.

11:9. land of milk and honey. See comment on 6:3.

11:10. irrigation methods in Egypt. The contrast here does not favor rainfall over irrigation, for everyone recognized the value and success of irrigation methods and technology. Furthermore, it is not suggested that the often-sparse rainfall of Palestine is superior to the regular abundant annual flooding of the Nile. There is no known irrigation method that would be identified as "watering by foot," but that phrase is used as a euphemism for urinating in the reading preserved in some manuscripts of 2 Kings 18:27. If that is the meaning here, the contrast would have to do not with technologies of irrigation or abundance of water supply but with the purity of the water used to grow food.

11:11-15. seasons in Israel. Israel has a rainy season (winter months) and a dry season (summer months). The rainy season begins with the autumn rains ("early rains," October-November) and ends with the spring rains ("latter rains," early April). These are important for what they contribute to the overall moisture levels in the earth and for softening the ground for plowing. Grain is harvested in the spring (barley in May, wheat in June), and the summer months (July and August) are for threshing and winnowing. Grapes are harvested in the fall, while the olive harvest stretches into the winter.

11:18. symbols on hands, foreheads and doorframes. See comment on 6:8-9.

11:24. Lebanon to the Euphrates. For the general boundaries of the land, see the comment on 1:7.

11:29. Gerizim and Ebal. Gerizim and Ebal are the mountains that flank the town of Shechem in the central hill country, Gerizim (elevation 2,849 feet) to the south, Ebal (elevation 3,077 feet) to the north. This site was chosen for the ceremony because it was believed to represent the center of the land (Judg 9:37) and because from here a large portion of the land could be seen. The valley that runs between the two mountains, Wadi Nablus, was one of the only passageways through the region. The valley at its southeastern end is quite narrow (the lower flanks of the hills are separated by little over a quarter of a mile) and would easily accommodate the antiphonal ceremony anticipated here.

11:29. blessings and curses. The international treaties of this time featured blessings and curses on the parties responsible for keeping the terms of the *covenant. The blessings and curses typically were seen as to be carried out by the deities in whose name the agreement had been made. The blessing formulas are rarer and the curse formulas grow longer between the second and first millennia.

11:30. Gilgal. This is not the same Gilgal that the Israelites use as a base in the book of Joshua but is farther north in the vicinity of Shechem. One possibility is the site of El-Unuk, about four miles east of Shechem along the Wadi Far'ah.

12:1-32
Central Place of Worship

12:2-3. outdoor shrines. Apparently the use of outdoor shrines was common among the Canaanites. These local *cult sites were considered abhorrent to the writer because they promoted a "popular" brand of religion that contained elements of Canaanite worship that deviated from the established *Yahweh-only doctrine. Thus local altars, sacred poles dedicated to *Asherah, sacred groves and any place associated with a Canaanite god (*Baal, *El, etc.) and the worship of God outside of Jerusalem, "the place the Lord your God will choose" (Deut 12:5), were forbidden. There is a difference between these outdoor *cultic places and the "high place" (*bamah*) often mentioned as a religious center in the local towns and cities (1 Kings 11:7; Jer 7:31; Ezek 16:16; 2 Chron 21:11; Mesha's inscription). The "high place" was apparently an indoor facility, built to house sacred furniture, an altar and precincts large enough to accommodate a priesthood. A clear differentiation is drawn between these two types of religious sites in 2 Kings 17:9-11.

12:3. sacred stones. See comment on 7:5.

12:3. Asherah poles. One common feature of Canaanite worship and of *syncretized Israelite worship on "high places" and in city shrines is the erection of *Asherah poles (Judg 3:7; 1 Kings 14:15; 15:13; 2 Kings 13:6). There is some uncertainty about whether these were simply wooden poles erected to symbolize trees, perhaps containing a carved image of the *fertility goddess, or part of a sacred grove. The reference in 2 Kings 17:10, which refers to Asherah poles beside "every spreading tree," seems to indicate that these were poles erected for *cultic purposes rather than planted trees. As the consort of *El, Asherah was clearly a popular goddess (see 2 Kings 18:19), and her worship is mentioned in *Ugaritic texts (1600-1200 B.C.). Her prominent appearance in the biblical narrative indicates that her *cult was a major rival to *Yahweh worship (see the prohibition in Ex 34:13; Deut 16:21). This explains the number of examples in which Asherah poles are erected and venerated, the strong condemnations of this practice and the depictions of these poles being cut down and burned (Judg 6:25-30; 2 Kings 23:4-7). For more information see the comment on Deuteronomy 7:5.

12:4, 30-31. their way of worshiping. The prohibited aspects of Canaanite religion would have included the use of idols to manipulate the deity, *fertility practices (perhaps including *ritual sex with temple prostitutes, but see comment on 23:17-18), child sacrifice, *divination and appeasement rituals.

12:3-5. wipe out their names, the Lord establishing his name. The potency and power associated with names and name giving are clearly demonstrated in the biblical narrative (see Gen 17:5; 41:45; Ex 3:13-15; Deut 5:11). One sign of this is found in the practice of erasing the names of discredited officials and even pharaohs from their monuments in an-

cient Egypt. Names were also used in *execration formulas throughout the Near East to curse enemies and to call down divinely inspired disaster (Num 22:6; Jer 19:3-15). *Execration texts are known in Egypt throughout the second millennium and consist of names of rulers or cities written on objects that were then smashed. When the Israelites are called on to wipe out the names of the Canaanites and their gods, the command is to wipe them from the pages of history. Utter destruction, in a world tied to the service of named persons and gods, could only come if all memory of these names was obliterated. Once that was done, only one name would remain, and there would be no reason or desire to worship another (see Is 42:8).

12:5-7. sacrifices in the presence of deity. Throughout the ancient Near East it was a common understanding that deities had their own realms of influence and thus were tied to particular sites (e.g., *Marduk of *Babylon or Baalzebub of Ekron). It was expected that devotees of these gods would come to the principal shrines, where they could offer sacrifices, take vows, formalize contracts or treaties, or provide legal testimony within the sacred precinct of the god (as in the Code of *Hammurabi and the *Middle Assyrian laws). By doing this, the supplicant could draw on the god as a witness and thus add force to the act being performed. It also provided validity to the shrine, marking it as the place where God's presence was made manifest.

12:11. vows. See comment on Leviticus 27:2-13.

12:16. pouring out blood before eating meat. Sacred literature from *Ugarit and Mesopotamia identified blood as the life force of any animal. In Israelite tradition, blood as the life force belonged to the life-giver, the Creator God *Yahweh. Therefore, the Israelites were prohibited from consuming meat which still contained blood. This sacred fluid had to be drained from the meat and "poured on the ground like water" so that it returned to the earth. In sacrificial contexts, the blood was to be poured on the altar (see Lev 17:11-12).

12:20. eating meat. The promise that the Israelites would be able to eat their fill of meat is tied to the *covenantal promise of land and fertility. This society, however, was generally never so rich in animals that they could be slaughtered indiscriminately. Animal sacrifice was therefore both a sacred and a solemn occasion. The meat of the sacrifice might be the only meat eaten for weeks at a time.

13:1-18
Those Who Encourage the Worship of Other Gods

13:1-3. prophet urging worship of other gods. In its effort to delineate a *Yahweh-only religion, Deuteronomy had to discredit and disavow the teachings and pronouncements of all other gods and their prophets. Prophets, diviners and priests for these other gods were present among the Canaanites and other neighboring groups (mentioned in *Mari texts, the account of Balaam in Numbers 22—24 and the Deir 'Alla inscriptions). However, what seems most heinous here are Israelites who speak in the name of other gods. This type of internal proselytizing was particularly frightening since it had a stronger degree of credibility and could therefore be most effective (see Num 25:5-11). Should the words or the predictions of prophets come true (a sign of their validity as prophets, Deut 18:22), the Israelites were to be alert to whether they attributed the signs to Yahweh. If not, it was a test of their faithfulness, and they must reject the prophet and condemn him to death as a corrupting influence.

13:1-5. foretelling by dreams in ancient Near East. Dreams were one of the standard means for receiving messages from a god in the ancient Near East (see Jacob in Gen 28:12; Joseph in Gen 37:5-11; Nebuchadnezzar in Dan 2, 4). They appear in *Old Babylonian omen texts, along with reports of the examination of sheep livers, anomalies in the weather and birth of animals, and other presumed signs of divine will. Among the most famous is the dream of Gudea of *Lagash (c. 2150 B.C.), who was commanded in a dream to build a temple by a figure reminiscent of the apocalyptic figures in Daniel's dreams and Ezekiel's call narrative (Dan 7; Ezek 1:25-28). The royal correspondence from *Mari (c. 1750 B.C.) contains around twenty prophetic utterances involving dreams, always from nonprofessional personnel. These portents were taken quite seriously and studied. The professional priesthood in both Mesopotamia and Egypt included instruction in the interpretation of dreams and other omens (see the appearance of wise men, mediums and astrologers in Gen 41:8 and Dan 2:4-11).

13:10. stoning as capital punishment. Aside from the ready availability of stones in Israel, stoning was chosen as a form of execution because it was communal. No one person was responsible for the death of the condemned criminal, but in the case of public offenses (apostasy, blasphemy, sorcery, stealing from the *herem) every citizen was required to take a hand in purging the community of evil (see Deut 17:5; Lev 20:27; 24:14; Josh 7:25). Familial offenses such as adultery and recurrent disobedience also were punishable by stoning, and again the entire community was involved (Deut 21:21; 22:21). Stoning is not mentioned as a form of capital punishment outside the Bible. Ancient Near Eastern law codes list only drowning, burning, impalement and beheading, and in each case it is an official body, not the community at large, that is charged with carrying out the punishment.

13:16. plunder as burnt offering. There are two types of plunder reckoned as belonging solely to God: that taken in a *herem* (holy war, Josh 6:18-19) and that gathered from a village condemned for its apostasy. To keep any of these objects corrupts the one who takes them and brings down God's wrath on the people (Josh 7).

13:16. ruin. The Hebrew word NIV translates as "ruin" is *tel*, and it has come into English as *"tell," referring to a mound made up of the layers of the accumulated ruins of ancient settlements.

14:1-21
Clean and Unclean Food

14:1-2. ritual for the dead. Ancestor worship and *rituals associated with mourning and memorializing the dead were common in ancient Israel. The assumption behind them was that the dead, although having a rather shadowy existence, could for a time have some effect on the living (see 1 Sam 28:13-14). Thus libations were poured out during meals, and special garments were worn by the mourner. Unlike public worship, however, the rituals for the dead were private and thus more difficult to control. These practices were specifically targeted in the late monarchy period as efforts were made to nationalize *Yahweh worship and move toward strict monotheism in the reigns of Hezekiah and Josiah (2 Kings 23:24). The specific practices (such as lacerating the skin) prohibited in Deuteronomy are also mentioned in the *Baal cycle of stories and in the *Aqhat epic from *Ugarit (c. 1600-1200 B.C.). Their association with magic and with polytheistic cultures would have made them prime targets

for the Israelite writers. See comments on Numbers 3:12-13 and Deuteronomy 26:14.

14:2. treasured possession. The phrase "treasured possession" uses a word common in other languages of the ancient Near East to describe accumulated assets, whether through division of spoils or inheritance from estate. That people can be so described is evident in a royal seal from *Alalakh, where the king identifies himself as the "treasured possession" of the god Hadad. Likewise in a *Ugaritic text the king of Ugarit's favored status as a vassal is noted by naming him a "treasured possession" of his *Hittite overlord. Additionally, the Israelites are identified as a "kingdom of priests," which identifies the nation as serving a priestly role among the nations as intermediary between the peoples and God. Additionally there is a well-attested concept in the ancient Near East that a city or group of people may be freed from being subject to a king and placed in direct subjection to a deity. So Israel, freed from Egypt, is now given sacred status.

14:3-21. dietary restrictions. In Mesopotamia there were numerous occasions on which certain foods were prohibited for a short period. There is also evidence in *Babylonia that there were certain restrictions concerning animals that particular gods would accept for sacrifice. But there is no overriding system such as that found here. Yet though there is no known parallel in the ancient world to anything like the Israelite system of dietary restrictions, the permitted animals generally conform to the diet common in the ancient Near East.

14:6-10. criteria for classification of animals. The main criteria are (1) means of locomotion and (2) physical characteristics. Nothing is mentioned of their eating habits or the conditions of their habitat. Anthropologists have suggested that animals were considered clean or unclean depending on whether they possessed all the features that made them "normal" in their category. Other suggestions have concerned health and hygiene. The weakness of each of these is that there are too many examples that do not fit the explanation. A popular traditional explanation suggested that the animals prohibited had some connection to non-Israelite *rituals. In fact, however, the sacrificial practices of Israel's neighbors appear strikingly similar to Israel's. A recent promising suggestion is that the Israelite diet is modeled after God's "diet"—that is, if it could not be offered in sacrifice to God, then it was not suitable for human consumption either.

14:8. pigs. *Assyrian wisdom literature calls the pig unholy, unfit for the temple and an abomination to the gods. There is also one dream text in which eating pork is a bad omen. Yet it is clear that pork was a regular part of the diet in Mesopotamia. Some *Hittite *rituals require the sacrifice of a pig. Milgrom observes, however, that in such rituals the pig is not put on the altar as food for the god but absorbs *impurity and then is burned or buried as an offering to underworld deities. Likewise in Mesopotamia it was offered as a sacrifice to demons. There is evidence in Egypt of pigs being used for food, and Herodotus claims they were used for sacrifice there as well. Egyptian sources speak of herds of swine being kept on temple property, and pigs were often included in donations to the temples. The pig was especially sacred to the god Seth. Most evidence for the sacrifice of pigs, however, comes from Greece and Rome, there also mostly to gods of the underworld. In urban settings pigs, along with dogs, often scavenged in the streets, making them additionally repulsive. The attitude toward the pig in Israel is very clear in Isaiah 65:4; 66:3,17, the former showing close connection to worship of the dead. It is very possible then that sacrificing a pig was synonymous with sacrificing to demons or the dead.

14:21. disposal of roadkill. In a protein-starved area such as ancient Israel, it would have been almost criminal to let good meat go to waste. However, since the carcass would not have been drained of its blood, Israelites might not eat it (see Deut 12:16; Lev 11:40; 17:50). The meat could be distributed as charity to resident aliens (one of the protected classes, Deut 1:16; 16:11; 26:11). It could also be sold to foreigners who were not settlers in Israel.

14:21. goat in its mother's milk. See comment on Exodus 23:19.

14:22-29
Tithes

14:22-29. tithes and taxes. In the ancient Near East there was little difference between tithes and taxes. Both were exacted from villages as payment to the government and usually stored in temple complexes, from which the grain, oil and wine were then redistributed to maintain royal and religious officials. In collecting and redistributing the tithe, the distinction between sacred and secular was blurred. The kings were considered divinely chosen, and the storage centers were religious centers. The services that were provided in exchange for the tithe/tax included both administrative and sacred tasks. The process is well laid out in 1 Samuel 8:10-17, a text describing how the king will "take a tenth . . . and give it to his officials and attendants." This is precisely the same procedure outlined in *Ugaritic economic texts and royal correspondence. There too specialists (artisans, bureaucrats, temple personnel) are listed, along with their ration. State building throughout the ancient Near East required assessing the annual production of their lands and villages. The harvesting of the tithe is a reflection of that type of state planning. See comment on Numbers 18:21-32 for further information.

14:23. eating the tithe. It is unlikely that the one who is tithing is expected to eat the entire tithe. That would frustrate its purpose of providing for the priestly community and serving as a reserve for the destitute. The injunction probably has more to do with bringing the tithe (or its value in silver) to God's sanctuary in Jerusalem and thereby demonstrating devotion (see Deut 14:24-26). What is eaten would serve as a *covenantal meal, similar to that eaten in Exodus 24:9-11.

14:27-29. provision for the Levites. As spelled out more completely in 18:1-8, the Levites were to receive a portion of the sacrificial tithe because they were not apportioned any section of the land after the conquest. As religious specialists, they would be allotted a ration from the land's produce in much the same way that bureaucrats and artisans are assigned specific grain and wine rations in the *Ugaritic economic documents (see comment on 14:22-29). It is therefore to be expected that the Levites would be paid for services rendered.

14:29. provision for the vulnerable. A major aspect of Israelite legal tradition involves making provision for groups classified as weak or poor: widows, orphans and the resident alien (see Ex 22:22; Deut 10:18-19; 24:17-21). Thus the tithe from the third year (not an additional tithe in that year) is to be set aside and used to support the vulnerable of society. Concern for the needy is evident in Mesopotamian legal collections as early as the mid-third millennium, but this generally addresses protection of rights and guarantee of justice in the courts rather than financial provision.

15:1-18
Cancellation of Slavery and Debts

15:1-11. financial systems in the ancient Near East. Since the wealth of the nations of the ancient Near East was based on the dual economic foundations of natural resources (mines and agriculture) and trade, an intricate financial system had to be developed to support these ventures. For instance, risk capital (in the form of gold, silver, precious stones, spices, etc.) was provided by kings and entrepreneurs in Egypt and Mesopotamia to mariners plying the Mediterranean routes to Cyprus and Crete and the trade routes south along the Red Sea to Arabia, Africa and India. Loans were also made to merchants leading caravans throughout the Near East (with an expected yield on investment of at least 100 percent) and to farmers to provide seed and equipment for the growing season. These loans were generally made at interest (although there was an interest-free category of loan within a set payment period). *Hammurabi's code contains numerous examples governing the rate of interest and even prescribing forfeiture of investment if the creditor charged more than 20 percent. Individual farmers who experienced a bad harvest would often have to incur debt in order to provide food for the coming year and supplies for the next year's planting. Continuing bad harvests would lead to the indenturing of the land or the sale of his family and eventually himself into debt slavery.

15:2-3. debt remission. In granting an absolute remission of all debt at the end of the seventh year, the Deuteronomic law expands on the original sabbatical year legislation (Ex 23:10-11), which related to the fallowing of the land. As the economy expanded, this required broadening the law to include debt as well as the return of property that had been given as collateral for debt (see the Jubilee law in Lev 25). The likelihood that this is total remission of debt rather than a suspension of debt for the year is confirmed by the *misharum* decree of the *Old Babylonian king Ammisaduqa (1646-1626 B C). This document prohibits creditors from pursuing the payment of debt after the decree has been issued, on pain of death. However, as in Deuteronomic law, merchants, who were often foreign nationals or new settlers (foreigners in 15:3), are still required to repay investors, since this is a transaction rather than a debt.

15:1-6. sabbatical year. The fallowing of the land in the seventh year, as an acknowledgment of the Creator's work and an example of good husbandry, is first found in Exodus 23:10-11. An expansion of that law is later found in Leviticus 25:2-7, providing more specificity about how it affects the land and the people. The Deuteronomic legislation is more concerned with debt remission, manumission of slaves (15:12-18) and the educational process of reading the law publicly (31:10-13) during the sabbatical year. Although there is no direct parallel to either sabbath or sabbatical-year legislation outside the Bible, the *Ugaritic epic of *Baal contains a seven-year agricultural cycle that may be related. In *Hammurabi's laws women and children sold into slavery would be freed after three years.

15:12. Hebrew. It may well be that originally *Hebrew*, like *Habiru* in *Akkadian texts, was a generic term for landless, stateless persons who contracted themselves as mercenaries, laborers and servants. This is not necessarily a pejorative designation. There are some negative connotations present, since persons in the ancient world tended to identify themselves with a group or place. But considering the fact that the first "Hebrew," Abram, was a landless immigrant,

something like "gypsy" might give a general idea of meaning. Israelite villagers considered themselves to be free landowners. *Hebrew*, therefore, would refer to an Israelite who had become destitute (compare Jer 34:9) or was living in foreign lands (Judg 19:16). The Hebrew had to work his full six-year term in order to regain his mortgaged land and landowner status. Thus the Hebrew in Exodus 21:2, Deuteronomy 15:12 and Jeremiah 34:9 would be an Israelite, who, unlike the non-Israelite, could not be sold into permanent slavery. It was his right to release that distinguished him from the non-Israelite.

15:16-17. ear-piercing ceremony. See the comment on Exodus 21:5-6. The only difference in the description of the ceremony is that Deuteronomy has added the phrase "Do the same for your maidservant" in verse 6, since this version of the manumission law deals more fully with both male and female slaves.

15:19-23
Firstborn Animals

15:19-23. treatment of firstborn animals. Dedication of firstborn animals to deity is without firm attestation in the other cultures of the ancient Near East, though some claim to have found such a practice in the *Ugaritic texts. If it is there, the texts give us little information to understand the reasoning behind the practice.

15:23. eating blood. See the comments on Leviticus 17:11 and Deuteronomy 12:16, 20, regarding the prohibition against consuming the blood of animals along with their meat.

16:1-17
The Three Major Festivals

16:1-17. Israel's sacred calendar. Other versions of the calendar are found in Exodus 23:12-19; 34:18-26; Leviticus 23; and Numbers 28—29 (see the comments there).

16:1. Abib. The month of Abib (March-April) is considered the first month in the Israelite calendar and is tied to the exodus event (see Ex 13:4; 23:15). It is one of the month names that is often thought to have been brought over from the Canaanite month names. The first month later came to be known as the month of Nisan when the names were adopted from the *Babylonian calendar. In Exodus 23:15, Abib is tied to the Feast of Unleavened Bread, while in the Deuteronomic law it is keyed to the Passover.

16:1-8. Passover. Compare the comment on the Passover in Exodus 12. This Deuteronomic legislation makes allowance for the changes in Israelite society that have taken place since the exodus and centralizes the celebration of the Passover in "the place [God] will eventually choose as a dwelling for his Name" (v. 5), that is, Jerusalem.

16:8. sacred assembly. Sacred assemblies or proclamations were an important part of most religious practice in the ancient world. They refer to local or national gatherings for public, corporate worship. The people were summoned together away from their occupational work.

16:9. standing grain. The Feast of Weeks (see Ex 23:16) is tied to the wheat harvest of March-April. The Gezer calendar notes this as the month to "reap and feast." Since the grain would have matured at different times in the various locales of the country, the harvest of "standing grain" would have required the prescribed seven-week period to complete.

16:9-12. Feast of Weeks. This second of the three major harvest festivals comes seven weeks after the harvest of the early grain (Ex 34:22) and is also known as the Feast of Harvest or Pentecost (Ex 23:16). In the agricultural cycle it marks the end of the wheat harvest season, and by tradition it is tied to the giving of the law on Mount Sinai. It is also associated with *covenant renewal and pilgrimage. Celebration includes the bringing of a "wave offering" of two loaves of bread, animal sacrifices (seven year-old lambs, one bull and two rams) and a drink offering in thanksgiving for a good harvest. A goat is also to be sacrificed as a sin offering for the people.

16:13-17. Feast of Tabernacles. The final harvest of the year occurred in the autumn prior to the onset of the rainy season and marked the beginning of a new agricultural year (fifteenth day of the seventh month). At this time the last of the ripening grain and fruits were gathered and stored. The seven-day event is also known as the Feast of Ingathering (Ex 23:16) and is symbolized by the construction of booths decorated with greenery for the harvesters. The use of the term *booths* for this festival appears first in Deuteronomy and is probably a reflection of the practice of harvesters of setting up shelters in the fields so that they could work throughout the day without returning to their homes (see Lev 23:42). The festival was tied into Israelite tradition as a commemoration of the wilderness wanderings. It was also the occasion for the dedication of Solomon's temple in Jerusalem (1 Kings 8:65).

16:16. pilgrimage feasts. See the comment on Exodus 23:17 regarding the obligation imposed on the Israelites to come before the Lord as pilgrims three times a year. In the rest of the ancient world each town had its patron deities and its local temples. Festivals and other worship activities would therefore not require lengthy pilgrimage. Nevertheless festivals such as the great Akitu (new year's) festival of *Marduk in *Babylon would undoubtedly have drawn pilgrims from near and far. One of the primary aspects of the ancient Near Eastern festivals was procession, where the image of the God was carried through various symbolic stages. Instead of finding its parallels in other religions' festivals, the pilgrimage aspect of Israel's festivals finds similarity to the *Hittite treaty documents that require the vassal king to travel periodically to the suzerain in order to reaffirm his loyalty (and pay the annual tribute).

16:18—17:13
Establishing Justice

16:18-20. judiciary institutions in ancient Near East. As evidenced by the preface to the Code of *Hammurabi (c. 1750 B.C.) and the statements made by the "Eloquent Peasant" in Egyptian wisdom literature (c. 2100 B.C.), those in authority were expected to protect the rights of the poor and weak in society. "True justice" (see Lev 19:15) was required of kings, officials and local magistrates. In fact, the "world turned upside down" theme found in the book of Judges and in prophetic literature (Is 1:23) describes a society in which "laws are enacted, but ignored" (for example in the Egyptian *Visions of Neferti* [c. 1900 B.C.]). An efficiently administered state in the ancient Near East depended on the reliability of the law and its enforcement. To this end, every organized state created a bureaucracy of judges and local officials to deal with civil and criminal cases. It was their task to hear testimony, investigate charges made and evaluate evidence, and then execute judgment (detailed in the *Middle Assyrian laws and the Code of Hammurabi). There were some cases, however, that required the attention of the king (see 2 Sam 15:2-4), and appeals were occasionally forwarded to that highest magistrate (as in the *Mari texts).

16:19. bribes in the ancient world. The temptation for judges and government officials to accept bribes is found in every time and place (see Prov 6:35; Mic 7:3). Taking bribes becomes almost institutionally accepted in bureaucratic situations as competing parties attempt to outmaneuver each other (see Mic 3:11; Ezra 4:4-5). However, at least on the ideal level, arguments and penalties are imposed to eliminate or at least lessen this problem. Thus *Hammurabi's code places harsh penalties on any judge who alters one of his decisions (presumably because of a bribe), including stiff fines and permanent removal from the bench. Exodus 23:8 forbids the taking of bribes and the perversion of justice as an offense against God, the weak and innocent, and the entire community (see Is 5:23; Amos 5:12).

16:21. Asherah poles. See the comments on Exodus 34:13 and Deuteronomy 7:5; 12:3.

16:22. sacred stones. See the comments on Exodus 23:24 and Deuteronomy 12:3.

17:3. astral worship. The worship of the celestial bodies (sun, moon, planets, stars) was common throughout the ancient Near East. One of the principal gods of *Assyria and *Babylonia was a sun god (Shamash), and a moon god (Thoth in Egypt; Sin in Mesopotamia; Yarah in Canaanite religion) was widely worshiped. During most of their history the Israelites would have been familiar with and heavily influenced by Assyrian culture and religion (see Deut 4:19; 2 Kings 21:1-7; 23:4-5). These forbidden practices continued to be a source of condemnation during the Neo-Babylonian period, as Israelites burned incense on altars placed on the roofs of their houses to the "starry hosts" (Jer 19:13). Because worship of the elements of nature diminished *Yahweh's position as the sole power in creation, they were outlawed. However, the popular nature of this type of worship continues to appear in prophetic literature and in Job (see Job 31:26-28; 38:7). For additional information see comment on Deuteronomy 4.

17:5. stoning as capital punishment. See the comment on 13:10.

17:6-7. witnesses in the ancient court system. The task of serving as a witness occurs in a variety of legal contexts and is a solemn duty which is not to be abused (Ex 20:16; Num 35:30; Deut 19:16-19). It can involve hearing testimony, signing commercial or civil documents, or testifying on a legal matter (laws of *Ur-Nammu, Code of *Hammurabi and the *Middle Assyrian laws). Witnesses serve an essential purpose in verifying business transactions (Jer 32:44; Hammurabi), such as the sale of property, marriages and changes in social status (*Middle Assyrian laws). Occasionally, they function as representatives of the people in matters brought before a god (Ex 24:9-11; Hammurabi).

17:8-13. verdict by omen in ancient Near East. In situations where physical evidence was not present or was insufficient, a verdict could be determined by the reading of omens. This meant that plaintiffs had to consult religious professionals (Levitical priests in 17:9), whose service included seeking divine verdicts. Among the *divination methods used in the ancient Near East were the examination of a sheep's liver (hepatoscopy), the interpretation of dreams (specific *Babylonian texts contain lists of dreams and what they portend—accidents, deaths, military defeats or victories; see Dan 2:9), the noting of freak occurrences in nature and the use of astrological charting (especially during the period of the *Assyrian empire in the tenth to seventh centuries B.C.). In the biblical text, the Urim and Thummim (Ex 28:30; Num 27:21) were used to help divine God's will, and a number of the prophets point to famines, droughts and other natural calamities as a sign of God's judgment on an unfaithful people (Amos 4:10-12; Hag 1:5-11).

17:14-20
The King

17:14-20. king chosen by deity. The *Sumerian King List, which purports to contain the names of kings from before the flood until the end of the *Ur III dynasty (c. 2000 B.C.), begins with the line, "When the kingship was lowered from heaven." The assumption throughout Mesopotamian history is that every ruler received his certification to reign from the gods. Thus *Hammurabi (1792-1750 B.C.) speaks in the prologue to his law code of the gods' establishment of "an enduring kingship" in *Babylon and how the gods Anum and *Enlil specifically chose him to rule on behalf of the people. The result is an obligation imposed on the king to rule wisely and with justice, never abusing his power and being responsible to the commands and requirements of the gods. The situation is slightly different in Egypt, where each pharaoh was considered to be a god.

17:16. proliferation of horses. Since horses were used primarily to draw chariots and carry horsemen into battle, the acquisition of large numbers of these animals implies either an aggressive foreign policy or a monarch who wishes to impress his people and his neighbors with his wealth and power. The reference to Egypt is suggestive of dependence on that nation as an ally and a supplier of horses for war (Is 36:6-9). Such alliances in the late monarchy period proved disastrous for Israel and Judah and were roundly condemned by the prophets (Is 31:1-3; Mic 5:10).

17:17. royal marriage as alliance. Marriage was a tool of diplomacy throughout the ancient Near East. For instance,

Zimri-Lim, the king of *Mari (eighteenth century B.C.), used his daughters to cement alliances and establish treaties with his neighboring kingdoms. Similarly, Pharaoh Thutmose IV (1425-1412 B.C.) arranged a marriage with a daughter of the *Mitannian king to demonstrate good relations and end a series of wars with that middle Euphrates kingdom. Solomon's seven hundred wives and three hundred *concubines (1 Kings 11:3) were a measure of his power and wealth (just as horses are in Deut 17:16), especially his marriage to the daughter of the pharaoh (1 Kings 3:1). While the political advantages were quite evident, the danger of such marriages is demonstrated in the introduction of the worship of other gods by Solomon's wives (1 Kings 11:4-8).

17:17. royal treasuries. The theme of excessive acquisition of royal symbols of power (horses, wives, gold and silver) continues in this admonition against overtaxing the people simply to fill the royal treasury. All of the categories of wealth are said to lead to excessive pride, apostasy and a rejection or diminution of *Yahweh's role (compare 8:11-14). The vanity of kings who amass wealth without purpose other than pride is found in Ecclesiastes 2:8-11 and Jeremiah 48:7. The treasuries typically contained the precious metal assets of temple and state, including contributions as well as plunder. Though coinage or bullion may have been included, much of it would be in the form of jewelry, vessels for *ritual use, religious objects or the various accessories of royal or wealthy households. Payment of tribute at times required drawing from or even emptying the treasuries (see 1 Kings 14:26; 2 Kings 18:15). Excavations or descriptions of temples and palaces often indicate rooms as treasuries, and royal officers included keepers of the treasuries.

17:18-20. king subject to the law. In Egypt and Mesopotamia the king was the fountainhead of law. It was his task to perceive and maintain the order that was built into the universe (Egyptian *ma'at*; Mesopotamian *me*). The king could not be "brought to justice," except by the gods. He was not above the law, but there was no mechanism by which he could be tried in a human court. Judicially this may have been no different in Israel, though the prophets, as spokesmen for the deity, could call the king to account.

18:1-13
Priests and Levites

18:1-5. provision for Levites. Whether or not the worshiper ate a portion of the sacrifice, a number of the sacrifices provided an opportunity for the priests to eat. This was also true in *Babylonian practice, where the king, the priest and other temple personnel received portions of the sacrifices. As early as *Sumerian texts it was considered a grievous crime to eat that which had been set apart as holy. See also the comment on Numbers 18:12-19 for tithes paid to the priests.

18:6-8. function of the Levites in the towns. During the early settlement period, Levites officiated at local shrines and altars. It would have been their role to serve as religious professionals, performing sacrifices and instructing the people on the law. While some Levites may have been tied to these places for generations (1 Sam 1:3), there is also evidence of itinerant Levites, who traveled about the country and were hired to serve for a time at a local shrine or high place (Judg 17:7-13). Without an inheritance of their own (Josh 14:3-4), the Levites stood out within a society that was territorial. The Levites were supposed to instruct the people in proper worship, though the book of Judges makes it clear that sometimes they were a major part of the problem rather than the solution. They were supposed to be preservers of tradition and law and would have often served as judges.

18:9-22
Receiving Information from Deity

18:10. children passing through fire. The remainder of this list of "detestable ways" centers on *divination practices. Although "passing through" might suggest a form of trial by ordeal (referred to in a number of the Mesopotamian law collections), and thus a form of divination, that interpretation is uncertain in this case. Evidence of child sacrifice has been recovered from Phoenician sites in North Africa (Carthage) and Sardinia, and it was also practiced in Syria and Mesopotamia during the *Assyrian period (eighth and seventh centuries B.C.). Dedicating children to a god as a form of sacrifice is found in several biblical narratives. It can be explained as a means of promoting fertility (Mic 6:6-7) or as a way of obtaining a military victory (Judg 11:30-40; 2 Kings 3:27). In no case, however, is this considered acceptable as a sacrifice to *Yahweh under biblical law (Deut 18:10). Many scholars consider Molech to be a netherworld deity whose *rituals had Canaanite origins and focused on dead ancestors.

18:10. divination. See the comment on Leviticus 19:26. *Divination involves a variety of methods used by prophets (Mic 3:11), soothsayers, mediums and sorcerers to determine the will of the gods and to predict the future. These included the examination of the entrails of sacrificial animals, the analysis of omens of various types and the reading of the future in natural and unnatural phenomena (see Gen 44:5). While there were acceptable divination practices among the Israelites (use of the Urim and Thummim), what is being condemned here is a group of practitioners, who served as professional fortunetellers.

18:10. sorcery. Since magic in the ancient world was a means of contacting the supernatural realm, it was considered to have two facets: good magic and evil. In Mesopotamia and among the *Hittites harmful magic was practiced by sorcerers and was punishable by death. It involved the use of potions, figurines and curses designed to bring death, disease or bad luck to the victim. This was distinguished from the practical and helpful magic of professional exorcists and "old women," whose role included the rites involved in temple construction and dedication, as well as medical aid. Only in Egypt was there no distinction between white and black magic. There the practitioners' job involved intimidating demons and other divine powers to perform required tasks or to remove curses. The Israelite law totally rejected all these practices because of their polytheistic character and the diminishing of *Yahweh's role as lord of creation (see Ex 22:18).

18:10. omens. One of the priestly classes mentioned in Mesopotamian texts is the *baru*-diviners. It was their task to perform extispicy (generally on lambs), examining the liver and interpreting this omen for the person who has asked for a reading of the future. The *baru* might be consulted by a king who wished to go to war (compare 1 Kings 22:6), a merchant about to send out a caravan or a person who had become ill. Government officials often included the report of omens in their letters (*Mari texts). However, since omens were not always clear, several groups of diviners might be used before action was taken. An entire body of omen texts (with descriptions of past events and predictions) were archived in temples and palaces for consultation by staff diviners. Even clay models of livers were used in schooling apprentices in the trade.

18:10. witchcraft. Like sorcery, witchcraft was generally classed as an illegitimate use of magic. Its practitioners might serve in royal courts or temples or as local herbalists and itinerant diviners, who would, for a price, provide the means to harm or destroy an enemy (see Lev 19:26; 20:6; 2 Kings 21:6). The Mesopotamian distinction between good and evil magic is lost in Israelite law, where the female witch is condemned (Ex 22:18) and the words of sorcerers are declared to be unreliable (Jer 27:9; Mal 3:5).

18:11. spells, medium, spiritist. The practitioners of spiritism and sorcery are condemned because of their association with Canaanite religion and because their "art" attempted to circumvent *Yahweh by seeking knowledge and power from spirits. They represented a form of popular religion that was closer to the folk practices of the common people and served as a form of "shadow religion" for many. Sometimes, because of its association with *divination, their *rituals and methods stood in direct opposition to official religion or as an alternative to be used in times of desperation (see Saul's use of the outlawed witch of Endor in 1 Sam 28). Sorcery and potions used in the practice of magic were also banned in the Code of *Hammurabi and the *Middle Assyrian laws, suggesting that the prohibition and fear of these practices were not unique to Israel.

18:11. consulting the dead. Although there was no clear sense of an afterlife in ancient Mesopotamia, no envisioning of a place of reward or punishment, ancestor worship did exist, and offerings were made to the spirits of the dead. A group of magical practitioners created a means for consulting the spirits of the dead to find out about the future (see the witch of Endor in 1 Sam 28:7-14). This was called necromancy and could involve consulting a particular or "familiar" spirit, or it could be the raising of any ghost attracted by the spells of the medium. Ritual pits, stuffed with bread and blood, were commonly used in *Hittite ritual by diviners, and the Greek hero Odysseus used a pit filled with blood to attract the shades of his dead companions. It was believed that if libations were poured out to them, the spirits of dead ancestors could offer protection and help to those still living. In *Babylon the disembodied spirit (*utukki*) or the ghost (*etemmu*) could become very dangerous if not cared for, and such spirits were often the objects of incantations. Proper care for the dead would begin with proper burial and would continue with ongoing gifts and honor of the memory and name of the deceased. The firstborn was responsible for maintaining this ancestor worship and therefore inherited the family gods (often images of deceased ancestors).

18:10-13. worldview basis for prohibiting divination. The worldview promulgated in the Old Testament maintains that *Yahweh is the sole God and is the ultimate power and authority in the universe. In stark contrast, the polytheistic religions of the ancient Near East did not consider their gods (even as a group) to represent the ultimate power in the universe. Instead they believed in an impersonal primordial realm that was the source of knowledge and power. *Divination attempted to tap into that realm for the purposes of gaining knowledge; incantations tried to utilize its power. Both *divination and incantation can therefore be seen to assume a worldview that was contradictory to Yahweh's revealed position.

18:14-22. function of the prophet. These individuals were more than simple religious practitioners. While some of them were members of the priestly community, they stood outside that institution. Their role was to challenge the establishment and the social order, to remind the leadership and the people of their obligation to the *covenant with *Yahweh and to provide warning of the punishment that went with violation of the covenantal agreement. The prophet is invested with special powers, a message and a mission, and there is a special compulsion associated with being called as a prophet. It can be denied for a time (see Jonah's flight) but ultimately must be answered. It should also be noted that prophets may be reluctant to speak harsh words or condemnations of their own people. When this occurs, the prophet will experience a compulsion to speak that cannot be resisted (Jer 20:9). Since they speak a message that comes from God, they separate themselves from the words and thus cannot be charged with treason, sedition or doomsaying. The message is thus the most important thing about the prophet, not the prophet himself or herself. Certainly, there were some prophets like Balaam and Elijah who acquired a personal reputation, but this was based on their message or their ability to speak for God. For a prophet to gain credibility with the people, the message must come true. Although sometimes the prophets are mentioned as part of the *cult community (Isaiah and Ezekiel) and as court prophets (Nathan), they always seem to be able to stand apart from these institutions to criticize them and to point out where they have broken the *covenant with God. In the early periods of the monarchy, the prophets primarily addressed the king and his court, much like their ancient Near Eastern counterparts did (they have been termed "preclassical" prophets). Beginning in the eighth century, however, they turned their attention increasingly to the people and became the social/spiritual commentators whom we most readily identify with the prophetic institution (the "classical" prophets and the "writing" prophets). Their role was not to predict as much as it was to advise of God's policies and plans.

18:20-22. false prophecy. Like Deuteronomy 13:1-3 and its discussion of persons urging the worship of other gods, false prophets are generally those who speak in the name of other gods. Deuteronomy discounts the existence of these other gods and thus the veracity of their prophets. In cases where prophets presume to speak in *Yahweh's name without permission, the test of true prophecy is whether what they say actually occurs. There are a number of examples of false prophecy cited in the biblical text. Jeremiah rails against it in his accusation against Hananiah (Jer 28:12-17) and in his warning against other prophets who predicted a quick end to the exile (29:20-23). In some cases, the potential for confusion involved is such that events must take their course before the true prophet is revealed (see 1 Kings 22). The Israelites were not alone in their caution concerning false prophecy. In other cultures, however, they generally used *divination to try to confirm the message of the prophet, but this was not permissible for Israel.

18:14-22. prophecy in the ancient Near East. Texts from Mesopotamia, Syria and Anatolia contain a large number of prophetic utterances, demonstrating the existence of prophets throughout much of ancient Near Eastern history. While some of these texts may actually fall into the realm of wisdom literature or omen reports, many involve individuals who claim to have received a message from a god. Most famous among these texts are about fifty texts from *Mari (eighteenth century B.C.) that contain reports from both male and female prophets: warnings about plots against the king, admonitions from a god to build a temple or to provide a *funerary offering, and assurances of military victory. These prophets present divine messages received in dreams or through omens. Others are said to fall into a trance state and speak as ecstatic prophets. This type of prophecy is also found in the eleventh-century B.C. Egyptian tale of *Wenamon and in 1 Samuel 10:5-11 and 2 Kings 3:15.

19:1-21
Capital Punishment Cases

19:1. Late Bronze Canaanite cities. Most of what is known about *Late Bronze Canaanite cities comes from archaeological excavations and surveys and the inscriptions of the Egyptian Pharaohs who ruled that region. Evidence suggests that the major cities of this period (Jerusalem, Shechem, Megiddo) were walled, but settlements were spaced fairly far apart. The central hill country was sparsely inhabited prior to 1200 B.C. The population was mixed, containing peoples who had come from the *Hittite kingdom, Syria, Mesopotamia and the desert areas of Arabia. The Egyptians apparently had some difficulty governing the area and were required on numerous occasions to send military expeditions to quell revolts and end brigandage (reported in the fourteenth-century B.C. *Amarna letters as well as in the victory inscriptions of Amenophis II [c. 1450-1425 B.C.] and of Merneptah [c. 1208 B.C.]).

19:2-3. refuge cities in ancient Near East. See the comment on Numbers 35:6-34 for a discussion of the cities of refuge in Israel. The concept of asylum and refuge is quite old. *Babylonian and *Hittite texts both speak of sacred space where all are to be protected. The inhabitants of the great temple cities of Nippur,

Sippar and Babylon were granted special status because of the protection afforded by patron deities of these places. The principle was that only the god could withdraw protection from persons here, and thus no one could shed their blood without an omen or sign from the god (Herodotus has an example from the classical period). Egyptian tradition regarding asylum appears to apply only to the temple precinct rather than to the entire city. This would parallel the biblical examples in which a fugitive takes refuge at the altar (1 Kings 1:50-53; 2:28-34).

19:6. avenger of blood and the justice system. See the comment on Numbers 35:9-34 for a discussion of the responsibility of the family to avenge a death. It is possible that the title "avenger of blood" evolved out of the family obligation to engage in blood revenge when one of their clan members was slain. Such a process, while typical of tribal society, is extremely disruptive to the maintenance of order within an organized state. As a result, the "avenger of blood" (a term which appears only in the context of the cities of refuge) may have been appointed by the government to serve the needs of both the family and the state by apprehending the accused and then carrying out the sentence if the verdict was murder.

19:11-13. capital punishment. In the Bible capital punishment is the sentence imposed for apostasy (Lev 20:2), blasphemy (Lev 24:14), sorcery (Lev 20:27), violation of the sabbath (Num 15:35-36), stealing from the *herem (Josh 7:25), gross disobedience to parents (Deut 21:21), adultery (Deut 22:21), incest (Lev 20:14) and deliberate homicide (Num 35:9). While stoning is the most common form of capital punishment, some offenses require burning or stabbing with a sword. In every case the purpose is to eliminate contaminating elements from society and thereby purge the evil that threatened to draw the people away from the *covenant.

19:14. moving boundary stones. Since the land had been given to the people by God and apportioned according to a God-given formula, to move boundary stones and thus appropriate territory unlawfully was a crime of theft against God. The antiquity of laws concerning property rights is affirmed by inscriptions on sixteenth-century B.C. Kassite *kudurru* boundary stones, admonitions in eleventh-century B.C. Egyptian wisdom literature against relocating a surveyor's stone *(Teachings of Amenemope)* and in the curse in Hosea 5:10. Each example calls on the gods to protect the owner's rights against encroachment.

19:15-20. the role of witnesses in the ancient judicial system. Witnesses were an essential part of the judicial system in the ancient world. One sign of this is that Israelite law required two witnesses to convict a person of a crime (Num 35:30; Deut 17:6; 1 Kings 21:13). Both *Hammurabi's code and the *Middle Assyrian laws rely heavily on the presence of witnesses to certify business transactions and to testify in civil and criminal cases.

19:21. *lex talionis.* The legal principle of "an eye for an eye" or *lex talionis* ("law of retaliation") is found in both the biblical law codes and the codes of Mesopotamia. Biblical examples (Ex 21:24; Lev 24:20) express the desire to eliminate a corrupting or unclean element in society. The admonition is to have "no mercy" on the culprit. Mesopotamian law contains both the idealized version of *lex talionis* and an amelioration to set limits of compensation. For instance, the law collection of *Eshnunna sets a fine of one mina of silver for the loss of an eye. In the personal liability laws found in *Hammurabi's code, reciprocity for injury may be an exactly equivalent injury, a fine or mutilation, depending on the

social status of the injured party and the accused. Even in the cases where exact reciprocity is required by Mesopotamian law, it is quite possible that a monetary equivalent was taken in compensation (if not explicitly included in the law), rather than an eye or a tooth being actually removed.

20:1-20
Rules for Warfare

20:2. priest addressing the army. Since warfare was considered a religious enterprise, it was expected that priests and other religious functionaries would accompany the army. *Assyrian texts and reliefs depict the roles performed by priests accompanying the troops. They carried or attended the images and emblems of the gods (see Josh 6:4-5; 1 Sam 4:4), performed religious *rituals and sacrifices, and undoubtedly addressed the army in the name of the gods. This latter task may have involved interpreting of omens, assuring the aid of the gods and exhorting the troops to fight for the god's chosen king (as in the annals of Tukulti-Ninurta I [1244-1208 B.C.] and Ashurnasirpal II [883-859 B.C.]).

20:5-9. exemptions from military duty. While every able-bodied free man was expected to serve in the military, in practice exemptions were allowed for special categories, such as priests (in the *Mari texts), newlyweds (Deut 24:5) and those who have religious duties to perform (see Lev 19:23-25). Conscription of troops was necessary to fulfill feudal obligations to kings and took various forms, including census taking and coercion (at Mari). The biblical injunction to allow the "frightened" to leave the army may have had its basis in maintaining discipline in the ranks, but it is also an assurance that those who fight are certain of Yahweh's aid in battle (see Judg 7:1-3). The law codes are at times contradictory on the matter of hiring substitutes for service in the military. The *Hittite code allows this practice, but it is outlawed in the Code of *Hammurabi. This latter case is based on a direct order to join the king's campaign. It is possible that arrangements could be made for members of the nobility that would preempt any awkward legal problems. In the Canaanite *Keret Epic the king raises an army in a cause so important that normal exemptions (newlywed among them) are abandoned.

20:10-15. normal warfare practices. In the ancient world, the standard procedure was not to pay soldiers a wage. Instead they were given a portion of the loot taken in the capture of villages and towns. Because warfare was also seen as a divine mission, ordered by the god(s) and facilitated by divine intervention, all plunder taken in battle was technically the sacred property of the god(s). As a result strict procedures had to be followed in its division in order to prevent a violation of sacred taboos. For instance, in the *Mari texts officers took an oath not to "eat the *asakkum*" (i.e., infringe on the rights) of their peers or of lesser ranks. Violators were punished with heavy fines. Following this pattern, Mesopotamian as well as Israelite armies commonly took women and children as spoils, along with animals and moveable property, while the men were killed (see Gen 34:25-29; *Assyrian Annals of Sennacherib). In this way the efforts of the victorious were rewarded, and the psychological effect of the sight of devastated cities served the purpose of enhancing the reputation of the conquering nation and its god(s).

20:16-18. holy war procedures. In unusual circumstances, an army chose to forego taking prisoners or spoils and dedicated it entirely to the god who had given them the victory. This practice is known as *herem* in Hebrew and is used very sparingly as a method of warfare. Only in a few instances is the total destruction of a city called for: Jericho in Joshua 6:17-24, Hazor in Joshua 11:10-11, Zephath in Judges 1:17 and the Amalekites in 1 Samuel 15:3. There are several instances where some variation on utter destruction is allowed, as in Deuteronomy 2:34-35 and 3:6-7 (people killed, livestock taken as spoil). Outside the Bible, this perspective on war is attested as early as the ninth century B.C. in the war against the tribe of Gad by the Moabite king Mesha. A similar concept may be reflected in the annals of several of the *Assyrian kings, who used total destruction as a psychological ploy to make revolting nations submissive.

20:20. siege works. To capture a walled city, it was necessary to employ a variety of siege works, including ramps (2 Sam 20:15; 2 Kings 19:32), towers (Is 23:13; Ezek 21:22) or perimeter walls to prevent escape (Ezek 26:8; Mic 5:1). Battering rams (Ezek 26:9) as well as supports for tunnels undermining the walls also required the use of timbers. This explains the dispensation allowed in Deuteronomy for the cutting of trees during a siege. The *Assyrian reliefs of Ashurnasirpal II (883-859 B.C.) at Nimrud portray many of these siege engines and simultaneous methods of warfare.

21:1-9
Unsolved Murder

21:1-9. innocent blood procedures and concepts. See the comments on Numbers 19 dealing with the significance of the purification *ritual and the use of the red heifer. These comments also deal with the importance of expiation for the shedding of "innocent blood." In *Hittite law if a body was found out in the open country, the person's heir was entitled to some property from the town nearest the place where the body was found, up to three leagues' distance. This legislation is more concerned with the rights of the heir than with the issue of innocent bloodshed.

21:10-14
Rights of Captive Women

21:10-14. treatment of captive women. Part of warfare is the disposition of prisoners. Some female captives could expect to serve as slaves (2 Kings 5:2-3), but many would also be taken as wives by the soldiers. The Deuteronomic law deals with the transformation process as these women were adopted into Israelite society. This included the shaving of the head, a change of clothing and a period of mourning marking the death of the woman's old life and the beginning of a new one (compare Joseph's transformation in Gen 41:41-45). The *Mari texts also provide clothing and a job to captive women. The rights extended to the former captive after she has married are similar to those of Israelite women and are designed to demonstrate that there is no reduction of her status if a divorce occurs. Similar concerns are reflected in the *Middle Assyrian laws, which require former captives who are now married to dress like all Assyrian women of that class.

21:15-21
Treatment of Sons

21:15-17. right of the firstborn. Inheritance rights are based on the law of primogeniture. This stipulates that the firstborn son is to receive a double share of his father's property. That this was the normal situation in the ancient Near East can be seen in Middle Assyrian texts, *Larsa, *Mari and *Nuzi documents, just to name a few. The intent of such laws is to insure orderly transmission of property from one generation to the next. *Hammurabi's law gives the father the right to favor whichever son

he chooses. In the Nuzi texts the father had the option of altering the firstborn rights. In the ancient Near East the closest legislation to that found here is the stipulation in Hammurabi's law that says the children of the slave wife, if acknowledged as children during the father's lifetime, have an equal share in the inheritance with the full wife's children.

21:18-21. execution of a rebellious son. When a breakdown of family coherence occurred and a son refused to give his parents the obedience and support they were entitled to, it became a threat to the community as a whole. The language used here makes it clear that a repudiation of the *covenant is involved. The references to gluttony and drunkenness are considered indications that the son is beyond reform. Due process includes parental witness of the offense, and then a communal form of execution is prescribed (see comment on Deut 13:10). This offense is as grave a threat to the covenant as worshiping other gods. Mesopotamian law also defends the rights of parents, but only extending to disinheritance or mutilation. See the comment on Exodus 21:17. The legislation limits the authority of the parents in that they have to bring such a matter before the elders rather than having the freedom to act independently.

21:22-23
Treatment of Executed Criminals

21:22-23. exposure of executed criminals. Since the Deuteronomic laws are seldom concerned with matters of ritual *purity and polluting elements (see Lev 13—17 and comments on Lev 20:10-16; 22:3-9), it may be that the sense of "desecrating" the land is based on either the sight or the smell of an exposed and decaying body. The corpse was considered a defiling object (Lev 22:8; Num 5:2) and thus a danger to the living. Very few narratives describe the practice of exposing a body (Josh 8:29; 10:26-7; 2 Sam 4:12; 21:8-13). It is unlikely that hanging was the form of execution used here. Rather, a tree or pole was used to impale the bodies for public display. *Assyrian reliefs from the palace of Sennacherib in *Nineveh (704-681 B.C.) depict soldiers erecting stakes holding the impaled bodies of men of Lachish. It is possible that the horror of this form of shameful display is the basis for the Israelite law requiring the body to be removed and buried at sunset rather than leaving it to be devoured by birds and other animals (Gen 40:19; 2 Sam 21:10).

22:1-12
Miscellaneous Laws

22:1-3. lost property. Just as in Exodus 23:4, it is expected that an Israelite will either return lost property (animals, clothing, etc.) or keep it safe until the owner reclaims it. Taking the two laws together, this maxim applies to fellow Israelites as well as enemies. The laws of *Eshnunna and *Hammurabi also deal with lost property, but they broaden the legislation to include both the responsibilities of the finder and the legal rights of the owner when property is resold.

22:5. transvestism in the ancient Near East. Just as clothing served as a status marker in the ancient world, it also distinguished gender. In classical contexts, cross-dressing occurred in the theater, where women were not allowed to perform, and was also an aspect of homosexual practice. Most instances in which cross-dressing or transvestism are mentioned in ancient Near Eastern texts are *cultic or legal in nature. For instance, when the *Ugaritic hero *Aqhat is murdered, his sister Paghat puts on a male garment under her female robes in order to assume the role of blood avenger in the absence of a male relative. An *Assy-

rian wisdom text contains a dialogue between husband and wife who propose to exchange their clothing and thus assume each other's gender roles. This may be a *fertility rite or perhaps a part of a religious drama honoring a goddess. It may be this association with other religions that made transvestism an "abomination" in Deuteronomy, but the issue may also be the blurring of gender distinctions. *Hittite texts use gender-related objects as well as clothing in a number of magical rites used to influence one's sexual status or diminish or alter the gender status of an adversary. The objects of the female were mirror and distaff; those of the male, various weapons.

22:6-7. treatment of bird's nest. Aside from the apparent humanitarian concern for the welfare of the creatures involved here, conservation of nature is found in leaving the mature bird to breed again. One might compare this with the prohibition against cutting down fruit trees in Deuteronomy 20:19-20. In both instances, future sources of food are preserved while an alternative is suggested for immediate needs.

22:8. parapet on house. Since roofs were considered living space (see 2 Sam 11:2; 2 Kings 4:10), a parapet would have been an appropriate safety measure. This law deals with the liability of a homeowner for injury to a visitor in the case of negligent building practices. *Hammurabi's code (laws 229-33) cautions builders against doing a substandard or unsafe job that could lead to injury or death. Penalties ranged from fines to capital punishment.

22:9-11. mixing. Some mixtures were considered to be reserved for sacred use. The mixture of wool and linen was used in the tabernacle and in the high priest's outer garments, and was reserved for those uses. This interpretation is offered in the Dead Sea Scrolls (4QMMT). Sowing of two types of seed is also prohibited in the *Hittite laws with a death threat to violators. While it is not entirely clear why these mixtures are prohibited, it is possible that their origin is based on either religious or cultural taboos. The fact that the crop is "defiled" or forfeited to the priesthood suggests religious implications and perhaps a reaction to a Canaanite *fertility *ritual or practice. In Leviticus 19:19 the prohibition is against mating two kinds of animals, while here it concerns plowing with them together. Experiments with hybridization and crossbreeding are attested as early as the third millennium B.C.

22:12. tassels. All adult male Israelites were commanded to sew blue cords into the four quarters of the hem of their robes as a perpetual reminder of God's commandments (Num 15:37-41). Decorative hems are common in ancient Near Eastern fashion as many reliefs, paintings and texts attest. Hem design was often an indication of a person's status or office. The tassels are symbolic and are designed to promote right action, not to serve as an *amulet to ward off danger or temptation.

22:13-30
Laws Concerning Marriage

22:13-21. proof of virginity. Virginity prior to marriage was prized as a means of insuring that one's children and heirs were actually one's own. The integrity of the woman's household was based on her being able to show proof of her virginity. The physical evidence demanded in this case could be either the sheets from the initial consummation (bloodied by the breaking of the hymen) or possibly rags used during the woman's last menstrual period, showing that she was not pregnant prior to the marriage. **22:19. one hundred shekels of silver.** The fine imposed here for false accusation amounts to about two and one-half

pounds of silver. *Hammurabi's laws include cases of false accusation of sexual misconduct, but these do not concern the wedding context, and monetary fines are not set. Based on the bride price paid in Deuteronomy 22:29 of fifty shekels, this penalty amounts to twice the bride price and thus would be a real deterrent to such accusations. It would be the equivalent of about ten years of normal wages.

22:22. adultery. Having sexual relations with another man's wife was punishable by death in both the biblical and ancient Near Eastern codes. The Egyptian *Tale of Two Brothers* calls it a "great crime" that no honest man or woman would consider. This was an attack on a man's household, stealing his rights to procreate and endangering the orderly transmission of his estate to his heirs (see comment on Ex 20:14). The act itself defiles both participants (Lev 18:20; Num 13:5). Since it is not only an attack on the sanctity of the household but also a source of general contamination, adultery serves as a reason for God to expel the people from the land (Lev 18:24-25).

22:23-24. "in town" criterion. The rape of a virgin within a town brings an automatic death penalty because the woman had the opportunity to cry out and could expect to receive assistance. This is based on implied consent on her part. Mesopotamian codes also include locale as part of the rape law. However, in the *Sumerian laws, the focus is more on whether her parents were aware that she was out of the household and whether the rapist knew whether she was slave or free (laws of *Ur-Nammu and *Eshnunna impose fines for raping a virgin slave woman). *Hammurabi's law most closely resembles the Deuteronomic law. In this case the rapist is to be executed if he attacks a woman in the street and witnesses testify that she defended herself. *Middle Assyrian laws allow the parents of the victim to take the rapist's wife and have her raped. There is also provision for the rapist to marry the victim, if the family chooses, for a premium bride price.

22:23, 25. "pledged" status. A marriage contract was a sacred compact, comparable to the *covenant agreement made with Yahweh (see Ezek 16:8). The "pledge" agreement (1) set a bride price as well as the amount of the dowry, (2) guaranteed that the bride would be a virgin at the time of marriage and (3) required complete fidelity of the parties. Marriage was such an important economic and social factor in the ancient Near East that it was the basis of a huge amount of legislation. For instance, the laws of *Eshnunna and *Hammurabi explain the importance of having an official marriage contract. Hammurabi's laws also provide guidance on payment of the bride price and instances when one party or the other wishes to break the contract (see 2 Sam 3:14). Once an agreement is in place, it is expected that other persons will respect the betrothed status of the woman as technically already married (see Gen 20:3). Thus the laws of adultery are in full force even before the actual ceremony and consummation of the marriage.

22:25-27. "in the country" criterion. In this case, Israelite law adds another criterion by specifying the guiltlessness of the woman who is raped in the countryside, where her screams were unlikely to attract assistance. The assumption of her innocence is based on implied resistance to the rape in this circumstance. It is likely that the law applied to married as well as to betrothed women, even though only the latter are mentioned. A similar statement appears in *Hittite law, which condemns the man only if he seizes a woman "in the mountains" and condemns the woman only if the crime occurs "in (her) house" (see the adulter-

ous woman in Prov 5:3-14).

22:29. fifty shekels. The bride price probably varied depending on the status and wealth of the bride-to-be's family. Fifty shekels of silver may have been a standard amount (equivalent to the value of the bride's virginity, according to *Middle Assyrian laws), but there were probably other items exchanged as well (compare Ex 22:16-17). To provide one measure of these transactions, in the *Ugaritic religious texts the moon god Yarih offers one thousand shekels of silver as a bride price for the moon goddess Nikkal. These amounts should be measured against the fact that the standard annual wage in the ancient world was ten shekels.

22:29. divorce in ancient Near East. The most straightforward statement on divorce in the ancient Near Eastern law codes is Middle Assyrian law 37, which simply says that it is a man's right to divorce his wife and that he may choose whether or not to provide her with a settlement. Other legal clauses, however, at least provide grounds for divorce: wife neglects household duties to go into business (Hammurabi); wife's desertion of her husband (*Middle Assyrian laws); failure to produce children (Hammurabi). General indications are that men in both Egypt and Mesopotamia could divorce their wives on almost any grounds. There are also a number of sources that prescribe a fixed settlement: one mina of silver to a primary wife and one-half mina of silver to a former widow (Ur-Nammu); one mina of silver if no bride price was paid (Hammurabi). It should be noted that women did have some rights in divorce proceedings: to keep the bride price (*Middle Assyrian laws); to have dowry returned (Hammurabi); to receive a share of the inheritance as a dowry (Hammurabi). There is also one case in which a woman was able to leave an unsatisfactory marriage, taking her dowry with her (Hammurabi). However, this was based on an examination of her character, which could lead to her execution if she was found to be at fault (Hammurabi).

22:30. incest. Incest was equally abhorrent in most other societies (e.g., the prohibitions in *Hittite laws). The most well-known exception is Egypt, where it was a common practice in the royal family (but little attested elsewhere) as a means to strengthen or consolidate royal authority. This concept is also seen among *Elamite kings. *Hammurabi's laws call for the execution of a son who has intercourse with his mother after the death of his father.

23:1-14
Defiling the Assembly and the Camp

23:1-8. exclusions from the assembly. "Assembly of the LORD," like the more common "assembly of Israel," is a technical term for all those adult males who are enfranchised to make decisions, participate in *cultic activities and serve in the military of Israel (Mic 2:5). Because they were a chosen people, who were required to maintain their *ritual purity as part of the *covenant (Ex 19:6), the unclean and the stranger were excluded from the activities of the assembly. The examples listed include persons who were sexually impaired (probably eunuchs) and thus incapable of procreation, men of illegitimate birth (including incest and intermarriage) and certain national groups who were excluded from ever being adopted into the assembly.

23:4. Balaam's home. The exact location of Balaam's home is unknown. Numbers 22:5, 23:7 and Deuteronomy 23:4 seem to indicate the area of the upper Euphrates, perhaps the site of Pitru, twelve miles south of Carchemish, mentioned in the monolith inscription of the

*Assyrian king Shalmaneser III (858-824 B.C.). However, the journey of Balaam described in Numbers 22:21-35 suggests a shorter distance, possibly a journey from Ammon.

23:9-14. sanitation in the camp. Since the army is engaged in a holy war, they must maintain themselves in a state of ritual purity consistent with God's holiness. Thus matters of personal hygiene are elevated to reinforce the need to keep both person (see Lev 15:16-17) and place clean. Obviously, there would be health value in digging latrines outside the camp, but such mundane activities here are keyed to preventing the ritual *impurity that would cause God to abandon them (see Deut 8:11-20).

23:15-25
Miscellaneous Laws

23:15-16. slavery. Although debt slavery occurred in ancient Israel, it had a term limit of six years and then the slave was freed. Perpetual slavery did exist as well, but that involved foreign captives and Israelites who had made the decision to accept that condition (Ex 21:2-11; Deut 15:12-18). It is most likely this latter class of persons that is mentioned in this law, since debt slaves could expect to be released eventually. Israel's fugitive slave law is unusual in the context of ancient Near Eastern law. However it is tied to Israel's former condition as slaves in Egypt and thus is based on a national hatred of the institution (see Ex 22:21). The Code of *Hammurabi makes hiding a runaway slave a capital crime and sets a bounty of two shekels of silver for the return of a slave. Similarly, the international treaty between Pharaoh Rameses II and the *Hittite king Hattusilis III (c. 1280 B.C.) includes an extradition clause requiring the return of fugitive slaves.

23:17-18. cultic *prostitution. One can distinguish between several different categories. In "sacred" prostitution, the proceeds go to the temple. In "cultic" prostitution, the intent is to insure *fertility through sexual *ritual. We must also differentiate between occasional sacred/cultic prostitution (as in Gen 38) and professional sacred/cultic prostitution (as in 2 Kings 23:7). The evidence for cultic prostitution in ancient Israel or elsewhere in the ancient Near East is not conclusive. Canaanite texts list prostitutes among the temple personnel, and *Akkadian literature attests those who were dedicated for life to serve the temple in this way. Although the Hebrew word used here is related to an Akkadian word for prostitute, this does not prove that any religious ritual or cultic practice is involved. It is quite possible for prostitutes to be employed by temples as a means of raising funds without their having any official status as priestesses. Furthermore, since women often did not have personal assets, sometimes the only way of earning money by which to pay a vow appeared to be prostitution. The injunction against bringing the wages of a prostitute to the temple may, however, be a reaction against practices like that of the *Ishtar temple servants in the Neo-Babylonian period, who hired out female members of their community as prostitutes. Their wages would have been placed in the temple treasury. All of this demonstrates the existence of sacred prostitution, both occasional and professional, in Israel and the ancient Near East. But the existence of cultic prostitution on either level is more difficult to prove. Cultic prostitution is not easily confirmed in Mesopotamia, unless one includes the annual sacred marriage ritual. But it is hard to imagine that prostitutes serving at the temple of Ishtar (who personified sexual force) were not viewed as playing a sacred role in the fertility cult. The translation "male prostitute" in Deuteronomy 23:18 is based on the use of the Hebrew word that usually means "dog." In the fourth-century B.C. Kition inscription, this term is used to describe a group that receives temple rations. It is possible, but not certain, that this refers to a temple official or priest. Recent study has shown that, at least by the Persian period (sixth-fifth century), dogs had some significant role in Phoenician *cultic practice. *Kalbu* (dog) has a more positive meaning of "faithful one," as can be seen in its use in personal names (like the biblical Caleb). (See Ex 34:16.)

23:19-20. charging interest. See the comment on Exodus 22:25. In Deuteronomy, though not in Exodus, it is explicitly stated that interest may be charged on loans to non-Israelites.

23:21-23. vows. In the Decalogue is the commandment that no one should "misuse the name of the Lord" (Ex 20:7). When a vow using God's name is spoken, it brings God into contract with that person. Thus any failure to carry out the stipulations of the vow breaks the contract and subjects that person to divine wrath (see Judg 11:35-36). The instruction about vows contained in Deuteronomy is a wisdom statement similar in form to Ecclesiastes 5:4-7. It is designed as a caution against unwise speech and has many parallels in ancient Near Eastern wisdom literature. For instance, the seventh-century B.C. *Assyrian *Instructions of *Ahiqar* notes that "a human word is a bird; once released it can never be recaptured." Similarly, the Egyptian *Admonitions of Amenemope* state that "to stop and think before you speak . . . is a quality pleasing to the gods" (c. 1100 B.C.). For more information on vows, see comments on Leviticus 27 and Numbers 30.

23:24-25. hand gleaning. Just as widows may glean in a ripe field or orchard to sustain themselves from the harvest provided by God, it is permissible for a traveler to refresh himself with a handful of fruit or grain, taken in passing from a field (see Deut 24:19-21). However, it is theft if a person purposefully harvests from a neighbor's field. The hospitality rights of travelers are also discussed in the Egyptian *Tale of the Eloquent Peasant* (c. 2100 B.C.).

24:1-22
Protection of Dignity

24:1-4. divorce. The basis for divorce in the biblical text is the dissatisfaction of the husband with his wife (as in the *Middle Assyrian Laws). In that sense there must be clear grounds for the divorce (as in *Hammurabi and the *Middle Assyrian Laws). A "bill of divorcement" is drawn up specifying these particulars (see Jer 3:8), which, if it follows the manner of other legal proceedings, would be reviewed by a body of elders, and testimony would be given (as in Hammurabi's laws). For further information see the comment on Deuteronomy 22:29.

24:4. defilement. The very unusual form of the Hebrew verb used in verse 4 makes it clear that the woman in this case is the victim, not the guilty party. She has been forced to declare her uncleanness by the uncharitable actions of the first husband, and the second marriage demonstrates that another husband has been capable of accommodating whatever *impurity she was plagued with. The prohibition is aimed at preventing the first husband from marrying the woman again (in which case he might be able to realize some financial gain), whereas if the woman were impure the prohibition would be against her and would preclude a marriage relationship with anyone.

24:5. newlywed rule. This humanitarian law could be compared to the recruitment law in Deuteronomy 20:7. The latter exempts men who are betrothed from service, while this one specifically exempts the newly married man. In both cases the object is to give him time to father an heir and establish a household. However, the law in chapter 24 also concerns itself with the right of the individual to take pleasure in the joys of life before going to war.

24:6. millstone as necessary for survival. The millstone was made up of two stones, usually basalt. The lower millstone was heavy (sometimes nearly one hundred pounds), a flat or slightly curved stone upon which the grain was laid and then ground into flour with the upper, lighter stone (weighing four or five pounds), which was shaped to the hand of the worker. The poor, who could not buy processed grain from others, had to grind it themselves each day. If they were forced to give their millstone in pledge for a day's labor, they could be left without the means to feed themselves.

24:7. slave trade in ancient Near East. While slaves were bought and sold throughout the ancient Near East (see Gen 37:28-36), it was forbidden by law for persons to kidnap free citizens and sell them as slaves (compare Ex 21:16). Both the Deuteronomic law and *Hammurabi's laws condemned the kidnapper to death. In this way some restraint was placed on slave traders adding to their stock by simply taking stray children or unlucky adults. The vast majority of persons who did end up on the slave block either were sold to the slavers by their own families or were prisoners of war.

24:8-9. leprosy. See the comments on the diagnosis of skin diseases by the priests in Leviticus 13:1-46. The Deuteronomic injunction simply reinforces the prerogatives and authority of the priests to determine whether a person had the skin condition (probably psoriasis or other skin disease, since Hansen's disease was unknown in the Near East until the Hellenistic period) and, when it was cured, to perform a purification *ritual.

24:10-15. regulations concerning a pledge. It was a common business practice in the ancient Near East for a person to "make a pledge" (i.e., offer as collateral) a portion of his property as a guarantee of paying off a debt or other financial obligation. For instance, the Code of *Hammurabi and *Hittite laws stipulate the pledging of land or planted fields. Hammurabi and *Middle Assyrian laws both deal with the legal rights of persons who have been taken in pledge for a debt. What is distinctive about the Deuteronomic law, as compared to the older version in the *covenant code (Ex 22:26-27), is its emphasis on protecting both the humanitarian rights and the personal honor of the debtor. Thus the creditor may not enter the debtor's house to take an object in pledge. Instead, the debtor's dignity is preserved by maintaining the sanctity of his personal dwelling and by giving him the opportunity to choose what will be offered. In this way the poor are treated on a par with all other Israelites.

24:16. family culpability. This legal concept of personal responsibility is cited in 2 Kings 14:6 as the basis for sparing the sons of condemned men. What is unclear is this principle's relationship to the concept of *corporate responsibility, evidenced in Deuteronomy 13:12-17 and 21:1-9. In the latter cases, the entire nation was expected to maintain their ritual purity by eliminating contaminating elements. If individual and corporate responsibility were coexisting legal ideas, then the instances where entire families were slain because of the sin of the father (Josh 7:24-26; 2 Sam 21:1-9; 2 Kings 9:26) would be viewed as cases of divine punishment rather than the actions of the civil legal system.

24:17-18. justice for the vulnerable. Once again the legal rights of the "pro-tected classes" of society (widows, orphans, resident aliens) are listed (see Ex 22:21-24; Deut 26:12). The basis for protecting and providing for these persons is God's compassion during the exodus event, as well as the *covenant promise of a fertile land. The theme of legal protection for the vulnerable is quite common in the ancient Near East (Ex 23:6), especially in wisdom literature. For example, in the Egyptian *Teachings of Amenemope* appears the admonition not to "steal from the poor, nor cheat the cripple . . . nor poach on the widow's field." Among the titles that the "Eloquent Peasant" of Egyptian literature uses for the local governor is "father of the orphan" and "husband of the widow," reminding him of his responsibilities to uphold the rights of the weak in society.

24:19-22. provision for the needy. Since the bounty of the harvest is a reflection of God's *covenant promise, it is only just that the owners of fields and orchards share a portion of their harvest (see comments on Ex 22:22-24 and Deut 23:24-25). Such a provision served several purposes. It insured that the entire community participated in the humanitarian efforts to sustain the poor (see Lev 23:22). The practice of leaving a portion of a field unharvested may also be tied into the regular fallowing of fields (Ex 23:10-11), which allowed the land to rest and regain its fertility. In the ancient Near East in general it is likely that what was left in the fields was originally associated with sacrificial offerings to local *fertility gods. By designating this produce for the poor, rather than local deities, the biblical writer both removes the taint of false worship and establishes a practical welfare system.

25:1-19
Individual Rights

25:1-3. punishments meted out by courts. In complex societies, when a legal dispute arises, it is necessary to take it to the judicial system. This system must include judges and a place for the hearing of testimony. On the village level this simply means drawing together the "elders" at the gate or threshing floor (see Deut 21:18-21; Ruth 4:1-12). In towns and cities, the judges were officials appointed by the government, who could hear appeals from village courts (Deut 17:9-10) or try cases within their own jurisdiction (2 Sam 15:3; Jer 26:10-19). Their responsibility included hearing testimony, making a judgment based on the law and officiating to insure that punishment was meted out exactly as the law decreed (in the *Middle Assyrian laws the judges are expected to observe the punishment).

25:2-3. limitation on number of lashes. Ancient Near Eastern law (*Middle Assyrian laws and *Hammurabi) stipulate that both men and women be flogged for various crimes. The number of lashes ranges from twenty to sixty. In Deuteronomy, however, forty lashes serves as the upper limit. This limit may be based on either the symbolic value of forty or the degree of mutilation and personal humiliation permissible for an Israelite to bear without being permanently excluded from social and religious activities.

25:4. role of oxen in grain processing. Oxen were used to plow fields and to pull threshing sleds to crush the stocks of grain once they were harvested. At the threshing floor, the grain would be laid in such a way that a heavy sled could be driven over it. The hooves of the oxen would also aid in the processing of the grain. The injunction that the ox not be muzzled follows the humanitarian pattern of previous laws and allows the animal to eat a portion of the grain as its wage. Since few farmers owned their own team of oxen, they were provided by government officials (observed in *Mari texts) or hired from wealthier farmers or even other villages (as in *Lipit-Ishtar laws and *Hammurabi, which include statutes regarding the hire and liability for oxen).

25:5-10. levirate marriage. For additional information on this practice, see the comment on Genesis 38:6-26. *Hittite law 193 and *Middle Assyrian law 33 have very similar legislation, though neither offers an explanation in terms of providing a family heir or of passing on property in an orderly fashion. Both of these concerns are referred to in Deuteronomy. Thus the law, although it is also designed to provide the widow with the security attendant upon marriage and having a son, is primarily focused on the rights of the deceased husband. The obligation owed to the deceased by his brother (defined best as nearest male kin) can be an economic hardship (see Ruth 4). Thus the second part of this law allows the levir to renounce his obligation publicly and thus, judging by the example in Ruth, presumably allow the widow to marry whomever she wishes. Even though the levir must submit to public humiliation and be labeled uncooperative, the financial factors involved might make it justifiable.

25:7-8. elders at town gate. Because of the constant traffic at the gate as people went to and from the fields, it became the place of judgment and business transaction in ancient Near Eastern towns. Merchants would set up collapsible booths or simply sit under an umbrella while their customers came to them (see Lot in Gen 19:1). When a legal matter came up, a group of the town elders either could be found sitting in the gate (Prov 31:23) or could be gathered from those passing by (Ruth 4:1-2).

25:9. removing sandal. Sandals were the ordinary footwear in the ancient Near

East, but they were also a symbolic item of clothing, especially in the relationship between the widow and her legal guardian or levir. This is due to the fact that land was purchased based on whatever size triangle of land one could walk off in an hour, a day, a week or a month (1 Kings 21:16-17). Land was surveyed in triangles, and a benchmark was constructed of fieldstones to serve as a boundary marker (Deut 19:14). Since they walked on the land in sandals, the sandals became the movable title to that land. By removing the sandals of her guardian (Ruth 4:7), a widow removed his authorization to administer the land of her household.

25:11-12. law. There is a very close parallel to this law in the *Middle Assyrian code, in which the degree of physical punishment on the woman is dependent on whether one or both testicles are damaged. It would appear that punishment in the Deuteronomic law is based not on the degree of injury inflicted on the man's genitals but on the act of immodesty displayed by the woman. Her hand is severed because it is the offending appendage (see the comment on the laws of talion in Deuteronomy 19:21). Although she is attempting to help her husband, by grasping another man's genitals she has committed a sexual act that disonors her and her husband.

25:13-16. weights and measures standards. Commerce in a society without coined money is dependent on standard weights and measures. Examples of stone and metal weights, marked with specific symbols designating weight values, have been found in Egyptian tombs as well as at several sites in Israel and Mesopotamia (stylized lion-weights were found in eighth-century B.C. levels of Nimrud in *Assyria). The merchant who used a heavier weight to buy than to sell defrauded his suppliers and customers (see Prov 11:1; 20:23;

Amos 8:5). Although this was condemned as an abhorrent practice, it was common enough in the ancient world. A good example is in the Egyptian *Tale of the Eloquent Peasant,* which accuses government officials and grain distributors of "shorting" the people.

25:17-19. Amalekites. See the comment on Numbers 24:20. The Amalekites wandered through vast stretches of land in the Negev, Transjordan and Sinai peninsula. They are unattested outside the Bible, and no archaeological remains can be positively linked to them. However, archaeological surveys of the region have turned up ample evidence of nomadic and seminomadic groups like the Amalekites during this period. Despite several attempts to eliminate the Amalekites (Ex 17:8-13; 1 Sam 15:2-3), they reappear as enemies of Israel on an alarming number of occasions (Judg 6:3; 1 Sam 30:1; 2 Sam 8:12; 1 Chron 4:43). Their refusal to aid the Israelites as they crossed Sinai functions, as it does here, as the basis for the original enmity, but subsequent disputes are probably based on territorial clashes and raiding of each others' villages.

26:1-18
First Fruits

26:1-15. first-fruit offering in ancient Near East. The religious principle involved in offering the "first fruits" (animal, vegetable or human) to the gods is based on the promotion of fertility. From earliest times the assumption was made that the gods created life in its various forms and that they expected to receive as their due offering the first of the harvest or the first fruit of the womb. Israelite religion tempered this by allowing for the redemption of some animals and all human firstborn males (Ex 13:11-13; Num 18:14-15). The giving of the first fruits could also take on a political character.

The *Assyrian annals of Sennacherib (705-681 B.C.) contain his command that conquered peoples pay their first-fruit offerings of sheep, wine and dates to the gods of Assyria.

26:5. wandering Aramean. The creedal statement contained here emphasizes the nomadic character of Israel's ancestors. The original homeland of Abraham and his family is generally identified as Paddan Aram or Aram Naharaim (see comment on Gen 11:28). The mention of Arameans in relation to Abraham and Jacob is likely a reference to scattered tribes of peoples in upper Mesopotamia who had not yet coalesced into the nation of *Aram that appears in later texts. Based on other examples from *cuneiform literature, the name Aram may in fact have originally been that of a region (cf. Sippar-Amnantum of the *Old Babylonian period) that was later applied to people living there. For more on the Arameans see comment on Genesis 28:5.

26:8. mighty hand and outstretched arm as Egyptian metaphors. These two attributes of God also appear together in 4:34; 5:15; 7:19; 11:2; and 26:8, and in the prophetic literature (Jer 32:21; Ezek 20:33). Its origin may be found in Egyptian royal hymns and official correspondence. For example, in the fourteenth-century B.C. *Amarna letters, Abdi-Heba, the governor of Jerusalem, refers to "the strong arm of the king" as the basis for his government appointment. Similarly, the Eighteenth-Dynasty "Hymn to *Osiris" equates Osiris's growing to majority with the phrase "when his arm was strong," and Haremhab's "Hymn to *Thoth" describes the moon god as guiding the divine bark through the sky with "arms outstretched."

26:9. milk and honey. See comment on 6:3.

26:11. sharing with Levites and aliens. Once again the "protected classes" are listed, and the command is made to share a portion of the sacrificial offering with them. In the case of Levites and aliens, neither group is allowed to own land, and thus both are economically impaired (see 1:16; 12:18; 14:29; 16:11). Their receipt of aid is balanced in the case of the Levites by their service as priests and in the case of aliens by their itinerant labor service.

26:12-15. tithing in ancient Near East. See the comments on tithing in 14:22-29 and Numbers 18:31-32.

26:12. third year, year of the tithe. See comment on 14:29.

26:12-13. provision for the needy. The four categories of needy persons are the Levites, aliens, widows and orphans. Because they lack either land or the protection of a household, it becomes the obligation of the nation to provide food and legal protection to these vulnerable people (see 1:16). In this case, the form of support which they are to receive is the tithe in the third year. However, it may be presumed that additional provision was made throughout the year, every year, for them (see Ruth 2:2-18).

26:14. eating while mourning or unclean. This threefold litany of ritual purity and obedience, similar in form to Job's "oath of clearance" (Job 31), maintains that the offerer has not contaminated the sacred meal by being in an impure state. For example, persons who had come in contact with the dead were considered unclean (Lev 5:2). *Hittite *ritual for the preparation of the king's food and meal offerings for the gods included meticulous attention to physical cleanliness as well as the exclusion of ritually impure animals (dogs and pigs) and ritually unclean persons. The Deuteronomic statute may also be tied to ritual meals associated with the ancestor *cult or with Canaanite or Mesopotamian *fertility rituals (see women mourning for *Dumuzi/Tammuz in Ezek 8:14).

26:14. offerings for the dead. See the comments on Numbers 3 and Deuteronomy 14:1-2 on *rituals associated with the ancestor *cult. In this case the assurance is given that the sacrificial meal has not been contaminated by unclean persons or polluting actions, such as giving a portion as an offering to the dead. This might include food provided for the spirit of a dead person, to strengthen it for its journey to Sheol (as seen in Tobit 4:17) or to learn something of the future (Deut 18:11). In addition, an association between eating "sacrifices offered to the dead" and the worship of the Canaanite god *Baal is made in Psalm 106:28. Either purpose would place reliance on powers other than *Yahweh, and both were therefore condemned by the biblical writer as polluting and leading to destruction.

27:1-8
Setting Up the Altar on Mount Ebal

27:2. monuments on stones coated with plaster. Ancient writing techniques included ink on papyrus (Egypt), a stylus on clay tablets (Mesopotamia), an inscribing tool on stone and a stick on wax-coated wooden boards. Engraving in stone could be very time-consuming, so one variation for longer inscriptions was to coat the stone surface with plaster and then write in the soft plaster. Inscriptions of this type have been found in the Palestine region at Deir Allah (see comment on Num 22:4-20) and Kuntillet Ajrud (see the comment on Asherah poles in 7:5).

27:4. Mount Ebal. Gerizim and Ebal are the mountains that flank the town of Shechem in the central hill country, Gerizim (elevation 2,849 feet) to the south, Ebal (3,077 feet) to the north. The altar spoken of here is actually constructed in

Joshua 8. Some archaeologists believe that the remains of this altar have been found. It is a structure on one of the peaks of Mount Ebal about twenty-five by thirty feet with walls about five feet thick and nine feet high made of fieldstones. The fill is dirt and ashes, and what appears to be a ramp leads up to the top. The structure is surrounded by a courtyard, and animal bones litter the site. Pottery on the site goes back to 1200 B.C.

27:5. altar built with fieldstones; no iron tool. These instructions parallel those found in Exodus 20:25. Iron tools were used for dressing the stone—shaping it to make a sturdier structure. Altars of dressed stone have been found in Judah (the best example is at Beersheba). This altar was not supposed to be attached to a sanctuary, and perhaps the use of unhewn stone helped keep that distinction. There is a fieldstone altar in the court of the Arad fortress sanctuary dating from the monarchy period.

27:6-7. purpose of the altar. It appears that this altar was not intended to be a permanent installation (another reason to use fieldstones), but was set up for the purpose of the celebration ceremonies of this occasion. It is specifically fellowship offerings (see comment on Lev 3) that are offered here—no purification or reparation offerings.

27:8. law on monumental stones. *Hammurabi's laws were inscribed on a diorite stele eight feet tall and displayed publicly for all to see and consult. Royal inscriptions often were placed in prominent locations. Memorial inscriptions in our culture are used on tombstones, cornerstones of buildings and at various historical sites. The purpose in these cases is for people to see, take note and remember. Treaty documents in the Near East, in contrast, were often stationed in holy places that were not accessible to the public. Here the purpose was to put the agreement in writing before the gods in whose name the agreement had been sworn.

27:9-26
The Recitation of Covenant Curses

27:12. Mounts Gerizim and Ebal. See comment on 11:29.

27:15-26. curse recitation. The curses here are not statements of what will happen to the one breaking the *covenant but statements calling down unspecified curses on particular types of covenant-breaking conduct. This section constitutes a solemn oath entered into by the people concerning secret violations. Such oath-taking ceremonies regularly accompanied international treaties.

27:15. use of idols. See comment on 4:15-18.

27:16. dishonoring parents. Honoring and respecting parents consists of respecting their instruction in the *covenant. This assumes that a religious heritage is being passed on. The home is seen as an important and necessary link for the covenant instruction of each successive generation. Honor is given to parents as representatives of God's authority and is for the sake of covenant preservation. If parents are not heeded or their authority is repudiated, the covenant is in jeopardy. In this connection, notice that this commandment comes with covenant promise: living long in the land. In the ancient Near East it is not the religious heritage but the fabric of society that is threatened when there is no respect for parental authority and filial obligations are neglected. Violations would include striking parents, cursing parents, neglecting the care of elderly parents and failing to provide adequate burial. (See Ex 20:12.)

27:17. importance of boundary stones. See comment on 19:14.

27:19. justice for vulnerable classes. A major aspect of Israelite legal tradition involves making provision for groups classified as weak or poor: widows, orphans and the resident alien (see Ex 22:22; Deut 10:18-19; 24:17-21). Concern for the needy is evident in Mesopotamian legal collections as early as the mid-third millennium and generally addresses protection of rights and guarantee of justice in the courts.

27:20-23. incest and bestiality. Incest was abhorrent in most other societies as well (see, for example, the prohibitions in *Hittite laws). The exception is Egypt, where it was a common practice in the royal family (but little attested elsewhere) as a means to strengthen or consolidate royal authority. This concept is also seen among *Elamite kings. Bestiality was practiced in the context of *ritual or magic in the ancient Near East. It occurs in the mythology of *Ugarit (and was probably ritually imitated by the priests) and is banned in legal materials (especially the Hittite laws).

27:25. taking bribe to kill innocent. What is uncertain in this context is whether the curse concerns a payment made to an assassin (thus giving a variation on the previous verse) or a bribe made to a judge or witness in order to condemn an innocent man of a capital crime and thus have him executed (cf. 1 Kings 21:8-14). The temptation for judges and government officials to accept bribes is found in every time and place (see Prov 6:35; Mic 7:3). Taking bribes becomes almost institutionally accepted in bureaucratic situations as competing parties attempted to outmaneuver each other (see Mic 3:11; Ezra 4:4-5). However, at least on the ideal level, arguments and penalties are imposed to eliminate or at least lessen this problem. Thus *Hammurabi's code (law

5) places harsh penalties on any judge who alters one of his decisions (presumably because of a bribe), including stiff fines and permanent removal from the bench. Exodus 23:8 forbids the taking of bribes and the perversion of justice as an offense against God, the weak and innocent, and the entire community (see Is 5:23; Amos 5:12).

28:1-14
Covenant Blessings
28:2-11. ancient Near Eastern treaty curses and blessings. Curses and blessings are standard elements of the ancient treaties of the third, second and first millennia B.C., though they vary in specificity and proportion from one period to another. Since the treaty documents were confirmed by oath in the names of deities, the curses and blessings were usually those that were to be brought by the deities rather than by the parties to the treaty. Here that is of little difference because God is a party to the *covenant rather than simply the enforcer of it. Many of the curses found here are found in similar wording in the *Assyrian treaties of the seventh century B.C. Similarities can also be seen in the Atrahasis Epic, where, prior to sending the flood, the gods send various plagues on the land. These include the categories of disease, drought and famine, sale of family members into slavery, and cannibalism.

28:15-68
Covenant Curses
28:22. pathology in the ancient Near East. Affliction by various diseases is one of the curses found in *Assyrian treaty texts. Pathology in the ancient Near East was always considered in the light of supernatural cause and effect. Generally either hostile demons or gods angry at the violation of some taboo were considered responsible. "Wasting disease" probably included tuberculosis (rare in ancient Israel) as well as other diseases characterized by the same outward symptoms; verse 22 also includes categories of diseases characterized by fevers and inflammation; verse 27 describes a variety of skin diseases; and the symptoms of verse 28 are common with syphilis (in the ancient Near East generally the nonvenereal type). The categories of pathology can therefore be seen to be symptom related.

28:23. bronze sky, iron ground. An *Assyrian treaty curse from the seventh century B.C. (Esarhaddon) is very similar to this, not only using the analogies of bronze and iron but elaborating that there is no fertility in iron ground and no rain or dew comes from bronze skies.

28:25-29. devoured, infected, insane, plundered. Esarhaddon's treaties likewise include a series very similar to this and in nearly the same order. These, then, were typical ingredients of a curse section of a document such as this.

28:27. boils. Boils again represent a symptom, not a disease. The symptoms are not given in enough detail for specific diagnosis (guesses have included smallpox, chronic eczema, skin ulcers, syphilis and scurvy), but it is the symptom more than the disease that is the curse. This same symptom is the sixth plague in Egypt (Ex 9:8-11) and the affliction that tormented Job (Job 2:7-8), as well as being named among the skin diseases in Leviticus 13 (vv. 18-23).

28:40. olives dropping off. The oil of the olive is derived only from the black, ripe fruit. Olive trees normally lose a large percentage of the potential fruit due to the blossoms or the green olives dropping off the tree. The small proportion left can be further depleted by drought or disease, causing heavier dropping off. This curse is not found in *Assyrian texts because sesame seed oil was used in Mesopotamia.

28:42. locusts. The Aramaic Sefire treaty

has a seven-year locust curse included in its list. Locusts were all too common in the ancient Near East and were notorious for the devastation and havoc they brought. The locusts breed in the region of the Sudan. Their migration would strike in February or March and would follow the prevailing winds either to Egypt or Palestine. A locust will consume its own weight each day. Locust swarms have been known to cover as many as four hundred square miles, and even one square mile can teem with over one hundred million insects.

28:48. iron yoke. Yokes, usually made of wood, consisted of a bar across the nape of the animals' necks. The bar had pegs placed down through it on either side of each animal's head. The pegs were then tied together under the chin. The iron yoke would likely be one that featured iron pegs, the part most liable to break.

28:51. grain, new wine, oil as staple products. Besides being the three most significant staple products of the region, grain, new wine and oil represent the main produce of the three major harvesting seasons (grain in the spring-summer, grapes in the fall and olives in the winter). The oil referred to here is olive oil. It was also one of the principal exports of the region, since olives were not grown in either Egypt or Mesopotamia.

28:53. cannibalism. Cannibalism is a standard element of curses in *Assyrian treaties of the seventh century B.C. It was the last resort in times of impending starvation. This level of desperation could occur in times of severe famine (as illustrated in the Atrahasis Epic) or could be the result of siege, when the food supply had become depleted, as mentioned in this text and anticipated in the treaty texts. Siege warfare was common in the ancient world, so this was not as rare an occasion as might be presumed. An example of this drastic measure can be seen in the biblical record in 2 Kings 6:28-29.

28:56. touch the ground with the sole of her foot. The author is showing that the most genteel, refined woman imaginable, one who would not even dream of walking around barefoot, would be so desperate that she would begin cannibalizing her family.

28:58. book. We tend to think of a book as having pages, a binding and a cover. Books of that sort did not exist in the ancient world. The term used here can refer to any document from inscription to scroll, from papyrus to clay tablet to stone.

28:68. returning to Egypt in ships. *Assyrian kings of the seventh century coerced their vassals into supplying troops for their military campaigns. One way then for Israelites to return to Egypt in ships would be in the Assyrian campaigns launched from the Phoenician coast in which they were obliged to take part. This represents continued oppression by foreign enemies, as the curses have detailed. Another possibility would include falling victim to Egypt's slave trade in Syro-Palestine, where the slaves were often transported by ship.

29:1-29
Covenant Renewal

29:5. clothes and sandals not wearing out. See comment on 8:4.

29:6. no bread or wine. The Lord's provision for them instead of bread and wine was manna and water. The inclusion of strong drink here is unusual—the only individuals restricted from this were serving priests (Lev 10:9) and those under a *Nazirite vow (Num 6:3).

29:7. Sihon and Og. These battles are initially recorded in Numbers 21. Sihon is known only from the biblical records, and archaeology has little information to offer regarding his capital city or his kingdom. There is also no extrabiblical information from historical sources or archaeology to shed light on Og. For information about Heshbon and Bashan, see comments on Numbers 21:25-28, 33 and Deuteronomy 3:1.

29:19-21 the secret violator. The concept that one who keeps a violation secret will nevertheless be vulnerable to the curses is found in Aramaic (Sefire) and *Hittite treaties, where the curse includes the destruction of the violator's name (family).

29:23. land of salt and sulfur. Salt and sulfur (sometimes translated "brimstone"; see Gen 19) are both minerals that are detrimental to the soil. They are the two most evident in the Dead Sea region known for its infertility and associated with the destruction of Sodom and Gomorrah.

29:24-25. reason identified for punishment. This same question and similar answer are found in an *Assyrian text of the seventh century where the Assyrian king Assurbanipal describes his reasons for putting down an Arab revolt that had violated the terms of a treaty. The Arabs had broken the oaths they made before the Assyrian gods.

30:1-20
Response to Curses and Blessings

30:2-5. forgiveness clause. Unlike the treaties of the ancient Near East, the *covenant as represented in Deuteronomy has a forgiveness clause that offers second chances when the covenant has been violated. Repentance and recommitment to the terms of the covenant would result in restoration. Such mercy was not impossible with ancient treaties, but there is no example of such a possibility being explicitly included in the written document.

30:6. circumcise the heart. This is of course not asking for a physical surgical procedure. *Circumcision had been adopted as a sign of commitment to the *covenant and acceptance of its terms. As such it could be applied to the heart as a reflection that the outer *ritual had permeated the inner being.

30:19. heaven and earth as witness. See comment on 4:26.

31:1-8
Commissioning of Joshua as Moses' Successor

31:2. life expectancy in ancient Near East. In Egypt the ideal length of life was 110 years; in a wisdom text from *Emar in Syria it was 120. Examination of mummies has demonstrated that the average life expectancy in Egypt in this general period was between 40 and 50, though texts speak of some reaching 70 and 80. Mesopotamian texts of several different periods mention individuals who lived into their seventies and eighties, and the mother of the *Babylonian king Nabonidus was reported to have lived 104 years.

31:4. Sihon and Og. For details on these two kings and the battles against them, see comments on Numbers 21.

31:9-13
Instructions for the Reading of the Law

31:9. writing down laws. From the laws of *Ur-Nammu (probably compiled in actuality by his son Shulgi) around 2000 B.C. through the laws of *Lipit-Ishtar, *Eshnunna and *Hammurabi and the *Hittite laws in the first half of the second millennium, to the *Middle Assyrian laws toward the end of the second millennium, rulers made it a practice to compile laws and write them down as evidence that they were fulfilling their duty of maintaining justice.

31:10. reading the law every seven years. Several *Hittite treaties contain clauses requiring periodic public reading of the document—one stipulates three times a year, while others are less specific, saying "always and constantly."

31:10. year of canceling debts. The sabbatical year featured remission of debts. See comment on 15:1-6.

31:10. Feast of Tabernacles. The Feast of Tabernacles is the fall harvest feast that commemorates the wandering in the wilderness. See comment on 16:13-17.

31:14-29
Future Rebellion

31:15. pillar at the entrance of the tent of meeting. Prior to the construction of the tabernacle in Exodus, the tent of meeting was outside the camp and served as a place of revelation (see the comment on Ex 33:7-10). However, now that the tabernacle is in operation, it also is referred to as the tent of meeting. The Lord again appears in a pillar of cloud. In the ancient world a bright or flaming aura surrounding deity is the norm. In Egyptian literature it is depicted as the winged sun disk accompanied by storm clouds. *Akkadian uses the term *melammu* to describe this visible representation of the glory of deity, which in turn is enshrouded in smoke or cloud. It has been suggested that in Canaanite mythology the *melammu* concept is expressed by the word *'anan*, the same Hebrew word here translated "cloud," but the occurrences are too few and obscure for confidence. See comment on Exodus 13:21-22.

31:22. covenant song. Songs of all sorts are known throughout the ancient Near East from the first half of the third millennium. One *Assyrian list of songs about a century before David includes titles of about 360 songs in dozens of different categories. Songs concerning the *covenant are also present in the book of Psalms (e.g., Ps 89).

31:26. contents of the ark. The only objects placed inside the ark were the tab-

lets with the law on them (10:2, 5). In Egypt it was common for important documents that were confirmed by oath (e.g., international treaties) to be deposited beneath the feet of the deity. The Book of the Dead even speaks of a formula written on a metal brick by the hand of the god being deposited beneath the feet of the god. There were a number of objects placed *before* the ark, including a jar of manna (Ex 16:33-34) and Aaron's rod that budded (Num 17:10). Here the book of the law is added to them.

32:1-43
The Covenant Song of Moses

31:30. covenant song. See comment on 31:22.

32:4. rock metaphor. Used in 2 Samuel 22:3 as a divine epithet, *rock* could also carry the meaning "mountain" or "fortress." It is used in Israelite names both as a metaphor for God (Zuriel, Num 3:35, "God is my Rock") and as a divine name (Pedahzur, Num 2:20, "Rock is my redeemer"). It is used of other deities in *Aramaic and *Amorite personal names, and its application to other gods is hinted at here in verses 31 and 37. As a metaphor it speaks of safety and deliverance.

32:8. Most High (Elyon). In the Old Testament the term *Elyon* is usually used as an epithet for *Yahweh (see comments on Gen 14:17-24). There is no convincing evidence thus far of *Elyon* as the name of a deity in the ancient Near East, but it is fairly common as an epithet for various gods, particularly *El and *Baal, the principal gods in the Canaanite pantheon.

32:8. deity granting nations inheritance. In Israelite theology *Yahweh had assigned each nation its inheritance (5:2, 9, 19; Amos 9:7), though there is also some accommodation to the concept that each god gave territory to his people

(Judg 11:24). It was not uncommon for kings in the ancient Near East seeking expansion of territories to claim that deity had assigned or delivered land to them. In Israel the territorial assignment was uniquely based on a *covenantal bond with *Yahweh.

32:10. apple of the eye metaphor. "Apple" is the English idiom, not the Hebrew one. The pupil is referred to here as a sensitive, protected and significant part of the body.

32:11. eagle behavior. Though the eagle cannot be ruled out, the bird named here is more usually taken to be the griffin vulture, with a wingspan of eight to ten feet. While Bible reference books often report how the eagle carries its young on its wings when they grow weary of flying, or catches them on their wings when they are fluttering in failure, this behavior has been difficult for naturalists to confirm through observation. In fact most eagles and vultures do not take their first flight until three or four months of age, at which time they are nearly full grown. Furthermore, observations by naturalists have consistently confirmed that the first flight is usually taken while the parents are away from the nest. Alternatively, if the metaphor here concerns a vulture, it may be political in nature. In Egypt, Nekhbet was the vulture goddess who represented Upper Egypt and served as a protecting deity for Pharaoh and the land. Israel was protected in Egypt until Yahweh brought them to himself. Nekhbet was depicted as particularly maternal and was believed to assist at royal and divine births. Significant building of her temple in el-Kab (capital of third nome in Upper Egypt) took place in the Eighteenth Dynasty toward the end of the Israelite stay in Egypt, so we know that she was a popular goddess at that time. It is conceivable that the imagery of this verse was not drawn from actual observation of the behavior of vultures but from elements in the depiction of the vulture goddess, Nekhbet, whose characteristics are here transferred to *Yahweh (see v. 12, "no foreign god was with him"). The first half of the verse would then introduce the metaphor of the vulture that cares for and protects its young. The second half of the verse speaks of the Lord's care and protection of his people using the imagery that was familiar from Egyptian metaphors of care and protection. Additionally, in Mesopotamia the *Tale of Etana* includes an eagle that carries *Etana and then repeatedly lets him go and catches him on its wings. (See Ex 19:4.)

32:13. heights of the land metaphor. Cities were typically built on hills because of their natural defensibility, and armies chose hills as strategic points of control. The metaphor of treading on the heights therefore is one that speaks of victory and security.

32:13. source of honey and oil. While most honey spoken of in the Old Testament is the syrup from the date palm, mention of the rock here suggests bees' honey from honeycombs in the rocks. Olive trees, which were the main source of oil, were able to grow in rocky soil because they could thrive with minimal amounts of water.

32:14. rams of Bashan. The region of Bashan (see comment on Deut 3:1) was well known for its choice livestock. The prime grazing land of the area provided a natural diet that produced animals of the highest quality.

32:15. Jeshurun. The word *Jeshurun* is built from a root related to the one used in the name Israel, and it is a poetic way to refer to Israel.

32:17. sacrifice to demons. This word for demon is used elsewhere in the Old Testament only in Psalm 106:37, but it is a well-known type of spirit/demon (*shedu*) in Mesopotamia, where it describes a protective guardian mostly concerned with the individual's health and welfare. It is not the name of a deity, but a category of being (like *cherub* would be in the Old Testament). A *shedu* could destroy one's health just as easily as it could protect it, so sacrifices to keep it placated were advisable. They are depicted as winged creatures (similar to the cherub; see comments on Gen 3:24 and Ex 25:18-20), but they do not have idols (as the gods have idols) by which they are worshiped (see comment on Deut 4:28 for how this worked).

32:22. foundations of the mountains. In the ancient worldview the netherworld, the realm of the dead, was down beneath the earth where one found the foundations of the mountains, especially those mountains that were believed to support the dome of the heavens. Though the Israelites clearly use the language of this conceptual worldview, it is difficult to distinguish between beliefs and poetic usage.

32:23-25. divine punishment in the ancient Near East. Famine, disease, wild beasts, war—these are the tools of the gods when they desire to punish their human subjects. Throughout history and literature the apparent randomness of these "acts of God" led them to be considered signs of divine displeasure. Atrahasis and the *Gilgamesh Epic both contain accounts of the gods trying to reduce human population through these means prior to the flood. In contrast to the Old Testament, where the offenses are identified that would lead to these judgments, in the ancient Near East the judgments would indicate only that some deity was angry about something, leaving the people to figure out what offense might have been committed. Examples include the *Hittite prayer of Mursilis, where he prays that a plague might be abated, several *Sumerian and *Akkadian texts of lam-

entations over the fall of a major city, and Egyptian Wisdom Admonitions (Ipuwer). These all view various national calamities as the punishment of the gods. Perhaps the most striking example is the Erra Epic, in which civilization itself is threatened by the anarchy and havoc wreaked by the violence of Erra (the *Babylonian deity Nergal). The text of Deuteronomy 32, however, must also be understood in the context of its treaty form, where the punishments are not random, arbitrary or unexplained. Rather, they are commensurate with the violation of the terms of the agreement.

32:33. poisonous serpents. The allusions in the second half of verse 24 are generic, speaking of carnivorous or ferocious beasts on the one hand and creatures with poisonous bites or stings on the other. The latter are not limited to snakes, of which there were a few poisonous species around, but could also include scorpions.

32:38. food and drink of the gods. A common view of sacrifices in the ancient Near East was that they served as food and drink for the gods, who needed their sustenance (see comments on Lev 1:2). This view was rejected in the ideal Israelite worldview (see Ps 50:7-15), though many Israelites would have probably accepted the concept. This text is mocking the idea that gods who have needs would be adequate for deliverance.

32:39. no pantheon. Most religions of that day had a pantheon, a divine assembly that ruled the realm of the gods, the supernatural and, ultimately, the human world. There would typically be a deity who was designated head of the pantheon, and he, like the other gods, would have at least one consort (female partner). The first commandment forbids Israel to think in these terms. *Yahweh is not the head of a pantheon, and he does not have a consort—there are no gods in his presence. This verse goes further to insist that there is no other god exercising power or competing for jurisdiction and authority. Just as blessing and prosperity is not the result of a benevolent deity's managing to hold back demonic forces and chaos, so punishment is not the surge of malevolent power to overwhelm the protector. All happens within Yahweh's plan—an impossible concept in the pagan polytheism of the rest of the world.

32:44-52
Conclusion and Instructions to Moses

32:49. Abarim range and Mount Nebo. The Abarim range extends east of the mouth of the Jordan River and on around the northern end of the Dead Sea (see Deut 32:49). It forms the northwestern rim of the Moabite plateau. The specific peak in this range from which Moses will view the Promised Land is Mount Nebo, 2,740 feet in height. Pisgah and Nebo are identified as the two peaks of Jebel Shayhan, about five miles northwest of Medeba and about a mile and a half apart. They stand about ten miles from the Jordan River.

32:50. Mount Hor. The death site for Aaron (although 10:6 identifies his death with Moseroth). The traditional location is near Petra at Jebal Nabi Harun, but this is not "on the border of Edom." Another possibility is Jebal Madrah, west of Kadesh and near the Edomite border, but it lacks sufficient water sources.

32:51. Meribah Kadesh in the Desert of Zin. Kadesh Barnea is in the wilderness of Zin (see comment on Num 13:26). This is where the incident in Numbers 20 occurred when Moses struck the rock for water. Meribah means "quarreling," and it is a name applied to both instances

when water was brought from the rock.

33:1-29.
The Blessing on the Tribes

33:1. patriarchal pronouncements. In the biblical material the patriarchal pronouncement generally concerns the destiny of the sons with regard to fertility of the ground, fertility of the family and relationships between family members. Blessings or curses pronounced by the patriarch of the family were always taken seriously and considered binding, even though they were not presented as prophetic messages from God. They were usually given when the patriarch was on his deathbed. This chapter is most reminiscent of Genesis 49, when Jacob blessed his sons, the forefathers of the tribes Moses now blesses.

33:2. Seir. Seir is generally considered the mountainous central region of Edom (elevations generally over 5,000 feet) between Wadi al-Ghuwayr on the north and Ras en-Naqb on the south.

33:2. Mount Paran. Mount Paran is considered by most a poetic variation for Mount Sinai/Horeb.

33:5. Jeshurun. See comment on 32:15.

33:8. Thummim and Urim. These were devices used by the priests to give *oracular messages. See the comment on Exodus 28:30.

33:17. bull/ox metaphor. The bull and ox are symbols of fertility and strength. As such, the latter term is used as a title of *El, the head of the Canaanite pantheon. Both elements are included in this blessing on the Joseph tribes, Manasseh and Ephraim. One *Ugaritic text describes the gods *Baal and Mot as strong, goring like wild bulls, and the *Babylonian king *Hammurabi describes his own military might in terms of an ox goring the foe.

33:22. Bashan. The region of Bashan is centered in the area of the upper Yarmuk River, east of the Sea of Galilee. Its northern border is Mount Hermon. Dan's territory was originally in the south by the

Philistine coast, but the Danites moved north to the region of the city called Dan north of the Sea of Galilee and contiguous to Bashan.

33:24. bathing feet in oil. Washing feet was a constant need and an act of hospitality in the dusty terrain. Only the wealthy and genteel, however, would regularly make use of (olive) oil for the washing. Compare John 12:3. This metaphor speaks of prosperity.

33:25. bolts of the gates. The locking system on gates and doors usually included a bar (wood or metal) that slid into openings in the posts. Brackets that held the bar firmly to the doors are probably what is referred to by the "bolts" of this passage. The gate could be breached by applying a battering ram to the center where the doors met in order to break the bar. Brackets would make the bar much harder to break, but they in turn could break. Brackets of bronze or iron could make a gate much harder to break through.

34:1-12
The Death of Moses
34:1. Nebo and Pisgah. See comment on 32:49.

34:1-3. view from Mount Nebo. At this point the Mediterranean Sea is about sixty miles west, but it cannot be seen because the hills on the west side of the Jordan obscure the view. On a clear day one can see Mount Hermon, about a hundred miles to the north, the mountains to the northwest that flank the Jezreel Valley (Tabor and Gilboa), the mountains of the central hill country (Ebal and Gerizim) and to the southwest as far as Engedi.

34:1-3. the boundaries of the land. Even though the land has not been distributed yet, this viewing of the land is described partially by tribal territories, to be distinguished from the geographical descriptions given in Deuteronomy 1:7. The description moves from Moses' point toward the north and then counterclockwise through the land.

34:6. Baal Peor. The Wadi Ayun Musa at the foot of Mount Nebo is generally considered to be the Valley of Beth Peor, with the site Khirbet Ayun Musa as probably the town.

34:7. apocryphal literature concerning the death of Moses. Jude 9 speaks of a dispute over the body of Moses, and apocryphal and rabbinic literature speculated about it in a number of places, particularly in *The Assumption of Moses* (of which manuscripts are no longer known) and *The Testament of Moses* (known from one Latin manuscript from the sixth century A.D.). The former speaks of Moses ascending directly to heaven, while in the latter it is implied that he dies a natural death. Deuteronomy makes it very clear that he died, and there is nothing remarkable in the account. The text leaves it somewhat ambiguous who buried Moses, but it is clear that the grave site is unmarked and unknown.

34:8. plains of Moab. This is the broad plain or steppe region immediately north of the Dead Sea and east of the Jordan River, just opposite the "plains of Jericho" (Josh 4:13). Its location serves as the jumping-off point for entrance into Canaan. (See Num 22:1.)

GLOSSARY

Adapa: a priest of the god Ea in the Sumerian city of Eridu. The story about him tells how he was tricked out of the opportunity to obtain immortality when he was advised not to eat divine food.

Ahiqar: an adviser to the Assyrian king Sennacherib (704-681 B.C.) who was exiled and wrote a set of teachings on "wise" and "foolish" men that parallels some of the saying in Proverbs.

Akkad: Semitic peoples who entered Mesopotamia after 2400. They first served the dominant Sumerian rulers, but they were united under Sargon I (c. 2350 B.C.) as he conquered the non-Semitic cities of Sumer in southern Mesopotamia. His successor Naram-Sin (2250 B.C. to about 2220 B.C.) brought the Akkadian empire to its height.

Akkadian: term applied to Mesopotamian culture and language from about 2500 B.C. to about 500 B.C.

Alalakh: northern Syrian city, in the southern part of the plain of Antioch, which flourished in the early second millennium. It has produced numerous records that describe the politics and economy of the area, and it is mentioned in texts from Mari, Nuzi and the Hittite kingdom.

Amarna: see El Amarna.

amulet: a carved ornament worn around the neck designed to ward off evil, cure disease or bring good luck to the owner.

Amorite/Amurru: a group of Semitic peoples who lived in an area west of Mesopotamia, including the Mediterranean seacoast, during the second millennium B.C.

Anat: goddess of fertility and warfare, and principal consort of the god Baal in Canaanite and Ugaritic religion.

anachronism: a detail or word in a story that does not fit the time period of the story. Often can be understood as a clarification or adjustment to the text made at a later time.

annunciation: a birth announcement.

apodictic law: a type of legal statement which is in the form of a command, without explanation.

apostasy: any action which allows or condones false worship.

apotropaic: an action taken or a symbol used to drive away evil.

Aqhat: the son of Danil, and the hero of a Ugaritic epic in which he is portrayed as a mighty hunter and is murdered by the goddess Anat when he refuses to give her his bow. The story has parallels with the ancestral narratives and the book of Judges.

Aram: the northwestern half of Mesopotamia and the Mediterranean coast, home of the Arameans in the late second and early first millennia B.C.

Aramaic: a northwest Semitic dialect that was the primary language of diplomacy and literature throughout the Near East from c. 700 B.C. to A.D. 700. Sections of the Bible written in Aramaic are found in Daniel 2:4—7:28; Ezra 4:8-68 and 7:12-26.

Asherah: Canaanite fertility goddess, consort of Baal, often associated with sacred groves or represented by sacred poles in the Bible.

Assyria: northern Mesopotamian area centered on the Tigris River. It has several periods of prominence, the most important from 1000 to 612 B.C., when the Assyrians conquered all of the Near East and produced a law code (Middle Assyrian code) that parallels biblical law.

Astarte: a Canaanite and Phoenician goddess, consort of the god Baal, associated with fertility and known as the goddess of war.

Baal: Canaanite and Ugaritic god of storms and fertility.

Babylon: major Mesopotamian city located at the closest conjunction of the Tigris and Euphrates Rivers, which dominated the history of that area during several periods.

Bronze Age: the era (divided into Early, Middle and Late periods) from approximately 3000 to 1200 B.C., characterized by bronze technology.

bulla: a clay stamp used to seal a papyrus document. The seal impression prevented tampering and also provided the name or the rank of the official who wrote the document.

casuistic law: a form of legal statement based on an "if—then" structure.

Chalcolithic Age: the era from 4300 to 3000 B.C., characterized by use of copper technology.

Chaldean: period of Mesopotamian history from approximately 700 to 540 B.C. and associated with the Neo-Babylonians and King Nebuchadnezzar.

Chemosh: Moabite national god, often associated with war.

circumcision: the religious ritual of removing the foreskin from the penis. It was employed by the Israelites to mark

them as members of the covenant community.

colophon: a statement or phrase placed at the end of a document or a literary segment that may serve as a summary or simply as an end marker.

concubine: a secondary wife, who may have come to the marriage without a dowry and whose children may not inherit from their father unless he publicly declares them his heirs.

corporate identity: a group is treated as a single unit. Reflected in a legal principle that rewards or punishes an entire household for the righteousness or the sins of the head of the household.

covenant: a contractual agreement associated in the Bible with the agreement between Yahweh and the Israelites that promises land and children in exchange for exclusive worship and obedience.

cult: the organization and activities of a religious group, including sacrifice and other rituals.

cuneiform: the wedge-shaped, syllabic script invented by the Sumerians and used by every subsequent civilization in Mesopotamia until the coming of the Greeks.

Dilmun: an Eden-like land in Mesopotamian mythology. Utnapishtim, the hero of the Gilgamesh flood epic, was taken here to live eternally after the flood.

divination: a process of determining the will of the god(s) through the examination of natural phenomena (cloud formations, the entrails of sheep) or by casting lots.

Dumuzi/Tammuz: a Mesopotamian god, consort of the goddess Ishtar, whose death and incarceration in the underworld represented the changes of the seasons.

Ea: Mesopotamian god of rivers and streams who figures in the flood story of the Gilgamesh Epic and in the Babylonian creation story, Enuma Elish.

Early Bronze Age: the era from approximately 3300 to 2300 B.C., characterized by the emergence of cities, the high civilization of early dynastic Egypt and Sumer, as well as bronze technology.

El: the high god in the Ugaritic pantheon and also a generic term for a god. It would be added to a place name (e.g., Bethel or El Elohe Israel) to distinguish it as a place where a god has made his power manifest.

Elam: country to the east of the Tigris River in modern Iran.

El Amarna: the capital of Pharaoh Akhenaton (fourteenth century B.C.), in which archaeologists have discovered hundreds of royal dispatches describing rather chaotic events in Canaan during this period.

Elohim: one of the names for the Israelite god, translated as "God" in English.

Emar: a Bronze Age city (Tell Meskene/ Balis) located on the northern reaches of the Euphrates River in Syria. Texts found here from the Late Bronze period provide insights into daily life during the fourteenth-twelfth centuries B.C.

Enki and Ninhursag: a Sumerian myth providing an explanation for the life-giving properties of river water (Enki) and the types of vegetation engendered as the water passed through and nourished the land (Ninhursag and her children).

Enlil: Mesopotamian storm god, the head of the divine assembly and instigator of the flood in the Gilgamesh Epic.

Enuma Elish: the Babylonian creation story.

Eshnunna: Mesopotamian city in the Diyala region east of modern Baghdad, which produced a short-lived kingdom between 2100 and 2000 B.C. and a law code which contains some parallels to Hammurabi's code and biblical law.

Etana: ancient Mesopotamian king, the subject of a legend in which he obtains a plant from heaven that provides fertility and thus is able to father a son to continue his rule. His flight to heaven is on the back of an eagle, and thus he is depicted on ancient seals.

etiology: a story that attempts to explain the origin of a name, a custom or a current reality, such as death or painful childbirth.

execration: a method of cursing an enemy by fashioning a doll or an incantation bowl that contains the name of the accursed party.

exorcism: a ritual, including spells and incantations, designed to cast out or remove demons from persons or places.

fertility worship: in a society dominated by farming and herding, fertility is of utmost importance. This worship dominated religious practice in much of the ancient world. The principal gods were paired as male and female, and their rites were designed to insure plentiful rain, plant growth and bountiful harvests and herds. This worship could include sacrifices as well as sacred prostitution.

funerary: rituals and objects involved with the interment of the dead. Funerary rites were also part of a larger system of ancestor worship.

Gilgamesh: Sumerian king of Uruk, who is the prototypical hero of Mesopotamian literature. His epic contains a quest for the secret of immortality and a flood story.

Habiru: a term used in Mesopotamian texts for stateless persons.

Hammurabi: Babylonian king (1792-1750 B.C.) who compiled a law code that has a number of parallels with biblical law.

henotheism: acknowledging the existence of other gods but often insisting on the supremacy of one's own god.

herem: "holy war" or the "ban," which required the complete destruction of all persons, animals and property as a dedicatory sacrifice to Yahweh.

hieroglyphic: the pictographic, syllabic script developed by the ancient Egyptians.

Hittites: an Indo-European people who migrated into Anatolia after 2000 B.C. and created an empire that challenged Egypt for control of Syro-Palestine during the mid-second millennium. They also produced a law code with parallels to biblical law.

Hurrian: a non-Semitic people who created a kingdom in Mitanni, central Mesopotamia, during the mid-second millennium.

Hyksos: an alliance of Semitic peoples, perhaps from the resurgent cities of Middle Bronze Canaan, who settled in Egypt and gained control of major portions of the country c. 1750 B.C. They eventually ruled most of Lower Egypt, with their capital at Avaris, until c. 1570 B.C.

impurity: a state of being in which an individual, a group or an object has been polluted through an unlawful act or through contact with an impure person or thing. The result is ritual impurity, which prohibits a person or group from participating in religious activities and may (in the case of leprosy) require expulsion. Rituals of purification are required to remove this stigma and restore the person or group to full participation.

in situ: a term applied to the resting place or "find spot" of an artifact that has been uncovered and recorded by archaeologists.

Iron Age: the era in ancient Near Eastern history from 1200 to 300 B.C., characterized by the use of iron technology.

Ishtar: Mesopotamian goddess of love, who is prominent in myths such as Gilgamesh's flood story.

Kassites: a people originally from the mountainous region in northern Mesopotamia who conquered the Old Babylonian kingdom about 1595 B.C. and ruled in Babylon until 1157 B.C.

Keret: the king hero of a Ugaritic tale in which he receives instructions from the gods concerning how to acquire a wife and an heir to his throne. This family crisis is only one of a series that includes illness and rebellion by one of his sons.

Lagash: third-millennium Sumerian city-state (el-Hiba) containing several urban centers that contested for control of the region with Ur, Uruk and Kish.

Larsa: early second-millennium Sumerian city, ten miles east of Uruk and twenty miles north of Ur.

Late Bronze Age: the chronological era from 1550 to 1200 B.C., which is marked by the Amarna age and New Kingdom in Egypt, the Hittite empire in Anatolia and the invasion of the Sea Peoples.

Leviathan: a sea serpent associated with the chaotic powers of the sea. The name is found in Ugaritic mythological texts as well as the Psalms.

Lipit-Ishtar: king of the Ur III dynasty in Mesopotamia who produced a law code that parallels some aspects of biblical law.

Marduk: principal god of Babylon, who defeats Tiamat in the creation story, Enuma Elish, and becomes the head of the divine assembly.

Mari: Mesopotamian city on the northern reaches of the Euphrates River that thrived from 2500 to 1700 B.C. and produced thousands of cuneiform documents describing political events, prophetic activity and the pastoral nomadic peoples of northern Syria.

Middle Assyrian (laws): published by Tiglath-Pileser I (1115-1077 B.C.), this code of laws contains many parallels with biblical law.

Middle Bronze Age: The chronological era from 2300 to 1550 B.C., which includes the period of Israel's ancestors, the Old Babylonian period and Egyptian control of Syro-Palestine.

Mitanni: the kingdom of the Hurrians in central Mesopotamia during the mid-second millennium B.C.

monolatry: a situation where a person or group has determined to worship only one god regardless of whether other gods exist.

Nazirite: an Israelite (either male or female) who takes an oath to refrain from consuming any product of the grape, from coming in contact with the dead and from cutting his or her hair.

New Kingdom (Egyptian): spanning 1570-1150 B.C., this period of Egyptian history was marked by an expansion of empire and the El Amarna period. It was ended by the invasion of the Sea Peoples.

Nineveh: the capital of the Assyrian empire on the upper reaches of the Tigris River.

Nuzi: a Hurrian city of the sixteen-fifteenth centuries B.C. It has left family and business documents that reflect marriage and inheritance customs similar to those in the ancestral stories.

Old Babylonian: a period of Mesopotamian history from 2025 to 1595 B.C., highlighted by the reign of Hammurabi (1792-1750 B.C.), who produced a law code and united all of the city-states under his rule.

oracle: a prophetic speech or a reading of divine will through the use of divination.

Osiris: the Egyptian god of the underworld.

pollution (unclean): ritual impurity is caused by contact with or consumption of polluted items, such as blood, and can be removed only through ritual acts designed to transform the person's impurity to a clean state.

purity: to be in a state of purity is to be in compliance with the law and to be free to participate in religious and social activities. This state may be achieved through proper action, ritual purification or sacrifices.

ritual acts: a prescribed set of actions taken for religious purposes, such as a sacrifice.

ritual prostitution: the practice of sexual acts as part of a religious ceremony, to promote fertility or to enrich a sanctuary.

Sea Peoples: a mixed group of peoples from throughout the Mediterranean area who served as mercenaries in the Egyptian and Hittite armies until about 1200 B.C., when they made a collective attack on the major civilizations of the Near East and disrupted them enough to allow for the emergence of new peoples in Canaan.

Sinuhe: an official of Pharaoh Amenemhat I (1991-1962 B.C.) who was exiled in Canaan for many years before being pardoned and allowed to return to Egypt. His story contains some parallels to that of the ancestors in Genesis as well as the story of Moses.

Sumer: the southernmost area of ancient Mesopotamia, which produced the first true civilization in that country about 3500 B.C., invented cuneiform script and created many of the myths that sustained religion for the next several millennia.

syncretism: the borrowing of cultural ideas, practices and beliefs and combining them with one's own.

tell: an artificial hill that has been created by successive layers of settlements on that site.

theophany: the appearance of God to a human being, as in the "burning bush."

Thoth: the Egyptian moon god.

Tiamat: primordial Mesopotamian goddess of salt water, the consort of Apsu, god of fresh water. She is Marduk's opponent in the creation story Enuma Elish.

Ugarit: northern Syrian seaport city which controlled the Mediterranean carrying trade from approximately 1600 to 1200 B.C., when it was destroyed by the Sea Peoples. Several Ugaritic epic stories have been discovered that help illumine biblical stories from the ancestral and settlement periods. Ugaritic culture is thought to approximate Canaanite culture.

Ur: an ancient Sumerian city located at the extreme southern end of Mesopotamia, on the Euphrates River. The name means "city" and was also used as the name for cities in northern Mesopotamia.

Ur III: the period of Mesopotamian history from 2120 to 1800 B.C., founded by Ur-Nammu, centered in the city of Ur and characterized by a brief revival of Sumerian culture.

Ur-Nammu: Ur III king, father of Shulgi, who produced a law code that has some parallels with biblical law.

Uruk: third- and early-second-millennium Sumerian city ruled by Gilgamesh.

Utnapishtim: hero of the flood story in the Gilgamesh Epic.

Wenamon: a priest of the Egyptian god Amon (c. 1100 B.C.), sent as an envoy to obtain logs for the royal barge from the rulers of Syria and the Phoenician coast. His mission was delayed by the weak stature of Egypt at that time and the chaotic political conditions following the invasion of the Sea Peoples.

Yahweh: one of the names for the Israelite God, sometimes anglicized as Jehovah. It is normally translated in English as "LORD."

Major Tablets of Old Testament Significance

NAME	NUMBER OF TABLETS	LANGUAGE	DIS-COVERER	LOCATION FOUND	DATE FOUND	SUBJECT	DATE OF ORIGIN	BIBLICAL SIGNIFI-CANCE
Ebla	17,000	Eblaite	Matthiae	Tell-Mardikh	1976	Royal archives containing many types of texts	24th c.	Provide historical background of Syria in late 3rd millennium
Atrahasis	3	Akkadian	Many found different parts	different parts in different sites	1889 to 1967	Account of creation, population growth and flood	1635 copy	Parallels to Genesis accounts
Mari	20,000	Akkadian (Old Babylo-nian)	Parrot	Tell-Harırı	1933	Royal archives of Zimri-Lim containing many types of texts	18th c.	Provide his-torical back-ground of the period and largest collection of prophetic texts
Enuma Elish	7	Akkadian (Neo-Assyrian)	Layard	Nineveh (library of Ashurban-ipal)	1848-1876	Account of Marduk's ascension to the head of the pantheon	7th c. copy	Parallels to Genesis creation accounts
Gilga-mesh	12	Akkadian (Neo-Assyrian)	Rassam	Nineveh (library of Ashurban-ipal)	1853	The exploits of Gilga-mesh and Enkidu and the search for immor-tality	7th c. copy	Parallels to Genesis flood accounts
Boghaz-Köy	10,000	Hittite	Winckler	Boghaz-Köy	1906	Royal archives of Neo-Hittite Empire	16th c.	Hittite his-tory and il-lustrations of inter-national treaties
Nuzi	4000	Hurrian dialect of Akkadian	Chiera and Speiser	Yorghun Tepe	1925 to 1941	Archive containing family records	15th c.	Source for contempo-rary cus-toms in mid-2nd millennium
Ugarit	1400	Ugaritic	Schaeffer	Ras Shamra	1929 to 1937	Royal archives of Ugarit	13th c.	Canaanite religion and literature
Amarna	380	Akkadian (W. Semitic dialect)	Egyptian peasant	Tell el-Amarna	1887	Correspon-dence between Egypt and her vassals in Canaan	1370 to 1340	Reflects conditions in Palestine in the mid-2nd millen-nium
Baby-lonian Chron-icles	4	Akkadian (Neo-Babylo-nian)	Wiseman	Babylon	1956	Court re-cords of Neo-Babylonian Empire	626 to 594	Record of capture of Jerusalem in 597 and history of the period
Emar	800	Akkadian	Margueron	Tell-Meskene	1975	Royal Temple, and family archives	13th c.	family cus-toms; religi-ous rituals
Alalakh	500	Akkadian	Woolley	Tell-Atchana	1939	Royal Temple archive; Statute of Idrimi	18th-17th c.	Treaties and contracts of-fer cultural background

Major Inscriptions of Old Testament Significance

NAME	LANGUAGE	DISCOVERER	LOCATION FOUND	DATE FOUND	SUBJECT	DATE OF ORIGIN (B.C.)	BIBLICAL SIGNIFICANCE
Beni Hasan Tomb Painting	Hieroglyphic Egyptian	Newberry	Beni Hasan	1900	Tomb painting of Khnumhotep II	1920	Picures Semites in Egypt
Laws of Hammurabi	Akkadian (Old Babylonian)	deMorgan	Susa	1901	Collection of Babylonian laws	1725	Illustrates ancient Near Eastern law
Merenptah Stela	Hieroglyphic Egyptian	Petrie	Thebes	1896	Military accomplishments of Merenptah	1207	First mention of the name "Israel"
Sheshonq Inscription	Hieroglyphic Egyptian		Karnak Temple	1825	Military accomplishments of Sheshonq	920	Confirmation of raid against Rehoboam
"House of David" Inscription	Aramaic	Biran	Dan	1993	Syrian conquest of region	9th c.	Earliest mention of David in contemporary records
Mesha Inscription	Moabite	Klein	Dibon	1868	Military accomplishments of Mesha of Moab	850	Moabite-Israelite relations in 9th century
Black Stela	Akkadian (Neo-Assyrian)	Layard	Nineveh	1845	Military accomplishments of Shalmaneser III	840	Picture Israelites paying tribute
Balaam Texts	Aramaic	Franken	Deir Alla (Succoth)	1967	Prophecy of Balaam about the displeasure of the divine council	8th c.	Connected to a famous seer known from the Bible
Silver Scrolls	Hebrew	Barkay	Hinnom Valley Tomb	1979	Amulet containing the text of Num 6:24-26	7th c.	Earliest copy of any portion of the Bible
Siloam Inscription	Hebrew	Peasant boy	Jerusalem	1880	Commemoration of the completion of Hezekiah's water tunnel	701	Contemporary example of Hebrew language
Sennacherib Prism	Akkadian (Neo-Assyrian)	Taylor	Nineveh	1830	Military accomplishments of Sennacherib	686	Describes siege of Jerusalem
Lachish Ostraca	Hebrew	Starkey	Tell ed-Duweir	1935	18 letters from the captain of the fort of Lachish	588	Conditions during the final Babylonian siege
Cyrus Cylinder	Akkadian	Rassam	Babylon	1879	Decree of Cyrus allowing the rebuilding of temples	535	Illustrates the policy by which Judah also benefited

Legal Texts of the Ancient Near East

	NAME	CENTURY B.C.	DESCRIPTION
SUMERIAN	Reform of Uruinimgina (King of Lagash)	24th Early Dynastic III	Social reform
	Laws of Ur-Nammu (King of Ur)	21st (Ur III)	About 31 laws remain. Fragmented
	Laws of Lipit-Ishtar (King of Isin)	19th (Isin-Larsa)	Parts of 38 laws with prologue and epilogue: civil law only
AKKADIAN	Laws of Eshnunna	18th (Old Baby-lonian)	60 paragraphs civil and criminal law
	Laws of Hammurabi (King of Babylon)	18th (Old Baby-lonian)	282 laws remaining (35-40 erased) plus prologue and epilogue
	Middle Assyrian laws (Tiglath-Pileser I?)	12th (Middle Assyrian)	About 100 laws on 11 tablets civil and criminal law
HITTITE	Hittite laws (Murshilish I or Hattushilish I)	17th (Old Hittite)	About 200 laws civil and criminal law

Ancient Near Eastern Literature
Containing Parallels to the Old Testament

LITERARY WORK	LANGUAGE	DATE	OT BOOK	NATURE OF PARALLEL
Atrahasis Epic	Akkadian	~1635	Genesis	Creation, population growth and flood with ark
Enuma Elish	Akkadian	~1100	Genesis	Account of creation
Gilgamesh Epic	Sumerian Akkadian	~2000	Genesis	Account of the flood complete with ark and birds
Memphite Theology	Egyptian	~13th c.	Genesis	Creation by spoken word
Hammurabi's Laws	Akkadian	~1750	Exodus	Laws similar to those given at Sinai in form and content
Hymn to the Aten	Egyptian	~1375	Psalm 104	Wording used in motifs and analogies; subject matter
Ludlul bel Nemeqi	Akkadian	~13th c.	Job	Sufferer questions justice of deity
Babylonian Theodicy	Akkadian	~1000	Job	Dialogue between sufferer and friend concerning the justice of deity
Instruction of Amenemope	Egyptian	~1200	Proverbs 22:17—24:22	Vocabulary, imagery, subject matter, structure
Hittite Treaties (36)	Hittite	2nd m.	Deuteronomy; Joshua 24	Format and content
Lamentations over the fall of Sumerian Cities (5)	Sumerian	20th c.	Lamentations	Phrasing, imagery and subject matter
Egyptian Love Songs (54)	Egyptian	1300-1150	Song of Solomon	Content and literary categories employed
Mari Prophecy Texts (~50)	Akkadian	18th c.	Preclassical Prophecy	Addressed similar subjects (military undertakings and cultic activity)

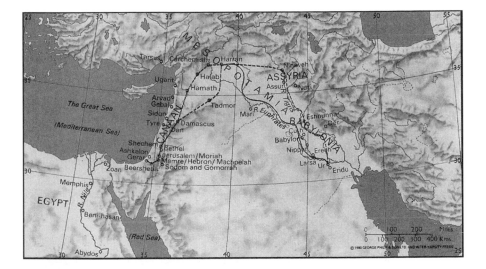

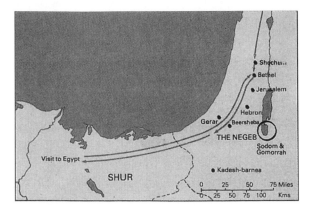

Map 1. Abraham's Travels

The map above traces the possible routes of Abraham's journey from Ur to Canaan (Gen 11:31—12:6). The map shows two possible routes to Haran (Harran), with the southern route (solid line) being more likely, and two possible routes from Haran to Damascus.

The map below traces Abraham's travel through Canaan to Egypt and back to Canaan (Gen 12:6—13:4).

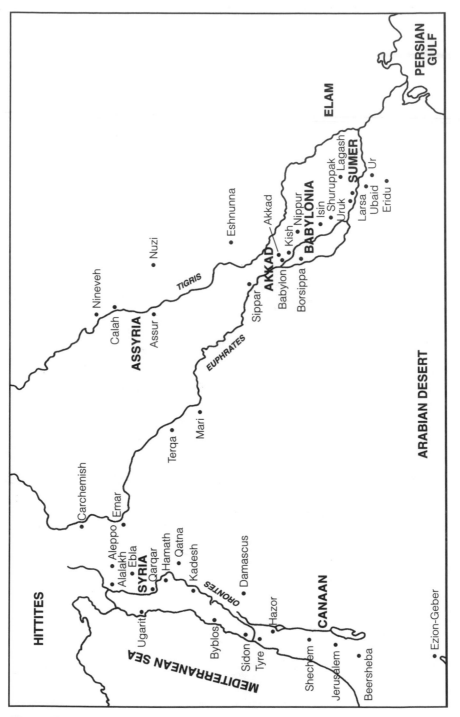

Map 2. The Ancient Near East
This map locates important sites of the Old Testament world.

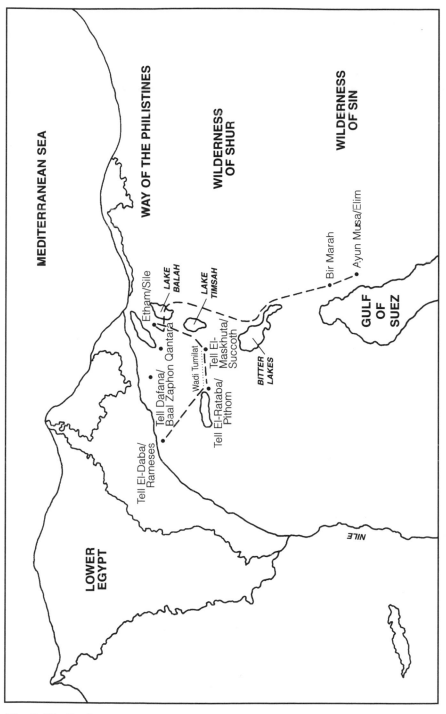

Map 3. The Exodus
This map traces the possible route of the exodus from Egypt.

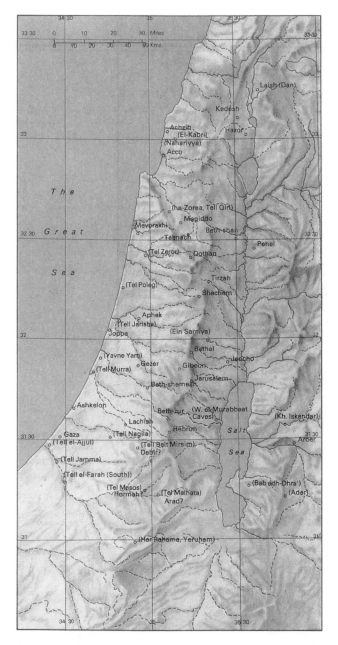

Map 4. Archaeological Sites of Palestine: Middle Bronze Age